CONSUMER GUIDE®
1996 CARS

All rights reserved under International and Pan American copyright conventions. Copyright © 1996 Publications International, Ltd. This publication may not be reproduced or quoted in whole or in part by mimeograph or any other printed or electronic means, or for presentation on radio, television, videotape, or film without written permission from Louis Weber, C.E.O. of Publications International, Ltd., 7373 N. Cicero Ave., Lincolnwood, Illinois 60646. Permission is never granted for commercial purposes. Printed in U.S.A.

CONTENTS

Introduction.....................5	Chevrolet Caprice/ Impala SS.................44
Shopper's Guide............7	Chevrolet Cavalier.......46
	Chevrolet Corsica........48
Model Groups..............10	Chevrolet Corvette.......50
	Chevrolet Lumina Minivan.....................52
Acura Integra...............12	Chevrolet Lumina/ Monte Carlo...........54
Acura SLX 120	
Acura TL Sedan...........14	Chrysler Cirrus...........56
Audi A4......................16	Chrysler Concorde.......66
Audi A6/S6.................18	Chrysler LHS/ New Yorker 58
BMW 5-Series 20	
BMW 7-Series 22	Chrysler Sebring..........62
Buick Century 190	Chrysler Town & Country.....................60
Buick LeSabre 194	
Buick Park Avenue 24	Dodge Avenger............62
Buick Regal 26	Dodge Caravan 64
Buick Riviera...............28	Dodge Intrepid.............66
Buick Roadmaster 44	Dodge Neon 68
Buick Skylark...............30	Dodge Stealth............170
Cadillac De Ville/ Concours.................32	Dodge Stratus..............70
	Eagle Talon 166
Cadillac Eldorado 34	Eagle Vision.................66
Cadillac Fleetwood 36	Ford Aspire.................72
Cadillac Seville 38	Ford Contour 74
Chevrolet Beretta.........48	Ford Crown Victoria.....76
Chevrolet Blazer..........40	Ford Escort.................78
Chevrolet Camaro 42	Ford Explorer..............80

CONSUMER GUIDE®

Ford Mustang	82	Lexus LX 450	230
Ford Probe	84	Lexus SC 300/400	136
Ford Taurus	86	Lincoln Continental	138
Ford Thunderbird	88	Lincoln Mark VIII	140
Ford Windstar	90	Lincoln Town Car	142
Geo Metro	92	Mazda Miata	144
Geo Prizm	94	Mazda Millenia	146
Geo Tracker	96	Mazda MPV	148
GMC Jimmy	98	Mazda MX-6	150
Honda Accord	100	Mazda Protege	152
Honda Civic	102	Mazda 626	154
Honda Odyssey	104	Mercedes-Benz C-Class	156
Honda Passport	118	Mercedes-Benz E-Class	158
Hyundai Accent	106	Mercedes-Benz S-Class	160
Hyundai Sonata	108	Mercury Cougar	88
Infiniti G20	110	Mercury Grand Marquis	76
Infiniti I30	112	Mercury Mountaineer	80
Infiniti J30	114	Mercury Mystique	74
Infiniti Q45	116	Mercury Sable	162
Isuzu Oasis	104	Mercury Tracer	78
Isuzu Rodeo	118	Mercury Villager	164
Isuzu Trooper	120	Mitsubishi Eclipse	166
Jaguar XJ Sedan	122	Mitsubishi Galant	168
Jeep Cherokee	124	Mitsubishi 3000GT	170
Jeep Grand Cherokee	126	Nissan Altima	172
Kia Sportage	128	Nissan Maxima	174
Lexus ES 300	130	Nissan Pathfinder	176
Lexus GS 300	132		
Lexus LS 400	134		

CONSUMER GUIDE®

Nissan Quest	178
Nissan Sentra	180
Nissan 200SX	182
Oldsmobile Achieva	184
Oldsmobile Aurora	186
Oldsmobile Bravada	188
Oldsmobile Cutlass Ciera	190
Oldsmobile Cutlass Supreme	192
Oldsmobile Eighty Eight	194
Oldsmobile Ninety Eight	24
Oldsmobile Silhouette	52
Plymouth Breeze	70
Plymouth Neon	68
Plymouth Voyager	196
Pontiac Bonneville	198
Pontiac Firebird	42
Pontiac Grand Am	200
Pontiac Grand Prix	202
Pontiac Sunfire	204
Pontiac Trans Sport	52
Range Rover 4.0 SE/ 4.6 HSE	206
Saab 900	208
Saab 9000	210
Saturn Coupe	212
Saturn Sedan/ Wagon	214
Subaru Legacy	216
Suzuki Esteem/ Swift	218
Suzuki Sidekick	220
Toyota Avalon	222
Toyota Camry	224
Toyota Celica	226
Toyota Corolla	228
Toyota Land Cruiser	230
Toyota Paseo	232
Toyota Previa	234
Toyota RAV4	236
Toyota Tercel	238
Toyota 4Runner	240
Volkswagen Jetta/ Golf	242
Volkswagen Passat	244
Volvo 850	246
Volvo 960	248
Prices	250

INTRODUCTION

1996 Cars covers more than 140 passenger cars, minivans, and sport-utility vehicles that are currently on sale or will be in the next few months. Major changes for 1996, key features, and latest available prices are included for each model, along with ratings for specific models stested by the auto editors of Consumer Guide®.

To help readers compare direct competitors, vehicles are divided into 10 model groups based on their size, price, and market position. A complete list of model groups, including vehicles not covered in this issue, follows the Shopper's Guide. Each report lists the model group to which the vehicle belongs and mentions similar vehicles built from the same design.

How Cars Are Rated

The Rating Guide with each report has numerical ratings in 16 categories. These ratings apply only to the vehicle as it was tested by the editors. For example, the ratings for the Ford Contour apply only to the SE model, which has a standard V-6 engine and was tested with the optional anti-lock brakes (ABS). A Contour without ABS or the V-6 engine may not score as highly in braking or acceleration. The chart below the Rating Guide lists major specifications for the vehicle that was tested.

In addition to the ratings, the editors have selected Best Buys in each of the 10 model groups as the best overall choices. In some groups, there are models labeled Recommended and Budget Buy that also are worthy of attention. Road test results play a major role in the editors' decisions. Other factors include price, cost of ownership, reputation for reliability and durability, warranties, and safety features.

Price Information

The latest available prices are provided for all models (and optional equipment) in this issue. In most cases, this includes dealer invoice prices and our estimated fair price. In some cases, only suggested retail prices were available. With some models that hadn't yet gone on sale when this book was printed (such as the Toyota RAV4), no prices were available.

The dealer invoice prices are what the dealer pays the manufacturer for the car, including its factory- or port-installed options. The dealer's cost of preparing a car for delivery to the consumer is included in the invoice price of all domestic cars. On some imported vehicles, this cost may not be included in the dealer invoice. In most cases, the destination charge is not included in either the suggested retail or dealer invoice prices, so it must be added to the cost of the vehicle.

The fair prices listed in this book are estimates based on national market conditions for each model. Since market conditions can vary greatly in different parts of the country, the fair prices should only be used as a guide. If possible, it's best to price the same car at three or more dealers to get a better idea of the fair price in your area.

Fair prices aren't listed for some models because of insufficient information about market conditions for that particular vehicle.

While we have done all we can to see that the prices in this issue are accurate, car companies are free to change their prices at any time. Most car companies have raised their prices more than once during recent model years.

Many dealers tell our readers that the prices we publish are incorrect so they can eliminate dealer-invoice price from consideration. Once they accomplish that, then they're back in the driver's seat on price negotiations. If a dealer claims our prices are incorrect or the information in this issue doesn't match what you see in showrooms, contact us and we'll do our best to help you out.

Advertising fees are not included in the price lists because they vary greatly in different parts of the country and not all dealers try to charge their customers for advertising. We think it's unfair for consumers to reimburse dealers for their advertising expenses, so we strongly suggest you argue against paying such a fee. It's their cost of doing business, not yours.

Two federal taxes affect car prices. First, a gas-guzzler tax is levied on cars that average less than 22.5 mpg in combined city/highway mileage based on EPA estimates. Some manufacturers include the gas-guzzler tax in the base prices; others list it separately. Guzzler taxes range from $1000 to more than $3000, so they can have a substantial impact on the purchase price.

Second, a 10 percent "luxury tax" is levied on cars selling for more than $32,000. The tax applies only to the amount over $32,000, so a car that sells for $38,000 will carry a tax of $600 and one that sells for $50,000 will be hit with an $1800 tax. The tax applies to the *transaction* or sale price of the vehicle, not the suggested retail price. In addition, the tax is figured on the full purchase price before any trade-in value is deducted.

The editors invite your questions and comments. Address them to:

Consumer Guide®
7373 N. Cicero Ave.
Lincolnwood, IL 60646

KEY TO SPECIFICATIONS

Dimensions and capacities are supplied by the manufacturers. **Body types: notchback** = coupe or sedan with a separate trunk; **hatchback** = coupe or sedan with a rear liftgate. **Wheelbase** = distance between the front and rear wheels. **Curb weight** = weight of base models, not including optional equipment. **Engine types: ohv** = overhead valve; **ohc** = overhead camshaft; **dohc** = dual overhead camshafts; **I** = inline cylinders; **V** = cylinders in V configuration; **flat** = horizontally opposed cylinders. **Engine size, (l/cu. in.)** = liters/cubic inches. **Rpm** = revolutions per minute. **Brakes: ABS** = anti-lock braking system. **NA** = not available.

SHOPPER'S GUIDE

Before you venture out to test drive and compare some of the new models, here are some suggestions to get you started on the right road:

- Determine how much you are willing to pay—or can afford to pay. If you plan on buying a car (instead of leasing) you should shop for a loan at a bank or other lending institution before you shop for a car. It's better to figure out how much you can afford at a bank than in a dealer's showroom, where they can juggle numbers faster than you can count.

- Decide which vehicle or type of vehicle best suits your needs and pocketbook. Start price shopping after you've narrowed the field to three or four vehicles.

- If you have an old car you intend to sell, you'll almost always get more money by selling it yourself instead of trading it in. Dealers want to make money on your old car, so they'll only give you wholesale value or less. You might be able to sell it for close to its retail value, which can put hundreds of dollars into your pocket.

Showroom Strategies

If you intend to buy a new vehicle instead of leasing one, here are some suggestions for planning your shopping strategy:

- There are no formulas for calculating a "good deal." You can't just "knock 10 percent off the sticker." It all depends on supply and demand for a particular model in your area and how much competition there is among dealers.

- Don't tell a car salesman how much you're willing to pay. Your price might be higher than what others are paying. Even if it's right on target, a salesman might reject it by saying, "We couldn't possibly sell it for that."

It's their job to price the products they sell. It's your privilege to accept or reject their price.

- Once you've settled on which vehicle you want to buy, shop at least three dealers—more if you can—to compare prices on the same model with the same equipment. Let them know you're comparison shopping and that you'll buy from the dealer who gives you the lowest price and the best treatment.

- Keep your trade-in out of the new-car price. If you're thinking about trading in your old vehicle, get a written trade-in value after you settle on a price for the new car.

When the dealer asks if you're trading in your old car, tell him, "Maybe. We can talk about that later." Some dealers will try to lure you with the offer of a high trade-in allowance and then inflate the price of the new vehicle. Concentrate on the price of the new car before you talk trade-in value.

"One-Price" Models

If you're uneasy—or terrified—about negotiating a price from a dealer, then shop for a "one-price" model, such as a Ford Escort or a Saturn, or go to dealers that advertise "no-dicker" sales practices. "One-price" isn't necessarily the lowest price for a particular car, but it can reduce the stress and let you concentrate on finding the model that best meets your needs.

In addition to Ford and Saturn, Oldsmobile, Chevrolet, and others offer one-price and so-called "value-priced" models that typically have more standard features for less money than a base model. For example, the Chevrolet Corsica has a base price of $14,385 and a destination charge of $500 that the consumer must pay. The Special Value version of the Corsica costs $13,995, including the destination charge, and comes with additional features such as intermittent wipers, a rear defogger, floor mats, and a trunk cargo net.

Many manufacturers also offer option packages that lump several options into one group at a lower price than if you ordered the items individually. These packages may include things you don't want, but why quibble if you're saving money?

Lease Instead of Buy?

Leasing has become a popular alternative to buying as tax laws have changed, eliminating deductions for interest on car loans. Also, prices of new cars have soared to where many people can no longer afford to buy. Recent estimates indicate that leases account for about 25 percent of new car sales overall and well over 50 percent of luxury models that cost $30,000 or more.

Is leasing right for you? It depends on your particular financial situation, so sit down with an accountant or tax adviser for a heart-to-heart talk on whether leasing is the best way to go. Some people still buy simply because they're more comfortable with "owning" a vehicle than "renting" one. However, some financial advisers argue that most advantages to owning a car have disappeared, making leasing more attractive.

Here are some guidelines to help you decide whether you should lease or buy:

● One of leasing's major advantages is that a large down payment isn't needed, though some leases require a substantial initial payment (often called a "capital cost reduction"). Also, monthly lease payments are generally lower than the monthly loan payment for an equivalent car.

When you buy a car, banks typically want a down payment of at least 20 percent. With the average price of a new car close to $20,000, that requires $5000 in cash or trade-in value. If you don't have that much, then leasing might be a better bet.

● The major disadvantage to leasing is that unless you eventually buy a car, you'll always be making a monthly payment. At the end of a lease you have the option of giving it back to the leasing company or buying it. Either way, you're going to have to dig into your pocket again to have a car.

Think ahead two or three years. Will your financial situation allow you to lease another new car or take out a loan to buy one?

● While the monthly payments may be lower on a lease, in the long run it is usually cheaper to buy if you keep cars five years or longer. For example, if you pay off a car loan in four years and keep the car another three years, your only expenses once the car is paid for will be for maintenance and repairs.

If your car needs few repairs—and that can be a big "if"—then you'll be thousands of dollars ahead because you won't be making a monthly payment.

● On the other hand, would you rather drive a 7-year-old car or a much newer one? A 2- or 3-year lease gives you the option of having a new car more often. The car you drive will always be under warranty and you don't have the hassle of selling or trading in an old car. After two or three years, you simply turn it in to the leasing agent.

● Leasing often is less expensive than buying for those who claim their car as a business expense. You can write off more of the expense of a leased vehicle than one that is purchased, and you tie up less capital. However, this may not be the best choice for everyone.

How do you find out if it is for you? Talk to your accountant or financial adviser—not the guy next door. Because everyone has a different situation, leasing can be a great deal for your next-door neighbor but of no real benefit to you.

Read the Fine Print on Leases

If you're enticed by leasing ads that tout "No money down, $299 a month" for a $25,000 car, read the fine print. It should explain some of the following:

● Most leases allow 10,000 to 15,000 miles a year. Go over the mileage limit and you'll pay a penalty of 10 to 15 cents a mile.

● On most leases, you have to pay up front the first month's payment and a refundable security deposit.

● Some states require that the lessee—that's you—pay sales tax on the full suggested retail price of the car. If the sales tax is eight percent in your area and you're leasing a $30,000 car, that's $2400 you have to pay. You usually have the option of rolling the sales tax into your monthly payment.

In addition, if you purchase the car at the end of the lease, you may have to pay sales tax on that amount. Check your local tax laws to be sure.

● You'll also probably have to pay an "acquisition fee" if you buy the car or a "disposition fee" if you return it at the end. The amount is usually between $250 and $500.

● Early termination and purchase options: Before signing, learn whether you can terminate the lease early and how much of a penalty you must pay. It might cost hundreds of dollars to terminate a lease early.

● End-of-lease costs: You'll be liable for "excessive wear" or may be charged for having the car prepped for resale. It pays to take good care of a leased car so it passes inspection when you turn it in.

MODEL GROUPS

Subcompact Cars
Chevrolet Cavalier
Dodge Neon
Eagle Summit
Ford Aspire
Ford Escort
Geo Metro
Geo Prizm
Honda Civic
Hyundai Accent
Hyundai Elantra
Kia Sephia
Mazda Protege
Mercury Tracer
Mitsubishi Mirage
Nissan Sentra
Plymouth Neon
Pontiac Sunfire
Saturn Sedan/Wagon
Subaru Impreza
Suzuki Esteem/Swift
Toyota Corolla
Toyota Tercel
Volkswagen Jetta/Golf

Compact Cars
Buick Skylark
Chevrolet Corsica
Ford Contour
Mazda 626
Mercury Mystique
Mitsubishi Galant
Nissan Altima
Oldsmobile Achieva
Pontiac Grand Am
Subaru Legacy
Toyota Camry
Volkswagen Passat

Mid-size Cars
Buick Century
Buick Regal
Chevrolet Lumina/Monte Carlo
Chrysler Cirrus
Dodge Stratus
Ford Taurus
Ford Thunderbird
Honda Accord
Hyundai Sonata
Mercury Cougar
Mercury Sable
Oldsmobile Cutlass Ciera
Oldsmobile Cutlass Supreme
Plymouth Breeze
Pontiac Grand Prix

Full-size Cars
Buick LeSabre
Buick Roadmaster
Chevrolet Caprice/Impala SS
Chrysler Concorde
Dodge Intrepid
Eagle Vision
Ford Crown Victoria
Mercury Grand Marquis
Oldsmobile Eighty Eight
Pontiac Bonneville
Toyota Avalon

Premium Coupes
Audi Cabriolet
BMW 8-Series
Buick Riviera
Cadillac Eldorado
Jaguar XJS
Lexus SC 300/400
Lincoln Mark VIII
Mercedes-Benz SL
Mercedes-Benz S500/600

Premium Sedans
Acura TL Sedan
Audi A4
Audi A6/S6
BMW 3-Series
BMW 5-Series
BMW 7-Series
Buick Park Avenue
Cadillac De Ville/Concours
Cadillac Fleetwood
Cadillac Seville
Chrysler LHS/New Yorker
Infiniti G20
Infiniti I30

Infiniti J30
Infiniti Q45
Jaguar XJ Sedan
Lexus ES 300
Lexus GS 300
Lexus LS 400
Lincoln Continental
Lincoln Town Car
Mazda Millenia
Mercedes-Benz C-Class
Mercedes-Benz E-Class
Mercedes-Benz S-Class
Mitsubishi Diamante
Nissan Maxima
Oldsmobile Aurora
Oldsmobile Ninety Eight
Saab 900
Saab 9000
Volvo 850
Volvo 960

Sports Coupes
Acura Integra
Chevrolet Beretta
Chrysler Sebring
Dodge Avenger
Eagle Talon
Ford Probe
Honda del Sol
Honda Prelude
Mazda MX-6
Mitsubishi Eclipse
Nissan 200SX
Nissan 240SX
Saturn Coupe
Toyota Celica
Toyota Paseo
Volkswagen Cabrio

Sports and GT Cars
Acura NSX
BMW Z3
Chevrolet Camaro
Chevrolet Corvette
Dodge Stealth
Dodge Viper
Ford Mustang
Mazda Miata
Mazda RX-7
Mitsubishi 3000GT

Nissan 300ZX
Porsche 911
Pontiac Firebird
Subaru SVX
Toyota Supra

Sport-Utility Vehicles
Acura SLX
Chevrolet Blazer
Ford Explorer
Geo Tracker
GMC Jimmy
Honda Passport
Isuzu Rodeo
Isuzu Trooper
Jeep Cherokee
Jeep Grand Cherokee
Jeep Wrangler
Kia Sportage
Land Rover Defender 90
Land Rover Discovery
Lexus LX 450
Mercury Mountaineer
Mitsubishi Montero
Nissan Pathfinder
Oldsmobile Bravada
Range Rover 4.0 SE/4.6 HSE
Suzuki Sidekick
Suzuki X-90
Toyota Land Cruiser
Toyota RAV4
Toyota 4Runner

Minivans
Chevrolet Astro
Chevrolet Lumina Minivan
Chrysler Town & Country
Dodge Caravan
Ford Aerostar
Ford Windstar
GMC Safari
Honda Odyssey
Isuzu Oasis
Mazda MPV
Mercury Villager
Nissan Quest
Oldsmobile Silhouette
Plymouth Voyager
Pontiac Trans Sport
Toyota Previa

ACURA INTEGRA **RECOMMENDED**
Sports Coupe

Acura Integra LS 3-door

Acura's front-drive Integra returns for 1996 with minor equipment updates for both the 3-door hatchback and 4-door notchback sedan. Acura is the luxury division of Honda and the Integra is its least-expensive model line. The top-of-the-line GS-R gets new standard 15-inch alloy wheels, while the LS and base RS models, which have standard 14-inch wheels, wear new wheel covers for 1996. The LS model also gets body-color (instead of black) side moldings this year. All models have new green-tinted glass that is designed to reflect radiant heat to keep the interior cooler. In addition to the RS, LS, and GS-R models, there also is a Special Edition, which has standard leather upholstery and 15-inch alloy wheels. All models are available in both body styles. The hatchback is nearly two inches shorter in wheelbase and six inches shorter overall than the sedan. All models except the GS-R come with a 142-horsepower 1.8-liter 4-cylinder with dual overhead camshafts. The GS-R uses a 170-horsepower dual-cam 1.8-liter engine with Honda's variable-valve timing system. A 5-speed manual transmission is standard on all models and a 4-speed automatic is optional except on the GS-R. Dual air bags are standard across the board. Anti-lock brakes are standard on all models except the RS, where they aren't available. Prices start at around $16,000 and climb above $22,000, so the Integra isn't the best choice for consumers on a tight budget. However, the Integra should be reliable and have good resale value. The 142-horsepower engine revs like crazy but doesn't have enough low-speed torque to show much gusto with the automatic transmission. With the 5-speed manual, all models are quick. All models have commendable cornering ability and sharp steering, but the ride is rather bouncy on the 3-door versions because of the shorter wheelbase.

Acura Integra prices are on page 250.

ACURA INTEGRA LS

Rating Guide	1	2	3	4	5

Performance

Acceleration	4
Economy	3
Driveability	3
Ride	3
Steering/handling	4
Braking	5
Noise	3

Accommodations

Driver seating	4
Instruments/controls	4
Visibility	4
Room/comfort	3
Entry/exit	3
Cargo room	3

Workmanship

Exterior	4
Interior	4

Value 4

Total Points 58

Rating scale 5=Exceptional; 4=Above average; 3=Average; 2=Below average; 1=Poor

Specifications

Body type	3-door hatchback
Wheelbase (in.)	101.2
Overall length (in.)	172.4
Overall width (in.)	67.3
Overall height (in.)	52.6
Curb weight (lbs.)	2529
Seating capacity	4
Front head room (in.)	38.5
Max. front leg room (in.)	42.7
Rear head room (in.)	35.0
Min. rear leg room (in.)	28.1
Cargo volume (cu. ft.)	13.3
Engine type	dohc I-4
Engine size (l/cu. in.)	1.8/112
Horsepower @ rpm	142 @ 6300
Torque @ rpm	127 @ 5200
Transmission	manual/5-sp.
Drive wheels	front
Brakes, F/R	disc/disc (ABS)
Tire size	195/60HR14
Fuel tank capacity (gal.)	13.2
EPA city/highway mpg	25/31
Test mileage (mpg)	24.8

Warranties The entire car is covered for 4 years/50,000 miles. Body perforation rust is covered for 5 years/unlimited miles.

Built in Japan.

CONSUMER GUIDE®

ACURA TL SEDAN
Premium Sedan

Acura 2.5TL

Acura, the luxury division of Honda, introduced the TL sedan last spring as a replacement for the Vigor and a rival for cars such as the BMW 3-Series, Lexus ES 300, Mazda Millenia, and Mercedes C-Class. The front-drive TL ("Touring-Luxury") comes in two versions. The base 2.5TL has a 176-horsepower 2.5-liter 5-cylinder engine, which was used in the Vigor. The 3.2TL has the 200-horsepower 3.2-liter V-6 used in the larger Acura Legend. Both models come with a 4-speed automatic transmission. Standard equipment includes dual air bags, anti-lock brakes, automatic climate control, cassette and CD players, and power locks and windows. Leather upholstery is standard on the 3.2TL and optional on the 2.5TL, which has a firmer suspension and is marketed as the sportier of the two. Both models are available with optional Premium Packages. On the 3.2TL, the Premium Package includes traction control, a power moonroof, heated front seats and outside mirrors, and a power front passenger's seat. On the 2.5TL, major features of the package include leather upholstery and the moonroof. The 2.5TL isn't that much different from the Vigor in features or driving feel. The automatic transmission is slow to downshift for passing and often shifts harshly in hard acceleration. The 5-cylinder engine is quieter and smoother than it was in the Vigor but still has a coarse growl most of the time. The 2.5TL is no slouch, but the 3.2TL is much livelier and the V-6 is quieter. Though the TL is roomier than the Vigor, head room all around and rear leg room are just adequate for 6-footers. Among the TL's good points are an accommodating driving position and simple, intuitive instruments and controls. Acura bolstered its customer service programs recently to try to retain customers who were defecting to other luxury brands, so give the TL a look.

Acura TL Sedan prices are on page 251.

ACURA 2.5TL

Rating Guide	1	2	3	4	5
Performance					
Acceleration				▓	
Economy		▓			
Driveability			▓		
Ride			▓		
Steering/handling				▓	
Braking				▓	
Noise			▓		
Accommodations					
Driver seating				▓	
Instruments/controls				▓	
Visibility			▓		
Room/comfort		▓			
Entry/exit			▓		
Cargo room			▓		
Workmanship					
Exterior				▓	
Interior				▓	
Value			▓		

Total Points...59

Rating scale 5=Exceptional; 4=Above average; 3=Average; 2=Below average; 1=Poor

Specifications

Body type ....4-door notchback	Engine type ....ohc I-5
Wheelbase (in.) 111.8	Engine size (l/cu. in.)....2.5/152
Overall length (in.)................191.5	Horsepower @ rpm ...176 @ 6300
Overall width (in.) 70.3	Torque @ rpm ....170 @ 3900
Overall height (in.) 55.3	Transmission................auto/4-sp.
Curb weight (lbs.) 3252	Drive wheels ....front
Seating capacity 5	Brakes, F/R...........disc/disc (ABS)
Front head room (in.) 39.1	Tire size 205/60HR15
Max. front leg room (in.) 43.7	Fuel tank capacity (gal.) 17.2
Rear head room (in.) 36.9	EPA city/highway mpg 20/25
Min. rear leg room (in.)..........35.2	Test mileage (mpg) 19.2
Cargo volume (cu. ft.).............14.1	

Warranties The entire car is covered for 4 years/50,000 miles. Body perforation rust is covered for 5 years/unlimited miles.

Built in Japan.

CONSUMER GUIDE®

AUDI A4
Premium Sedan

Audi A4

Audi replaces the 90 sedan this year with the A4, a compact sedan with more daring styling and a roomier interior. Compared to the 90, the A4's 103-inch wheelbase is slightly longer than the 90's, while the 178-inch overall length is slightly shorter. The A4 is about two inches wider, which combines with a shorter engine bay to create more space for the passenger compartment. A 172-horsepower 2.8-liter V-6 returns as standard. A 5-speed manual transmission is standard and a new 5-speed automatic is optional. The A4 comes with front-wheel drive or Audi's permanently engaged 4-wheel drive Quattro system. Standard features include dual air bags, anti-lock brakes, automatic climate control, and a tilt and telescopic steering wheel. Leather upholstery and a CD changer are optional. The $26,500 base price for 1996 is $830 more than the 1995 Audi 90. The A4 addresses most of the 90's shortcomings while offering some pleasant surprises. Audi's V-6 feels like a new engine in the A4: It's smoother, quieter, and much more responsive. The new 5-speed automatic transmission has such smooth gear shifts that it may set new standards for the industry. Noise levels are low and the A4 has a smooth ride. There's more passenger room in the A4 than the Audi 90, but tall people still don't have much leg room in back and head room is only adequate with the optional moonroof, which steals about two inches of clearance. The gauges and most controls are easy to see and intuitive. An exception is the climate control panel, which is too small and low for easy reading. The A4 is good enough to stand comparison with the BMW 3-Series, Mercedes-Benz C-Class, and Lexus ES 300. Though the roomier Nissan Maxima goes for less, we think the A4 represents good value with prices starting at $26,500. It also is the only "near-luxury" sedan to offer all-wheel drive, plus free scheduled maintenance for 3 years/50,000 miles.

Audi A4 prices are on page 252.

AUDI A4 (Preliminary)

Rating Guide	1	2	3	4	5
Performance					
Acceleration			■■■		
Economy		■■			
Driveability			■■■		
Ride			■■■		
Steering/handling			■■■		
Braking			■■■		
Noise			■■■		
Accommodations					
Driver seating			■■■		
Instruments/controls		■■			
Visibility			■■■		
Room/comfort			■■■		
Entry/exit			■■■		
Cargo room			■■■		
Workmanship					
Exterior			■■■		
Interior			■■■		
Value		■■			

Total Points..59

Rating scale 5=Exceptional; 4=Above average; 3=Average; 2=Below average; 1=Poor

Specifications

Body type ....4-door notchback	Engine type.......................ohc V-6
Wheelbase (in.) 103.0	Engine size (l/cu. in.)..........2.8/169
Overall length (in.)................178.0	Horsepower @ rpm ...172 @ 5500
Overall width (in.) 68.2	Torque @ rpm ....184 @ 3000
Overall height (in.) 55.8	Transmission..................auto/5-sp.
Curb weight (lbs.) 2980	Drive wheels ....front
Seating capacity..........................5	Brakes, F/R...........disc/disc (ABS)
Front head room (in.) 38.1	Tire size 205/55HR16
Max. front leg room (in.) 41.3	Fuel tank capacity (gal.) 16.4
Rear head room (in.) 36.8	EPA city/highway mpg 18/28
Min. rear leg room (in.)...........33.4	Test mileage (mpg) ....NA
Cargo volume (cu. ft.).............13.7	

Warranties The entire car is covered for 3 years/50,000 miles. Body perforation rust is covered for 10 years/unlimited miles.

Built in Germany.

CONSUMER GUIDE®

AUDI A6/S6
Premium Sedan

Audi A6 Quattro 4-door

Audi adds new standard features this year to its A6 sedan and wagon, including a differential lock and one-touch power window operation. The A6 returns with a 2.8-liter V-6 engine and a standard 4-speed automatic transmission. The 5-speed manual transmission that was standard on the A6 sedan last year has been dropped. Front-wheel drive is standard and Audi's permanently engaged 4-wheel-drive Quattro system is optional. There are no 1996 versions of the high-performance S6 sedan and wagon, but 1995 models should still be available. The S6 comes with a 227-horsepower 2.2-liter 5-cylinder engine, a 5-speed manual transmission, and the Quattro 4WD system. On all models, the standard anti-lock brake system gains an electronic differential lock that engages in low-speed acceleration to improve traction on slippery surfaces. The anti-lock system can now apportion braking force between the front and rear wheels based on driving conditions. The power window system has been revised so that all windows can be lowered or raised by a single touch of the controls. The windows will reverse direction if they encounter an obstacle while being raised. Both body styles have front bucket seats and a 3-place second seat. The wagon also has a rear-facing 2-place child seat. Dual air bags are standard on all models. Last year prices on the A6 were cut nearly $5000, so it is now less expensive than some Japanese luxury sedans. In addition, Audi throws in free maintenance for the first 3 years/50,000 miles. However, the A6 doesn't match most rivals in acceleration. The 2.8-liter V-6 doesn't produce much torque at low speeds, so it requires a heavy throttle foot for good pickup. Handling and roadholding are commendable, and the A6 has a soft, absorbent ride. All models have ample room for four passengers and their luggage. Dealers should be discounting and offering subsidized leases on the A6.

Audi A6/S6 prices are on page 253.

AUDI A6 QUATTRO

Rating Guide	1	2	3	4	5
Performance					
Acceleration			▓▓▓		
Economy		▓▓▓			
Driveability				▓▓▓	
Ride				▓▓▓	
Steering/handling			▓▓▓		
Braking				▓▓▓	
Noise			▓▓▓		
Accommodations					
Driver seating				▓▓▓	
Instruments/controls				▓▓▓	
Visibility		▓▓▓			
Room/comfort			▓▓▓		
Entry/exit			▓▓▓		
Cargo room			▓▓▓		
Workmanship					
Exterior				▓▓▓	
Interior				▓▓▓	
Value			▓▓▓		
Total Points					61

Rating scale 5=Exceptional; 4=Above average; 3=Average; 2=Below average; 1=Poor

Specifications

Body type ....4-door notchback
Wheelbase (in.) 105.8
Overall length (in.) 192.6
Overall width (in.) 70.0
Overall height (in.) 56.3
Curb weight (lbs.) 3428
Seating capacity 5
Front head room (in.) 38.4
Max. front leg room (in.) 42.4
Rear head room (in.) 37.6
Min. rear leg room (in.) 34.8
Cargo volume (cu. ft.):.............16.8

Engine type........................ohc V-6
Engine size (l/cu. in.) 2.8/169
Horsepower @ rpm ...172 @ 5500
Torque @ rpm ....184 @ 3000
Transmission..................auto/4-sp.
Drive wheels ....all
Brakes, F/R............disc/disc (ABS)
Tire size 195/65HR15
Fuel tank capacity (gal.) 21.1
EPA city/highway mpg 19/25
Test mileage (mpg) 18.0

Warranties The entire car is covered for 3 years/50,000 miles. Body perforation rust is covered for 10 years/unlimited miles.

Built in Germany.

BMW 5-SERIES
Premium Sedan

BMW 540i

A redesigned 5-Series sedan is scheduled to go on sale in the U.S. in the spring as an early 1997 model and a station wagon will follow by next fall. Styling for the new 5-Series sedan is evolutionary from the current model, with BMW's trademark "twin-kidney" grille a returning feature. BMW hasn't released much information on the 1997 models, which will retain rear-wheel drive. They will have new side air bags with two elements, one to protect the chest and hips and another to protect the heads of front-seat occupants. There will not be any 1996 models. Until the 1997 models arrive, BMW will sell carryover 1995 5-Series models and one new model, the limited-production 540i Sport. The 540i Sport has a 282-horsepower 4.0-liter V-8 engine, a choice of 6-speed manual or 5-speed automatic transmissions, and some features borrowed from the European M5 model, a performance-oriented sedan. Among the M5 components are the Electronic Damping Control suspension and Servotronic variable-assist power steering. Returning 1995 models include the 525i sedan and station wagon with a 189-horsepower 2.5-liter 6-cylinder engine; the 530i sedan and wagon with a 215-horsepower 3.0-liter V-8; and the 540i with the 282-horsepower 4.0-liter V-8. All models come with dual front air bags and anti-lock brakes. With new models scheduled to arrive next spring and arch rival Mercedes-Benz introducing a new E-Class sedan this fall, BMW dealers should be heavily discounting prices on the 1995 5-Series cars. Among the current crop we prefer the V-8 models. We clocked a 540i with the automatic at 7.1 seconds to 60 mph. However, we averaged just 15.7 mpg from a mix of city and highway driving, and premium gas is required. The 6-cylinder 525i and 525i Touring trade somewhat higher mileage for a noticeable loss of acceleration, especially with the automatic transmission.

BMW 5-Series prices are on page 254.

BMW 540i

Rating Guide	1	2	3	4	5
Performance					
Acceleration				|||||	
Economy	|||||				
Driveability			|||||		
Ride			|||||		
Steering/handling			|||||		
Braking			|||||		
Noise			|||||		
Accommodations					
Driver seating			|||||		
Instruments/controls			|||||		
Visibility			|||||		
Room/comfort		|||||			
Entry/exit		|||||			
Cargo room			|||||		
Workmanship					
Exterior			|||||		
Interior			|||||		
Value			|||||		

Total Points..61

Rating scale 5=Exceptional; 4=Above average; 3=Average; 2=Below average; 1=Poor

Specifications

Body type ....4-door notchback	Engine type....................dohc V-8
Wheelbase (in.) 108.7	Engine size (l/cu. in.)........4.0/243
Overall length (in.) 185.8	Horsepower @ rpm ...282 @ 5800
Overall width (in.) 68.9	Torque @ rpm ....295 @ 4500
Overall height (in.) 55.6	Transmission.................auto/5-sp.
Curb weight (lbs.) 3804	Drive wheels ....rear
Seating capacity..........................5	Brakes, F/R ....disc/disc (ABS)
Front head room (in.) 36.9	Tire size 225/60HR15
Max. front leg room (in.) 41.6	Fuel tank capacity (gal.) 21.1
Rear head room (in.) 36.4	EPA city/highway mpg 17/25
Min. rear leg room (in.) 37.0	Test mileage (mpg) 15.7
Cargo volume (cu. ft.)............16.2	

Warranties The entire car is covered for 4 years/50,000 miles. Body perforation rust is covered for 6 years/unlimited miles.

Built in Germany.

BMW 7-SERIES
Premium Sedan

BMW 740iL

BMW plans to import only the long-wheelbase version of its rear-drive 7-Series sedan this year, so the 740i model stays home in Germany. The returning 740iL and 750iL ride a 120.9-inch wheelbase, 5.5 inches longer than the 740i. The other big change for BMW's flagship sedan, which was redesigned last year, is that the 740iL will trade last year's 4.0-liter V-8 for a 4.5-liter version. Despite the larger displacement, the model name will continue to be 740iL. Power ratings for the new engine weren't available, but BMW estimated horsepower will remain nearly the same as the 4.0-liter's 282, while torque is expected to be greater than last year's 295 pounds/feet. The 750iL returns with a 323-horsepower 5.4-liter V-12 engine. A 5-speed automatic transmission, dual air bags, and anti-lock brakes are standard on both models. Traction control is standard instead of optional this year on the 740iL (it was already standard on the 750iL) and Electronic Damping Control, which automatically adjusts suspension firmness based on driving conditions, is a new option. The 750iL also has an anti-skid system called Dynamic Stability Control, which uses the sensors for the anti-lock brakes and traction-control system to detect when any wheel is locking or slipping. It then reduces engine power and applies individual brakes to maintain traction and steering control. The 7-Series sedans are quiet, comfortable, and enjoyable to drive. The 740iL and 750iL have more passenger room than most luxury sedans, and the seats are supportive and comfortable on long drives. Though both models have more exhaust and road noise than the Lexus LS 400, they're still quieter than most other rivals. The 740iL has enough low-end power to accelerate briskly from a standing start and abundant passing power at highway speeds. In fact, the V-8 is strong enough that we see little need to pay the hefty premium on the V-12-powered 750iL.

BMW 7-Series prices are on page 255.

BMW 750iL

Rating Guide	1	2	3	4	5

Performance

Acceleration	5
Economy	1
Driveability	4
Ride	4
Steering/handling	4
Braking	4
Noise	4

Accommodations

Driver seating	4
Instruments/controls	4
Visibility	4
Room/comfort	5
Entry/exit	4
Cargo room	4

Workmanship

Exterior	5
Interior	5

Value	3

Total Points..66

Rating scale 5=Exceptional; 4=Above average; 3=Average; 2=Below average; 1=Poor

Specifications

Body type	4-door notchback
Wheelbase (in.)	120.9
Overall length (in.)	201.7
Overall width (in.)	73.3
Overall height (in.)	56.1
Curb weight (lbs.)	4200
Seating capacity	5
Front head room (in.)	37.7
Max. front leg room (in.)	41.9
Rear head room (in.)	37.2
Min. rear leg room (in.)	41.9
Cargo volume (cu. ft.)	13.0
Engine type	ohc V-12
Engine size (l/cu. in.)	5.4/328
Horsepower @ rpm	323 @ 5000
Torque @ rpm	362 @ 3900
Transmission	auto/5-sp.
Drive wheels	rear
Brakes, F/R	disc/disc (ABS)
Tire size	235/60HR16
Fuel tank capacity (gal.)	25.1
EPA city/highway mpg	15/20
Test mileage (mpg)	13.8

Warranties The entire car is covered for 4 years/50,000 miles. Body perforation rust is covered for 6 years/unlimited miles.

Built in Germany.

BUICK PARK AVENUE/ OLDSMOBILE NINETY EIGHT
Premium Sedan

Buick Park Avenue

The Park Avenue Ultra model has a more powerful supercharged V-6 engine for 1996, the 240-horsepower 3800 Series II, while the similar Ninety Eight has a short future. Ninety Eight, a name first used in 1941 and one of the oldest in the auto industry, will be retired after the 1996 model year. The Park Avenue will be redesigned for 1997. For 1996 the base Park Avenue returns with a 205-horsepower version of the 3800 Series II engine. For its final season the Ninety Eight returns in Series I and II price levels with the 205-horsepower engine. Both engines have new coolant designed to last 5 years/100,000 miles and spark plugs designed to last 100,000 miles, and they team with a 4-speed automatic transmission. Dual air bags and anti-lock brakes are standard on all models. Though these cars share major mechanical components they have different styling and interior features. The automatic door locks available on all models have a new feature that lets the owner program them to one of four operating modes. The remote keyless entry system has several new features, including a panic button that sounds the horn and flashes the lights. In addition, it can adjust the driver's seat and outside mirrors to one of two preset positions. Though the supercharged Ultra delivers more impressive acceleration, the base Park Avenue and the Ninety Eight have ample power and should be sufficient for most situations. Both engines have seamless power delivery through General Motors' smooth 4-speed automatic transmission. These cars are roomy and comfortable and have spacious trunks, but the suspension is too soft and allows too much body lean in turns and lots of bouncing at highway speeds. If you're considering either of these models, check out the Buick LeSabre or the Oldsmobile Eighty Eight. They offer most of the same features for less money.

Buick Park Avenue prices are on page 260.
Oldsmobile Ninety Eight prices are on page 403.

BUICK PARK AVENUE

Rating Guide	1	2	3	4	5

Performance

Acceleration	4
Economy	2
Driveability	4
Ride	3
Steering/handling	3
Braking	4
Noise	4

Accommodations

Driver seating	3
Instruments/controls	3
Visibility	3
Room/comfort	4
Entry/exit	4
Cargo room	4

Workmanship

Exterior	4
Interior	4

Value

Value	3

Total Points **60**

Rating scale 5=Exceptional; 4=Above average; 3=Average; 2=Below average; 1=Poor

Specifications

Body type	4-door notchback
Wheelbase (in.)	110.8
Overall length (in.)	205.9
Overall width (in.)	74.1
Overall height (in.)	55.1
Curb weight (lbs.)	3536
Seating capacity	6
Front head room (in.)	38.8
Max. front leg room (in.)	42.7
Rear head room (in.)	37.8
Min. rear leg room (in.)	40.7
Cargo volume (cu. ft.)	20.3
Engine	ohv V-6
Engine size (l/cu. in.)	3.8/231
Horsepower @ rpm	205 @ 5200
Torque @ rpm	230 @ 4000
Transmission	auto/4-sp.
Drive wheels	front
Brakes, F/R	disc/drum (ABS)
Tire size	205/70R15
Fuel tank capacity (gal.)	18.0
EPA city/highway mpg	19/29
Test mileage (mpg)	19.8

Warranties The entire car is covered for 3 years/36,000 miles. Body perforation rust is covered for 6 years/100,000 miles.

Built in Orion, Mich.

BUICK REGAL

Mid-Size

RECOMMENDED

Buick Regal Limited

The mid-size Regal has a new 3.8-liter V-6 engine and more standard features for 1996. The new 3800 Series II V-6 produces 205 horsepower, 35 more than last year's 3.8-liter engine. The 3800 Series II is standard on the Gran Sport and Limited models and optional on the Custom. Both the 3.8-liter and the 160-horsepower 3.1-liter V-6 (standard on the Custom) have new spark plugs designed to last 100,000 miles and engine coolant designed to last 5 years/100,000 miles. Both engines come with a 4-speed automatic transmission. Regal is built from the same design as the Chevrolet Lumina/Monte Carlo, Oldsmobile Cutlass Supreme, and Pontiac Grand Prix, all of which have front-wheel drive. Though they share most major mechanical features, each has different styling and interior features, and the Regal is the only one that offers the 3.8-liter V-6. The Regal Custom and Gran Sport come in 2-door coupe and 4-door sedan styling, and the Limited comes only as a sedan. Dual air bags and anti-lock 4-wheel disc brakes are standard on all models. The base 3.1-liter V-6 provides adequate acceleration and is smooth and generally quiet. We prefer the 3.8-liter V-6, which delivers considerably stronger acceleration and swift, safe passing. This year's Series II 3.8-liter is smoother and quieter than last year's, and it gives the Regal a performance edge over the similar General Motors cars. Figure on 19-21 mpg with the 3.1-liter engine in urban driving and about two mpg less with the 3.8-liter. With the base suspension, Regal rides softly but leans heavily in turns and the steering is too light. Body lean is reduced with the optional Gran Touring suspension. Buick says it went to great lengths to make its seats more comfortable, but we still find the seats too soft and poorly shaped for good support. However, there's ample space for four adults and a roomy trunk that holds plenty of luggage.

Buick Regal prices are on page 263.

BUICK REGAL LIMITED

Rating Guide	1	2	3	4	5
Performance					
Acceleration			▓		
Economy		▓			
Driveability			▓		
Ride			▓		
Steering/handling		▓			
Braking			▓		
Noise			▓		
Accommodations					
Driver seating			▓		
Instruments/controls			▓		
Visibility			▓		
Room/comfort			▓		
Entry/exit			▓		
Cargo room			▓		
Workmanship					
Exterior			▓		
Interior			▓		
Value			▓		
Total Points					62

Rating scale 5=Exceptional; 4=Above average; 3=Average; 2=Below average; 1=Poor

Specifications

Body type	4-door notchback
Wheelbase (in.)	107.5
Overall length (in.)	193.7
Overall width (in.)	72.5
Overall height (in.)	54.5
Curb weight (lbs.)	3340
Seating capacity	5
Front head room (in.)	38.5
Max. front leg room (in.)	42.4
Rear head room (in.)	37.8
Min. rear leg room (in.)	36.2
Cargo volume (cu. ft.)	15.9
Engine type	ohv V-6
Engine size (l/cu. in.)	3.8/231
Horsepower @ rpm	205 @ 5200
Torque @ rpm	230 @ 4000
Transmission	auto/4-sp.
Drive wheels	front
Brakes, F/R	disc/disc (ABS)
Tire size	205/70R15
Fuel tank capacity (gal.)	16.5
EPA city/highway mpg	19/30
Test mileage (mpg)	18.3

Warranties The entire car is covered for 3 years/36,000 miles. Body perforation rust is covered for 6 years/100,000 miles.

Built in Canada.

BUICK RIVIERA

RECOMMENDED

Premium Coupe

Buick Riviera

A new version of General Motors' supercharged 3.8-liter V-6 is optional on Riviera, Buick's front-drive luxury coupe. Called the 3800 Series II, it produces 240 horsepower, 15 more than last year's supercharged 3.8-liter V-6. A non-supercharged 205-horsepower version of the 3800 V-6 remains standard on Riviera, which was redesigned for the 1995 model year. Both engines team with a 4-speed automatic transmission and have new spark plugs designed to last 100,000 miles and coolant designed to last 5 years/100,000 miles. Though Riviera is built on the same front-drive platform as the Oldsmobile Aurora sedan, it shares none of its styling or interior features. In addition, the Aurora uses a V-8 engine. Riviera comes in a single price level with a standard 3-place front bench seat. Leather bucket seats are optional. Among the new standard features this year are a CD player and lockout protection that disables the lock on the driver's door when the key is in the ignition. Riviera has the performance and refinement of rival premium coupes that cost thousands more. We clocked a supercharged model at a brisk 7.9 seconds to 60 mph, the same league as V-8-powered rivals such as the Cadillac Eldorado. While we haven't timed a Riviera with the base engine, acceleration isn't as lively, though it's still more than adequate. The Riviera feels balanced and nimble in turns, with little body lean and good grip, and the suspension teams with the long wheelbase to provide a comfortable ride over bumps and broken pavement. The dashboard layout is one of the weakest areas. The speedometer and tachometer are spaced too far apart and the steering wheel blocks the headlamp and cruise control switches. Though the base price has climbed more than $1800 the past year to $29,475, the Riviera is still a bargain compared to most premium coupes.

Buick Riviera prices are on page 265.

BUICK RIVIERA

Rating Guide	1	2	3	4	5

Performance

Acceleration	||||||||||||||||||||||||||||||||||||||||||||||||
Economy	||||||||||||||||||||||
Driveability	||||||||||||||||||||||||||||||||||||
Ride	||||||||||||||||||||||||||||||||||||
Steering/handling	||||||||||||||||||||||||||||||||||||
Braking	||||||||||||||||||||||||||||||||||||
Noise	||||||||||||||||||||||||||||||||||||

Accommodations

Driver seating	||||||||||||||||||||||||||||||||||||||||||||||||
Instruments/controls	||||||||||||||||||||||
Visibility	||||||||||||||||||||||||||||||||||||
Room/comfort	||||||||||||||||||||||||||||||||||||
Entry/exit	||||||||||||||||||||||||||||||||||||
Cargo room	||||||||||||||||||||||||||||||||||||

Workmanship

Exterior	||||||||||||||||||||||||||||||||||||
Interior	||||||||||||||||||||||||||||||||||||

Value

|||||||||||||||||||||||||||||||||||||

Total Points..**59**

Rating scale 5=Exceptional; 4=Above average; 3=Average; 2=Below average; 1=Poor

Specifications

Body type ....2-door notchback
Wheelbase (in.) 113.8
Overall length (in.) 207.2
Overall width (in.) 75.0
Overall height (in.) 55.2
Curb weight (lbs.) 3748
Seating capacity 5
Front head room (in.) 38.2
Max. front leg room (in.) 42.6
Rear head room (in.) 36.2
Min. rear leg room (in.) 37.3
Cargo volume (cu. ft.) 17.4

Engine ....Supercharged ohv V-6
Engine size (l/cu. in.) 3.8/231
Horsepower @ rpm ...240 @ 5200
Torque @ rpm ....280 @ 3200
Transmission ....auto/4 sp.
Drive wheels ....front
Brakes, F/R...........disc/disc (ABS)
Tire size 225/60R16
Fuel tank capacity (gal.) 20.0
EPA city/highway mpg 18/27
Test mileage (mpg) 17.7

Warranties The entire car is covered for 3 years/36,000 miles. Body perforation rust is covered for 6 years/100,000 miles.

Built in Orion, Mich.

CONSUMER GUIDE®

BUICK SKYLARK
Compact

Buick Skylark Gran Sport 2-door

Buick's front-drive compact is extensively revised for 1996, with a new passenger-side air bag in a redesigned dashboard, a larger standard engine, and fresh styling. The new passenger-side air bag joins a driver-side air bag, which has been standard since 1994. The base engine this year is a dual-camshaft 150-horsepower 2.4-liter 4-cylinder that General Motors calls the Twin Cam. It is an enlargement of the 2.3-liter Quad 4 that was last year's base engine. A 4-speed automatic transmission replaces a 3-speed automatic as standard with the 4-cylinder and includes traction control as a new feature. Anti-lock brakes return as standard. Skylark Custom and Limited models come with the 4-cylinder standard. A 155-horsepower 3.1-liter V-6 is standard on the Gran Sport models and optional on the others. Both engines have new 5-year/100,000-mile coolant and 100,000-mile spark plugs. All three versions of the Skylark come in 2-door coupe and 4-door sedan body styles. All also have new grilles, fascias, hoods, and headlamps that give them closer resemblance to other Buicks. Skylark is built from the same design as the Oldsmobile Achieva and Pontiac Grand Am but has different exterior styling and interior features. The new 2.4-liter 4-cylinder is just as powerful as earlier versions and much smoother and quieter. We no longer recommend the V-6 as a necessary alternative. The V-6's big advantage is its greater torque at lower speeds, which gives the Skylark a quicker jump off the line. However, the 4-cylinder is more economical. There is adequate room for four adults in the Skylark, though entry/exit is tight to the rear seat even on the 4-door. The new dashboard groups clearly marked analog gauges directly in front of the driver, and controls for the climate and sound systems are easy to reach. Buick dealers should be offering big discounts on Skylark.

Buick Skylark prices appear on page 269.

BUICK SKYLARK GS

Rating Guide	1	2	3	4	5
Performance					
Acceleration				4	
Economy			3		
Driveability			3		
Ride			3		
Steering/handling			3		
Braking					5
Noise			3		
Accommodations					
Driver seating				4	
Instruments/controls			3		
Visibility			3		
Room/comfort			3		
Entry/exit			3		
Cargo room			3		
Workmanship					
Exterior			3		
Interior			3		
Value			3		
Total Points..**57**					

Rating scale 5=Exceptional; 4=Above average; 3=Average; 2=Below average; 1=Poor

Specifications

Body type ....2-door notchback
Wheelbase (in.) 103.4
Overall length (in.) 189.1
Overall width (in.) 68.7
Overall height (in.) 53.2
Curb weight (lbs.) 2888
Seating capacity 5
Front head room (in.) 37.8
Max. front leg room (in.) 43.3
Rear head room (in.) 36.5
Min. rear leg room (in.) 32.5
Cargo volume (cu. ft.).............13.3

Engine type ....dohc I-4
Engine size (l/cu. in.).........2.4/146
Horsepower @ rpm ...150 @ 6000
Torque @ rpm ....150 @ 4400
Transmission.................auto/4-sp.
Drive wheels ....front
Brakes, F/R ....disc/drum (ABS)
Tire size 205/55R16
Fuel tank capacity (gal.) 15.2
EPA city/highway mpg 22/32
Test mileage (mpg) ....NA

Warranties The entire car is covered for 3 years/36,000 miles. Body perforation rust is covered for 6 years/100,000 miles.

Built in Lansing, Mich.

CONSUMER GUIDE®

CADILLAC DE VILLE/ CONCOURS
Premium Sedan

Cadillac Concours

All of Cadillac's front-drive models are now powered by the 4.6-liter Northstar V-8 with dual overhead camshafts. Last year, the De Ville sedan used an overhead-valve 4.9-liter V-8 with 200 horsepower. This year, it has a 275-horsepower Northstar V-8, while the similar Concours sedan gets a 300-horsepower version. Last year, the Concours had the 275-horsepower Northstar engine. Both engines team with a 4-speed automatic transmission and have new coolant designed to last 5 years/100,000 miles. Dual air bags and anti-lock brakes also are standard on both models. Some interior features can be automatically set to one of two positions on the De Ville and Concours this year, including the automatic door locks and the driver's seat position, using either the remote keyless entry system or dashboard controls. New items standard on the Concours this year include Rainsense, a feature that automatically turns on the wipers when it rains. The base price on the De Ville has jumped about $1000 this year, but it remains a relative bargain at $35,995, more than $5000 cheaper than the Lincoln Continental. The overhead-valve V-8 used last year was no slouch, but the Northstar engine is smoother and furnishes stronger acceleration than some rivals that purport to be sports sedans. We clocked a 1995 Concours at 6.8 seconds to 60 mph. On paper, the Concours' 300-horsepower engine looks more impressive. On the road, however, the 275-horsepower version delivers more power at lower speeds, so it is more useful in the kind of driving most people do. Unfortunately, both engines use expensive premium gas—and lots of it. We averaged 17.2 mpg in a Concours, but that was inflated by an abundance of highway miles. With either model, there's ample space for six adults in the roomy interior and the trunk has a wide, flat floor that can hold lots of luggage.

Cadillac De Ville/Concours prices are on page 271.

CADILLAC CONCOURS

Rating Guide	1	2	3	4	5
Performance					
Acceleration				▓▓▓▓	
Economy	▓▓				
Driveability				▓▓▓▓	
Ride			▓▓▓		
Steering/handling		▓▓			
Braking				▓▓▓▓	
Noise			▓▓▓		
Accommodations					
Driver seating		▓▓			
Instruments/controls		▓▓			
Visibility		▓▓			
Room/comfort				▓▓▓▓	
Entry/exit			▓▓▓		
Cargo room		▓▓			
Workmanship					
Exterior			▓▓▓		
Interior			▓▓▓		
Value			▓▓▓		
Total Points					**63**

Rating scale 5=Exceptional; 4=Above average; 3=Average; 2=Below average; 1=Poor

Specifications

Body type ....4-door notchback	Engine type.....................dohc V-8
Wheelbase (in.).....................113.8	Engine size (l/cu. in.).........4.6/279
Overall length (in.)................209.7	Horsepower @ rpm ...300 @ 6000
Overall width (in.) 76.6	Torque @ rpm ....295 @ 4400
Overall height (in.).................56.3	Transmission.................auto/4-sp.
Curb weight (lbs.) 3959	Drive wheels ....front
Seating capacity 6	Brakes, F/R..........disc/disc (ABS)
Front head room (in.) 38.5	Tire size 225/60HR16
Max. front leg room (in.) 42.6	Fuel tank capacity (gal.) 20.0
Rear head room (in.) 38.4	EPA city/highway mpg 17/26
Min. rear leg room (in.)...........43.3	Test mileage (mpg) 17.2
Cargo volume (cu. ft.).............20.0	

Warranties The entire car is covered for 4 years/50,000 miles. Body perforation rust is covered for 6 years/100,000 miles.

Built in Hamtramck, Mich.

CONSUMER GUIDE®

CADILLAC ELDORADO
Premium Coupe

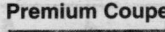

Cadillac Eldorado

The sporty Eldorado Touring Coupe has a new dashboard, while both the ETC and base model have new standard stereos and daytime running lights. The Eldorado, a 2-door coupe, is built from the same design as the Seville sedan but has different styling and a shorter front-drive chassis. A 275-horsepower version of Cadillac's 4.6-liter Northstar V-8 engine is standard on the base Eldorado. The ETC comes with a 300-horsepower version. Both engines have new coolant designed to last 5 years/100,000 miles. A 4-speed automatic transmission, dual air bags, and anti-lock brakes are standard on both models. The new dashboard in the ETC has larger analog gauges and new climate and stereo controls mounted above the center console. The base Eldorado retains the dashboard used previously by both models, but, like the ETC, it has a new stereo with a cassette player and 12 FM station and six AM station presets. In addition, both models have new redundant stereo and climate controls mounted on the steering wheel. The ETC has a new standard feature called Rainsense, which automatically activates the windshield wipers when needed. A new feature shared with all front-drive Cadillacs is lockout protection that disables the driver's door lock when the key is in the ignition. Don't judge the two Eldorado models entirely on horsepower. We prefer the base model's 275-horsepower version because it produces more torque at low speeds, which is what you need for quick acceleration and swift passing on the highway. The 300-horsepower engine in the Touring Coupe develops more power at higher engine speeds, which is less useful in the kind of driving most Americans do. Both engines use lots of premium gas. We averaged just 15 mpg with a Touring Coupe and 18 with a base model, and highway driving was included with both. Aside from the low mileage, our biggest complaint is that the massive rear roof pillars severely restrict visibility in the Eldorado.

Cadillac Eldorado prices are on page 273.

CADILLAC ELDORADO

Rating Guide

	1	2	3	4	5

Performance
Acceleration	5
Economy	2
Driveability	3
Ride	3
Steering/handling	3
Braking	3
Noise	3

Accommodations
Driver seating	3
Instruments/controls	3
Visibility	3
Room/comfort	4
Entry/exit	3
Cargo room	3

Workmanship
Exterior	5
Interior	4

Value
3

Total Points..**59**

Rating scale 5=Exceptional; 4=Above average; 3=Average; 2=Below average; 1=Poor

Specifications

Body type	2-door notchback
Wheelbase (in.)	108.0
Overall length (in.)	200.2
Overall width (in.)	75.5
Overall height (in.)	54.0
Curb weight (lbs.)	3774
Seating capacity	5
Front head room (in.)	37.4
Max. front leg room (in.)	42.6
Rear head room (in.)	38.3
Min. rear leg room (in.)	36.0
Cargo volume (cu. ft.)	15.3
Engine type	dohc V-8
Engine size (l/cu. in.)	4.6/279
Horsepower @ rpm	275 @ 5600
Torque @ rpm	300 @ 4000
Transmission	auto/4-sp.
Drive wheels	front
Brakes, F/R	disc/disc (ABS)
Tire size	225/60R16
Fuel tank capacity (gal.)	20.0
EPA city/highway mpg	17/26
Test mileage (mpg)	17.9

Warranties The entire car is covered for 4 years/50,000 miles. Body perforation rust is covered for 6 years/100,000 miles.

Built in Hamtramck, Mich.

CONSUMER GUIDE®

CADILLAC FLEETWOOD
Premium Sedan

Cadillac Fleetwood

This is the final season for the rear-drive Fleetwood, the longest production car built in America at 225 inches stem to stern. General Motors has announced that production of the Fleetwood, Buick Roadmaster, and Chevrolet Caprice/Impala SS will end in early 1996 so the plant in Arlington, Texas, where all three are built can be converted to produce trucks. Fleetwood returns in a single price level, but there also is a more luxurious Brougham option package. Standard equipment includes a 260-horsepower 5.7-liter V-8, 4-speed automatic transmission, dual air bags, anti-lock brakes, and traction control. The 5.7-liter V-8, derived from the engine used in the Chevrolet Corvette, has new coolant designed to last 5 years/100,000 miles. Fleetwood sales have declined in recent years as buyers switch to smaller front-drive cars and luxurious sport-utility vehicles. Because it's so big and heavy, you don't expect the Fleetwood to be a sprinter. With a Corvette engine under the hood it has quick takeoffs and strong passing power. Fuel economy, however, is no bargain: 14.8 mpg in our last test. We tested a Fleetwood during the winter and found that the standard traction control system makes this rear-drive sedan an all-weather vehicle. At nearly 4500 pounds, this car isn't designed for zipping around winding roads. There's too much body lean and the soft suspension allows lots of bouncing on wavy roads. There's room for adults to stretch their legs at the four outboard seating positions. The interior is wide enough to fit three people across, but those in the middle won't have much leg room. The roomy trunk can hold several suitcases or a foursome's golf bags. Though Cadillac updated its rear-drive sedan considerably the past few years, the rival Lincoln Town Car remains more popular. If you'd rather have a Fleetwood, Cadillac dealers should be cutting their prices.

Cadillac Fleetwood prices are on page 274.

CADILLAC FLEETWOOD

Rating Guide	1	2	3	4	5
Performance					
Acceleration					■
Economy	■				
Driveability			■		
Ride				■	
Steering/handling		■			
Braking				■	
Noise			■		
Accommodations					
Driver seating		■			
Instruments/controls		■			
Visibility		■			
Room/comfort				■	
Entry/exit			■		
Cargo room		■			
Workmanship					
Exterior			■		
Interior			■		
Value		■			
Total Points					59

Rating scale 5=Exceptional; 4=Above average; 3=Average; 2=Below average; 1=Poor

Specifications

Body type ....4-door notchback
Wheelbase (in.) 121.5
Overall length (in.) 225.0
Overall width (in.) 78.0
Overall height (in.) 57.1
Curb weight (lbs.) 4477
Seating capacity 6
Front head room (in.) 38.7
Max. front leg room (in.) 42.5
Rear head room (in.) 39.1
Min. rear leg room (in.) 43.9
Cargo volume (cu. ft.)..............21.1

Engine type ....ohv V-8
Engine size (l/cu. in.) 5.7/350
Horsepower @ rpm ...260 @ 5000
Torque @ rpm ....335 @ 2400
Transmission ....auto/4-sp.
Drive wheels ....rear
Brakes, F/R ....disc/drum (ABS)
Tire size 235/70R15
Fuel tank capacity (gal.) 23.0
EPA city/highway mpg 17/26
Test mileage (mpg) 14.8

Warranties The entire car is covered for 4 years/50,000 miles. Body perforation rust is covered for 6 years/100,000 miles.

Built in Arlington, Tex.

CONSUMER GUIDE®

CADILLAC SEVILLE
Premium Sedan

✓ **BEST BUY**

Cadillac Seville STS

A new dashboard for the sporty STS model is the biggest change this year on the front-drive Seville. Both the STS (Seville Touring Sedan) and the SLS (Seville Luxury Sedan) have new standard stereos and daytime running lights. The Seville is a 4-door sedan built from the same design as the Eldorado, a 2-door coupe, but it has different styling and a longer chassis. A 275-horsepower version of Cadillac's 4.6-liter Northstar V-8 engine is standard on the SLS. The STS comes with a 300-horsepower version. Both engines have new coolant designed to last 5 years/100,000 miles. A 4-speed automatic transmission, dual air bags, and anti-lock brakes are standard on both models. The STS's new dashboard has larger analog gauges and new climate and stereo controls grouped in the center. Both models have new redundant stereo and climate controls mounted on the steering wheel. The STS has a new standard feature called Rainsense, which automatically activates the windshield wipers when needed. The STS's 300-horsepower engine provides a performance advantage only at higher speeds. The SLS's 275-horsepower version produces more power at low speeds, making it more usable in urban driving. Both Seville engines require premium gas and neither is an economy champ. We averaged 16.8 mpg with an STS, with more than half of our driving on highways. Ride quality is where the STS and SLS differ most, though this year the STS has softer tires that have reduced the differences somewhat. The STS's firmer suspension transmits some harshness into the interior, while by contrast the SLS easily absorbs rough pavement. Seville has a roomy, elegantly styled interior and ample cargo space. With base prices well below rivals such as the Lexus LS 400 and BMW 740iL, Seville is a worthy alternative to Japanese and European luxury sedans.

Cadillac Seville prices appear on page 275.

CADILLAC SEVILLE STS

Rating Guide	1	2	3	4	5
Performance					
Acceleration					▉
Economy	▉				
Driveability				▉	
Ride			▉		
Steering/handling				▉	
Braking				▉	
Noise			▉		
Accommodations					
Driver seating				▉	
Instruments/controls				▉	
Visibility			▉		
Room/comfort			▉		
Entry/exit			▉		
Cargo room			▉		
Workmanship					
Exterior				▉	
Interior				▉	
Value				▉	
Total Points					62

Rating scale 5=Exceptional; 4=Above average; 3=Average; 2=Below average; 1=Poor

Specifications

Body type	4-door notchback
Wheelbase (in.)	111.0
Overall length (in.)	204.1
Overall width (in.)	74.2
Overall height (in.)	54.5
Curb weight (lbs.)	3892
Seating capacity	5
Front head room (in.)	38.0
Max. front leg room (in.)	43.0
Rear head room (in.)	38.3
Min. rear leg room (in.)	39.1
Cargo volume (cu. ft.)	14.4
Engine type	dohc V-8
Engine size (l/cu. in.)	4.6/279
Horsepower @ rpm	300 @ 6000
Torque @ rpm	295 @ 4000
Transmission	auto/4-sp.
Drive wheels	front
Brakes, F/R	disc/disc (ABS)
Tire size	225/60HR16
Fuel tank capacity (gal.)	20.0
EPA city/highway mpg	17/26
Test mileage (mpg)	16.8

Warranties The entire car is covered for 4 years/50,000 miles. Body perforation rust is covered for 6 years/100,000 miles.

Built in Hamtramck, Mich.

CONSUMER GUIDE®

CHEVROLET BLAZER

RECOMMENDED

Sport-Utility Vehicle

Chevrolet Blazer LT

Chevrolet's compact sport-utility vehicle gets a new engine for 1996. Blazer is similar to the GMC Jimmy, both of which were redesigned for 1995. Oldsmobile also uses this design for the 1996 Bravada, a luxury version (see separate reports). Blazer continues as a 3- and 5-door wagon in base and LS price levels, with top-line LT trim reserved for the 5-door. Both body styles are offered with rear-wheel drive or an on-demand, part-time 4-wheel drive system (not for use on dry pavement). A permanently engaged 4WD system is optional on the LT. Anti-lock brakes and a driver-side air bag are standard. Blazer's new 4.3-liter V-6 is called the Vortec. Horsepower drops by five, to 190, and torque decreases by 10 pounds/feet, to 250, but peak torque is produced at 2800 rpm, 600 rpm lower than before. Engine coolant designed to last 5 years/100,000 miles and spark plugs designed to last 100,000 miles are new features. A 4-speed automatic transmission is standard and gains an interlock that requires applying the brake pedal before shifting into a drive gear. The Blazer has some advantages over the rival Ford Explorer, including a stronger V-6 engine, a more comfortable ride, and lower prices. However, Explorer has dual air bags and now offers an optional V-8 engine. There's ample room for four adults in both Blazer body styles, and five in a pinch in the larger 5-door. Cargo room is ample and the rear seat folds flat in a simple, easy motion. The engine is loud in hard acceleration but quieter and smoother than Explorer's V-6. Road and wind noise are moderate. Fuel economy is no bargain. We averaged 15.2 mpg with a 5-door Blazer, even though nearly half our driving was on expressways and most of it was in 2WD. Chevy missed the boat by not providing a passenger-side air bag, but the Blazer is competitive with the Explorer and Jeep Grand Cherokee in most areas and beats them on price.

Chevrolet Blazer prices are on page 278.

CHEVROLET BLAZER

Rating Guide	1	2	3	4	5
Performance					
Acceleration				4	
Economy	1				
Driveability			3		
Ride			3		
Steering/handling			3		
Braking			3		
Noise			3		
Accommodations					
Driver seating			3		
Instruments/controls			3		
Visibility			3		
Room/comfort			3		
Entry/exit			3		
Cargo room			3		
Workmanship					
Exterior			3		
Interior			3		
Value			3		
Total Points					59

Rating scale 5=Exceptional; 4=Above average; 3=Average; 2=Below average; 1=Poor

Specifications

Body type	5-door wagon
Wheelbase (in.)	107.0
Overall length (in.)	181.2
Overall width (in.)	67.8
Overall height (in.)	67.0
Curb weight (lbs.)	4071
Seating capacity	5
Front head room (in.)	39.6
Max. front leg room (in.)	42.5
Rear head room (in.)	38.2
Min. rear leg room (in.)	36.2
Cargo volume (cu. ft.)	74.1
Engine type	ohv V-6
Engine size (l/cu. in.)	4.3/262
Horsepower @ rpm	190 @ 4500
Torque @ rpm	250 @ 2800
Transmission	auto/4-sp.
Drive wheels	rear/all
Brakes, F/R	disc/drum (ABS)
Tire size	235/70R15
Fuel tank capacity (gal.)	19.0
EPA city/highway mpg	16/21
Test mileage (mpg)	15.2

Warranties The entire vehicle is covered for 3 years/36,000 miles. Body perforation rust is covered for 6 years/100,000 miles.

Built in Moraine, Ohio, and Linden, N.J.

CHEVROLET CAMARO/ PONTIAC FIREBIRD
Sports and GT

RECOMMENDED

Chevrolet Camaro convertible

Base versions of the rear-drive Camaro and Firebird get a new standard V-6 engine this year, while V-8 models gain additional power. Both come as 3-door hatchbacks and 2-door convertibles with a power top and glass rear window. Camaro is available in base and high-performance Z28 trim; Firebird comes in base, Formula, and Trans Am price levels. Dual air bags and anti-lock brakes are standard on all models. The base models now come with a 200-horsepower 3.8-liter V-6, which replaces a 160-horsepower 3.4-liter V-6. The Camaro Z28 and Firebird Formula and Trans Am continue with a 5.7-liter V-8, but horsepower increases by 10 this year to 285. A 5-speed manual transmission is standard with the V-6 and a 6-speed manual is standard with the V-8. A 4-speed automatic transmission is optional with both engines. A new high-performance package is available on V-8 models. It is produced by an outside firm, SLP Engineering, and includes wider wheels and tires, styling and suspension modifications, and a functional hood scoop that boosts horsepower to 305. Chevrolet calls its version the SS Package, while Pontiac's is called the Ram Air Performance and Handling Package. There used to be a huge performance gap between V-6 and V-8 versions of these cars, but it has narrowed considerably with the arrival of the 3.8-liter V-6. This 200-horsepower engine feels more like a V-8, and it nearly matches the Ford Mustang's new 4.6-liter V-8 in acceleration. Against the Mustang's base V-6 engine, it's no contest. The V-6 Camaro and Firebird win by a mile. If high performance is your top priority, the V-8 models are still better choices. Camaro and Firebird beat the rival Mustang on a performance basis, but the Mustang is quieter, roomier, and easier to live with as a daily vehicle.

Chevrolet Camaro prices are on page 281.
Pontiac Firebird prices are on page 410.

CHEVROLET CAMARO CONVERTIBLE

Rating Guide	1	2	3	4	5
Performance					
Acceleration				4	
Economy		2			
Driveability			3		
Ride			3		
Steering/handling			3		
Braking				4	
Noise			3		
Accommodations					
Driver seating				4	
Instruments/controls				4	
Visibility			3		
Room/comfort		2			
Entry/exit		2			
Cargo room			3		
Workmanship					
Exterior			3		
Interior			3		
Value			3		
Total Points					53

Rating scale 5=Exceptional; 4=Above average; 3=Average; 2=Below average; 1=Poor

Specifications

Body type	2-door convertible
Wheelbase (in.)	101.1
Overall length (in.)	193.2
Overall width (in.)	74.1
Overall height (in.)	52.0
Curb weight (lbs.)	3440
Seating capacity	4
Front head room (in.)	38.0
Max. front leg room (in.)	43.0
Rear head room (in.)	39.0
Min. rear leg room (in.)	26.8
Cargo volume (cu. ft.)	7.6
Engine type	ohv V-6
Engine size (l/cu. in.)	3.8/231
Horsepower @ rpm	200 @ 5200
Torque @ rpm	225 @ 4000
Transmission	auto/4-sp.
Drive wheels	rear
Brakes, F/R	disc/disc (ABS)
Tire size	235/55R16
Fuel tank capacity (gal.)	15.5
EPA city/highway mpg	19/29
Test mileage (mpg)	18.4

Warranties The entire car is covered for 3 years/36,000 miles. Body perforation rust is covered for 6 years/100,000 miles.

Built in Canada.

CONSUMER GUIDE®

CHEVROLET CAPRICE AND IMPALA SS/ BUICK ROADMASTER
Full-Size

Chevrolet Impala SS

These full-size rear-drive cars will be discontinued after 1996, along with the Cadillac Fleetwood (see separate report). All three share the same basic body-on-frame design and are built at the same Texas assembly plant. The Caprice comes as a 4-door sedan and 5-door wagon. The Impala SS is a high-performance sedan with a rear spoiler, firmer suspension, alloy wheels with 255/50ZR17 tires, and other unique features. Standard on the Caprice sedan is a 200-horsepower 4.3-liter V-8. Standard on the wagon and the Impala SS and optional on the Caprice sedan is a 260-horsepower 5.7-liter V-8. Roadmaster, which has different styling than the Caprice, comes as a 4-door sedan and Estate 5-door wagon, both available in base and Limited price levels. All Roadmasters use the 5.7-liter V-8. A 4-speed automatic transmission is standard with both engines, and all versions of these cars have standard dual air bags and anti-lock brakes. The Caprice and Roadmaster sedans seat six and the wagons add a 2-place rear-facing bench seat for 8-passenger capacity. The Impala SS has front bucket seats for 5-passenger capacity. Though we prefer General Motor's front-drive full-size cars, such as the Buick LeSabre, because they handle better and use less gas, none matches the 5000-pound towing ability of these cars or comes as a wagon. Both V-8s are smooth, strong performers that run on regular rather than premium gas. However, don't expect to average more than 20 mpg except in straight highway driving. The rear-drive Ford Crown Victoria and Mercury Grand Marquis are the closest rivals, though they only come as sedans and have less power. Big discounts should be available on the Caprice and Roadmaster models but probably not on the Impala SS.

Chevrolet Caprice and Impala SS prices are on page 284.
Buick Roadmaster prices are on page 266.

CHEVROLET IMPALA SS

Rating Guide	1	2	3	4	5
Performance					
Acceleration					▮
Economy		▮			
Driveability			▮		
Ride			▮		
Steering/handling			▮		
Braking				▮	
Noise			▮		
Accommodations					
Driver seating			▮		
Instruments/controls			▮		
Visibility		▮			
Room/comfort				▮	
Entry/exit			▮		
Cargo room			▮		
Workmanship					
Exterior			▮		
Interior			▮		
Value			▮		

Total Points 61

Rating scale 5=Exceptional; 4=Above average; 3=Average; 2=Below average; 1=Poor

Specifications

Body type	4-door notchback
Wheelbase (in.)	115.9
Overall length (in.)	214.1
Overall width (in.)	77.5
Overall height (in.)	55.7
Curb weight (lbs.)	4061
Seating capacity	5
Front head room (in.)	39.2
Max. front leg room (in.)	42.2
Rear head room (in.)	39.7
Min. rear leg room (in.)	39.5
Cargo volume (cu. ft.)	20.4
Engine type	ohv V-8
Engine size (l/cu. in.)	5.7/350
Horsepower @ rpm	260 @ 4800
Torque @ rpm	330 @ 2400
Transmission	auto/4-sp.
Drive wheels	rear
Brakes, F/R	disc/disc (ABS)
Tire size	255/50ZR17
Fuel tank capacity (gal.)	23.0
EPA city/highway mpg	17/26
Test mileage (mpg)	17.0

Warranties The entire car is covered for 3 years/36,000 miles. Body perforation rust is covered for 6 years/100,000 miles.

Built in Arlington, Tex.

CONSUMER GUIDE®

CHEVROLET CAVALIER

RECOMMENDED

Subcompact

Chevrolet Cavalier Z24

A new dual-camshaft 4-cylinder engine, traction control, and daytime running lights top the changes to Chevrolet's front-drive subcompact. Cavalier was redesigned for 1995, gaining a longer wheelbase, fresh styling, and a new interior with standard dual air bags. The Pontiac Sunfire has different styling but is built from the same design (see separate report). Cavalier comes as a 2-door coupe in base and sporty Z24 form, as a 2-door convertible in LS trim, and as a 4-door sedan in base and LS trim. Base models use a 120-horsepower 2.2-liter overhead-valve 4-cylinder engine. Standard on the Z24 and optional on the LS sedan and convertible is a 150-horsepower 2.4-liter 4-cylinder with dual overhead camshafts. Called the Twin Cam, the new engine is derived from General Motors' 2.3-liter Quad 4, which has been discontinued. Both engines have new 5-year/100,000-mile coolant and 100,000-mile spark plugs. A 5-speed manual transmission is standard on base models and the Z24 and optional on the convertible with the Twin Cam engine. A 3-speed automatic is optional on base models. A 4-speed automatic is standard on the LS sedan and convertible and optional on other Cavaliers. Traction control is now included with the 4-speed automatic. Cavalier doesn't have the refinement of the Toyota Corolla or the fun-to-drive character of the Dodge and Plymouth Neon. However, with dual air bags and anti-lock brakes standard, the base price of $10,500 is a bargain. The 2.2-liter engine gives the Cavalier adequate acceleration with the automatic transmission. The new 2.4-liter Twin Cam engine is noticeably improved over the Quad 4. It's smoother at all speeds and works better with the automatic transmission. The well-designed dashboard has clear gauges and controls that are easy to reach and use. Six-footers have adequate room in front, but head room in back is sufficient only for those under about 5-foot-8.

Chevrolet Cavalier prices are on page 285.

CHEVROLET CAVALIER Z24

Rating Guide	1	2	3	4	5
Performance					
Acceleration				▓	
Economy			▓		
Driveability			▓		
Ride			▓		
Steering/handling				▓	
Braking				▓	
Noise			▓		
Accommodations					
Driver seating			▓		
Instruments/controls				▓	
Visibility			▓		
Room/comfort		▓			
Entry/exit		▓			
Cargo room			▓		
Workmanship					
Exterior			▓		
Interior			▓		
Value			▓		

Total Points **58**

Rating scale 5=Exceptional; 4=Above average; 3=Average; 2=Below average; 1=Poor

Specifications

Body type ....2-door notchback	Engine type ....dohc I-4
Wheelbase (in.) 104.1	Engine size (l/cu. in.)..........2.4/146
Overall length (in.) 180.3	Horsepower @ rpm ...150 @ 6000
Overall width (in.) 67.4	Torque @ rpm ....150 @ 4400
Overall height (in.) 53.2	Transmission ....manual/5-sp.
Curb weight (lbs.) 2617	Drive wheels ....front
Seating capacity 5	Brakes, F/R ....disc/drum (ABS)
Front head room (in.) 37.6	Tire size 205/55R16
Max. front leg room (in.) 42.3	Fuel tank capacity (gal.) 15.2
Rear head room (in.) 36.6	EPA city/highway mpg 23/33
Min. rear leg room (in.) 33.2	Test mileage (mpg) 21.3
Cargo volume (cu. ft.)..............13.2	

Warranties The entire car is covered for 3 years/36,000 miles. Body perforation rust is covered for 6 years/100,000 miles.

Built in Lansing, Mich., and Lordstown, Ohio.

CHEVROLET CORSICA/ BERETTA
Compact/Sports Coupe

Chevrolet Corsica

Longer service intervals for both engines are the only changes of note for the final year for these front-drive cars. For 1997, a new 4-door compact sedan called the Malibu will replace the Corsica sedan. No replacement is planned for the Beretta, a 2-door sports coupe built from the same design as Corsica but with different styling. Corsica comes in a single trim level with a standard driver-side air bag and anti-lock brakes. There also are "value-priced" Special Value versions. A 120-horsepower 2.2-liter 4-cylinder engine is standard and a 155-horsepower 3.1-liter V-6 is optional. Both engines gain coolant designed to last 5 years/100,000 miles and spark plugs designed to last 100,000 miles. The 4-cylinder comes with a 3-speed automatic transmission and the V-6 with a 4-speed automatic. Beretta comes in base and Z26 models, and in Special Value versions of both. The 4-cylinder engine is standard on the base Beretta, and the V-6 is standard on the Z26 and optional on the base model. If you're interested in a Corsica or Beretta, we recommend you spring for the optional V-6 because the noisy 4-cylinder engine barely delivers adequate acceleration. You'll lose some fuel economy with the V-6 but gain much better performance. The Corsica has ample room in front but rear leg room is marginal for tall passengers. Trunk space is adequate and the optional split, folding rear seatback increases versatility. Beretta has more interior space than most sports coupes and also costs less than most. However, sports coupes are sold largely on style and image, and the Beretta is the oldest model in that category, so it looks old-hat compared to most rivals. With prices starting at $13,995, Corsica costs considerably less than comparably equipped imports, though it doesn't match the assembly quality or refined driving feel of its Japanese rivals.

Chevrolet Beretta prices are on page 277.
Chevrolet Corsica prices are on page 287.

CHEVROLET CORSICA

Rating Guide	1	2	3	4	5
Performance					
Acceleration			▓		
Economy			▓		
Driveability			▓		
Ride			▓		
Steering/handling			▓		
Braking					▓
Noise			▓		
Accommodations					
Driver seating		▓			
Instruments/controls		▓			
Visibility			▓		
Room/comfort			▓		
Entry/exit			▓		
Cargo room			▓		
Workmanship					
Exterior			▓		
Interior			▓		
Value			▓		
Total Points					**54**

Rating scale 5=Exceptional; 4=Above average; 3=Average; 2=Below average; 1=Poor

Specifications

Body type ....4-door notchback
Wheelbase (in.) 103.4
Overall length (in.) 183.4
Overall width (in.) 68.5
Overall height (in.) 54.2
Curb weight (lbs.) 2745
Seating capacity 5
Front head room (in.) 38.1
Max. front leg room (in.) 43.4
Rear head room (in.) 37.4
Min. rear leg room (in.) 35.5
Cargo volume (cu. ft.).............13.5

Engine type......................ohv V-6
Engine size (l/cu. in.)..........3.1/191
Horsepower @ rpm ...155 @ 5200
Torque @ rpm ....185 @ 4000
Transmission..................auto/4-sp.
Drive wheels ....front
Brakes, F/R ....disc/drum (ABS)
Tire size 195/70R14
Fuel tank capacity (gal.) 15.2
EPA city/highway mpg 21/29
Test mileage (mpg) 19.6

Warranties The entire car is covered for 3 years/36,000 miles. Body perforation rust is covered for 6 years/100,000 miles.

Built in Wilmington, Del.

CONSUMER GUIDE®

CHEVROLET CORVETTE
Sports and GT

Chevrolet Corvette Collector Edition convertible

Chevrolet's sports car marks the final year of the current design with two special models and a new high-output engine. A redesigned Corvette will arrive during the 1997 model year with new styling, a V-8 engine, and a 2-seat cabin. The current design debuted as a 1984 model and continues in coupe and convertible form. Production ended on the 405-horsepower ZR-1 coupe last spring, so the new Grand Sport takes over as Corvette's performance leader. It has blue paint with a white stripe, red "hash marks" on the left front fender, and black 5-spoke alloy wheels. The second special model, the Collector Edition, comes in both body styles with silver paint, silver 5-spoke wheels, and special emblems and seat trim. The Corvette's 5.7-liter V-8 comes in two versions this year. Standard on all models except the Grand Sport is a 300-horsepower version called the LT1. Standard on the Grand Sport and optional on the other models is a new 330-horsepower version called the LT4. The LT1 is available only with a 4-speed automatic transmission and the LT4 only with a 6-speed manual. Dual air bags, traction control, and antilock 4-wheel disc brakes are standard. Corvette has always been a car for those who enjoy life in the fast lane and are willing to sacrifice some comfort. It has become more civilized in recent years and improved assembly quality has greatly reduced the number of squeaks and rattles. Though the suspension no longer jars your teeth over bumps, it's still quite firm, and noise levels are high in all models. It's also a challenge to get in or out of the low-mounted bucket seats, fuel economy remains poor, and luggage space is precious. Wide tires, a firm suspension, and a low center of gravity allow Corvette to handle like a race car, and acceleration is magnificent. Both engines deliver a seamless rush of power from virtually any speed.

Chevrolet Corvette prices are on page 288.

CHEVROLET CORVETTE COLLECTOR EDITION

Rating Guide	1	2	3	4	5
Performance					
Acceleration					▬▬
Economy	▬				
Driveability				▬	
Ride			▬		
Steering/handling				▬	
Braking				▬	
Noise		▬			
Accommodations					
Driver seating				▬	
Instruments/controls			▬		
Visibility			▬		
Room/comfort			▬		
Entry/exit		▬			
Cargo room		▬			
Workmanship					
Exterior			▬		
Interior			▬		
Value			▬		
Total Points					**48**

Rating scale 5=Exceptional; 4=Above average; 3=Average; 2=Below average; 1=Poor

Specifications

Body type ....2-door convertible
Wheelbase (in.) 96.2
Overall length (in.) 178.5
Overall width (in.) 73.1
Overall height (in.) 47.3
Curb weight (lbs.) 3383
Seating capacity 2
Front head room (in.) 37.0
Max. front leg room (in.) 42.0
Rear head room (in.) ....—
Min. rear leg room (in.) ....—
Cargo volume (cu. ft.) 6.6

Engine type ....ohv V-8
Engine size (l/cu. in.) 5.7/350
Horsepower @ rpm ...330 @ 5800
Torque @ rpm ....340 @ 4500
Transmission ....manual/6-sp.
Drive wheels ....rear
Brakes, F/R...........disc/disc (ABS)
Tire size.....................285/40ZR17
Fuel tank capacity (gal.) 20.0
EPA city/highway mpg 16/27
Test mileage (mpg) ....NA

Warranties The entire car is covered for 3 years/36,000 miles. Body perforation rust is covered for 6 years/100,000 miles.

Built in Bowling Green, Ky.

CONSUMER GUIDE®

CHEVROLET LUMINA MINIVAN/OLDSMOBILE SILHOUETTE/PONTIAC TRANS SPORT

Minivan

Chevrolet Lumina Minivan

General Motors' front-drive minivans have a new standard engine for the final year for the current design. All three versions have plastic body panels, a sliding door on the passenger side, and a standard driver-side air bag and anti-lock brakes. They will be replaced for 1997 by a front-drive minivan that will have steel body panels, dual air bags, and sliding doors available on both sides. For 1996 all three come with a 180-horsepower 3.4-liter V-6 and a 4-speed automatic transmission. Last year a 120-horsepower 3.1-liter V-6 was standard on the Lumina and Trans Sport, and a 170-horsepower 3.8-liter V-6 was standard on the Silhouette and optional on the others. Seven bucket seats are available on all three models, and integrated child safety seats for the two middle buckets are optional. A power sliding side door, which is unique to GM's front-drive minivans, is optional on all three. It opens and closes at the push of a button on the remote entry key fob or inside the vehicle. We've driven the new 3.4-liter engine only briefly and found it adequate for this vehicle. It has more muscle than the 3.1-liter engine but doesn't feel as lively as the 3.8-liter V-6, which had more torque (225 pounds/feet) and better performance at low speeds. The GM minivans have a car-like driving feel and flexible seating and cargo arrangements, and the middle and rear bucket seats weigh just 34 pounds each. One of the big reasons they haven't sold well is that forward visibility is severely compromised by the sloped nose, front roof pillars, and expansive shelf on top of the dashboard. Discounts should be available on all three.

Chevrolet Lumina Minivan prices are on page 290.
Oldsmobile Silhouette prices are on page 403.
Pontiac Trans Sport prices are on page 420.

CHEVROLET LUMINA MINIVAN

Rating Guide	1	2	3	4	5
Performance					
Acceleration				▨	
Economy		▨			
Driveability			▨		
Ride			▨		
Steering/handling			▨		
Braking				▨	
Noise			▨		
Accommodations					
Driver seating			▨		
Instruments/controls		▨			
Visibility		▨			
Room/comfort			▨		
Entry/exit		▨			
Cargo room			▨		
Workmanship					
Exterior			▨		
Interior			▨		
Value			▨		
Total Points					**59**

Rating scale 5=Exceptional; 4=Above average; 3=Average; 2=Below average; 1=Poor

Specifications

Body type	4-door van
Wheelbase (in.)	109.8
Overall length (in.)	191.5
Overall width (in.)	73.9
Overall height (in.)	65.7
Curb weight (lbs.)	3686
Seating capacity	7
Front head room (in.)	39.2
Max. front leg room (in.)	40.1
Rear head room (in.)	39.0
Min. rear leg room (in.)	36.1
Cargo volume (cu. ft.)	112.6
Engine type	ohv V-6
Engine size (l/cu. in.)	3.4/207
Horsepower @ rpm	180 @ 5200
Torque @ rpm	205 @ 4000
Transmission	auto/4-sp.
Drive wheels	front
Brakes, F/R	disc/drum (ABS)
Tire size	205/70R15
Fuel tank capacity (gal.)	20.0
EPA city/highway mpg	19/26
Test mileage (mpg)	NA

Warranties The entire vehicle is covered for 3 years/36,000 miles. Body perforation rust is covered for 6 years/100,000 miles.

Built in Tarrytown, N.Y.

CHEVROLET LUMINA/ MONTE CARLO

RECOMMENDED

Mid-Size

Chevrolet Lumina LS

Chevrolet adds power and creature comforts to its front-drive mid-size sedan and coupe, which were redesigned last year. The Lumina sedan and Monte Carlo coupe have slightly different styling but share mechanical features and have similar interiors with standard dual air bags. The same basic front-drive platform also is used for the Buick Regal, Oldsmobile Cutlass Supreme, and Pontiac Grand Prix. Lumina returns in base and LS price levels, both with a standard 160-horsepower 3.1-liter V-6 engine. A 3.4-liter V-6 is optional on the LS. The base Monte Carlo LS comes with the 3.1-liter V-6 and the sportier Z34 comes with the 3.4-liter V-6. The 3.4-liter engine has 215 horsepower and 220 pounds/feet of torque; both ratings are up by five over last year. A 4-speed automatic transmission is standard on all models. Anti-lock brakes are standard except on the base Lumina, where they are optional. A child safety seat that folds out of Lumina's rear seatback is a new option. The Lumina is a pleasant, competent family sedan that deserves a look among mid-size cars. The 3.1-liter engine feels a little slow initially but delivers adequate acceleration. The 4-speed automatic changes gears smoothly and downshifts promptly when passing power is needed. Chevy's 3.4-liter V-6 has a more potent passing punch. However, it isn't much stronger at low speeds and is louder in hard acceleration. There's ample room for four people in the Monte Carlo and for as many as six in the Lumina, though that squeezes everyone. Entry to the Lumina's rear seat is easy through the tall doors. Monte Carlo requires lots of room to fully open the wide doors and then you have to bend to get into the back seat. Both have ample cargo space.

Chevrolet Lumina/Monte Carlo prices are on page 291.

CHEVROLET LUMINA LS

Rating Guide	1	2	3	4	5
Performance					
Acceleration			3		
Economy		2			
Driveability			3		
Ride			3		
Steering/handling			3		
Braking				4	
Noise			3		
Accommodations					
Driver seating			3		
Instruments/controls			3		
Visibility			3		
Room/comfort			3		
Entry/exit			3		
Cargo room			3		
Workmanship					
Exterior			3		
Interior			3		
Value			3		
Total Points..61					

Rating scale 5=Exceptional; 4=Above average; 3=Average; 2=Below average; 1=Poor

Specifications

Body type ....4-door notchback	Engine type......................ohv V-6
Wheelbase (in.) 107.5	Engine size (l/cu. in.)........3.1/191
Overall length (in.) 200.7	Horsepower @ rpm ...160 @ 5200
Overall width (in.) 72.5	Torque @ rpm ....185 @ 4000
Overall height (in.) 53.8	Transmission................auto/4-sp.
Curb weight (lbs.) 3451	Drive wheels ....front
Seating capacity...........................6	Brakes, F/R ....disc/drum (ABS)
Front head room (in.) 37.9	Tire size 205/70R15
Max. front leg room (in.) 42.4	Fuel tank capacity (gal.) 17.1
Rear head room (in.) 36.9	EPA city/highway mpg 20/29
Min. rear leg room (in.)...........34.9	Test mileage (mpg) 20.1
Cargo volume (cu. ft.).............15.7	

Warranties The entire car is covered for 3 years/36,000 miles. Body perforation rust is covered for 6 years/100,000 miles.

Built in Canada.

CONSUMER GUIDE®

CHRYSLER CIRRUS

RECOMMENDED

Mid-Size

Chrysler Cirrus LX

The front-drive Cirrus returns for its second model year in two versions, LX and LXi, with a new standard engine for the LX. The mid-size Cirrus sedan shares its design with the Dodge Stratus and new Plymouth Breeze (see separate report). The Cirrus LX now comes standard with a Chrysler 2.4-liter 4-cylinder engine that produces 150 horsepower. When the Cirrus was introduced last year, the only engine for both models was a Mitsubishi 2.5-liter V-6 with 168 horsepower. The V-6 remains standard on the LXi and is optional on the LX. Both engines come with a 4-speed automatic transmission. A programmable universal garage door is a new standard feature on both models. Both models also have dual air bags, anti-lock brakes, air conditioning, power windows and locks, and a folding rear seatback. An integrated child seat is optional on the LX. There's a great deal to like about Cirrus, including a sporty driving feel and a roomy interior. Cirrus is about two inches shorter overall than the compact Toyota Camry but rides a wheelbase that's a substantial five inches longer. The result is ample rear leg room—enough for some adults to ride with their legs crossed. Visibility to the rear is severely restricted by the narrow back window; otherwise, it's good. The V-6 has fairly lively acceleration but doesn't generate much torque below 4000 rpm. As a result, it initially feels flat in highway passing or when you need a quick burst of power in the 40-50-mph range. The 4-cylinder provides adequate acceleration. Noise suppression could be improved. Both engines are loud under hard throttle and road noise is prominent on the highway. Cirrus is a highly capable family sedan that equals Japanese competitors in many areas and soundly beats them on passenger space and price.

Chrysler Cirrus prices are on page 293.

CHRYSLER CIRRUS LX

Rating Guide	1	2	3	4	5
Performance					
Acceleration			▓▓▓▓		
Economy			▓▓▓▓		
Driveability			▓▓▓▓		
Ride			▓▓▓▓		
Steering/handling			▓▓▓▓		
Braking				▓▓▓▓	
Noise			▓▓▓▓		
Accommodations					
Driver seating				▓▓▓▓	
Instruments/controls				▓▓▓▓	
Visibility			▓▓▓▓		
Room/comfort				▓▓▓▓	
Entry/exit			▓▓▓▓		
Cargo room				▓▓▓▓	
Workmanship					
Exterior				▓▓▓▓	
Interior			▓▓▓▓		
Value				▓▓▓▓	
Total Points					**61**

Rating scale 5=Exceptional; 4=Above average; 3=Average; 2=Below average; 1=Poor

Specifications

Body type	4-door notchback
Wheelbase (in.)	108.0
Overall length (in.)	186.0
Overall width (in.)	71.0
Overall height (in.)	54.1
Curb weight (lbs.)	3150
Seating capacity	5
Front head room (in.)	38.1
Max. front leg room (in.)	42.3
Rear head room (in.)	36.8
Min. rear leg room (in.)	37.8
Cargo volume (cu. ft.)	15.7
Engine type	ohc V-6
Engine size (l/cu. in.)	2.5/152
Horsepower @ rpm	168 @ 5900
Torque @ rpm	170 @ 4350
Transmission	auto/4-sp.
Drive wheels	front
Brakes, F/R	disc/drum (ABS)
Tire size	195/65HR15
Fuel tank capacity (gal.)	16.0
EPA city/highway mpg	20/28
Test mileage (mpg)	21.0

Warranties The entire car is covered for 3 years/36,000 miles. Body perforation rust is covered for 7 years/100,000 miles.

Built in Sterling Heights, Mich.

CONSUMER GUIDE®

CHRYSLER LHS/ NEW YORKER
Premium Sedan

Chrysler LHS

The New Yorker name, first introduced in the 1938 model year and the oldest still in use in the U.S., will soon be history. Production of the 1996 New Yorker ended in the fall, so the name will disappear once dealers sell remaining stock. Production of the more-expensive LHS model will continue. These two cars ride the same 113-inch wheelbase as the Chrysler Concorde but have different styling and are about six inches longer overall. Both come with a 214-horsepower 3.5-liter V-6, a 4-speed automatic transmission, dual air bags, and anti-lock brakes. New Yorker differs from the LHS primarily in that it comes with a split front bench seat in place of the LHS's bucket seats and has fewer standard features. Chrysler says these cars are quieter this year thanks to additional sound insulation and revised structural engineering. Also new is a built-in transmitter that takes the place of a regular remote garage-door opener. Though we're generally impressed with these luxury versions of the LH sedans, there are a couple of sore spots that stand out against other cars in the $30,000 range. One is that both have a lot of road noise (the 1996 models aren't substantially quieter than previous versions). Another problem is that the interiors are trimmed with too much cheap-feeling plastic. In addition, the climate controls are too low in the center of the dashboard and visibility to the rear is restricted by the narrow back window. However, since these are stretched versions of the Concorde, they have all the same good points, plus limousine-like rear leg room. New Yorker and LHS aren't much heavier than the Concorde, so acceleration is nearly as brisk. These cars are agile for full-size sedans, but the suspension could be more compliant. They offer lots of room and loads of features at reasonable prices.

Chrysler LHS/New Yorker prices are on page 295.

CHRYSLER LHS

Rating Guide	1	2	3	4	5
Performance					
Acceleration				▓	
Economy		▓			
Driveability				▓	
Ride			▓		
Steering/handling			▓		
Braking			▓		
Noise			▓		
Accommodations					
Driver seating			▓		
Instruments/controls			▓		
Visibility			▓		
Room/comfort				▓	
Entry/exit			▓		
Cargo room			▓		
Workmanship					
Exterior				▓	
Interior			▓		
Value				▓	

Total Points..60

Rating scale 5=Exceptional; 4=Above average; 3=Average; 2=Below average; 1=Poor

Specifications

Body type ....4-door notchback	Engine type......................ohc V-6
Wheelbase (in.)....................113.0	Engine size (l/cu. in.).........3.5/215
Overall length (in.)................207.4	Horsepower @ rpm ...214 @ 5800
Overall width (in.) 74.4	Torque @ rpm ....221 @ 3100
Overall height (in.)..................55.9	Transmission.................auto/4-sp.
Curb weight (lbs.) 3592	Drive wheels ....front
Seating capacity...........................5	Brakes, F/R..........disc/disc (ABS)
Front head room (in.) 38.9	Tire size 225/60R16
Max. front leg room (in.).........42.3	Fuel tank capacity (gal.).........18.0
Rear head room (in.) 37.8	EPA city/highway mpg 18/26
Min. rear leg room (in.)...........41.7	Test mileage (mpg) 18.4
Cargo volume (cu. ft.).............17.9	

Warranties The entire car is covered for 3 years/36,000 miles. Body perforation rust is covered for 7 years/100,000 miles.

Built in Canada.

CONSUMER GUIDE®

CHRYSLER TOWN & COUNTRY
Minivan

Chrysler Town & Country LXi

A redesigned Town & Country bowed last spring as an early 1996 model. It meets 1998 federal passenger-car safety requirements and offers an optional sliding driver-side door—a minivan first. The similar Dodge Caravan and Plymouth Voyager also have been redesigned (see separate reports). The Town & Country line includes a standard-wheelbase LX model, a long-wheelbase base model, and a top-drawer long-wheelbase LXi all with front-wheel drive. The standard-wheelbase LX rides a 113.3-inch wheelbase and the long-wheelbase versions a 119.3-inch wheelbase. The base and LX use a 3.3-liter V-6 with 158 horsepower. A 166-horsepower 3.8-liter V-6 is standard on the LXi and optional on the others. Both engines team with a 4-speed automatic transmission. All-wheel drive will become optional on the LX and LXi later this year. All models have 7-passenger seating that includes two front buckets and a 3-place rear bench. The base and LX come with a 2-place middle bench and the LXi with twin center buckets. Both the middle and rear benches have new built-in rollers. Dual integrated child safety seats are optional on models with a middle bench seat and cloth upholstery. Standard equipment includes dual air bags and anti-lock brakes. Chrysler's new minivans are even more car-like than the old models, and they're roomier and more practical as well. They feel like big cars on the road, with a supple, well-controlled ride at highway speeds. There's ample cargo space at the rear in the long-wheelbase models and adequate space in the standard-size LX. The door sills have been lowered 1.4 inches to improve entry/exit, and the optional driver-side sliding door is a nifty feature. We favor the Caravan and Voyager over the Town & Country because they offer the same features at lower prices. If you don't mind paying premium prices, then the Town & Country also is a good choice.

Chrysler Town & Country prices are on page 297.

CHRYSLER TOWN & COUNTRY LXi

Rating Guide	1	2	3	4	5
Performance					
Acceleration			▮		
Economy			▮		
Driveability			▮		
Ride			▮		
Steering/handling			▮		
Braking			▮		
Noise			▮		
Accommodations					
Driver seating				▮	
Instruments/controls				▮	
Visibility				▮	
Room/comfort					▮
Entry/exit				▮	
Cargo room					▮
Workmanship					
Exterior				▮	
Interior				▮	
Value				▮	

Total Points 64

Rating scale 5=Exceptional; 4=Above average; 3=Average; 2=Below average; 1=Poor

Specifications

Body type ....5-door van	Engine type ....ohv V-6
Wheelbase (in.) 119.3	Engine size (l/cu. in.) 3.8/230
Overall length (in.) 199.6	Horsepower @ rpm ...166 @ 4300
Overall width (in.) 75.6	Torque @ rpm ....227 @ 3100
Overall height (in.) 68.5	Transmission..................auto/4-sp.
Curb weight (lbs.) 3951	Drive wheels ....front
Seating capacity...........................7	Brakes, F/R...........disc/disc (ABS)
Front head room (in.) 39.8	Tire size 215/65R16
Max. front leg room (in.) 41.2	Fuel tank capacity (gal.) 20.0
Rear head room (in.) 40.1	EPA city/highway mpg 17/24
Min. rear leg room (in.) 36.6	Test mileage (mpg) ....NA
Cargo volume (cu. ft.)..........167.0	

Warranties The entire vehicle is covered for 3 years/36,000 miles. Body perforation rust is covered for 7 years/100,000 miles.

Built in St. Louis, Mo., and Canada.

DODGE AVENGER/ CHRYSLER SEBRING
Sports Coupe

Dodge Avenger ES

The front-drive Avenger and Sebring sports coupes, which debuted last year, get few changes for 1996, but there is a new Sebring convertible. The convertible is derived from the design used for the Chrysler Cirrus/Dodge Stratus sedan and is not related to the Sebring coupe, which is built in Illinois by Mitsubishi. Prices weren't available on the Sebring convertible, which is built at a Chrysler plant in Mexico. It has different styling than the coupe and a longer wheelbase (106 inches instead of 103.7). Except for a different grille and taillights, the Avenger and Sebring are identical in appearance, but the Avenger has fewer standard features and lower prices. The base Avenger and Sebring LX coupe have a 140-horsepower 2.0-liter 4-cylinder, with either a 5-speed manual or 4-speed automatic transmission. The Avenger ES and Sebring LXi coupe come with a 2.5-liter V-6 and a 4-speed automatic. All models have dual air bags. Anti-lock brakes are standard on both Sebring coupes and the Avenger ES and optional on the base Avenger. The Avenger and Sebring are roomier than nearly all other sports coupes, and they almost match the spaciousness of mid-size coupes like the Chevrolet Monte Carlo. There's ample head room and leg room for the front bucket seats, and enough room in the rear seat for two adults to sit comfortably. Cargo space also is good. Acceleration is fairly lively with the V-6, but it doesn't produce much torque at low speeds. Step on the gas and there's a long pause before the automatic transmission downshifts. The 4-cylinder engine in the base model is noisy and, with the automatic, slow. Hitched to the standard 5-speed manual, the 4-cylinder provides adequate acceleration. These cars are reasonably priced and they offer something most coupes sorely lack: room for four adults.

Dodge Avenger prices are on page 299.
Chrysler Sebring standard equipment is on page 296.

DODGE AVENGER ES

Rating Guide	1	2	3	4	5
Performance					
Acceleration				▓	
Economy			▓		
Driveability			▓		
Ride			▓		
Steering/handling			▓		
Braking			▓		
Noise			▓		
Accommodations					
Driver seating			▓		
Instruments/controls			▓		
Visibility			▓		
Room/comfort			▓		
Entry/exit			▓		
Cargo room			▓		
Workmanship					
Exterior			▓		
Interior			▓		
Value			▓		

Total Points...57

Rating scale 5=Exceptional; 4=Above average; 3=Average; 2=Below average; 1=Poor

Specifications

Body type ....2-door notchback	Engine type......................ohc V-6
Wheelbase (in.).....................103.7	Engine size (l/cu. in.)..........2.5/152
Overall length (in.)................187.2	Horsepower @ rpm ...163 @ 5800
Overall width (in.) 68.5	Torque @ rpm ....170 @ 4400
Overall height (in.)..................53.0	Transmission..................auto/4-sp.
Curb weight (lbs.)..................2879	Drive wheels ....front
Seating capacity...........................5	Brakes, F/R..........disc/disc (ABS)
Front head room (in.) 39.1	Tire size 205/55HR16
Max. front leg room (in.).........43.3	Fuel tank capacity (gal.).........16.0
Rear head room (in.) 36.5	EPA city/highway mpg 20/27
Min. rear leg room (in.)...........35.0	Test mileage (mpg) 23.6
Cargo volume (cu. ft.).............13.1	

Warranties The entire car is covered for 3 years/36,000 miles. Body perforation rust is covered for 7 years/100,000 miles.

Built in Normal, Ill., and Mexico.

CONSUMER GUIDE®

DODGE CARAVAN
Minivan

✓ BEST BUY

Dodge Grand Caravan ES

Dodge rolled out a redesigned Caravan last spring as an early 1996 model with more aerodynamic styling, an optional sliding door on the driver's side, and removable seats with built-in rollers. The similar Chrysler Town & Country and Plymouth Voyager also have been redesigned (see separate reports). All three are available in standard-wheelbase (113.3 inches) and long-wheelbase (119.3 inches) body styles that hold up to seven people. All models initially have front-wheel drive; all-wheel drive will be added during 1996. Caravan comes in four price levels—base, SE, LE, and ES—in both the standard and long-wheelbase (called Grand Caravan) sizes. Dual air bags are standard on all, and anti-lock brakes are optional on the base models and standard on the rest. The base engine is a new 150-horsepower 2.4-liter 4-cylinder with dual overhead camshafts. Three V-6s are available: a 150-horsepower 3.0-liter; a 158-horsepower 3.3-liter; and a 166-horsepower 3.8-liter. The 2.4- and 3.0-liter engines come only with a 3-speed automatic transmission and the other engines only with a 4-speed automatic. All models have a standard passenger-side sliding door and a one-piece rear liftgate. Chrysler's new minivans are a clear step ahead of the 1995 versions, which were our Best Buys, so we're highly impressed with the 1996 models. So far, we've tested only the 3.3- and 3.8-liter V-6s. We prefer the 3.8-liter, though the 3.3-liter is adequate. The 1996 models are quieter and more car-like to drive. They handle more like big sedans than vans, and cruise highways with a stable, comfortable attitude. The built-in rollers for the removable seats are clever and handy. If you're shopping for a minivan, check out the new Caravan and its Chrysler and Plymouth cousins. They're at the head of the class. The closest competitor is the Ford Windstar.

Dodge Caravan prices appear on page 301.

DODGE GRAND CARAVAN ES

Rating Guide	1	2	3	4	5
Performance					
Acceleration				▓	
Economy		▓			
Driveability			▓		
Ride			▓		
Steering/handling			▓		
Braking				▓	
Noise			▓		
Accommodations					
Driver seating			▓		
Instruments/controls			▓		
Visibility			▓		
Room/comfort				▓	
Entry/exit				▓	
Cargo room					▓
Workmanship					
Exterior			▓		
Interior			▓		
Value				▓	
Total Points					**64**

Rating scale 5=Exceptional; 4=Above average; 3=Average; 2=Below average; 1=Poor

Specifications

Body type	5-door van
Wheelbase (in.)	119.3
Overall length (in.)	199.6
Overall width (in.)	75.6
Overall height (in.)	68.5
Curb weight (lbs.)	3680
Seating capacity	7
Front head room (in.)	39.8
Max. front leg room (in.)	41.2
Rear head room (in.)	40.1
Min. rear leg room (in.)	36.6
Cargo volume (cu. ft.)	172.3
Engine type	ohv V-6
Engine size (l/cu. in.)	3.3/201
Horsepower @ rpm	158 @ 4850
Torque @ rpm	203 @ 3250
Transmission	auto/4-sp.
Drive wheels	front
Brakes, F/R	disc/disc (ABS)
Tire size	215/65R15
Fuel tank capacity (gal.)	20.0
EPA city/highway mpg	18/24
Test mileage (mpg)	19.2

Warranties The entire vehicle is covered for 3 years/36,000 miles. Body perforation rust is covered for 7 years/100,000 miles.

Built in St. Louis, Mo., and Canada.

DODGE INTREPID/ CHRYSLER CONCORDE/ EAGLE VISION

RECOMMENDED

Full-Size

Dodge Intrepid

This family of front-drive sedans represents the three versions of Chrysler Corporation's full-size LH car. In all three lines, you can choose the model you want or choose the engine you want, but you can't choose both a model and an engine. A 161-horsepower 3.3-liter V-6 engine with overhead valves is standard on the base models of all three this year. The only way to get Chrysler's 214-horsepower 3.5-liter overhead camshaft V-6 is to buy one of the upscale models, the Intrepid ES, Concorde LXi, or Vision TSi. All models come with a 4-speed automatic transmission, but the Vision TSi is the only one with Chrysler's new Autostick transmission. Autostick can be used as a normal automatic, or it can be changed to a manual mode that allows the driver to shift up or down through the gears by tilting the shift lever left or right. Dual air bags are standard on all LH cars. Anti-lock brakes are standard on the Intrepid ES, both Concorde models, and the Vision TSi, and they are optional on the base Intrepid and Vision. The LH cars are full-size based on interior space, though they don't feel like big cars when you're driving them. Even the base models handle as well as some smaller sports sedans, zipping around tight turns with little body lean and commendable grip. The LH cars have more usable interior space than all rivals. The rear seat is wide enough for three adults to fit without crowding, plus there's generous leg room. The spacious trunk opens at bumper level. You won't win many drag races with the 3.3-liter V-6, but it provides adequate acceleration. The 3.5-liter V-6 has quicker highway passing and more steam going uphill. Overall, we're highly impressed with these cars and think they represent good value.

Dodge Intrepid prices are on page 305; Chrysler Concorde prices are on page 294; Eagle Vision prices are on page 313.

DODGE INTREPID

Rating Guide — 1 2 3 4 5

Performance

Category	Rating
Acceleration	3
Economy	3
Driveability	3
Ride	3
Steering/handling	3
Braking	5
Noise	3

Accommodations

Category	Rating
Driver seating	3
Instruments/controls	3
Visibility	3
Room/comfort	5
Entry/exit	4
Cargo room	4

Workmanship

Category	Rating
Exterior	3
Interior	3

Value

Category	Rating
Value	4

Total Points..59

Rating scale 5=Exceptional; 4=Above average; 3=Average; 2=Below average; 1=Poor

Specifications

Body type	4-door notchback
Wheelbase (in.)	113.0
Overall length (in.)	201.7
Overall width (in.)	74.4
Overall height (in.)	56.3
Curb weight (lbs.)	3318
Seating capacity	5
Front head room (in.)	38.4
Max. front leg room (in.)	42.3
Rear head room (in.)	37.5
Min. rear leg room (in.)	38.7
Cargo volume (cu. ft.)	16.7
Engine type	ohv V-6
Engine size (l/cu. in.)	3.3/201
Horsepower @ rpm	161 @ 5300
Torque @ rpm	181 @ 3200
Transmission	auto/4-sp.
Drive wheels	front
Brakes, F/R	disc/disc (ABS)
Tire size	225/60R16
Fuel tank capacity (gal.)	18.0
EPA city/highway mpg	19/27
Test mileage (mpg)	19.1

Warranties The entire car is covered for 3 years/36,000 miles. Body perforation rust is covered for 7 years/100,000 miles.

Built in Newark, Del., and Canada.

CONSUMER GUIDE®

DODGE/PLYMOUTH NEON
Subcompact

RECOMMENDED

Dodge Neon Sport 4-door

The front-drive Neon gets some price-cutting changes this year. Base, Highline, and Sport price levels are again offered, and base models get standard 14-inch wheels (versus 13s) and body-colored bumpers to replace last year's grey bumpers. Neon, which is sold in identical form through Dodge and Plymouth dealers, originally came as a 4-door sedan. A 2-door coupe was added last year in Highline and Sport versions. This year a lower-priced base coupe is added. Another move toward lowering prices is the deletion of anti-lock brakes and a rear spoiler as standard equipment on Sport models. Anti-lock brakes are now optional across the board. Dual air bags are standard. The standard engine is a 132-horsepower 2.0-liter overhead-camshaft 4-cylinder. Optional on Sport models is a dual-cam version of that engine with 150 horsepower. Both engines come with a standard 5-speed manual or optional 3-speed automatic transmission. New to the options list are an Expresso trim package for Highline models and a power moonroof. Neon is solid, roomy, fun to drive, and priced well below most Japanese rivals. It's a "must see" for anyone shopping for a compact or subcompact. The base engine is quick off the line with either transmission. Fuel economy is commendable. We averaged over 31 mpg with a 5-speed model in a mix of city and highway driving. We've driven a Sport with the base engine and automatic transmission more than 6000 miles and have averaged 24.2 mpg, with most of our driving in urban areas. Even the base models have agile, sporty handling. Neon has an impressive amount of passenger space for such a small package. The interior has enough head and leg room to seat four 6-footers without squeezing, and the trunk has a wide, flat cargo floor that provides good luggage space.

Dodge/Plymouth Neon prices are on page 306.

DODGE NEON SPORT

Rating Guide	1	2	3	4	5
Performance					
Acceleration			▓		
Economy			▓		
Driveability			▓		
Ride		▓			
Steering/handling			▓		
Braking			▓		
Noise		▓			
Accommodations					
Driver seating			▓		
Instruments/controls			▓		
Visibility			▓		
Room/comfort			▓		
Entry/exit			▓		
Cargo room			▓		
Workmanship					
Exterior			▓		
Interior			▓		
Value			▓		

Total Points 59

Rating scale 5=Exceptional; 4=Above average; 3=Average; 2=Below average; 1=Poor

Specifications

Body type ....4-door notchback	Engine type ....ohc I-4
Wheelbase (in.) 104.0	Engine size (l/cu. in.)..........2.0/122
Overall length (in.)................171.8	Horsepower @ rpm ......132 @ 6000
Overall width (in.) 67.5	Torque @ rpm ....129 @ 5000
Overall height (in.)..................54.8	Transmission.................auto/3-sp.
Curb weight (lbs.) 2416	Drive wheels ....front
Seating capacity...........................5	Brakes, F/R ....disc/drum (ABS)
Front head room (in.) 39.6	Tire size 185/65R14
Max. front leg room (in.) 42.5	Fuel tank capacity (gal.) 11.2
Rear head room (in.) 36.5	EPA city/highway mpg 25/33
Min. rear leg room (in.) 35.1	Test mileage (mpg) 24.2
Cargo volume (cu. ft.)..............11.8	

Warranties The entire car is covered for 3 years/36,000 miles. Body perforation rust is covered for 7 years/100,000 miles.

Built in Belvidere, Ill.

DODGE STRATUS/ PLYMOUTH BREEZE
Mid-Size

Dodge Stratus ES

Dodge's front-drive Stratus, which was introduced last winter, carries on with few changes for 1996. It is similar to the Chrysler Cirrus (see separate report) and the new Plymouth Breeze that will debut this winter (prices will be announced closer to the on-sale date). Cirrus is a more luxury-oriented model, while the Breeze is positioned as a low-price entry. Stratus comes in two versions: base and sportier ES. Standard on both is a 132-horsepower 2.0-liter 4-cylinder that comes only with a 5-speed manual transmission. Optional on both Stratus models is a 150-horsepower 2.4-liter dual-camshaft 4-cylinder, offered only with a 4-speed automatic. Also optional on the ES is a Mitsubishi 168-horsepower 2.5-liter V-6, which also comes only with a 4-speed automatic. The Breeze will come only with the 2.0-liter 4-cylinder but with a choice of 5-speed manual or 4-speed automatic transmissions. Dual air bags are standard on all versions. Anti-lock brakes are standard on the Stratus ES and optional on the base Stratus and the Breeze. Stratus has agile handling with little body lean and good grip. The 2.4-liter 4-cylinder available on the Stratus provides adequate acceleration and passing power. The 2.0-liter 4-cylinder is noisier and slower with the automatic but has adequate pep with the 5-speed manual. The smooth V-6 has the liveliest acceleration, but it's not the quietest engine around and it doesn't have much torque at low speeds. The interior is unusually roomy for the compact exterior dimensions. There's plenty of leg space fore and aft and sufficient rear-seat width for three medium-size adults to travel without feeling like sardines. The large trunk has ample luggage space. Stratus is a well-equipped compact-size sedan with mid-size room and reasonable prices, and we expect the Breeze to be priced even lower.

Dodge Stratus prices are on page 310.

DODGE STRATUS ES

Rating Guide	1	2	3	4	5
Performance					
Acceleration			3		
Economy			3		
Driveability			3		
Ride			3		
Steering/handling			3		
Braking			3		
Noise			3		
Accommodations					
Driver seating				4	
Instruments/controls			3		
Visibility			3		
Room/comfort			3		
Entry/exit			3		
Cargo room			3		
Workmanship					
Exterior			3		
Interior			3		
Value			3		

Total Points 61

Rating scale 5=Exceptional; 4=Above average; 3=Average; 2=Below average; 1=Poor

Specifications

Body type ....4-door notchback	Engine type ....ohc I-4
Wheelbase (in.) 108.0	Engine size (l/cu. in.) 2.0/122
Overall length (in.) 186.0	Horsepower @ rpm ...132 @ 6000
Overall width (in.) 71.7	Torque @ rpm ....129 @ 5000
Overall height (in.) 54.1	Transmission ....manual/5-sp.
Curb weight (lbs.) 2899	Drive wheels ....front
Seating capacity 5	Brakes, F/R...........disc/disc (ABS)
Front head room (in.) 38.1	Tire size 195/65HR15
Max. front leg room (in.) 42.3	Fuel tank capacity (gal.) 16.0
Rear head room (in.) 36.8	EPA city/highway mpg 25/36
Min. rear leg room (in.) 37.8	Test mileage (mpg) ....NA
Cargo volume (cu. ft.).............15.7	

Warranties The entire car is covered for 3 years/36,000 miles. Body perforation rust is covered for 7 years/100,000 miles.

Built in Sterling Heights, Mich.

CONSUMER GUIDE®

FORD ASPIRE
Subcompact

Ford Aspire 3-door

Ford's smallest car, the "minicompact" Aspire, returns in 3- and 5-door hatchback styling with few changes. Ford has dropped the SE 3-door hatchback, leaving only base versions of both body styles. The front-drive Aspire is built in Korea by Kia Motors and is based on a Mazda design. Ford owns a stake in Mazda and the two companies share other vehicles. Dual air bags are standard and anti-lock brakes are optional. The SE model included fog lamps, a rear spoiler, and a tachometer. All of these items are no longer available. Deleted from the option list for 1996 are aluminum wheels and the premium sound systems with cassette and CD players. The only option package available on the Aspire is the Interior Decor and Convenience group, which has intermittent wipers, a package tray cover, cargo light, manual remote mirrors, front door map pockets, upgraded cloth and vinyl seats, a split folding rear seat, and cloth door trim inserts. Stand-alone options include air conditioning and a rear window defroster. Aspire is an economical small car that could use more power. Though the 1.3-liter engine is adequate around town, on the highway there isn't enough torque for safe passing. Fuel economy is exceptional—more than 30 mpg in urban driving and over 40 mpg on the highway with the 5-speed manual. The automatic transmission isn't as stingy with gas because it lacks a fuel-saving overdrive gear. The manual transmission has vague and rubbery shift linkage, while the automatic shifts harshly in hard acceleration. The engine is loud under throttle and tolerably quiet when cruising. The driver's seat has enough travel to give 6-footers a workable driving position. Aspire's high fuel economy and low prices make it worth a look if you have a small budget.

Ford Aspire prices are on page 314.

FORD ASPIRE

Rating Guide	1	2	3	4	5

Performance

Acceleration	██
Economy	████
Driveability	██
Ride	██
Steering/handling	██
Braking	██
Noise	██

Accommodations

Driver seating	███
Instruments/controls	██
Visibility	████
Room/comfort	███
Entry/exit	███
Cargo room	███

Workmanship

Exterior	███
Interior	███

Value

███

Total Points..52

Rating scale 5=Exceptional; 4=Above average; 3=Average; 2=Below average; 1=Poor

Specifications

Body type	3-door hatchback	Engine type	ohc I-4
Wheelbase (in.)	90.7	Engine size (l/cu. in.)	1.3/81
Overall length (in.)	152.8	Horsepower @ rpm	63 @ 5000
Overall width (in.)	65.7	Torque @ rpm	74 @ 3000
Overall height (in.)	55.6	Transmission	manual/5-sp.
Curb weight (lbs.)	2004	Drive wheels	front
Seating capacity	4	Brakes, F/R	disc/drum
Front head room (in.)	37.8	Tire size	165/70R13
Max. front leg room (in.)	41.6	Fuel tank capacity (gal.)	10.0
Rear head room (in.)	35.5	EPA city/highway mpg	34/42
Min. rear leg room (in.)	33.6	Test mileage (mpg)	NA
Cargo volume (cu. ft.)	37.7		

Warranties The entire car is covered for 3 years/36,000 miles. Body perforation rust is covered for 5 years/unlimited miles.

Built in South Korea.

CONSUMER GUIDE®

FORD CONTOUR/ MERCURY MYSTIQUE

RECOMMENDED

Compact

Ford Contour SE

The front-drive Contour and Mystique last year replaced the Ford Tempo and Mercury Topaz. Though their 106.5-inch wheelbase is longer than some mid-size sedans, interior volume falls in the compact class. Contour and Mystique were most criticized last year for their lack of rear seat room. For 1996, Ford addresses this problem with two changes. First, the backs of the front seats have been scooped out to give rear passengers an additional inch of leg room. Second, the rear seat cushion will be repositioned later in the model year to provide more leg and head room. Though the styling is different for the Ford and Mercury versions, the front-drive platform, engines, transmissions, and other major components are shared. Contour comes in GL, LX, and SE price levels, and Mystique comes in GS and LS price levels. Dual air bags are standard on all models, and anti-lock brakes are optional. The base engine is a 125-horsepower 2.0-liter 4-cylinder. Standard on the Contour SE and optional on the others is a 170-horsepower 2.5-liter V-6. Both engines come with a standard 5-speed manual or optional 4-speed automatic transmission. Contour and Mystique have precise steering, sporty handling, and a firm ride that make them feel more German than American. The V-6 is well suited to the smooth-shifting automatic transmission and delivers lively acceleration (9.3 seconds to 60 mph in our test). The 4-cylinder is much noisier, feels sluggish going uphill, and requires a heavy throttle foot for brisk acceleration. There's ample head room and leg room for the front seats but surprisingly little leg room in the rear for a car with a 106.5-inch wheelbase, though this year's additional inch of leg space helps. Though the interior literally comes up short compared to some rivals, these cars have several good features and are well worth considering.

Ford Contour prices are on page 315.
Mercury Mystique prices are on page 380.

FORD CONTOUR SE

Rating Guide	1	2	3	4	5
Performance					
Acceleration			███		
Economy		███			
Driveability			███		
Ride			███		
Steering/handling			███		
Braking			███		
Noise			███		
Accommodations					
Driver seating		███			
Instruments/controls		███			
Visibility			███		
Room/comfort		███			
Entry/exit		███			
Cargo room			███		
Workmanship					
Exterior			███		
Interior			███		
Value			███		
Total Points					59

Rating scale 5=Exceptional; 4=Above average; 3=Average; 2=Below average; 1=Poor

Specifications

Body type	4-door notchback
Wheelbase (in.)	106.5
Overall length (in.)	183.9
Overall width (in.)	69.1
Overall height (in.)	54.5
Curb weight (lbs.)	2769
Seating capacity	5
Front head room (in.)	39.0
Max. front leg room (in.)	42.4
Rear head room (in.)	36.7
Min. rear leg room (in.)	34.3
Cargo volume (cu. ft.)	13.9
Engine type	dohc V-6
Engine size (l/cu. in.)	2.5/155
Horsepower @ rpm	170 @ 6250
Torque @ rpm	165 @ 4250
Transmission	auto/4-sp.
Drive wheels	front
Brakes, F/R	disc/disc (ABS)
Tire size	205/60R15
Fuel tank capacity (gal.)	14.5
EPA city/highway mpg	21/30
Test mileage (mpg)	18.9

Warranties The entire car is covered for 3 years/36,000 miles. Body perforation rust is covered for 5 years/unlimited miles.

Built in Kansas City, Mo., and Mexico.

CONSUMER GUIDE®

FORD CROWN VICTORIA/ MERCURY GRAND MARQUIS
Full-Size

Ford Crown Victoria LX

The Crown Victoria and similar Grand Marquis, which received interior and exterior upgrades last year, get only minor changes for 1996. Both are full-size rear-drive 6-passenger sedans with standard dual air bags and Ford's 4.6-liter overhead camshaft V-8 engine. It produces 190 horsepower in base form and 210 horsepower with the optional dual exhaust system. The only transmission available with either engine is an electronic 4-speed automatic, which Ford says has been revised for smoother shifts. Four-wheel disc brakes are standard, and anti-lock brakes with traction control are optional. A new standard steering wheel has a center-blow horn feature instead of buttons on the spokes (the horn can be activated by pressing anywhere on the steering wheel hub). The standard variable-assist power steering has been revised to provide more feel. As a modern interpretation of a traditional design, the Crown Vic and Grand Marquis are a lot of car for the money. The Chevrolet Caprice and Buick Roadmaster are the most direct rivals, but they're on the verge of extinction, so these will be the last full-size, rear-drive cars with body-on-frame construction. Though some drivers still favor rear-drive cars, most consumers have switched to smaller front-drive sedans with V-6s, such as the Dodge Intrepid and Oldsmobile Eighty Eight. They have less towing power but comparable interior room and performance. Ford's 4.6-liter V-8 provides brisk acceleration for these heavy sedans. We averaged 16 mpg in our most recent test of a Crown Vic, ranging from a low of 12 mpg in the city to a high of 22 in straight highway cruising. There's space for six adults and the trunk is huge. These cars wouldn't be our first choice in a full-size car, though they're hardly bad ones if you prefer rear-wheel drive.

Ford Crown Victoria prices are on page 317.
Mercury Grand Marquis prices are on page 378.

FORD CROWN VICTORIA LX

Rating Guide	1	2	3	4	5
Performance					
Acceleration			▓		
Economy	▓				
Driveability			▓		
Ride			▓		
Steering/handling			▓		
Braking			▓		
Noise			▓		
Accommodations					
Driver seating			▓		
Instruments/controls			▓		
Visibility			▓		
Room/comfort				▓	
Entry/exit			▓		
Cargo room			▓		
Workmanship					
Exterior			▓		
Interior			▓		
Value			▓		
Total Points					60

Rating scale 5=Exceptional; 4=Above average; 3=Average; 2=Below average; 1=Poor

Specifications

Body type ....4-door notchback
Wheelbase (in.) 114.4
Overall length (in.) 212.0
Overall width (in.) 77.8
Overall height (in.) 56.8
Curb weight (lbs.) 3780
Seating capacity.........................6
Front head room (in.) 39.4
Max. front leg room (in.) 42.5
Rear head room (in.) 38.0
Min. rear leg room (in.) 39.7
Cargo volume (cu. ft.)..............20.6

Engine..............................ohc V-8
Engine size (l/cu. in.).........4.6/281
Horsepower @ rpm ...210 @ 4600
Torque @ rpm ....270 @ 3400
Transmission.................auto/4-sp.
Drive wheels ....rear
Brakes, F/R...........disc/disc (ABS)
Tire size 215/70R15
Fuel tank capacity (gal.) 20.0
EPA city/highway mpg 17/25
Test mileage (mpg) 16.0

Warranties The entire car is covered for 3 years/36,000 miles. Body perforation rust is covered for 5 years/unlimited miles.

Built in Canada.

CONSUMER GUIDE®

FORD ESCORT/ MERCURY TRACER
Subcompact

BUDGET BUY

Ford Escort LX 4-door

Ford Motor Company's subcompacts carry over with only minor revisions for the 1996 model year. The front-drive Escort and Tracer are due to be replaced by new models next spring. Like the current models, the new ones will be built from the same design as the Mazda Protege but have different engines and styling. Escort comes as 3- and 5-door hatchbacks, a 4-door notchback sedan, and a 5-door wagon. The 3-door comes in Standard, LX, and sporty GT price levels, while the other body styles are available only in the high-volume LX trim. The Tracer comes as a sedan and wagon in a base price level and as a sporty LTS sedan. Dual air bags and motorized front shoulder belts are standard on all models. An integrated child safety seat is a $135 option on the Escort LX and base Tracer models. All models except the Escort GT and Tracer LTS use a Ford 1.9-liter 4-cylinder that produces 88 horsepower. The 1.9-liter engine has new platinum-tipped spark plugs designed to last 100,000 miles. The Escort GT and Tracer LTS come with a Mazda 1.8-liter 4-cylinder with dual camshafts and 127 horsepower. For both engines, a 5-speed manual transmission is standard and a 4-speed automatic is optional. Anti-lock brakes are optional on the GT and LTS. Escort and Tracer trail rivals such as the Geo Prizm, the similar Toyota Corolla, and the Honda Civic in refinement and performance. About 90 percent of Escorts are LX models purchased with a "one-price" package, which eliminates the traditional haggling that can make car buying unpleasant. With the one-price packages, all four body styles carry a suggested retail of $13,310 with the 4-speed automatic, including the $390 destination charge, air conditioning, power steering, a cassette player, rear defogger, and other features—hundreds less than most subcompact rivals. Buying a car on a tight budget? Check out the one-price Escort.

Ford Escort prices are on page 318.
Mercury Tracer prices are on page 384.

FORD ESCORT LX

Rating Guide	1	2	3	4	5
Performance					
Acceleration			3		
Economy				4	
Driveability			3		
Ride			3		
Steering/handling			3		
Braking			3		
Noise			3		
Accommodations					
Driver seating			3		
Instruments/controls			3		
Visibility				4	
Room/comfort			3		
Entry/exit			3		
Cargo room			3		
Workmanship					
Exterior			3		
Interior			3		
Value			3		

Total Points..**55**

Rating scale 5=Exceptional; 4=Above average; 3=Average; 2=Below average; 1=Poor

Specifications

Body type ....4-door notchback	Engine type ....ohc I-4
Wheelbase (in.) 98.4	Engine size (l/cu. in.) 1.9/114
Overall length (in.) 170.9	Horsepower @ rpm .....88 @ 4400
Overall width (in.) 66.7	Torque @ rpm ....108 @ 3800
Overall height (in.) 52.7	Transmission.................auto/4-sp.
Curb weight (lbs.) 2404	Drive wheels ....front
Seating capacity 5	Brakes, F/R.................disc/drum
Front head room (in.) 38.4	Tire size 175/65R14
Max. front leg room (in.) 41.7	Fuel tank capacity (gal.) 11.9
Rear head room (in.) 37.4	EPA city/highway mpg 26/34
Min. rear leg room (in.) 34.6	Test mileage (mpg) 26.8
Cargo volume (cu. ft.).............12.1	

Warranties The entire car is covered for 3 years/36,000 miles. Body perforation rust is covered for 5 years/unlimited miles.

Built in Wayne, Mich., and Mexico.

CONSUMER GUIDE®

FORD EXPLORER/MERCURY MOUNTAINEER
Sport-Utility Vehicle

✓ **BEST BUY**

Ford Explorer XLT

America's best-selling sport-utility vehicle, which was redesigned last year, gains an optional V-8 for 1996. Ford's 210-horsepower 5.0-liter V-8, used last year in the Mustang and some trucks, initially is a $760 option on the 2-wheel-drive XLT model and comes only with a 4-speed automatic transmission. Ford expects the V-8 to be available on the Eddie Bauer and Limited models and with 4-wheel drive by spring. All other models use a 160-horsepower 4.0-liter V-6 that comes with either a 5-speed manual transmission or 4-speed automatic. Mercury plans to join the booming sport-utility market this spring with the Mountaineer, a clone of the Explorer that will have the V-8 engine standard. The Mountaineer will have a different grille and interior trim, and it will come only as a 5-door wagon. Prices will be announced closer to the on-sale date. Explorer comes in 3- and 5-door styling, both available with 2- or 4-wheel drive. Dual air bags and 4-wheel anti-lock brakes are standard on all models. Ford's Control-Trac 4WD system sends power only to the rear wheels on smooth, dry surfaces. When wheel slip is detected the system automatically engages 4WD for improved traction. Compared to the Chevy Blazer and Jeep Grand Cherokee, the 6-cylinder Explorer is lethargic accelerating from stoplights, though passing power is more than adequate. The Explorer's V-6 also is louder and much rougher than the Blazer's. The new V-8 is much quicker off the line and delivers impressive passing power quickly. The V-8 is quieter and smoother than the V-6, and it feels much more muscular when climbing hills. There's ample room for five people in the 5-door model's spacious interior and more cargo room than Blazer. The Explorer earns the Best Buy among sport-utilities with its standard dual air bags, optional V-8, convenient 4WD system, and superior overall quality.

Ford Explorer prices are on page 321.
Mercury Mountaineer prices are on page

FORD EXPLORER XLT

Rating Guide	1	2	3	4	5
Performance					
Acceleration			3		
Economy		2			
Driveability			3		
Ride			3		
Steering/handling			3		
Braking				4	
Noise			3		
Accommodations					
Driver seating			3		
Instruments/controls			3		
Visibility			3		
Room/comfort			3		
Entry/exit		2			
Cargo room				4	
Workmanship					
Exterior			3		
Interior			3		
Value			3		

Total Points 61

Rating scale 5=Exceptional; 4=Above average; 3=Average; 2=Below average; 1=Poor

Specifications

Body type ....5-door wagon
Wheelbase (in.) 111.5
Overall length (in.) 188.5
Overall width (in.) 70.2
Overall height (in.) 67.3
Curb weight (lbs.) 4189
Seating capacity 5
Front head room (in.) 39.9
Max. front leg room (in.) 42.4
Rear head room (in.) 39.3
Min. rear leg room (in.) 37.7
Cargo volume (cu. ft.).............81.6

Engine type ....ohv V-6
Engine size (l/cu. in.) 4.0/245
Horsepower @ rpm ...160 @ 4400
Torque @ rpm ....225 @ 2800
Transmission.................auto/4-sp.
Drive wheels........................rear/all
Brakes, F/R..........disc/disc (ABS)
Tire size 225/70R15
Fuel tank capacity (gal.) 21.0
EPA city/highway mpg 15/20
Test mileage (mpg) 15.7

Warranties The entire vehicle is covered for 3 years/36,000 miles. Body perforation rust is covered for 5 years/unlimited miles.

Built in Louisville, Ky., and St. Louis, Mo.

CONSUMER GUIDE®

FORD MUSTANG
Sports and GT

RECOMMENDED

Ford Mustang GT 2-door

Ford gives the Mustang two new V-8 engines this year. Last year's 5.0-liter overhead-valve V-8 has been replaced by 4.6-liter overhead-camshaft engines. Standard on the Mustang GT this year is a single-cam 4.6-liter V-8 with 215 horsepower and 285 pounds/feet of torque, the same ratings as last year's overhead-valve V-8. The high-performance Cobra model has a dual-camshaft version with 305 horsepower and 300 pounds/feet of torque. The Cobra engine is available only with a 5-speed manual transmission, while the GT engine comes with the manual or a 4-speed automatic. Base Mustangs return with a 3.8-liter V-6 rated at 150 horsepower, five more than last year. A 5-speed manual transmission is standard and a 4-speed automatic is optional. All engines have new platinum-tipped spark plugs designed to last 100,000 miles. The base, GT, and Cobra models all are available as rear-drive 2-door notchback coupes and convertibles. Dual air bags and 4-wheel disc brakes are standard on all models. Anti-lock brakes are standard on the Cobra and optional on the others. With the power ratings for the GT's new overhead-cam V-8 the same as last year's, there's little improvement in acceleration. The biggest change is that the overhead-cam engine is smoother and more refined. The GT is certainly more spirited than V-6 Mustangs, but it's still not nearly as lively as the Chevrolet Camaro Z28 and little quicker than the new 3.8-liter V-6 Camaro. The new 305-horsepower V-8 in the Cobra, however, pulls noticeably stronger than the GT—perhaps as well as the Z28. Mustang's chief rival, the Camaro, feels like a toned-down race car, while Ford's car is more refined. Mustang and Camaro are priced competitively with each other, so shop both.

Ford Mustang prices are on page 324.

FORD MUSTANG GT

Rating Guide	1	2	3	4	5
Performance					
Acceleration				▓▓▓▓	
Economy		▓▓			
Driveability			▓▓		
Ride			▓▓		
Steering/handling			▓▓		
Braking				▓▓▓▓	
Noise		▓▓			
Accommodations					
Driver seating				▓▓▓▓	
Instruments/controls				▓▓▓▓	
Visibility			▓▓		
Room/comfort			▓▓		
Entry/exit			▓▓		
Cargo room			▓▓		
Workmanship					
Exterior			▓▓		
Interior			▓▓		
Value			▓▓		
Total Points					53

Rating scale 5=Exceptional; 4=Above average; 3=Average; 2=Below average; 1=Poor

Specifications

Body type	2-door notchback
Wheelbase (in.)	101.3
Overall length (in.)	181.5
Overall width (in.)	71.8
Overall height (in.)	52.9
Curb weight (lbs.)	3341
Seating capacity	4
Front head room (in.)	38.1
Max. front leg room (in.)	42.6
Rear head room (in.)	35.9
Min. rear leg room (in.)	30.3
Cargo volume (cu. ft.)	10.9
Engine type	ohc V-8
Engine size (l/cu. in.)	4.6/281
Horsepower @ rpm	215 @ 4400
Torque @ rpm	285 @ 3500
Transmission	auto/4-sp.
Drive wheels	rear
Brakes, F/R	disc/disc (ABS)
Tire size	225/55ZR16
Fuel tank capacity (gal.)	15.4
EPA city/highway mpg	17/24
Test mileage (mpg)	NA

Warranties The entire car is covered for 3 years/36,000 miles. Body perforation rust is covered for 5 years/unlimited miles.

Built in Dearborn, Mich.

CONSUMER GUIDE®

FORD PROBE
Sports Coupe

✓ **BEST BUY**

Ford Probe GT

Ford's front-drive sports coupe returns for 1996 with few changes. Probe is a 3-door hatchback that comes in base SE and GT models. Most SE models will be equipped with an option package that adds some of the GT's appearance features, a firmer suspension, and 205/55HR15 tires this year. The tire size is unchanged but the "H" denotes a speed rating of 129 mph. The GT has softer struts and springs that are supposed to provide a smoother ride without sacrificing handling. The Probe is built from the same design as the Mazda MX-6 coupe. Both use the same mechanical components but differ in interior design and exterior styling. The Probe, MX-6, and Mazda 626 sedan are built at a plant in Flat Rock, Michigan, that is jointly owned by Ford and Mazda. The base SE is powered by a 2.0-liter 4-cylinder engine with dual camshafts and 118 horsepower. The GT has a dual-cam 2.5-liter V-6 with 164 horsepower. Both engines are built by Mazda. A 5-speed manual transmission is standard and a 4-speed automatic is optional with both engines. Dual air bags are standard and anti-lock brakes are optional on both models. Probe is a smartly styled car that satisfies a range of tastes at reasonable prices. Our biggest beef with Probe's performance is how the optional automatic transmission saps the verve of both engines. Even the V-6 feels sluggish with the automatic: We timed an automatic GT at 9.8 seconds to 60 mph; a similar MX-6 with the 5-speed manual did it in 8.0 seconds. The V-6 has too little torque at low speeds for jackrabbit starts with the automatic. The 5-speed shifts smoothly and allows quicker engine response. Because Probe and the MX-6 are so similar, we suggest you consider both. They're the best choices in the competitive sports coupe class, and hefty discounts should be available on both.

Ford Probe prices are on page 326.

FORD PROBE GT

Rating Guide	1	2	3	4	5
Performance					
Acceleration				4	
Economy			3		
Driveability			3		
Ride		2			
Steering/handling			3		
Braking			3		
Noise		2			
Accommodations					
Driver seating			3		
Instruments/controls			3		
Visibility			3		
Room/comfort		2			
Entry/exit		2			
Cargo room			3		
Workmanship					
Exterior			3		
Interior			3		
Value			3		
Total Points					55

Rating scale 5=Exceptional; 4=Above average; 3=Average; 2=Below average; 1=Poor

Specifications

Body type ....3-door hatchback
Wheelbase (in.) 102.8
Overall length (in.) 178.7
Overall width (in.) 69.8
Overall height (in.) 51.6
Curb weight (lbs.) 2690
Seating capacity............................4
Front head room (in.) 37.8
Max. front leg room (in.) 43.1
Rear head room (in.) 34.8
Min. rear leg room (in.) 28.5
Cargo volume (cu. ft.).............18.0

Engine type....................dohc V-6
Engine size (l/cu. in.) 2.5/153
Horsepower @ rpm ...164 @ 5600
Torque @ rpm ....160 @ 4800
Transmission.................auto/4-sp.
Drive wheels ....front
Brakes, F/R...........disc/disc (ABS)
Tire size....................225/50VR16
Fuel tank capacity (gal.) 15.5
EPA city/highway mpg 20/26
Test mileage (mpg) 22.2

Warranties The entire car is covered for 3 years/36,000 miles. Body perforation rust is covered for 5 years/unlimited miles.

Built in Flat Rock, Mich.

CONSUMER GUIDE®

FORD TAURUS
Mid-Size

✓ **BEST BUY**

Ford Taurus GL 4-door

Taurus, America's best-selling car, and its cousin, the Mercury Sable (see separate report), are redesigned for 1996—their first complete overhaul since the originals were introduced a decade ago. Both cars are larger and have much more rounded styling than before. Taurus now rides a 108.5-inch wheelbase—2.5-inches longer than last year. Overall length increases more than five inches on the sedan and nearly six on the wagon. The front-drive Taurus comes as a sedan and wagon in base GL and deluxe LX price levels. A high-performance SHO sedan with a new 3.4-liter V-8 engine is scheduled to be added in the spring. The GL uses a revised version of last year's overhead-valve 3.0-liter V-6 with 145 horsepower. Last year's optional 3.8-liter V-6 has been replaced by the new 3.0-liter Duratec V-6 with dual overhead camshafts and 200 horsepower. The dual-cam engine is standard on the LX. Both engines team with a 4-speed automatic transmission. Dual air bags are standard, and anti-lock 4-wheel disc brakes are optional on all models. The new dashboard has an oval-shaped "integrated control panel" that houses the radio and climate controls. The new Taurus is quieter, handles more adeptly, and, in LX, form, accelerates with more authority. The new dual-cam V-6 is smooth, refined, and potent at higher engine speeds. By contrast, the overhead-valve engine in the GL is noisier, rougher, and slower, though acceleration and passing power are adequate. In addition to its head-turning exterior styling, the new Taurus has some innovative interior features. The modern-looking control panel for the climate and audio controls is easy to see and reach. There's more room for all seating positions, especially in the rear, where leg room has increased substantially. The new Taurus is more expensive than the old one, yet still a good value and an excellent choice among mid-size cars.

Ford Taurus prices are on page 327.

FORD TAURUS GL

Rating Guide	1	2	3	4	5
Performance					
Acceleration			▓▓▓		
Economy		▓▓			
Driveability			▓▓▓		
Ride				▓▓▓▓	
Steering/handling			▓▓▓		
Braking					▓▓▓▓▓
Noise			▓▓▓		
Accommodations					
Driver seating			▓▓▓		
Instruments/controls			▓▓▓		
Visibility			▓▓▓		
Room/comfort				▓▓▓▓	
Entry/exit				▓▓▓▓	
Cargo room				▓▓▓▓	
Workmanship					
Exterior			▓▓▓		
Interior			▓▓▓		
Value				▓▓▓▓	
Total Points					60

Rating scale 5=Exceptional; 4=Above average; 3=Average; 2=Below average; 1=Poor

Specifications

Body type ....4-door notchback	Engine type......................ohv V-6
Wheelbase (in.).....................108.5	Engine size (l/cu. in.)........3.0/182
Overall length (in.)................197.5	Horsepower @ rpm ...145 @ 5250
Overall width (in.) 73.0	Torque @ rpm ....170 @ 3250
Overall height (in.)..................55.1	Transmission.................auto/4-sp.
Curb weight (lbs.)..................3326	Drive wheels ....front
Seating capacity...........................6	Brakes, F/R...........disc/disc (ABS)
Front head room (in.) 39.2	Tire size 205/65R15
Max. front leg room (in.) 42.6	Fuel tank capacity (gal.) 16.0
Rear head room (in.) 36.2	EPA city/highway mpg 20/29
Min. rear leg room (in.) 38.9	Test mileage (mpg) 18.9
Cargo volume (cu. ft.)............15.8	

Warranties The entire car is covered for 3 years/36,000 miles. Body perforation rust is covered for 5 years/unlimited miles.

Built in Atlanta, Ga., and Chicago, Ill.

FORD THUNDERBIRD/ MERCURY COUGAR
Mid-Size

Ford Thunderbird LX

The high-performance Super Coupe model and its supercharged V-6 engine are gone, so the rear-drive Thunderbird is now sold only as a 2-door coupe in an LX price level. The similar Cougar returns in an XR7 price level. Both get extensive styling changes, including new front and rear fascias; headlights with a clear lens and complex reflectors; a new grille and hood; and a new front bumper. A new optional anti-theft system sounds the horn and flashes the lights if the hood, the side doors, or the trunk are opened without using the key to disengage the system. The standard 3.8-liter V-6 engine has been substantially revised this year and produces 145 horsepower, five more than last year. A 4.6-liter overhead-camshaft V-8 with 205 horsepower is optional. Both engines mate to a 4-speed automatic transmission and have new platinum-tipped spark plugs designed to last 100,000 miles. Dual air bags are standard, and anti-lock brakes and traction control are optional. At less than $18,000 for cars with dual air bags, air conditioning, a cassette player, and power windows and locks, the Thunderbird and Cougar are attractively priced. The biggest shortfall is the standard V-6, which can't move these cars with any verve. The V-8 is quieter and much stronger, though response in the 30-50 mph range is unimpressive. However, the V-8 has good acceleration off the line and strong highway passing power. Snow-belt residents should be aware that these rear-drive coupes have trouble coping with winter conditions. A V-8 LX we tested struggled for traction on ice and got stuck a couple of times in snow, despite having the optional traction control. Though these cars offer good value, so do the front-drive Chevrolet Monte Carlo and Pontiac Grand Prix. If you're interested in a mid-size coupe, check out those rivals, too.

Ford Thunderbird prices are on page 330.
Mercury Cougar prices are on page 376.

FORD THUNDERBIRD LX

Rating Guide	1	2	3	4	5
Performance					
Acceleration					5
Economy		2			
Driveability				4	
Ride				4	
Steering/handling				4	
Braking					5
Noise				4	
Accommodations					
Driver seating			3		
Instruments/controls			3		
Visibility			3		
Room/comfort			3		
Entry/exit			3		
Cargo room			3		
Workmanship					
Exterior				4	
Interior				4	
Value			3		

Total Points..57

Rating scale 5=Exceptional; 4=Above average; 3=Average; 2=Below average; 1=Poor

Specifications

Body type	2-door notchback*
Wheelbase (in.)	113.0
Overall length (in.)	200.3
Overall width (in.)	72.7
Overall height (in.)	52.5
Curb weight (lbs.)	3536
Seating capacity	5
Front head room (in.)	38.1
Max. front leg room (in.)	42.5
Rear head room (in.)	37.5
Min. rear leg room (in.)	35.8
Cargo volume (cu. ft.)	15.1
Engine type	ohc V-8
Engine size (l/cu. in.)	4.6/281
Horsepower @ rpm	205 @ 4500
Torque @ rpm	280 @ 3000
Transmission	auto/4-sp.
Drive wheels	rear
Brakes, F/R	disc/disc (ABS)
Tire size	205/70R15
Fuel tank capacity (gal.)	18.0
EPA city/highway mpg	17/25
Test mileage (mpg)	18.2

Warranties The entire car is covered for 3 years/36,000 miles. Body perforation rust is covered for 5 years/unlimited miles.

Built in Lorain, Ohio.

CONSUMER GUIDE®

FORD WINDSTAR **RECOMMENDED**
Minivan

Ford Windstar LX

Windstar, Ford's front-drive minivan, debuted for 1995 and gets major changes to its engine lineup for the 1996 model year. Standard equipment includes dual air bags and anti-lock brakes. Last year the only engine available was a 155-horsepower 3.8-liter V-6. The 3.8-liter has been heavily revised and is now standard on the top-line LX model and optional on the base GL. Horsepower increases by 45 to 200, and torque is up by 10 pounds/feet to 230. A 3.0-liter V-6 with 150 horsepower and 170 pounds/feet of torque is now standard on the GL. Both engines come with a 4-speed automatic transmission. Windstar comes in one size with a sliding passenger-side door, a rear liftgate, and seats for seven. The 120.7-inch wheelbase is the longest of any minivan, though the new long-wheelbase Chrysler minivans have slightly more interior room. Cargo volume is 144 cubic feet, about 28 cubic feet less than the Chrysler models. An all-speed traction control system, which applies the front brakes to prevent wheel slip during acceleration, is a new option. This year's 3.8-liter engine has stronger acceleration and passing power, and it's quieter and smoother. The 3.0-liter V-6 struggles to provide adequate acceleration and feels sluggish in passing situations. Windstar has an absorbent suspension that delivers a comfortable, stable ride at highway speeds and on bumpy urban streets. The 16-inch step-in height is among the lowest in the minivan field. It is almost as easy to get in or out of the front seats as in most passenger cars. There's adult-size room in all three rows, though the rear seat has to be pushed all the way back on its 7-inch track for adequate leg room. Chrysler's redesigned 1996 minivans are our Best Buys in this category, but the Windstar also is a good choice.

Ford Windstar prices are on page 331.

FORD WINDSTAR LX

Rating Guide	1	2	3	4	5

Performance
Acceleration	3
Economy	2
Driveability	3
Ride	4
Steering/handling	3
Braking	4
Noise	4

Accommodations
Driver seating	3
Instruments/controls	3
Visibility	3
Room/comfort	4
Entry/exit	3
Cargo room	4

Workmanship
Exterior	4
Interior	4

Value
Value	4

Total Points...61

Rating scale 5=Exceptional; 4=Above average; 3=Average; 2=Below average; 1=Poor

Specifications

Body type	4-door van
Wheelbase (in.)	120.7
Overall length (in.)	201.2
Overall width (in.)	75.4
Overall height (in.)	68.0
Curb weight (lbs.)	3800
Seating capacity	7
Front head room (in.)	39.3
Max. front leg room (in.)	40.7
Rear head room (in.)	38.9
Min. rear leg room (in.)	39.2
Cargo volume (cu. ft.)	144.0
Engine type	ohv V-6
Engine size (l/cu. in.)	3.8/232
Horsepower @ rpm	200 @ 5000
Torque @ rpm	230 @ 3000
Transmission	auto/4-sp.
Drive wheels	front
Brakes, F/R	disc/drum (ABS)
Tire size	215/70R15
Fuel tank capacity (gal.)	20.0
EPA city/highway mpg	17/23
Test mileage (mpg)	NA

Warranties The entire vehicle is covered for 3 years/36,000 miles. Body perforation rust is covered for 5 years/unlimited miles.

Built in Canada.

CONSUMER GUIDE®

GEO METRO
Subcompact

Geo Metro LSi 4-door

The larger of Metro's two engines is available on the entry-level model for 1996. Metro, sold by Chevrolet dealers with Geo franchises, is built from the same front-drive design used for the Suzuki Swift. Both cars are assembled at a General Motors/Suzuki assembly plant in Canada. They were redesigned last year and gained standard dual air bags, optional anti-lock brakes, and a 4-cylinder engine. Metro comes as a 3-door hatchback and a 4-door notchback sedan. With a curb weight of 1808 pounds, the hatchback is among the lightest cars sold in the U.S. Both body styles come in base and more upscale LSi trim. A 55-horsepower 1.0-liter 3-cylinder engine is standard on the 3-door models. Standard on the 4-door Metro and optional on both 3-door models this year is a 70-horsepower 1.3-liter 4-cylinder. A 5-speed manual transmission is standard on all models. A 3-speed automatic is optional except on the base hatchback. The new Metro feels far more substantial than its predecessor, which was a tin can by comparison. The light weight and modest dimensions are still evident, however. Bumps jar the suspension and create kickback through the steering wheel. Road noise is high and there's also lots of wind and mechanical noise. The 4-cylinder engine is much livelier than the 3-cylinder, yet it doesn't turn the Metro into a hot rod. Step on the gas and there's considerable noise—and only modest progress. Metro has a surprising amount of interior room for its petite dimensions. There's adequate leg room and generous head room for the front bucket seats, and the rear seat has adequate head room and leg room for two. However, it's difficult to get in or out of the rear on both body styles. Because there are many new-car shoppers on a tight budget, the economical Metro is worth considering if cost is the top priority.

Geo Metro prices are on page 333.

GEO METRO LSi

Rating Guide	1	2	3	4	5
Performance					
Acceleration	██				
Economy				██	
Driveability		██			
Ride		██			
Steering/handling		██			
Braking		██			
Noise		██			
Accommodations					
Driver seating		██			
Instruments/controls			██		
Visibility					██
Room/comfort		██			
Entry/exit			██		
Cargo room			██		
Workmanship					
Exterior		██			
Interior		██			
Value			██		

Total Points **50**

Rating scale 5=Exceptional; 4=Above average; 3=Average; 2=Below average; 1=Poor

Specifications

Body type	4-door notchback
Wheelbase (in.)	93.1
Overall length (in.)	164.0
Overall width (in.)	62.6
Overall height (in.)	55.7
Curb weight (lbs.)	1940
Seating capacity	4
Front head room (in.)	39.3
Max. front leg room (in.)	42.5
Rear head room (in.)	37.3
Min. rear leg room (in.)	32.8
Cargo volume (cu. ft.)	10.3
Engine type	ohc I-4
Engine size (l/cu. in.)	1.3/79
Horsepower @ rpm	70 @ 6000
Torque @ rpm	74 @ 3500
Transmission	auto/3-sp.
Drive wheels	front
Brakes, F/R	disc/drum
Tire size	155/80R13
Fuel tank capacity (gal.)	10.6
EPA city/highway mpg	39/43
Test mileage (mpg)	25.8

Warranties The entire car is covered for 3 years/36,000 miles. Body perforation rust is covered for 6 years/100,000 miles.

Built in Canada.

CONSUMER GUIDE®

GEO PRIZM
Subcompact

✓ **BEST BUY**

Geo Prizm

Additional safety and convenience items mark the 1996 edition of the Prizm, a front-drive subcompact that is a clone of the Toyota Corolla (see separate report). Prizm comes as a 4-door sedan in base and higher-priced LSi models. Dual air bags are standard and anti-lock brakes are optional on both models. The standard engine is a 105-horsepower 1.6-liter 4-cylinder. A 1.8-liter 4-cylinder is optional on the LSi. For 1996 the 1.8-liter is rated at 105 horsepower, 10 fewer than last year, but torque increases by two pounds/feet, to 117. A 5-speed manual transmission is standard with both engines. A 3-speed automatic transmission is optional with the 1.6-liter and a 4-speed automatic is optional with the 1.8-liter. Daytime running lights are a new standard feature. Designed to make the car more visible to other drivers, the headlights automatically illuminate when the ignition is on. A child safety seat that folds out of the right side of the rear backrest is a new option for LSi models. Prizm and Corolla differ in styling and dashboard design, and Corolla also comes as a 5-door wagon, but they use the same Japanese-built engines and transmissions. Most other components are built in North America. All Prizms and most Corolla sedans are assembled in California at a plant jointly owned by General Motors and Toyota. Prizm should be just as reliable as the Corolla. Prizm's starting price of $12,495 is about $230 less than the least-expensive Corolla, and a well-equipped LSi will cost less than a loaded Corolla DX. The 1.6-liter engine furnishes adequate acceleration, but the 1.8-liter provides noticeably more zip. There's ample room in the front seats. In back, there's limited head room and leg room. Though there are less-expensive small sedans, few are as well-made or polished.

Geo Prizm prices are on page 335.

GEO PRIZM

Rating Guide	1	2	3	4	5
Performance					
Acceleration			3		
Economy				4	
Driveability			3		
Ride			3		
Steering/handling			3		
Braking				4	
Noise			3		
Accommodations					
Driver seating				4	
Instruments/controls				4	
Visibility				4	
Room/comfort			3		
Entry/exit			3		
Cargo room			3		
Workmanship					
Exterior				4	
Interior				4	
Value					5

Total Points..**59**

Rating scale 5=Exceptional; 4=Above average; 3=Average; 2=Below average; 1=Poor

Specifications

Body type ....4-door notchback	Engine type ....dohc I-4
Wheelbase (in.) 97.0	Engine size (l/cu. in.)............1.6/97
Overall length (in.)................173.0	Horsepower @ rpm ...105 @ 5800
Overall width (in.) 66.3	Torque @ rpm ....100 @ 4800
Overall height (in.)..................53.5	Transmission..................auto/4-sp.
Curb weight (lbs.) 2359	Drive wheels ....front
Seating capacity..........................5	Brakes, F/R...........disc/disc (ABS)
Front head room (in.) 38.5	Tire size 175/65R14
Max. front leg room (in.) 41.7	Fuel tank capacity (gal.) 13.2
Rear head room (in.) 36.4	EPA city/highway mpg 28/34
Min. rear leg room (in.)...........33.1	Test mileage (mpg) 27.9
Cargo volume (cu. ft.).............12.7	

Warranties The entire car is covered for 3 years/36,000 miles. Body perforation rust is covered for 6 years/100,000 miles.

Built in Fremont, Calif.

GEO TRACKER
Sport-Utility Vehicle

Geo Tracker 5-door

Geo's pint-sized sport-utility vehicle gains a 5-door wagon body style and standard dual air bags for 1996. Tracker loses its 3-door hardtop body style in favor of the new 5-door wagon. A 2-door convertible returns. Tracker uses the same design and mechanical components as the Suzuki Sidekick, and both are built in Canada at a plant General Motors shares with Suzuki. The 5-door's wheelbase is 11 inches longer than the convertible's and the body is 15 inches longer. Both body styles come in base and upgraded LSi trim with a choice of rear-wheel drive or part-time 4-wheel drive (not for use on dry pavement). Anti-lock brakes that operate on all four wheels in both 2WD and 4WD are a new option. All models use a 95-horsepower 1.6-liter 4-cylinder with four valves per cylinder. A 5-speed manual transmission is standard. A 3-speed automatic is optional on the convertible and a 4-speed automatic is a new option for the 5-door. Chevrolet says the 5-door Tracker is aimed at drivers who need more room and utility than the convertible but can't afford a larger sport-utility such as the Blazer or Ford Explorer. The 5-door Tracker has loads of head room front and rear and adequate leg room for adults in the rear seat. There's also ample cargo space with the rear seat folded. The 5-door wagon is short of power, however. Acceleration is adequate with the 5-speed manual, though you have to downshift to fourth or even third gear for passing power. With the automatic transmission, the wagon feels sluggish and you have to plan passing maneuvers carefully. The 4WD wagon starts at an enticing $15,320, but the price climbs to more than $18,000 when you add the automatic transmission, air conditioning, automatic locking front hubs, and a stereo. At that price, you might as well look at the Jeep Cherokee, a more substantial vehicle with more power.

Geo Tracker prices are on page 336.

GEO TRACKER

Rating Guide	1	2	3	4	5
Performance					
Acceleration			▮		
Economy			▮		
Driveability			▮		
Ride		▮			
Steering/handling			▮		
Braking			▮		
Noise	▮				
Accommodations					
Driver seating			▮		
Instruments/controls				▮	
Visibility				▮	
Room/comfort		▮			
Entry/exit			▮		
Cargo room		▮			
Workmanship					
Exterior			▮		
Interior			▮		
Value			▮		
Total Points					51

Rating scale 5=Exceptional; 4=Above average; 3=Average; 2=Below average; 1=Poor

Specifications

Body type ....5-door wagon
Wheelbase (in.) 97.6
Overall length (in.) 158.7
Overall width (in.) 64.4
Overall height (in.) 65.7
Curb weight (lbs.) 2434
Seating capacity 4
Front head room (in.) 40.6
Max. front leg room (in.) 42.1
Rear head room (in.) 40.0
Min. rear leg room (in.) 32.7
Cargo volume (cu. ft.).............45.9

Engine type ....ohc I-4
Engine size (l/cu. in.)...........1.6/97
Horsepower @ rpm .....95 @ 5600
Torque @ rpm ....98 @ 4000
Transmission ....manual/5-sp.
Drive wheels......................rear/all
Brakes, F/R ....disc/drum (ABS)
Tire size 205/75R15
Fuel tank capacity (gal.) 14.5
EPA city/hiway mpg 24/26
Test mileage (mpg) ....NA

Warranties The entire vehicle is covered for 3 years/36,000 miles. Body perforation rust is covered for 6 years/100,000 miles.

Built in Canada.

CONSUMER GUIDE®

GMC JIMMY
Sport-Utility Vehicle

RECOMMENDED

GMC Jimmy 3-door

Jimmy, GMC's version of the compact sport-utility vehicle also sold as the Chevrolet Blazer and Oldsmobile Bravada, gets a new standard engine this year. Jimmy, which was redesigned last year, comes in 3- and 5-door wagon body styles in SL and SLS trim and also in SLE and SLT levels for the 5-door. Both body styles are offered with rear-wheel drive or on-demand, part-time 4-wheel drive (not for use on dry pavement). A permanently engaged 4WD system is optional on the SLT. Anti-lock brakes and a driver-side air bag are standard. Jimmy's only engine is again a 4.3-liter V-6, but extensive revisions, including a new fuel-injection system, 5-year/100,000-mile engine coolant and 100,000-mile spark plugs, make it part of GM's new family of Vortec truck engines. It's rated at 190 horsepower, five less than last year. Torque is now 250 pounds/feet, 10 less than last year, but it peaks at 2800 rpm, 600 rpm lower than before. A 4-speed automatic transmission is standard and gains an interlock that requires applying the brake pedal before shifting into a drive gear. A 5-speed manual transmission is a new option on the 3-door Jimmy. The Jimmy and Blazer trail most rivals in having only a driver-side air bag instead of dual air bags, but they are competitive in nearly all other areas. The well-designed interior has ample room for four adults in the 3-door and up to five in the larger 5-door. Getting in or out of the 3-door model's rear seat is a chore. Acceleration is brisk and there's ample passing power. Fuel economy is no bargain. We averaged 16.4 mpg with a 4WD Jimmy in 725 miles of driving, about half of which was on expressways and highways. Jimmy and Blazer are worth a close look, and they're less expensive than comparable versions of the Ford Explorer and Jeep Grand Cherokee.

GMC Jimmy prices are on page 338.

GMC JIMMY

Rating Guide	1	2	3	4	5
Performance					
Acceleration			▓▓▓		
Economy		▓▓▓			
Driveability			▓▓▓		
Ride			▓▓▓		
Steering/handling			▓▓▓		
Braking				▓▓▓	
Noise			▓▓▓		
Accommodations					
Driver seating			▓▓▓		
Instruments/controls			▓▓▓		
Visibility			▓▓▓		
Room/comfort			▓▓▓		
Entry/exit			▓▓▓		
Cargo room				▓▓▓	
Workmanship					
Exterior			▓▓▓		
Interior			▓▓▓		
Value			▓▓▓		
Total Points					**58**

Rating scale 5=Exceptional; 4=Above average; 3=Average; 2=Below average; 1=Poor

Specifications

Body type	3-door wagon
Wheelbase (in.)	100.5
Overall length (in.)	175.1
Overall width (in.)	67.8
Overall height (in.)	67.0
Curb weight (lbs.)	3825
Seating capacity	4
Front head room (in.)	39.6
Max. front leg room (in.)	42.5
Rear head room (in.)	38.2
Min. rear leg room (in.)	36.2
Cargo volume (cu. ft.)	66.9
Engine type	ohv V-6
Engine size (l/cu. in.)	4.3/262
Horsepower @ rpm	190 @ 4500
Torque @ rpm	250 @ 2800
Transmission	auto/4-sp.
Drive wheels	rear/all
Brakes, F/R	disc/drum (ABS)
Tire size	205/75R15
Fuel tank capacity (gal.)	20.0
EPA city/highway mpg	16/21
Test mileage (mpg)	16.4

Warranties The entire car is covered for 3 years/36,000 miles. Body perforation rust is covered for 6 years/100,000 miles.

Built in Moraine, Ohio, and Linden, N.J.

HONDA ACCORD
Mid-Size

✓ **BEST BUY**

Honda Accord EX 4-door

The front-drive Accord receives several appearance and equipment changes for 1996, the third year for the current design. Last year's big news was the addition of an optional V-6 engine for the LX and EX sedans. The V-6 continues to be available only on those two models this year. Among the styling changes are larger front and rear bumpers, new parking lamps, and new chrome grilles for 4-cylinder models to match the appearance of the V-6 sedans. The trunk opening has been enlarged on the coupe and sedan to make loading and unloading cargo easier, and the EX wagon gains a roof rack as a new standard feature. Other new standard features include a rear seat pass-through feature on the coupe and sedan for storing long items such as skis and a 6-way power driver's seat for the LX V-6 and all EX models equipped with the optional leather upholstery. This year's 4-cylinder lineup includes DX and LX models with a 130-horsepower 2.2-liter 4-cylinder engine and EX models with a 145-horsepower version. Both V-6 sedans come with a 170-horsepower 2.7-liter engine. Dual air bags are standard on all Accords. Anti-lock brakes are standard on the V-6 sedans and 4-cylinder EX models, and they're optional on the 4-cylinder LX Accords. Though there isn't a huge difference in acceleration between the 4-cylinder and V-6 models, the V-6 is quieter and smoother. We clocked a V-6 Accord at 8.9 seconds to 60 mph, versus 9.6 seconds for a 4-cylinder EX. All Accords have poised, sporty handling. They take tight corners with good grip and moderate body lean. The ride is on the firm side yet stable and comfortable. There's plenty of leg room front and rear in all models. Accord is an excellent choice among mid-size cars. The V-6 models are the most desirable, but the biggest discounts should be on the 4-cylinder models.

Honda Accord prices are on page 342.

HONDA ACCORD EX V-6

Rating Guide	1	2	3	4	5
Performance					
Acceleration				▓▓	
Economy			▓▓		
Driveability				▓▓	
Ride				▓▓	
Steering/handling				▓▓	
Braking					▓▓
Noise				▓▓	
Accommodations					
Driver seating			▓▓		
Instruments/controls			▓▓		
Visibility				▓▓	
Room/comfort				▓▓	
Entry/exit				▓▓	
Cargo room				▓▓	
Workmanship					
Exterior				▓▓	
Interior				▓▓	
Value				▓▓	
Total Points					**64**

Rating scale 5=Exceptional; 4=Above average; 3=Average; 2=Below average; 1=Poor

Specifications

Body type	4-door notchback
Wheelbase (in.)	106.9
Overall length (in.)	185.6
Overall width (in.)	70.1
Overall height (in.)	55.1
Curb weight (lbs.)	3285
Seating capacity	5
Front head room (in.)	38.4
Max. front leg room (in.)	42.7
Rear head room (in.)	36.7
Min. rear leg room (in.)	34.3
Cargo volume (cu. ft.)	13.0
Engine type	ohc V-6
Engine size (l/cu. in.)	2.7/163
Horsepower @ rpm	170 @ 5600
Torque @ rpm	165 @ 4500
Transmission	auto/4-sp.
Drive wheels	front
Brakes, F/R	disc/disc (ABS)
Tire size	205/60R15
Fuel tank capacity (gal.)	17.0
EPA city/highway mpg	19/25
Test mileage (mpg)	21.0

Warranties The entire car is covered for 3 years/36,000 miles. Body perforation rust is covered for 3 years/unlimited miles.

Built in Marysville, Ohio.

CONSUMER GUIDE®

HONDA CIVIC
Subcompact

✓ **BEST BUY**

Honda Civic EX 4-door

A redesigned Civic went on sale in the fall in three body styles with new styling, two new 1.6-liter 4-cylinder engines, and a continuously variable transmission (CVT). The Civic again comes with front-wheel drive in 2-door coupe, 3-door hatchback, and 4-door sedan body styles. The coupe and sedan are about 2.3 inches longer overall, and the hatchback grows 4.3 inches. A new model lineup includes DX, HX, and EX versions of the coupe; CX and DX hatchback models; and DX, LX, and EX sedans. Last year's 1.5-liter engines have been replaced by two new 1.6-liter 4-cylinders. The CX, DX, and LX use a 106-horsepower 1.6-liter engine available with a 5-speed manual or 4-speed automatic transmission. The HX coupe comes with a new 115-horsepower engine available with a 5-speed manual or the new CVT automatic transmission. Unlike conventional automatic transmissions, which have three or four forward gears, the CVT has an infinite number of gear ratios and operates like a dimmer instead of a 3-way light switch. The EX models use a 127-horsepower 1.6-liter engine available with 5-speed manual or 4-speed automatic. Dual air bags are standard on all Civics. Anti-lock brakes are standard on the EX sedan and optional on the LX sedan and EX coupe. The new Civic is roomier inside, has a more comfortable ride, and feels just as agile as the previous model. The EX models have livelier acceleration than the others, though all Civics have at least adequate performance. In a test of an EX with the automatic transmission we reached a peak of 36 mpg on the highway and averaged 29 mpg in suburban commuting. Prices on the 1996 models are only slightly higher than the 1995 versions. The new models should continue Civic's traditions for reliability, durability, and high resale value.

Honda Civic prices are on page 343.

HONDA CIVIC EX

Rating Guide	1	2	3	4	5
Performance					
Acceleration			▓		
Economy				▓	
Driveability				▓	
Ride			▓		
Steering/handling			▓		
Braking				▓	
Noise			▓		
Accommodations					
Driver seating				▓	
Instruments/controls				▓	
Visibility			▓		
Room/comfort			▓		
Entry/exit			▓		
Cargo room			▓		
Workmanship					
Exterior				▓	
Interior				▓	
Value				▓	
Total Points					61

Rating scale 5=Exceptional; 4=Above average; 3=Average; 2=Below average; 1=Poor

Specifications

Body type ....4-door notchback
Wheelbase (in.) 103.2
Overall length (in.) 175.1
Overall width (in.) 67.1
Overall height (in.) 54.7
Curb weight (lbs.) 2319
Seating capacity 5
Front head room (in.) 39.8
Max. front leg room (in.) 42.7
Rear head room (in.) 37.6
Min. rear leg room (in.) 34.1
Cargo volume (cu. ft.).............11.9

Engine type ....ohc I-4
Engine size (l/cu. in.) 1.6/97
Horsepower @ rpm ...127 @ 6600
Torque @ rpm ....107 @ 5500
Transmission.................auto/4-sp.
Drive wheels ....front
Brakes, F/R...........disc/disc (ABS)
Tire size 175/65R14
Fuel tank capacity (gal.) 11.9
EPA city/highway mpg 28/35
Test mileage (mpg) 29.2

Warranties The entire car is covered for 3 years/36,000 miles. Body perforation rust is covered for 3 years/unlimited miles.

Built in Liberty, Ohio, and Canada.

CONSUMER GUIDE®

HONDA ODYSSEY/ ISUZU OASIS

Minivan

Honda Odyssey EX

Honda joined the minivan market last year with the front-drive Odyssey, which is built on a stretched version of the Accord's platform and unchanged this year. Isuzu dealers will begin selling a clone of the Odyssey as the Oasis in early 1996. Oasis prices will be announced closer to the on-sale date. Odyssey and Oasis depart from most other minivans in having four swing-open side doors (instead of two front doors and a sliding passenger-side door) and a rear liftgate. Despite rumors that a V-6 engine would be optional this year, the only engine announced for 1996 is the 140-horsepower 2.2-liter 4-cylinder used last year. Both the engine and standard 4-speed automatic transmission are borrowed from the Accord, but the transmission shift lever is mounted on the steering column instead of the floor. LX and upscale EX versions of the Odyssey are again offered, both with standard dual air bags and anti-lock brakes. Seats for seven are standard on the LX, including two front bucket seats, a 3-place middle bench, and a 2-place rear seat that folds flush into the cargo floor. A pair of removable middle "captain's chairs" that weigh 38 pounds each are optional on the LX and standard on the EX for 6-passenger seating. Odyssey is about as long as the Mercury Villager and Nissan Quest but some three inches lower, which pays off in a lower step-in height that makes entry/exit easier. But Odyssey is also three to five inches narrower than other minivans, which makes for cramped seating in the 3-place middle bench on the 7-passenger version. There's ample space for six people in all versions. Odyssey is pleasant and competent on the road. However, it lacks a 6-cylinder engine, and it starts out at higher prices than most rivals. On the other hand, it's well-built, well-equipped, and likely to be reliable.

Honda Odyssey prices are on page 344.

HONDA ODYSSEY EX

Rating Guide	1	2	3	4	5
Performance					
Acceleration			3		
Economy			3		
Driveability			3		
Ride			3		
Steering/handling			3		
Braking				4	
Noise			3		
Accommodations					
Driver seating			3		
Instruments/controls			3		
Visibility			3		
Room/comfort			3		
Entry/exit			3		
Cargo room			3		
Workmanship					
Exterior			3		
Interior			3		
Value			3		
Total Points					61

Rating scale 5=Exceptional; 4=Above average; 3=Average; 2=Below average; 1=Poor

Specifications

Body type	5-door van
Wheelbase (in.)	111.4
Overall length (in.)	187.2
Overall width (in.)	70.6
Overall height (in.)	64.6
Curb weight (lbs.)	3450
Seating capacity	6
Front head room (in.)	40.1
Max. front leg room (in.)	40.7
Rear head room (in.)	39.3
Min. rear leg room (in.)	40.2
Cargo volume (cu. ft.)	102.5
Engine type	ohc I-4
Engine size (l/cu. in.)	2.2/132
Horsepower @ rpm	140 @ 5600
Torque @ rpm	145 @ 4500
Transmission	auto/4-sp.
Drive wheels	front
Brakes, F/R	disc/disc (ABS)
Tire size	205/65R15
Fuel tank capacity (gal.)	17.2
EPA city/highway mpg	20/24
Test mileage (mpg)	21.3

Warranties The entire vehicle is covered for 3 years/36,000 miles. Body perforation rust is covered for 3 years/unlimited miles.

Built in Japan.

HYUNDAI ACCENT
Subcompact

Hyundai Accent 4-door

The front-drive Accent was introduced last spring as Hyundai's new entry-level model, replacing the Excel. This year Hyundai adds a sporty version of the 3-door hatchback called the GT, while the returning models are unchanged. The Accent GT is powered by a new 105-horsepower 1.5-liter 4-cylinder engine with dual overhead camshafts. Other unique features for the GT include a firmer suspension and performance tires mounted on 14-inch alloy wheels (instead of 13-inch wheels). Other Accents use a 92-horsepower version of the 1.5-liter 4-cylinder with a single overhead camshaft. Both engines are available with a standard 5-speed manual or optional 4-speed automatic transmission. Returning from last year are an L hatchback, which is the least-expensive model, and base versions of the hatchback and 4-door sedan. Dual air bags are standard on all Accents. Anti-lock brakes are optional on the base and GT models. With a base price of $8285, the 1996 Accent L model retains its title as the least-expensive car sold in the U.S. The Accent feels much more solid and substantial than the Excel, the car it replaced, and is quieter as well. However, it's far from quiet. There's lots of road noise at highway speeds, and lots of engine racket in hard acceleration. Acceleration from the 92-horsepower engine is adequate with either transmission. Highway passing requires a long stretch of open road and the engine strains going up even small hills. We tested a 5-speed sedan that took nearly 11 seconds to reach 60 mph. We estimate it takes a second or two more with the automatic. Front head room is ample for 6-footers and the rear seat is big enough for occupants up to about 5-foot-10. Accent is acceptable low-cost transportation that is more satisfying to drive than some rivals.

Hyundai Accent prices are on page 346.

HYUNDAI ACCENT

Rating Guide	1	2	3	4	5
Performance					
Acceleration			███		
Economy				███	
Driveability			███		
Ride			███		
Steering/handling			███		
Braking			███		
Noise		███			
Accommodations					
Driver seating				███	
Instruments/controls				███	
Visibility				███	
Room/comfort			███		
Entry/exit			███		
Cargo room			███		
Workmanship					
Exterior				███	
Interior				███	
Value				███	
Total Points					**55**

Rating scale 5=Exceptional; 4=Above average; 3=Average; 2=Below average; 1=Poor

Specifications

Body type ....4-door notchback	Engine type ....ohc I-4
Wheelbase (in.) 94.5	Engine size (l/cu. in.)...........1.5/91
Overall length (in.) 162.1	Horsepower @ rpm .....92 @ 5500
Overall width (in.) 63.8	Torque @ rpm ....96 @ 3000
Overall height (in.)..................54.9	Transmission.................auto/4-sp.
Curb weight (lbs.) 2105	Drive wheels ....front
Seating capacity 5	Brakes, F/R....................disc/drum
Front head room (in.) 38.7	Tire size 175/70R13
Max. front leg room (in.)........42.6	Fuel tank capacity (gal.).........11.9
Rear head room (in.) 38.0	EPA city/highway mpg 28/37
Min. rear leg room (in.) 32.7	Test mileage (mpg)................30.1
Cargo volume (cu. ft.)............10.7	

Warranties The entire car is covered for 3 years/36,000 miles. Major powertrain components are covered for 5 years/60,000 miles. Body perforation rust is covered for 5 years/100,000 miles.

Built in South Korea.

HYUNDAI SONATA
Mid-Size

Hyundai Sonata GL

Hyundai's largest, most-expensive U.S. model, which was redesigned for the 1995 season, has minor equipment revisions for 1996. The front-drive Sonata is a mid-size sedan that comes in three price levels: base, GL, and GLS. Anti-lock brakes, previously available only as part of option packages, are now a separate option for the GLS. A split folding rear seatback, previously standard only on the top-line GLS model, is now standard on all versions. A 2.0-liter 4-cylinder engine with 137 horsepower is standard on the base and GL models. On the base model, it's available with a standard 5-speed manual or optional 4-speed automatic; on the GL it comes only with the automatic. A 142-horsepower 3.0-liter V-6 is standard on the GLS and optional on the GL and comes only with the 4-speed automatic. Dual air bags are standard on all models and anti-lock brakes are optional on models with the V-6. V-6 models have new liquid-filled engine mounts and additional sound insulation this year. Though the Sonata doesn't match mid-size class leaders such as the Ford Taurus and Honda Accord in overall quality, it is priced well below those rivals, making it worth considering by value-conscious shoppers. The 4-cylinder engine feels sluggish with the automatic transmission in standing-start acceleration but provides adequate passing power. The V-6 furnishes more than adequate acceleration (9.2 seconds in our test) and better passing response. Hyundai's automatic transmission is slow to downshift for passing and also shifts harshly during hard acceleration. The spacious rear seat looks huge compared to some rivals'. A trunk that opens at bumper level and has a wide, flat floor gives the Sonata generous cargo space. If you need a low-priced family car with lots of space, take a look at the Sonata.

Hyundai Sonata prices are on page 346.

HYUNDAI SONATA GL

Rating Guide	1	2	3	4	5
Performance					
Acceleration			3		
Economy			3		
Driveability			3		
Ride			3		
Steering/handling			3		
Braking				4	
Noise			3		
Accommodations					
Driver seating			3		
Instruments/controls			3		
Visibility			3		
Room/comfort			3		
Entry/exit			3		
Cargo room			3		
Workmanship					
Exterior			3		
Interior			3		
Value			3		

Total Points..**59**

Rating scale 5=Exceptional; 4=Above average; 3=Average; 2=Below average; 1=Poor

Specifications

Body type ....4-door notchback
Wheelbase (in.) 106.3
Overall length (in.) 185.0
Overall width (in.) 69.7
Overall height (in.) 55.3
Curb weight (lbs.) 3025
Seating capacity..........................5
Front head room (in.) 38.5
Max. front leg room (in.) 43.3
Rear head room (in.) ....NA
Min. rear leg room (in.) ....NA
Cargo volume (cu. ft.).............13.2

Engine type.......................ohc V-6
Engine size (l/cu. in.)..........3.0/181
Horsepower @ rpm ...142 @ 5000
Torque @ rpm ....168 @ 2400
Transmission.................auto/4-sp.
Drive wheels ....front
Brakes, F/R ....disc/drum (ABS)
Tire size 205/60R15
Fuel tank capacity (gal.) 17.2
EPA city/highway mpg 18/24
Test mileage (mpg) 17.8

Warranties The entire car is covered for 3 years/36,000 miles. Major powertrain components are covered for 5 years/60,000 miles. Body perforation rust is covered for 5 years/100,000 miles.

Built in South Korea.

CONSUMER GUIDE®

INFINITI G20
Premium Sedan

Infiniti G20

Infiniti's entry-level model is unchanged except for the addition of fake wood interior trim to the Leather Appointment Group and new exterior colors. The G20 is based on the Japanese-market Nissan Primera, which was redesigned recently. The U.S. model, however, continues to be built from the old design. Infiniti officials say they haven't decided whether the G20 will be replaced next year. Though they want a sedan priced below $25,000, the G20 has been sold at hefty discounts the past few years, which erodes resale value and hurts Infiniti's image in general. If it is dropped, the entry-level role at Infiniti will be filled by the new I30 sedan, which is based on the Nissan Maxima. Two versions of the G20 return for 1996: the base model and the G20t. The G20t includes a Touring Package that consists of a limited-slip differential, rear spoiler, fog lamps, a folding rear seat, and the Leather Appointment Group. Both models come with a 140-horsepower 2.0-liter 4-cylinder engine. A 5-speed manual transmission is standard and a 4-speed automatic is optional on both models, which come with dual air bags, anti-lock 4-wheel disc brakes, automatic climate control, and a 6-speaker sound system with cassette and CD players. Though the G20 comes with a long list of standard features, there are larger, more refined cars in the same price range, such as the Honda Accord and Toyota Camry (which are available with V-6 engines). However, the G20 comes with a longer warranty, roadside assistance, and other benefits that have helped Infiniti score at the top of customer satisfaction ratings. The G20's dual-cam engine is smooth and quiet in low-speed driving but grows raucous in hard acceleration. Slow sales mean Infiniti dealers are offering budget leases and huge discounts on the G20.

Infiniti G20 prices are on page 348.

INFINITI G20

Rating Guide	1	2	3	4	5
Performance					
Acceleration			▓		
Economy			▓		
Driveability			▓		
Ride			▓		
Steering/handling				▓	
Braking					▓
Noise			▓		
Accommodations					
Driver seating				▓	
Instruments/controls				▓	
Visibility				▓	
Room/comfort			▓		
Entry/exit			▓		
Cargo room		▓			
Workmanship					
Exterior				▓	
Interior				▓	
Value			▓		
Total Points					**58**

Rating scale 5=Exceptional; 4=Above average; 3=Average; 2=Below average; 1=Poor

Specifications

Body type ....4-door notchback	Engine type ....dohc I-4
Wheelbase (in.) 100.4	Engine size (l/cu. in.).........2.0/122
Overall length (in.)................174.8	Horsepower @ rpm ...140 @ 6400
Overall width (in.) 66.7	Torque @ rpm ....132 @ 4800
Overall height (in.)..................54.7	Transmission.................auto/4-sp.
Curb weight (lbs.) 2877	Drive wheels ....front
Seating capacity...........................5	Brakes, F/R..........disc/disc (ABS)
Front head room (in.) 38.8	Tire size 195/65HR14
Max. front leg room (in.)........42.0	Fuel tank capacity (gal.) 15.9
Rear head room (in.) 37.3	EPA city/highway mpg 22/28
Min. rear leg room (in.)...........32.2	Test mileage (mpg) 21.7
Cargo volume (cu. ft.).............14.2	

Warranties The entire car is covered for 4 years/60,000 miles. Major powertrain components are covered for 6 years/70,000 miles. Body perforation rust is covered for 7 years/unlimited miles.

Built in Japan.

CONSUMER GUIDE®

INFINITI I30
Premium Sedan

RECOMMENDED

Infiniti I30t

The I30 is a new "near-luxury" model for Infiniti, the luxury division of Nissan, that was an early arrival for the 1996 model year. The I30, a front-drive 4-door sedan based on the design used for the Nissan Maxima, is priced to compete with cars such as the Lexus ES 300, BMW 3-Series, and Mazda Millenia. The I30 and Maxima use the same 190-horsepower 3.0-liter V-6 engine with dual-overhead camshafts. A 5-speed manual transmission is standard and a 4-speed automatic is optional. Styling is where the I30 differs most from the Maxima. The I30's styling is shared with the Japanese-market Nissan Cefiro. A chrome, vertical-bar grille gives the front a strong resemblance to the Q45, Infiniti's flagship. Standard features on the I30 include dual air bags and anti-lock brakes. Three versions are offered: a base model, a "Leather-Appointed" model, and a sportier "Touring" model (designated I30t). The Leather-Appointed model and I30t come with leather upholstery, a power sunroof, and the HomeLink transmitter, which is built into the driver's sun visor. The transmitter can be programmed to open garage doors and electric gates and turn on home interior lights. The I30 has strong, refined performance and capable handling. The V-6 engine produces ample torque at low speeds, giving the I30 quick takeoffs. The suspension is firm yet soaks up most bumps easily. Visibility is good to the front and sides, but the large rear headrests block the driver's view directly back. The interior has ample room for four adults and the spacious trunk is augmented by a folding pass-through section that allows carrying long items like skis. The I30 has more standard features than the similar Maxima, plus a more-comprehensive warranty and the promise of better customer service that comes with owning an Infiniti.

Infiniti I30 prices are on page 348.

INFINITI I30t

Rating Guide

	1	2	3	4	5

Performance
Acceleration	4
Economy	3
Driveability	4
Ride	4
Steering/handling	4
Braking	4
Noise	4

Accommodations
Driver seating	4
Instruments/controls	4
Visibility	4
Room/comfort	4
Entry/exit	4
Cargo room	4

Workmanship
Exterior	5
Interior	5

Value
5

Total Points...62

Rating scale 5=Exceptional; 4=Above average; 3=Average; 2=Below average; 1=Poor

Specifications

Body type	4-door notchback
Wheelbase (in.)	106.3
Overall length (in.)	189.6
Overall width (in.)	69.7
Overall height (in.)	55.7
Curb weight (lbs.)	3001
Seating capacity	5
Front head room (in.)	40.1
Max. front leg room (in.)	43.9
Rear head room (in.)	37.4
Min. rear leg room (in.)	34.3
Cargo volume (cu. ft.)	14.1
Engine type	dohc V-6
Engine size (l/cu. in.)	3.0/181
Horsepower @ rpm	190 @ 5600
Torque @ rpm	205 @ 4000
Transmission	auto/4-sp.
Drive wheels	front
Brakes, F/R	disc/disc (ABS)
Tire size	215/60HR15
Fuel tank capacity (gal.)	18.5
EPA city/highway mpg	21/28
Test mileage (mpg)	18.6

Warranties The entire car is covered for 4 years/60,000 miles. Major powertrain components are covered for 6 years/70,000 miles. Body perforation rust is covered for 7 years/unlimited miles.

Built in Japan.

CONSUMER GUIDE®

INFINITI J30
Premium Sedan

Infiniti J30

The rear-drive J30 is unchanged for this year except for new exterior colors. The J30 is a mid-size 4-door that competes in the middle segment of the premium sedan market against rivals such as the Lexus ES 300 and GS 300, BMW 3- and 5-Series sedans, Mercedes-E-Class, and the Volvo 960. Infiniti is the luxury division of Nissan. Two models are available, the base J30 and the J30t, which has a Touring Package that includes performance tires, a firmer suspension, and a rear spoiler. Both models come with a 210-horsepower 3.0-liter V-6 engine, a 4-speed automatic transmission, dual air bags, and anti-lock brakes. Other standard features include a limited-slip differential, heated power front seats, leather upholstery, walnut interior trim, automatic climate control, a stereo with cassette and CD players and six speakers, a power glass sunroof, and remote keyless entry. The J30 comes with a full load of safety and convenience features but lacks the polish and refinement of rivals such as the less-expensive ES 300. With a 0-60 mph time of under nine seconds, it's competitive in acceleration among luxury sedans in the $40,000 price range, but in hard acceleration the engine is surprisingly loud and even a little coarse. It can be thirsty, too. We reached 24 mpg in highway driving but dropped below 16 mpg in the city. The firm suspension provides capable handling and a stable ride. The J30 is a few inches longer than an ES 300 but has less passenger and cargo room, with a cozy seating package that's practical only for four adults. With just 10.1 cubic feet of cargo space, the J30 has one of the smallest trunks among luxury sedans. Several good cars can be found in this price range, so also check out some competitors. Big discounts should be available whether you're buying or leasing.

Infiniti J30 prices are on page 349.

INFINITI J30

Rating Guide	1	2	3	4	5
Performance					
Acceleration				▓	
Economy		▓			
Driveability				▓	
Ride				▓	
Steering/handling			▓		
Braking					▓
Noise				▓	
Accommodations					
Driver seating			▓		
Instruments/controls			▓		
Visibility		▓			
Room/comfort			▓		
Entry/exit			▓		
Cargo room		▓			
Workmanship					
Exterior				▓	
Interior				▓	
Value			▓		

Total Points...**59**

Rating scale 5=Exceptional; 4=Above average; 3=Average; 2=Below average; 1=Poor

Specifications

Body type ....4-door notchback	Engine type.....................dohc V-6
Wheelbase (in.) 108.7	Engine size (l/cu. in.).........3.0/181
Overall length (in.)................191.3	Horsepower @ rpm ...210 @ 6400
Overall width (in.) 69.7	Torque @ rpm ....193 @ 4800
Overall height (in.)..................54.7	Transmission.................auto/4-sp.
Curb weight (lbs.) 3527	Drive wheels ....rear
Seating capacity..........................5	Brakes, F/R..........disc/disc (ABS)
Front head room (in.) 37.7	Tire size 215/60HR15
Max. front leg room (in.).........41.3	Fuel tank capacity (gal.) 19.0
Rear head room (in.) 36.7	EPA city/highway mpg 18/23
Min. rear leg room (in.) 30.5	Test mileage (mpg) 18.3
Cargo volume (cu. ft.).............10.1	

Warranties The entire car is covered for 4 years/60,000 miles. Major powertrain components are covered for 6 years/70,000 miles. Body perforation rust is covered for 7 years/unlimited miles.

Built in Japan.

INFINITI Q45
Premium Sedan

Infiniti Q45

Infiniti's flagship sedan loses its most-expensive model, the Q45a, and variable-valve timing has been deleted from the V-8 used in all models. The only additions announced for 1996 are new exterior colors. Infiniti is the luxury division of Nissan, and the rear-drive Q45, introduced as a 1990 model, is its flagship. A replacement for the Q45 is expected to be introduced in the spring as an early 1997 model. The Q45a has been dropped, along with its electronic Full-Active Suspension, which used electronic actuators instead of conventional shock absorbers to control body lean, pitch, and dive. Models returning this year are the base Q45 and the Q45t, which has a Touring Package that includes a rear spoiler, forged alloy wheels, larger stabilizer bars, performance tires, a trunk-mounted CD changer, and heated front seats. Both use a 4.5-liter V-8 engine, which this year loses its variable valve-timing feature—another victim of cost cutting. The engine still is rated at 278 horsepower and 292 pounds/feet of torque. A 4-speed automatic transmission, limited-slip differential, anti-lock brakes, and dual air bags are standard on both models. Traction control is the only major option, and it includes all-season tires and, on the base model, heated front seats. While the Q45 has the athletic feel of a European luxury sedan, the rival Lexus LS 400 provides more luxurious isolation. Though the Q45's suspension is firmer than the LS 400's, it doesn't ride harshly. The Q45 has a stable, comfortable highway ride yet most bumps are absorbed with little notice. We timed a Q45 at 8.5 seconds to 60 mph, which is slower than some competitors. However, passing power is outstanding. Q45 sales have slowed as some key rivals, such as the LS 400, have been redesigned and offer new features. That means big discounts should be available whether you're buying or leasing.

Infiniti Q45 prices are on page 350.

INFINITI Q45

Rating Guide	1	2	3	4	5
Performance					
Acceleration				▓	
Economy	▓				
Driveability			▓		
Ride			▓		
Steering/handling			▓		
Braking				▓	
Noise			▓		
Accommodations					
Driver seating				▓	
Instruments/controls				▓	
Visibility			▓		
Room/comfort			▓		
Entry/exit			▓		
Cargo room			▓		
Workmanship					
Exterior				▓	
Interior				▓	
Value			▓		
Total Points					63

Rating scale 5=Exceptional; 4=Above average; 3=Average; 2=Below average; 1=Poor

Specifications

Body type ....4-door notchback
Wheelbase (in.) 113.4
Overall length (in.) 199.8
Overall width (in.) 71.9
Overall height (in.) 56.5
Curb weight (lbs.) 4039
Seating capacity 5
Front head room (in.) 38.2
Max. front leg room (in.) 43.9
Rear head room (in.) 36.3
Min. rear leg room (in.) 32.0
Cargo volume (cu. ft.) 14.8

Engine type ....dohc V-8
Engine size (l/cu. in.).........4.5/274
Horsepower @ rpm ...278 @ 6000
Torque @ rpm ....292 @ 4000
Transmission ....auto/4-sp.
Drive wheels ....rear
Brakes, F/R...........disc/disc (ABS)
Tire size.....................215/65VR15
Fuel tank capacity (gal.) 22.5
EPA city/highway mpg 17/22
Test mileage (mpg) 16.6

Warranties The entire car is covered for 4 years/60,000 miles. Major powertrain components are covered for 6 years/70,000 miles. Body perforation rust is covered for 7 years/unlimited miles.

Built in Japan.

CONSUMER GUIDE®

ISUZU RODEO/ HONDA PASSPORT
Sport-Utility Vehicle

Isuzu Rodeo LS

Rodeo and Passport, which are similar U.S.-built sport-utility vehicles, are scheduled to get a more powerful V-6 engine, a new 4-wheel-drive system with shift-on-the-fly capability, and 4-wheel anti-lock brakes as a new option when the 1996 models arrive in January. The interior for both models was revamped last spring, when they received standard dual air bags and a new dashboard. Honda buys the Passport from Isuzu. Both vehicles come only as 5-door wagons and are built in Lafayette, Indiana, at a plant Isuzu shares with Subaru. The base 2-wheel-drive models in both lines come with a 120-horsepower 2.6-liter 4-cylinder engine and a 5-speed manual transmission. All other models come with a 190-horsepower 3.2-liter V-6. Last year, the V-6 made 175 horsepower. The V-6 teams with either a 5-speed manual or 4-speed automatic. Details on the new 4WD system weren't available, but Isuzu estimated it will allow changing in and out of 4WD High at speeds up to 60 mph without stopping. The current 4WD system allows engaging 4WD at speeds up to five mph, but the vehicle must be stopped and reversed to fully disengage 4WD. Anti-lock rear brakes were standard on all 1995 models. For 1996, a new anti-lock system that operates on all four wheels will be optional. Though Rodeo and Passport have some good points, a well-equipped 4WD model is in the same price range as a Ford Explorer, Jeep Grand Cherokee, or a Chevy Blazer/GMC Jimmy, which are roomier and have standard 4-wheel anti-lock brakes. The interior has ample head room and leg room, but entry to the back seat is tight through the narrow doors. While Isuzu's V-6 doesn't have the low-speed muscle of the larger Ford, General Motors, and Jeep 6-cylinders, it works well with the automatic transmission.

Isuzu Rodeo prices are on page 350.
Honda Passport prices are on page 345.

ISUZU RODEO LS

Rating Guide	1	2	3	4	5
Performance					
Acceleration			|||||||		
Economy	|||||||				
Driveability			|||||||		
Ride		|||||||			
Steering/handling		|||||||			
Braking			|||||||		
Noise		|||||||			
Accommodations					
Driver seating		|||||||			
Instruments/controls		|||||||			
Visibility		|||||||			
Room/comfort		|||||||			
Entry/exit		|||||||			
Cargo room		|||||||			
Workmanship					
Exterior			|||||||		
Interior			|||||||		
Value		|||||||			
Total Points					**54**

Rating scale 5=Exceptional; 4=Above average; 3=Average; 2=Below average; 1=Poor

Specifications

Body type	5-door wagon
Wheelbase (in.)	108.7
Overall length (in.)	176.5
Overall width (in.)	66.5
Overall height (in.)	65.4
Curb weight (lbs.)	3545
Seating capacity	5
Front head room (in.)	38.2
Max. front leg room (in.)	42.5
Rear head room (in.)	37.8
Min. rear leg room (in.)	36.1
Cargo volume (cu. ft.)	74.9
Engine type	ohc V-6
Engine size (l/cu. in.)	3.2/193
Horsepower @ rpm	190 @ 5200
Torque @ rpm	188 @ 4000
Transmission	auto/4-sp.
Drive wheels	rear/all
Brakes, F/R	disc/disc (ABS)
Tire size	225/75R15
Fuel tank capacity (gal.)	21.9
EPA city/highway mpg	15/18
Test mileage (mpg)	13.9

Warranties The entire vehicle is covered for 3 years/50,000 miles. Major powertrain components are covered for 5 years/60,000 miles. Body perforation rust is covered for 6 years/100,000 miles.

Built in Lafayette, Ind.

ISUZU TROOPER/ ACURA SLX

Sport-Utility Vehicle

Isuzu Trooper LS

The Trooper will be the basis for a new sport-utility vehicle that will be introduced this spring by Acura, the luxury division of Honda. Acura's version, which will be called the SLX, will differ only in styling details and interior furnishings. SLX prices weren't announced in time for this issue. Honda also sells the Isuzu Rodeo as the Passport, while Isuzu sells the Honda Odyssey as the Oasis. All versions of the Trooper and SLX have a new 190-horsepower engine and a new 4-wheel-drive system that allows changing in and out of 4WD High on the move. Last year, the base S and LS Troopers used a 175-horsepower 3.2-liter V-6 with a single overhead camshaft and the top-shelf Limited came with a dual-cam version of the 3.2-liter that produced 190 horsepower. For 1996, all models have a single-camshaft 3.2-liter V-6 with 190 horsepower. The new 4WD system allows engaging or disengaging 4WD High at speeds up to about 60 mph. Isuzu's old 4WD system allowed engaging 4WD at speeds up to five mph, but the vehicle had to be stopped and reversed to fully disengage it. The Trooper and SLX comes as 4-door wagons with swing-out rear doors that are split 70/30. Anti-lock rear brakes are standard on all models. An anti-lock system that operates on all four wheels is optional. The new 4WD system coming out this year is overdue. All of Trooper's domestic rivals and most imported rivals have had full shift-on-the-fly or permanently engaged 4WD for years. Trooper is one of the roomiest sport-utility vehicles. It has loads of head clearance front and rear, plus enough width in the rear for three adults to fit without squeezing. Isuzu's trademark 70/30 rear cargo doors (something like an upright refrigerator/freezer) open to a tall, long cargo area. Though Trooper's prices are pretty steep, Isuzu dealers should be discounting.

Isuzu Trooper prices are on page 352.
Acura SLX standard equipment is on page 251.

ISUZU TROOPER LS

Rating Guide	1	2	3	4	5
Performance					
Acceleration			3		
Economy	1.5				
Driveability				4	
Ride			3		
Steering/handling			3		
Braking					5
Noise			3		
Accommodations					
Driver seating				4	
Instruments/controls			3		
Visibility			3		
Room/comfort				4	
Entry/exit			3		
Cargo room					5
Workmanship					
Exterior				4	
Interior				4	
Value			3		
Total Points					**57**

Rating scale 5=Exceptional; 4=Above average; 3=Average; 2=Below average; 1=Poor

Specifications

Body type	4-door wagon
Wheelbase (in.)	108.7
Overall length (in.)	183.5
Overall width (in.)	68.7
Overall height (in.)	72.8
Curb weight (lbs.)	4210
Seating capacity	5
Front head room (in.)	39.8
Max. front leg room (in.)	40.8
Rear head room (in.)	39.8
Min. rear leg room (in.)	39.1
Cargo volume (cu. ft.)	90.0
Engine type	ohc V-6
Engine size (l/cu. in.)	3.2/193
Horsepower @ rpm	190 @ 5200
Torque @ rpm	188 @ 4000
Transmission	auto/4-sp.
Drive wheels	rear/all
Brakes, F/R	disc/disc (ABS)
Tire size	245/70R16
Fuel tank capacity (gal.)	22.5
EPA city/highway mpg	14/18
Test mileage (mpg)	15.8

Warranties The entire vehicle is covered for 3 years/50,000 miles. Major powertrain components are covered for 5 years/60,000 miles. Body perforation rust is covered for 6 years/100,000 miles.

Built in Japan.

CONSUMER GUIDE®

JAGUAR XJ SEDAN
Premium Sedan

Jaguar Vanden Plas

Jaguar redesigned its XJ sedan for 1995 and this year stretches the wheelbase by 4.9 inches on the Vanden Plas and XJ12 models. The base XJ6 and supercharged XJR models return on last year's 113-inch wheelbase, while the Vanden Plas and XJ12 ride a 117.9-inch wheelbase. Overall length also has grown 4.9 inches on the two stretched models. Most of the additional length has been used to increase leg room for rear passengers. Cargo volume is unchanged at 11.1 cubic feet for all models. The XJ6 and Vanden Plas come with a 245-horsepower 4.0-liter 6-cylinder engine. The XJR has a 322-horsepower supercharged version of this engine. The XJ12 uses a 313-horsepower 6.0-liter V-12 engine, and Jaguar has announced this is the final year for the venerable 12-cylinder. All models come with a 4-speed automatic transmission, dual air bags, and anti-lock brakes. The longer wheelbase means that instead of crowded, uncomfortable conditions, there's room to relax and stretch your legs in the rear seat of the Vanden Plas and XJ12. Most people should be able to sit in the rear with their legs crossed. Cargo space is still skimpy on all Jaguar sedans, with a trunk floor that is too short to carry much luggage. In other areas, the stretched versions feel the same as the shorter models. The base 6-cylinder engine provides brisk acceleration from a standing start and strong passing power. While the supercharged 6-cylinder gives the XJR a big performance boost, the V-12 doesn't offer a big enough gain in acceleration to justify its higher price. Jaguar has moved much closer to the leaders in the luxury sedan field in the past two years. The current lineup is well worth considering, especially if you're looking for a car with more character than rivals such as the Lexus LS 400.

Jaguar XJ Sedan prices are on page 353.

JAGUAR VANDEN PLAS

Rating Guide	1	2	3	4	5
Performance					
Acceleration				▓	
Economy		▓			
Driveability			▓		
Ride					▓
Steering/handling			▓		
Braking			▓		
Noise			▓		
Accommodations					
Driver seating			▓		
Instruments/controls		▓			
Visibility			▓		
Room/comfort			▓		
Entry/exit			▓		
Cargo room			▓		
Workmanship					
Exterior					▓
Interior				▓	
Value			▓		

Total Points..62

Rating scale 5=Exceptional; 4=Above average; 3=Average; 2=Below average; 1=Poor

Specifications

Body type ....4-door notchback
Wheelbase (in.) 117.9
Overall length (in.).................202.7
Overall width (in.) 70.8
Overall height (in.)..................53.1
Curb weight (lbs.) 4130
Seating capacity.........................5
Front head room (in.) 37.2
Max. front leg room (in.) 41.2
Rear head room (in.) 36.8
Min. rear leg room (in.) 39.2
Cargo volume (cu. ft.).............11.1

Engine type ....dohc I-6
Engine size (l/cu. in.)..........4.0/243
Horsepower @ rpm ...245 @ 4700
Torque @ rpm ....289 @ 4000
Transmission.................auto/4-sp.
Drive wheels ....rear
Brakes, F/R............disc/disc (ABS)
Tire size.....................225/60ZR16
Fuel tank capacity (gal.) 21.4
EPA city/highway mpg 17/23
Test mileage (mpg) ....NA

Warranties The entire car is covered for 4 years/50,000 miles. Body perforation rust is covered for 6 years/unlimited miles.

Built in England.

CONSUMER GUIDE®

JEEP CHEROKEE

BUDGET BUY

Sport-Utility Vehicle

Jeep Cherokee Sport 5-door

Cherokee, which gained a driver-side air bag last year, returns for its 13th model year in three price levels: SE, Sport, and Country. The SE and Sport are available in 3-door and 5-door wagon body styles, and the Country comes only as a 5-door. All three are available with rear-wheel drive or Command-Trac part-time 4-wheel drive, which is not for use on dry pavement. The Sport and Country are also available with Selec-Trac full-time 4WD, which can be used on dry pavement. The SE comes with a 2.5-liter 4-cylinder engine that produces 125 horsepower. The optional 3-speed automatic transmission has been dropped, so the 4-cylinder now comes only with a 5-speed manual transmission. Optional on the SE and standard on the Sport and Country is a 4.0-liter inline 6-cylinder that gets several internal improvements this year. Though horsepower and torque ratings are unchanged at 190 and 225, respectively, both are reached at lower engine speeds than before. In the SE and Sport, the 6-cylinder comes with a standard 5-speed manual or optional 4-speed automatic. In the Country, the automatic is standard. Despite its age, Cherokee is still a good choice among compact sport-utilities. It has convenient 4WD systems, commendable off-road capabilities, civilized on-road manners, and attractive prices. It isn't as roomy as a Grand Cherokee or Ford Explorer, but Cherokee can carry four adults in comfort. Cargo volume is ample and the cargo floor is flat and wide. Jeep's 4-cylinder is hard-pressed to provide even adequate performance. Most Cherokees are sold with the 6-cylinder engine, which allows you to scoot off the line and pass other vehicles quickly. Can't afford a Grand Cherokee or Explorer? The Cherokee is less expensive yet offers nearly as many features.

Jeep Cherokee prices are on page 354.

JEEP CHEROKEE SPORT

Rating Guide	1	2	3	4	5
Performance					
Acceleration			▓▓▓		
Economy		▓▓			
Driveability			▓▓▓		
Ride			▓▓▓		
Steering/handling			▓▓▓		
Braking					▓▓▓
Noise			▓▓▓		
Accommodations					
Driver seating		▓▓			
Instruments/controls		▓▓			
Visibility			▓▓▓		
Room/comfort			▓▓▓		
Entry/exit		▓▓			
Cargo room			▓▓▓		
Workmanship					
Exterior			▓▓▓		
Interior			▓▓▓		
Value			▓▓▓		
Total Points					**57**

Rating scale 5=Exceptional; 4=Above average; 3=Average; 2=Below average; 1=Poor

Specifications

Body type	5-door wagon
Wheelbase (in.)	101.4
Overall length (in.)	166.9
Overall width (in.)	67.7
Overall height (in.)	63.9
Curb weight (lbs.)	3090
Seating capacity	5
Front head room (in.)	38.3
Max. front leg room (in.)	41.4
Rear head room (in.)	38.5
Min. rear leg room (in.)	34.9
Cargo volume (cu. ft.)	71.8
Engine type	ohv I-6
Engine size (l/cu. in.)	4.0/242
Horsepower @ rpm	190 @ 4600
Torque @ rpm	225 @ 3000
Transmission	auto/4-sp.
Drive wheels	rear/all
Brakes, F/R	disc/disc (ABS)
Tire size	225/75R15
Fuel tank capacity (gal.)	20.2
EPA city/highway mpg	15/19
Test mileage (mpg)	16.4

Warranties The entire vehicle is covered for 3 years/36,000 miles. Body perforation rust is covered for 7 years/100,000 miles.

Built in Toldeo, Ohio.

CONSUMER GUIDE®

JEEP GRAND CHEROKEE
Sport-Utility Vehicle

RECOMMENDED

Jeep Grand Cherokee Laredo

Though it doesn't look much different on the outside, there are numerous changes to the 1996 edition of Jeep's flagship model. A restyled grille that dips into the front bumper and optional fog lights integrated into the bumper are the most notable visual changes. A redesigned dashboard adds a passenger-side air bag, so dual air bags are now standard. A new steering wheel contains the cruise-control switches and has a center horn pad. Four-wheel anti-lock brakes are standard on all models. Grand Cherokee comes as a 5-door wagon in two price levels: Laredo and Limited. A 4.0-liter inline 6-cylinder engine with 185 horsepower is standard and a 220-horsepower 5.2-liter V-8 is optional. A 4-speed automatic is the only transmission available. Both models can be ordered with rear-wheel drive, Selec-Trac full-time 4-wheel drive, or Quadra-Trac permanent 4-wheel drive. Though the Ford Explorer is the best-selling sport-utility vehicle and our Best Buy in this class, the Grand Cherokee also deserves strong consideration, along with the Chevrolet Blazer and GMC Jimmy. The optional V-8 engine gives the Grand Cherokee a noticeable boost in low-speed acceleration, but Jeep's 6-cylinder is all most people will need. It furnishes strong acceleration and brisk passing response. Grand Cherokee is smaller inside than the Explorer, yet head room and leg room are generous all around. With the rear seatback up, there's not much more luggage room than in a mid-size car—partly because the spare tire takes up a big chunk on the left side. The split rear seatback folds to create a long cargo floor. The Grand Cherokee has impressive performance on-road and off-road, plus a broader range of choices in engines and 4WD systems than most rivals.

Jeep Grand Cherokee prices are on page 357.

JEEP GRAND CHEROKEE LAREDO

Rating Guide	1	2	3	4	5
Performance					
Acceleration				▓	
Economy	▓				
Driveability				▓	
Ride			▓		
Steering/handling			▓		
Braking					▓
Noise			▓		
Accommodations					
Driver seating			▓		
Instruments/controls			▓		
Visibility		▓			
Room/comfort			▓		
Entry/exit		▓			
Cargo room				▓	
Workmanship					
Exterior				▓	
Interior				▓	
Value				▓	
Total Points					59

Rating scale 5=Exceptional; 4=Above average; 3=Average; 2=Below average; 1=Poor

Specifications

Body type	5-door wagon
Wheelbase (in.)	105.9
Overall length (in.)	177.1
Overall width (in.)	70.9
Overall height (in.)	64.7
Curb weight (lbs.)	3614
Seating capacity	5
Front head room (in.)	38.9
Max. front leg room (in.)	40.8
Rear head room (in.)	39.0
Min. rear leg room (in.)	35.7
Cargo volume (cu. ft.)	79.3
Engine type	ohv I-6
Engine size (l/cu. in.)	4.0/242
Horsepower @ rpm	185 @ 4600
Torque @ rpm	220 @ 2400
Transmission	auto/4-sp.
Drive wheels	rear/all
Brakes, F/R	disc/disc (ABS)
Tire size	215/75R15
Fuel tank capacity (gal.)	23.0
EPA city/highway mpg	15/20
Test mileage (mpg)	15.2

Warranties The entire vehicle is covered for 3 years/36,000 miles. Body perforation rust is covered for 7 years/100,000 miles.

Built in Detroit, Mich.

KIA SPORTAGE
Sport-Utility Vehicle

Kia Sportage EX

Early in 1996, a 3-door version of the Korean-built Sportage is scheduled to join the 5-door model that was introduced last January. The 3-door will be nearly a foot shorter in wheelbase and overall length than its big brother, making it a bit larger than a Geo Tracker. The 3-door Sportage will have 4-wheel drive, a 130-horsepower 2.0-liter 4-cylinder engine with dual-overhead camshafts, and a choice of 5-speed manual or 4-speed automatic transmissions. Until the 3-door model arrives, the big news is the addition of a standard driver-side air bag for the 5-door version. The 5-door Sportage is available with rear-wheel drive or 4WD. The rear-drive model comes with a 94-horsepower 2.0-liter 4-cylinder with a single overhead camshaft and a 5-speed manual transmission. The 4WD model has the dual-cam engine with 130 horsepower and is available with a 5-speed manual or 4-speed automatic transmission. All models have standard anti-lock rear brakes that operate only in 2WD. Kia has about 140 dealers, mainly in Western and Southern states. Sportage is shorter than nearly all sport-utility wagons, yet it has adequate room for four adults. Sportage also is as capable off-road as most rivals. Unfortunately, the 4WD system has only limited shift-on-the-fly capability (up to 15 mph) for engaging or disengaging 4WD. It also requires backing up a few feet to fully disengage 4WD. The 5-speed EX 4x4 feels sluggish even at full throttle, though passing power is adequate. Handling ability is good enough to almost make you think you're in a sporty small sedan. The firm ride, however, is more typical of a sport-utility than a car. Sportage is small enough to easily maneuver through the urban jungle yet large enough to be a family hauler, and it's less-expensive than most rivals.

Kia Sportage prices are on page 359.

KIA SPORTAGE EX

Rating Guide	1	2	3	4	5
Performance					
Acceleration		■■			
Economy		■■			
Driveability			■■■		
Ride			■■■		
Steering/handling			■■■		
Braking				■■■■	
Noise			■■■		
Accommodations					
Driver seating			■■■		
Instruments/controls			■■■		
Visibility				■■■■	
Room/comfort			■■■		
Entry/exit		■■			
Cargo room			■■■		
Workmanship					
Exterior			■■■		
Interior			■■■		
Value			■■■		
Total Points					**55**

Rating scale 5=Exceptional; 4=Above average; 3=Average; 2=Below average; 1=Poor

Specifications

Body type	5-door wagon
Wheelbase (in.)	104.4
Overall length (in.)	159.4
Overall width (in.)	68.2
Overall height (in.)	65.2
Curb weight (lbs.)	3280
Seating capacity	5
Front head room (in.)	39.6
Max. front leg room (in.)	44.5
Rear head room (in.)	37.8
Min. rear leg room (in.)	31.1
Cargo volume (cu. ft.)	55.4
Engine type	dohc I-4
Engine size (l/cu. in.)	2.0/122
Horsepower @ rpm	130 @ 5500
Torque @ rpm	127 @ 4000
Transmission	manual/5-sp.
Drive wheels	rear/all
Brakes, F/R	disc/drum (ABS)
Tire size	205/75R14
Fuel tank capacity (gal.)	15.8
EPA city/highway mpg	18/22
Test mileage (mpg)	NA

Warranties The entire vehicle is covered for 3 years/36,000 miles. Major powertrain components are covered for 5 years/60,000 miles. Body perforation rust is covered for 5 years/100,000 miles.

Built in South Korea.

LEXUS ES 300
Premium Sedan

✓ BEST BUY

Lexus ES 300

The ES 300, the least expensive and most popular model in the Lexus line, is unchanged for 1996. This is supposed to be the last year for the current design, which debuted in 1992. The ES 300 is built from the same front-drive design as the Toyota Camry (see separate report), which is scheduled to be replaced by a new model next summer. Lexus is the luxury division of Toyota and the ES 300 is a "near-luxury" sedan that competes with cars such as the Acura TL Sedan, Infiniti I30, BMW 3-Series, Mazda Millenia, and others. Though the ES 300 shares its structure and major mechanical components with the Camry, it has different styling and more standard features. The ES 300 comes with a 3.0-liter V-6 engine with 188 horsepower and an electronic 4-speed automatic transmission. Dual air bags and anti-lock brakes are standard. The ES 300 is the best-selling Lexus model because it has many of the attributes of the larger LS 400 sedan at a much lower price. The ES 300 accelerates swiftly, smoothly, and quietly, and has more than adequate passing power at highway speeds. We timed one at 8.5 seconds to 60 mph. Fuel economy has been under 20 mpg in our tests, except in straight highway driving, and the engine requires premium gas. On twisting roads the ES 300 doesn't feel as sporty as a BMW 325i or Mazda Millenia. The soft suspension allows moderate body roll, but the tires grip well and the steering is precise. The supple suspension absorbs bumps well. The ES 300 has more passenger space than its exterior dimensions imply. Leg room is more than adequate front and rear. Despite sharing its basic design and most mechanical features with the Camry, the ES 300 is different enough to justify its higher price. Because it's a Lexus, it also comes with a promise of better customer service.

Lexus ES 300 prices are on page 360.

LEXUS ES 300

Rating Guide	1	2	3	4	5
Performance					
Acceleration				▓	
Economy		▓			
Driveability				▓	
Ride				▓	
Steering/handling				▓	
Braking					▓
Noise				▓	
Accommodations					
Driver seating				▓	
Instruments/controls				▓	
Visibility			▓		
Room/comfort				▓	
Entry/exit			▓		
Cargo room		▓			
Workmanship					
Exterior				▓	
Interior				▓	
Value				▓	
Total Points					64

Rating scale 5=Exceptional; 4=Above average; 3=Average; 2=Below average; 1=Poor

Specifications

Body type	4-door notchback
Wheelbase (in.)	103.1
Overall length (in.)	187.8
Overall width (in.)	70.0
Overall height (in.)	53.9
Curb weight (lbs.)	3374
Seating capacity	5
Front head room (in.)	37.8
Max. front leg room (in.)	43.5
Rear head room (in.)	36.6
Min. rear leg room (in.)	33.1
Cargo volume (cu. ft.)	14.3
Engine type	dohc V-6
Engine size (l/cu. in.)	3.0/181
Horsepower @ rpm	188 @ 5200
Torque @ rpm	203 @ 4400
Transmission	auto/4-sp.
Drive wheels	front
Brakes, F/R	disc/disc (ABS)
Tire size	205/65VR15
Fuel tank capacity (gal.)	18.5
EPA city/highway mpg	20/29
Test mileage (mpg)	19.4

Warranties The entire car is covered for 4 years/50,000 miles. Major powertrain components are covered for 6 years/70,000 miles. Body perforation rust is covered for 6 years/unlimited miles.

Built in Japan.

LEXUS GS 300
Premium Sedan

Lexus GS 300

The rear-drive GS 300 has a new 5-speed automatic transmission as its major change for 1996. The 5-speed transmission replaces a 4-speed automatic as standard on the GS 300, the mid-priced sedan in the lineup at Lexus, the luxury division of Toyota. This is the first use of a 5-speed automatic by Lexus. The company says it is the smallest and lightest 5-speed automatic in the world. The new transmission teams with a 220-horsepower 3.0-liter 6-cylinder engine that is unchanged from last year. However, Lexus says closer gear ratios and a different final drive ratio with the new transmission will result in quicker acceleration and better passing response. Exterior changes for 1996 on the GS 300 are limited to new taillights and new badging at the rear. In size and price, this rear-drive 4-door sedan fits between the flagship LS 400 and entry-level ES 300 sedans at Lexus. Standard equipment includes dual air bags, anti-lock brakes, automatic temperature control, and walnut interior trim. The GS 300 is a step up from the ES 300 in performance and features, and virtually all the amenities found on the LS 400 are offered on the GS 300 at a starting price that's about $7000 less. Despite that, the GS 300 is the least popular of the three Lexus sedans. The 6-cylinder engine feels sluggish off the line, but then pulls strongly and smoothly for brisk acceleration. There's ample passing power on the open road. The GS 300 handles deftly and has a firmer ride than the LS 400, though it's never harsh. It also lacks the library-quiet highway ride of the LS 400 or ES 300. The suspension and tires make prominent "thumps" over bumps and ruts, though road noise isn't objectionable. There's plenty of leg room all around but not much head room in the rear seat with the optional power moonroof.

Lexus GS 300 prices are on page 360.

LEXUS GS 300

Rating Guide	1	2	3	4	5
Performance					
Acceleration				▓	
Economy		▓			
Driveability				▓	
Ride				▓	
Steering/handling			▓		
Braking				▓	
Noise			▓		
Accommodations					
Driver seating				▓	
Instruments/controls				▓	
Visibility			▓		
Room/comfort			▓		
Entry/exit			▓		
Cargo room		▓			
Workmanship					
Exterior					▓
Interior					▓
Value				▓	
Total Points					61

Rating scale 5=Exceptional; 4=Above average; 3=Average; 2=Below average; 1=Poor

Specifications

Body type	4-door notchback
Wheelbase (in.)	109.4
Overall length (in.)	194.9
Overall width (in.)	70.7
Overall height (in.)	55.1
Curb weight (lbs.)	3660
Seating capacity	5
Front head room (in.)	36.9
Max. front leg room (in.)	44.0
Rear head room (in.)	35.6
Min. rear leg room (in.)	33.8
Cargo volume (cu. ft.)	13.0
Engine type	dohc I-6
Engine size (l/cu. in.)	3.0/183
Horsepower @ rpm	220 @ 5800
Torque @ rpm	210 @ 4800
Transmission	auto/5-sp.
Drive wheels	rear
Brakes, F/R	disc/disc (ABS)
Tire size	215/60VR16
Fuel tank capacity (gal.)	21.1
EPA city/highway mpg	18/24
Test mileage (mpg)	NA

Warranties The entire car is covered for 4 years/50,000 miles. Major powertrain components are covered for 6 years/70,000 miles. Body perforation rust is covered for 6 years/unlimited miles.

Built in Japan.

CONSUMER GUIDE®

LEXUS LS 400
Premium Sedan

✓ **BEST BUY**

Lexus LS 400

The LS 400, flagship of the Lexus fleet, was redesigned last year and is unchanged for this year, except for one new exterior color ("deep jewel green pearl"). Though the current model closely resembles the 1990-94 model, it is different inside and outside. Lexus retained major styling cues from the previous generation while giving the current one sharper edges and creases. The nose has a larger grille and new headlamps. Overall length and body width were unchanged, but the wheelbase was stretched 1.4 inches to 112.2 and the interior was widened by two inches. The rear-drive LS 400 has a 4.0-liter V-8 with 260 horsepower and a 4-speed automatic transmission. Standard equipment includes dual air bags, anti-lock brakes, automatic climate control, and leather upholstery. Compared to the original LS 400, the current model is quicker, roomier, and even quieter. An additional 10 horsepower and a 209-pound weight reduction last year translated into noticeably better acceleration and livelier passing response. We averaged 19.5 mpg in our test from an even mix of rush-hour commuting and highway driving. Premium gas is required. The current LS 400 feels more agile and has less body lean in turns. The suspension is slightly firmer, yet still absorbent, and the steering feels crisper. On the original model, the steering was too light at high speeds and required frequent corrections. With the longer wheelbase there is ample room for adults to stretch their legs in the back seat and space for their feet under the front seats. The LS 400 starts at $52,900 and can top $60,000 when loaded with options. That's a lot, but the current version is better than the original, and high resale value should reduce the cost of ownership over the long term.

Lexus LS 400 prices are on page 361.

LEXUS LS 400

Rating Guide	1	2	3	4	5
Performance					
Acceleration					▓
Economy	▓				
Driveability				▓	
Ride					▓
Steering/handling				▓	
Braking				▓	
Noise				▓	
Accommodations					
Driver seating				▓	
Instruments/controls				▓	
Visibility			▓		
Room/comfort			▓		
Entry/exit			▓		
Cargo room		▓			
Workmanship					
Exterior					▓
Interior					▓
Value				▓	
Total Points					**68**

Rating scale 5=Exceptional; 4=Above average; 3=Average; 2=Below average; 1=Poor

Specifications

Body type ....4-door notchback
Wheelbase (in.) 112.2
Overall length (in.) 196.7
Overall width (in.) 72.0
Overall height (in.) 55.7
Curb weight (lbs.) 3650
Seating capacity 5
Front head room (in.) 38.9
Max. front leg room (in.) 43.8
Rear head room (in.) 36.8
Min. rear leg room (in.) 36.9
Cargo volume (cu. ft.) 14.9

Engine type ....dohc V-8
Engine size (l/cu. in.) 4.0/242
Horsepower @ rpm ...260 @ 5300
Torque @ rpm ....270 @ 4500
Transmission ....auto/4-sp.
Drive wheels ....rear
Brakes, F/R ....disc/disc (ABS)
Tire size.....................225/60VR16
Fuel tank capacity (gal.) 22.5
EPA city/highway mpg 19/26
Test mileage (mpg) 19.5

Warranties The entire car is covered for 4 years/50,000 miles. Major powertrain components are covered for 6 years/70,000 miles. Body perforation rust is covered for 6 years/unlimited miles.

Built in Japan.

CONSUMER GUIDE®

LEXUS SC 300/400
Premium Coupe

✓ **BEST BUY**

Lexus SC 400

The SC 400 coupe has a new engine for 1996, the 260-horsepower 4.0-liter V-8 that debuted last year in the LS 400 sedan. It replaces a similar engine that produced 250 horsepower. With the new engine, torque increases 10 pounds/feet to 270. As before, the V-8 comes only with a 4-speed automatic transmission. The SC 300 returns with a 225-horsepower 3.0-liter 6-cylinder engine and a choice of 5-speed manual or 4-speed automatic transmissions. Both these rear-drive coupes come with standard dual air bags, anti-lock brakes, and automatic climate control. Leather upholstery is standard on the SC 400 and optional on the SC 300. Both models gain as standard a handful of features that debuted last year on the LS 400. Among them are inside and outside mirrors that automatically dim in high-glare situations; a radio antenna mounted in the rear window; and a trunk opener and panic alarm for the remote keyless entry system. The SC coupes have a sportier personality than the Lexus sedans. They're agile and have commendable grip in tight turns, and though they have a much firmer ride than the Lexus sedans, they're never harsh. Both models are quick. We timed a 1995 SC 400 at 7.3 seconds to 60 mph and an SC 300 with automatic at 8.1 seconds to 60. We averaged 17.2 mpg with the SC 400 and 18 with the SC 300 from a similar mix of city and highway driving. Both engines require premium gas. We expect the 1996 SC 400 to be quicker without using more gas. Lexus accurately describes its coupes as "2+2s." Rear head room is skimpy and rear leg room vanishes if the front seats are pushed back more than halfway. Though there are good alternatives available for less money, the Lexus coupes rank at the top in quality and customer satisfaction.

Lexus SC 300/400 prices are on page 362.

LEXUS SC 400

Rating Guide	1	2	3	4	5
Performance					
Acceleration				▓▓▓▓	
Economy		▓▓▓▓			
Driveability				▓▓▓▓	
Ride			▓▓▓▓		
Steering/handling			▓▓▓▓		
Braking				▓▓▓▓	
Noise				▓▓▓▓	
Accommodations					
Driver seating				▓▓▓▓	
Instruments/controls				▓▓▓▓	
Visibility			▓▓▓▓		
Room/comfort		▓▓▓▓			
Entry/exit		▓▓▓▓			
Cargo room		▓▓▓▓			
Workmanship					
Exterior				▓▓▓▓	
Interior				▓▓▓▓	
Value			▓▓▓▓		
Total Points					**61**

Rating scale 5=Exceptional; 4=Above average; 3=Average; 2=Below average; 1=Poor

Specifications

Body type	2-door notchback
Wheelbase (in.)	105.9
Overall length (in.)	191.1
Overall width (in.)	70.5
Overall height (in.)	52.4
Curb weight (lbs.)	3575
Seating capacity	4
Front head room (in.)	38.3
Max. front leg room (in.)	44.1
Rear head room (in.)	36.1
Min. rear leg room (in.)	27.2
Cargo volume (cu. ft.)	9.3
Engine type	dohc V-8
Engine size (l/cu. in.)	4.0/242
Horsepower @ rpm	260 @ 5300
Torque @ rpm	270 @ 4500
Transmission	auto/4-sp.
Drive wheels	rear
Brakes, F/R	disc/disc (ABS)
Tire size	225/55VR16
Fuel tank capacity (gal.)	20.6
EPA city/highway mpg	18/23
Test mileage (mpg)	NA

Warranties The entire car is covered for 4 years/50,000 miles. Major powertrain components are covered for 6 years/70,000 miles. Body perforation rust is covered for 6 years/unlimited miles.

Built in Japan.

CONSUMER GUIDE®

LINCOLN CONTINENTAL
Premium Sedan

Lincoln Continental

A redesigned Continental debuted last winter and this year is available with two new security packages. In addition, an anti-theft alarm is standard instead of optional. The new Personal Security Package includes Michelin Securitires, 225/60HR16 tires that can run flat for up to 20 miles at a constant speed of 50 mph without loss of handling or control. Available as an additional feature for the Personal Security Package is Remote Emergency Satellite Cellular Unit (RESCU), which consists of a voice-activated cellular telephone, two emergency buttons mounted in the overhead console, and a global positioning satellite receiver in the trunk. One button summons roadside assistance and the other police or medical assistance. An emergency answering service receives the emergency call and dispatches the appropriate assistance, using the global positioning satellite to pinpoint the location. Prices for the two security packages weren't available. The redesigned Continental retains front-wheel drive but has more rounded styling. It comes only as a 4-door sedan with a 260-horsepower 4.6-liter V-8 with dual overhead camshafts. The new Continental is much quicker, a little more agile, and loaded with electronic gizmos. V-8 muscle makes the new Continental far more energetic than the old. We timed one at just 7.4 seconds to 60 mph; the old Continental had trouble breaking 10 seconds in the 0-60 sprint. The interior has plenty of leg space front and rear, and head room is adequate for 6-footers with the optional moonroof. Lincoln seems to have tried to make the Continental both a sports sedan and a traditional American luxury car, and it ends up being not quite either. It's still worth a look. Sales have been far from brisk, so dealers should be discounting.

Lincoln Continental prices are on page 363.

LINCOLN CONTINENTAL

Rating Guide	1	2	3	4	5
Performance					
Acceleration				4	
Economy		2			
Driveability			3		
Ride				4	
Steering/handling			3		
Braking					5
Noise				4	
Accommodations					
Driver seating				4	
Instruments/controls			3		
Visibility			3		
Room/comfort				4	
Entry/exit				4	
Cargo room			3		
Workmanship					
Exterior					5
Interior				4	
Value			3		
Total Points					61

Rating scale 5=Exceptional; 4=Above average; 3=Average; 2=Below average; 1=Poor

Specifications

Body type ....4-door notchback
Wheelbase (in.) 109.0
Overall length (in.) 206.3
Overall width (in.) 73.3
Overall height (in.) 55.9
Curb weight (lbs.) 3969
Seating capacity 6
Front head room (in.) 39.1
Max. front leg room (in.) 41.8
Rear head room (in.) 38.0
Min. rear leg room (in.) 39.2
Cargo volume (cu. ft.).............18.1

Engine type ....dohc V-8
Engine size (l/cu. in.).........4.6/281
Horsepower @ rpm ...260 @ 5750
Torque @ rpm ....265 @ 4750
Transmission................auto/4-sp.
Drive wheels ....front
Brakes, F/R..........disc/disc (ABS)
Tire size 225/60R16
Fuel tank capacity (gal.) 18.0
EPA city/highway mpg 17/25
Test mileage (mpg) 16.3

Warranties The entire car is covered for 4 years/50,000 miles. Body perforation rust is covered for 5 years/unlimited miles.

Built in Wixom, Mich.

CONSUMER GUIDE®

LINCOLN MARK VIII
Premium Coupe

Lincoln Mark VIII LSC

Several options have been lumped into a new Touring Package for this rear-drive luxury coupe, and a special edition denoting the 75th anniversary of the Lincoln brand will arrive later in the model year. The Mark VIII returns with a 280-horsepower 4.6-liter V-8 engine with dual overhead camshafts, 4-speed automatic transmission, dual air bags, and anti-lock brakes. The new Touring Package consists of traction control, the JBL audio system, a trunk-mounted CD changer, and electrochromatic automatic dimming mirrors. There also is a high-performance LSC Package (Luxury Sport Coupe) that includes a 290-horsepower version of the 4.6-liter V-8, a dual exhaust system, firmer suspension, directional aluminum wheels (designed to be mounted on one side of the car), and monochrome exterior trim. In the spring a Diamond Anniversary Edition will arrive to mark Lincoln's 75th anniversary. It will be available in silver or cordovan paint, grey leather upholstery with cordovan accents, the JBL sound system, a voice-activated cellular phone, and other features. Similar anniversary models also will be available on the Lincoln Continental and Town Car. The Mark VIII is quick off the line and once above 15 mph it really flies. We clocked one at 6.8 seconds to 60 mph. We tested this car on snow and ice and were disappointed with the performance of the optional traction control system. The rear wheels spun readily in snow, making takeoffs slow and laborious. Interior space isn't a strong point. Tall passengers don't have much head room, rear leg room is limited, and two adults is the comfortable maximum in back. Though the Mark VIII is a good car, don't buy one without first testing a Cadillac Eldorado, Lexus SC 400, or Buick Riviera, rivals that we rate higher overall.

Lincoln Mark VIII prices are on page 364.

LINCOLN MARK VIII

Rating Guide	1	2	3	4	5
Performance					
Acceleration				▓	
Economy	▓				
Driveability			▓		
Ride				▓	
Steering/handling			▓		
Braking				▓	
Noise				▓	
Accommodations					
Driver seating				▓	
Instruments/controls				▓	
Visibility			▓		
Room/comfort			▓		
Entry/exit			▓		
Cargo room		▓			
Workmanship					
Exterior					▓
Interior				▓	
Value			▓		
Total Points					**58**

Rating scale 5=Exceptional; 4=Above average; 3=Average; 2=Below average; 1=Poor

Specifications

Body type	2-door notchback
Wheelbase (in.)	113.0
Overall length (in.)	207.3
Overall width (in.)	74.8
Overall height (in.)	53.6
Curb weight (lbs.)	3768
Seating capacity	5
Front head room (in.)	38.1
Max. front leg room (in.)	42.6
Rear head room (in.)	37.5
Min. rear leg room (in.)	32.5
Cargo volume (cu. ft.)	14.4
Engine type	dohc V-8
Engine size (l/cu. in.)	4.6/281
Horsepower @ rpm	280 @ 5500
Torque @ rpm	285 @ 4500
Transmission	auto/4-sp.
Drive wheels	rear
Brakes, F/R	disc/disc (ABS)
Tire size	225/60VR16
Fuel tank capacity (gal.)	18.0
EPA city/highway mpg	18/26
Test mileage (mpg)	17.9

Warranties The entire car is covered for 4 years/50,000 miles. Body perforation rust is covered for 5 years/unlimited miles.

Built in Wixom, Mich.

CONSUMER GUIDE®

LINCOLN TOWN CAR
Premium Sedan

Lincoln Town Car Signature Series

Lincoln celebrates its 75th anniversary in 1996 and will mark the occasion with a Diamond Anniversary Edition of the Town Car. Due to arrive next spring, the anniversary edition will come in two color schemes: cordovan exterior with a charcoal interior or silver exterior with a red interior. The anniversary model also will include the JBL audio system, a voice-activated telephone, power moonroof, and other features. Similar versions of the Lincoln Continental and Mark VIII also will be available. The Town Car uses a 4.6-liter V-8 engine with 210 horsepower and dual overhead camshafts. The rear-drive Town Car comes in three price levels: Executive Series, Signature Series, and Cartier Designer Series. Dual air bags, anti-lock brakes, automatic climate control, and remote keyless entry are standard on all three. All three models have new seatbelts that eliminate the need for clips when child safety seats are installed. With its pillowy ride, isolation from mechanical noise, and expansive interior, Town Car delivers all the indulgences a car of this type should. However, the rival Cadillac Fleetwood matches Town Car in spaciousness and luxury and has a 260-horsepower V-8. In addition, Fleetwood comes with standard traction control—all for a lower base price. However, the Town Car has a future beyond 1996, and the Fleetwood doesn't. The Town Car is wide enough to accommodate three adults in both the front and rear, it has large doors that allow nearly effortless entry and exit. This is one of the biggest sedans available and it has huge rear roof pillars that hinder the driver's view when backing up, which can make parallel parking an adventure. We prefer cars that are more agile and take up less space on the road than the Town Car and Fleetwood. If you're interested, there should be hefty discounts on both.

Lincoln Town Car prices are on page 365.

LINCOLN TOWN CAR

Rating Guide	1	2	3	4	5
Performance					
Acceleration			▐▐▐		
Economy			▐▐▐		
Driveability			▐▐▐		
Ride				▐▐▐	
Steering/handling			▐▐▐		
Braking				▐▐▐	
Noise				▐▐▐	
Accommodations					
Driver seating				▐▐▐	
Instruments/controls				▐▐▐	
Visibility			▐▐▐		
Room/comfort					▐▐▐
Entry/exit				▐▐▐	
Cargo room				▐▐▐	
Workmanship					
Exterior			▐▐▐		
Interior				▐▐▐	
Value				▐▐▐	
Total Points					**60**

Rating scale 5=Exceptional; 4=Above average; 3=Average; 2=Below average; 1=Poor

Specifications

Body type	4-door notchback
Wheelbase (in.)	117.4
Overall length (in.)	218.9
Overall width (in.)	76.7
Overall height (in.)	56.9
Curb weight (lbs.)	4050
Seating capacity	6
Front head room (in.)	39.0
Max. front leg room (in.)	42.6
Rear head room (in.)	38.0
Min. rear leg room (in.)	41.1
Cargo volume (cu. ft.)	22.3
Engine type	ohc V-8
Engine size (l/cu. in.)	4.6/281
Horsepower @ rpm	210 @ 4600
Torque @ rpm	270 @ 3400
Transmission	auto/4-sp.
Drive wheels	rear
Brakes, F/R	disc/disc (ABS)
Tire size	215/70R15
Fuel tank capacity (gal.)	20.0
EPA city/highway mpg	17/25
Test mileage (mpg)	17.0

Warranties The entire car is covered for 4 years/50,000 miles. Body perforation rust is covered for 5 years/unlimited miles.

Built in Wixom, Mich.

CONSUMER GUIDE®

MAZDA MIATA
Sports and GT

✓ **BEST BUY**

Mazda Miata

Mazda's 2-seat convertible gets minor changes for its seventh model year. Miata now meets 1997 federal standards for side-impact protection. Tuning for lower emissions has added five horsepower and four pounds/feet of torque to Miata's 1.8-liter dual-camshaft 4-cylinder engine, bringing respective outputs to 133 and 114. Miata has standard dual air bags, a manual convertible top, and 5-speed manual transmission. Anti-lock brakes and a 4-speed automatic are optional. Other options include air conditioning, power steering, a removable hardtop, a Popular Equipment Group (which includes cruise control, alloy wheels and power steering, mirrors, windows, and antenna), and leather cockpit trim. Though Mazda hasn't confirmed yet, a new special-edition Miata should arrive in spring 1996. It should be much like the 1995 M Edition, which had special paint, leather interior trim, and a full load of convenience and comfort features. While other sports cars wither away, the Miata remains popular. That's because it is lively, agile, fun, and affordable. Sales of rivals have shrunk as their prices have escalated, but Miata has flourished partly because Mazda has kept price increases to more moderate levels. The 1.8-liter engine doesn't have much kick at low speed, especially with the automatic transmission, but the free-revving 4-cylinder quickly gets into its power band for brisk acceleration. You feel nearly every bump in the firmly sprung Miata, though the suspension absorbs enough of the impact so the car doesn't skitter sideways or lose traction. The cozy cockpit has well-placed gauges and controls and enough space to give tall people adequate working room. Though Miata has been around more than six years, it still looks and feels as fresh as it did back when it arrived in 1989.

Mazda Miata prices are on page 367.

MAZDA MIATA

Rating Guide	1	2	3	4	5
Performance					
Acceleration				4	
Economy				4	
Driveability				4	
Ride			3		
Steering/handling					5
Braking				4	
Noise		2			
Accommodations					
Driver seating				4	
Instruments/controls				4	
Visibility				4	
Room/comfort			3		
Entry/exit			3		
Cargo room	1				
Workmanship					
Exterior				4	
Interior				4	
Value				4	
Total Points					**57**

Rating scale 5=Exceptional; 4=Above average; 3=Average; 2=Below average; 1=Poor

Specifications

Body type ....2-door convertible
Wheelbase (in.) 89.2
Overall length (in.) 155.4
Overall width (in.) 65.9
Overall height (in.) 48.2
Curb weight (lbs.) 2293
Seating capacity.........................2
Front head room (in.) 37.1
Max. front leg room (in.) 42.7
Rear head room (in.) .... —
Min. rear leg room (in.) .... —
Cargo volume (cu. ft.).............. 3.6

Engine type .... dohc I-4
Engine size (l/cu. in.).........1.8/112
Horsepower @ rpm ...133 @ 6500
Torque @ rpm ....114 @ 5500
Transmission .... manual/5-sp.
Drive wheels .... rear
Brakes, F/R............disc/disc (ABS)
Tire size 185/60HR14
Fuel tank capacity (gal.) 12.7
EPA city/highway mpg 23/29
Test mileage (mpg) 26.7

Warranties The entire car is covered for 3 years/50,000 miles. Body perforation rust is covered for 5 years/unlimited miles.

Built in Japan.

CONSUMER GUIDE®

MAZDA MILLENIA
Premium Sedan

Mazda Millenia S

This front-drive 4-door sedan was new last year, so changes for the sophomore edition are minor. The Millenia is based on the design for Mazda's 626 but is equipped and priced to compete against the Acura TL Sedan, the Lexus ES 300, Infiniti I30, and other "near-luxury" sedans. Three versions return: base, base model with a leather interior, and S. All have a V-6 engine, 4-speed automatic transmission, dual air bags, and anti-lock 4-wheel disc brakes. The S model uses a supercharged "Miller-cycle" 2.3-liter V-6 with 210 horsepower. The others use a 2.5-liter V-6 with 170 horsepower, similar to the engine used in the 626 sedan. All 1996 models get a new standard stereo with an in-dash CD player (replacing a cassette player) and a wire-element antenna in the rear window (replacing an external mast-type). The standard alloy wheels now include locks. The Millenia impresses us with its reassuring solidity over rough roads and first-rate finish inside and out. Refinement is top-notch too, with little wind noise or engine noise and moderate tire noise. Handling is responsive and surefooted, with little body lean and firm steering that has ample feedback. The base Millenia always feels rather "sleepy," and proved it by reaching 60 mph in 9.4 seconds. By contrast, an S model took just 7.8 seconds and felt much stronger, especially in mid-range passing sprints. The interior has adequate space for four adults and the dashboard is attractive and convenient. The base Millenia delivers lots of luxury for a few thousand less than most rivals but can't match their performance. The Millenia S is a sporty alternative to the ES 300, which is in the same price range. The Millenia is more fun to drive, but the ES 300 has higher overall quality and the promise of better service that comes with the Lexus brand.

Mazda Millenia prices are on page 368.

MAZDA MILLENIA S

Rating Guide	1	2	3	4	5
Performance					
Acceleration				▓▓	
Economy			▓▓		
Driveability				▓▓	
Ride				▓▓	
Steering/handling				▓▓	
Braking					▓▓
Noise				▓▓	
Accommodations					
Driver seating				▓▓	
Instruments/controls				▓▓	
Visibility			▓▓		
Room/comfort			▓▓		
Entry/exit			▓▓		
Cargo room		▓▓			
Workmanship					
Exterior				▓▓	
Interior				▓▓	
Value			▓▓		
Total Points					**59**

Rating scale 5=Exceptional; 4=Above average; 3=Average; 2=Below average; 1=Poor

Specifications

Body type	4-door notchback
Wheelbase (in.)	108.3
Overall length (in.)	189.8
Overall width (in.)	69.7
Overall height (in.)	54.9
Curb weight (lbs.)	3220
Seating capacity	5
Front head room (in.)	39.3
Max. front leg room (in.)	43.3
Rear head room (in.)	37.0
Min. rear leg room (in.)	34.1
Cargo volume (cu. ft.)	13.3
Engine	Supercharged dohc V-6
Engine size (l/cu. in.)	2.3/138
Horsepower @ rpm	210 @ 4800
Torque @ rpm	210 @ 3500
Transmission	auto/4-sp.
Drive wheels	front
Brakes, F/R	disc/disc (ABS)
Tire size	215/55VR16
Fuel tank capacity (gal.)	18.0
EPA city/highway mpg	20/28
Test mileage (mpg)	21.8

Warranties The entire car is covered for 3 years/50,000 miles. Body perforation rust is covered for 5 years/unlimited miles.

Built in Japan.

CONSUMER GUIDE®

MAZDA MPV
Minivan

Mazda MPV ES

Mazda's MPV (Multi-Purpose Vehicle) adds a standard passenger-side air bag and 4-wheel anti-lock brakes, revised styling, and another side door for its eighth season. Last year's MPV had only a driver-side air bag and rear-wheel anti-lock brakes. MPV also adds a standard swing-out left rear door. Previously, it had two front doors, a swing-out right rear door, and a one-piece liftgate. Sprucing up the MPV's appearance is new front styling that adds 7.7 inches to the overall length. Last year's base L and luxury LXE models are retitled DX and ES; the LX remains the in-between model. A 3-place middle bench replaces a 2-place seat for standard 8-passenger capacity in the DX and LX. The ES seats seven with new "quad captain's chairs" (front and middle bucket seats) that are optional on the LX. The ES also includes standard leather interior trim. A 3-person rear bench remains standard on all models, but it now has quick-release latches so you don't have to use a wrench to remove or install it. MPV comes with standard rear-wheel drive in a single size. The LX and ES are available with optional on-demand 4-wheel drive. All models again use a 155-horsepower 3.0-liter V-6 engine and a 4-speed automatic transmission. The MPV has gained weight (100 to 200 pounds, depending on model) this year without gaining power. The result is that the rear-drive version feels sluggish in hilly terrain, and the 4WD version is downright slow. The MPV handles more like a car than a van, with moderate body lean and good grip. The removable rear bench seat is a big improvement, and it weighs only about 65 pounds, which is a lot easier than wrestling with the 90-pound seats in some rivals. The MPV still lags well behind the class leaders, the new Chrysler minivans and the Ford Windstar, in overall room, performance, and value.

Mazda MPV prices are on page 369.

MAZDA MPV ES

Rating Guide	1	2	3	4	5
Performance					
Acceleration			3		
Economy		2			
Driveability				4	
Ride				4	
Steering/handling			3		
Braking				4	
Noise			3		
Accommodations					
Driver seating			3		
Instruments/controls			3		
Visibility				4	
Room/comfort			3		
Entry/exit			3		
Cargo room			3		
Workmanship					
Exterior				4	
Interior				4	
Value			3		
Total Points					57

Rating scale 5=Exceptional; 4=Above average; 3=Average; 2=Below average; 1=Poor

Specifications

Body type	5-door van
Wheelbase (in.)	110.4
Overall length (in.)	183.5
Overall width (in.)	71.9
Overall height (in.)	68.1
Curb weight (lbs.)	3970
Seating capacity	7
Front head room (in.)	40.0
Max. front leg room (in.)	40.4
Rear head room (in.)	39.7
Min. rear leg room (in.)	33.4
Cargo volume (cu. ft.)	37.5
Engine type	ohc V-6
Engine size (l/cu. in.)	3.0/180
Horsepower @ rpm	155 @ 5000
Torque @ rpm	169 @ 4000
Transmission	auto/4-sp.
Drive wheels	rear
Brakes, F/R	disc/disc (ABS)
Tire size	215/65R15
Fuel tank capacity (gal.)	19.6
EPA city/highway mpg	16/22
Test mileage (mpg)	NA

Warranties The entire vehicle is covered for 3 years/50,000 miles. Body perforation rust is covered for 5 years/unlimited miles.

Built in Japan.

CONSUMER GUIDE®

MAZDA MX-6
Sports Coupe

✓ **BEST BUY**

Mazda MX-6

Mazda's MX-6 sports coupe is all but unchanged for 1996 except that the higher-priced LS version is a separate model again after spending last year as an option package. Otherwise, the 1996s are distinguished only by new colors and seat trim. The front-drive MX-6 is an under-the-skin twin to the Ford Probe. Both are built at the Ford/Mazda plant in Michigan (as are Mazda 626 sedans), but the MX-6 is a 2-door notchback and the Probe a more-aggressive looking 3-door hatchback. The MX-6 also has different model and equipment offerings and higher prices. The base MX-6 uses a dual-camshaft 2.0-liter 4-cylinder engine with 114 horsepower and the LS a dual-cam 160-horsepower V-6. Both come with a standard 5-speed manual transmission or an optional 4-speed automatic. Dual air bags are standard and anti-lock brakes are optional on both. Two new features have been added to the optional Popular Equipment Group for 1996—a power antenna and remote keyless entry system. Despite rather high prices, the MX-6 is one of our Best Buys in the sports coupe segment. Mazda's smooth, potent V-6 gives the LS a leg up on most sports coupe rivals, which have 4-cylinder engines. Though we prefer the V-6, the 4-cylinder engine has adequate performance and better fuel economy. Acceleration isn't as lively with the automatic transmission, which saps a lot of verve from both engines. In addition, the transmission shifts harshly in hard acceleration. MX-6 is a snug "2+2" coupe. Front head and leg room are adequate for 6-footers, but the back seat is so small it's hard for even some children to fit. If you're attracted to the MX-6, also check out the Probe, which has the same mechanical features at lower prices. MX-6 and Probe are the cream of the crop among sports coupes, and both should be available at big discounts.

Mazda MX-6 prices are on page 370.

CONSUMER GUIDE®

MAZDA MX-6

Rating Guide	1	2	3	4	5
Performance					
Acceleration			■■■		
Economy			■■■		
Driveability			■■■		
Ride			■■■		
Steering/handling			■■■		
Braking				■■■	
Noise			■■■		
Accommodations					
Driver seating			■■■		
Instruments/controls			■■■		
Visibility			■■■		
Room/comfort		■■■			
Entry/exit		■■■			
Cargo room			■■■		
Workmanship					
Exterior			■■■		
Interior			■■■		
Value			■■■		
Total Points					55

Rating scale 5=Exceptional; 4=Above average; 3=Average; 2=Below average; 1=Poor

Specifications

Body type	2-door notchback
Wheelbase (in.)	102.8
Overall length (in.)	181.5
Overall width (in.)	68.9
Overall height (in.)	51.6
Curb weight (lbs.)	2625
Seating capacity	4
Front head room (in.)	38.1
Max. front leg room (in.)	44.0
Rear head room (in.)	34.7
Min. rear leg room (in.)	27.7
Cargo volume (cu. ft.)	12.4
Engine type	dohc I-4
Engine size (l/cu. in.)	2.0/122
Horsepower @ rpm	114 @ 5500
Torque @ rpm	124 @ 4500
Transmission	auto/4-sp.
Drive wheels	front
Brakes, F/R	disc/disc (ABS)
Tire size	195/65R14
Fuel tank capacity (gal.)	15.5
EPA city/highway mpg	23/31
Test mileage (mpg)	NA

Warranties The entire car is covered for 3 years/50,000 miles. Body perforation rust is covered for 5 years/unlimited miles.

Built in Flat Rock, Mich.

CONSUMER GUIDE®

MAZDA PROTEGE
Subcompact

Mazda Protege LX

Mazda has deleted anti-lock brakes as a standard feature on the top-line ES version of the Protege and cut the base price more than $1400. Prices also have been cut by $500 to $600 on the base DX and LX models as Mazda tries to spur sales of its front-drive subcompact. Anti-lock brakes are now optional on the ES and the LX and still not available on the DX. The DX and LX models use a 92-horsepower 1.5-liter 4-cylinder engine and the ES a 1.8-liter 4-cylinder with 122 horsepower. A 5-speed manual transmission is standard on all models and a 4-speed automatic is optional. Other standard features on all models include dual air bags, power steering, a tilt steering column, and dual outside mirrors. When the Protege was redesigned last year, the wheelbase grew more than four inches and the overall length three inches, making this one of the roomier subcompact sedans. There's ample space for four adults. The abundant front head room and rear leg room are especially noteworthy because they are often in short supply in subcompacts. However, the rear doors are narrow at the bottom, making it awkward to get in or out. The dashboard is generally well laid out, with clear gauges and stalk-mounted light and wiper controls. Mazda tuned the Protege's suspension more towards ride than handling. Bumps are easily absorbed. The 1.5-liter engine in the DX and LX is one of the smallest and least powerful in this class, but it manages to deliver adequate acceleration with either transmission. The 1.8-liter engine in the ES doesn't seem much stronger around town despite 30 more horsepower. This year's price cuts were necessary top make the Protege more competitive with rivals such as the Nissan Sentra, Dodge/Plymouth Neon, and Chevrolet Cavalier. Give it a look; Mazda dealers should be willing to bargain on the price.

Mazda Protege prices are on page 371.

MAZDA PROTEGE LX

Rating Guide	1	2	3	4	5
Performance					
Acceleration			▮▮▮		
Economy				▮▮▮	
Driveability				▮▮▮	
Ride			▮▮▮		
Steering/handling			▮▮▮		
Braking			▮▮▮		
Noise		▮▮▮			
Accommodations					
Driver seating				▮▮▮	
Instruments/controls				▮▮▮	
Visibility				▮▮▮	
Room/comfort			▮▮▮		
Entry/exit			▮▮▮		
Cargo room			▮▮▮		
Workmanship					
Exterior				▮▮▮	
Interior				▮▮▮	
Value			▮▮▮		
Total Points					**57**

Rating scale 5=Exceptional; 4=Above average; 3=Average; 2=Below average; 1=Poor

Specifications

Body type	4-door notchback
Wheelbase (in.)	102.6
Overall length (in.)	174.8
Overall width (in.)	67.3
Overall height (in.)	55.9
Curb weight (lbs.)	2385
Seating capacity	5
Front head room (in.)	39.2
Max. front leg room (in.)	42.2
Rear head room (in.)	37.4
Min. rear leg room (in.)	35.6
Cargo volume (cu. ft.)	13.1
Engine type	dohc I-4
Engine size (l/cu. in.)	1.5/91
Horsepower @ rpm	92 @ 5500
Torque @ rpm	96 @ 4000
Transmission	manual/5-sp.
Drive wheels	front
Brakes, F/R	disc/drum
Tire size	175/70R13
Fuel tank capacity (gal.)	14.5
EPA city/highway mpg	32/39
Test mileage (mpg)	30.2

Warranties The entire car is covered for 3 years/50,000 miles. Body perforation rust is covered for 5 years/unlimited miles.

Built in Japan.

CONSUMER GUIDE®

MAZDA 626
Compact

✓ **BEST BUY**

Mazda 626 LX

Though Mazda's family compact sedan sees no great changes for 1996, the 4-year-old design wears a different face with a more prominent grille surrounded by chrome and a hood with a raised center section. There are also minor changes to the rear-end appearance and the usual crop of new exterior colors. All models now meet the more stringent 1997 federal side-impact standards. The front-drive 626 is a 4-door notchback sedan available in four models: base 4-cylinder DX, 4-cylinder LX, V-6 LX, and V-6 ES. The 4-cylinder is a dual-camshaft 2.0-liter engine with 114 horsepower and the V-6 is a dual-cam 2.5-liter with 160 horsepower. Both engines team with a standard 5-speed manual or optional 4-speed automatic transmission. Dual air bags are standard across the board. Anti-lock brakes (with rear discs instead of drums) are standard on the top-line ES and optional on both LX models. The 626 is built at a plant in Michigan that is jointly owned by Mazda and Ford. The Mazda MX-6 and Ford Probe sports coupes are built at the same plant. The 626 is a highly competitive entry in the compact sedan segment. One of the principal rivals is the Toyota Camry, which is quieter and more luxurious. The 626, has sportier handling, more personality, and lower prices. There's adequate head room for tall people in the 626 even with the power sunroof and ample leg room for all seats. Cargo space is generous for a compact sedan. However, the trunk opening is too small to easily load bulky items. Though the V-6 engine is the performance leader in the 626 line, the 4-cylinder engine is no slouch. The 626 is a competent family car with a sporty flair. The LX versions offer the best combination of features and value. There's lots of competition, so you won't have to pay full retail price.

Mazda 626 prices are on page 372.

MAZDA 626 LX

Rating Guide	1	2	3	4	5
Performance					
Acceleration			|||	
Economy			|||	
Driveability			|||	
Ride			|||	
Steering/handling			|||	
Braking					|||
Noise			|||	
Accommodations					
Driver seating				|||	
Instruments/controls			|||	
Visibility			|||	
Room/comfort			|||	
Entry/exit			|||	
Cargo room			|||	
Workmanship					
Exterior			|||	
Interior			|||	
Value			|||	
Total Points					62

Rating scale 5=Exceptional; 4=Above average; 3=Average; 2=Below average; 1=Poor

Specifications

Body type	4-door notchback
Wheelbase (in.)	102.8
Overall length (in.)	184.4
Overall width (in.)	68.9
Overall height (in.)	55.1
Curb weight (lbs.)	2749
Seating capacity	5
Front head room (in.)	39.2
Max. front leg room (in.)	43.5
Rear head room (in.)	37.8
Min. rear leg room (in.)	35.8
Cargo volume (cu. ft.)	13.8
Engine type	dohc I-4
Engine size (l/cu. in.)	2.0/122
Horsepower @ rpm	114 @ 5500
Torque @ rpm	124 @ 4500
Transmission	manual/5-sp.
Drive wheels	front
Brakes, F/R	disc/disc (ABS)
Tire size	195/65R14
Fuel tank capacity (gal.)	15.9
EPA city/highway mpg	26/34
Test mileage (mpg)	25.1

Warranties The entire car is covered for 3 years/50,000 miles. Body perforation rust is covered for 5 years/unlimited miles.

Built in Flat Rock, Mich.

CONSUMER GUIDE®

MERCEDES-BENZ C-CLASS
Premium Sedan

Mercedes-Benz C280

The entry-level sedan in the Mercedes-Benz stable gets a handful of new standard features for its third model year. All C-Class models have a new infrared remote entry system that operates the lock for the trunk as well as all four doors. The system changes its access code each time it is used to prevent others from copying the signal. Seatbelts with automatic locking retractors also are standard on both models, eliminating the need to use locking clips with child safety seats. Dual air bags and anti-lock brakes are standard on both models as well. In a bow to America's desire for beverages on the road, dual cup holders have been added to the center console. The compact-size C-Class sedan has rear-wheel drive. The C220 uses a 147-horsepower 2.2-liter 4-cylinder engine with dual camshafts and the C280 a 194-horsepower 2.8-liter 6-cylinder, also with dual camshafts. The high-performance, limited-production C36 sedan, introduced last spring, uses a dual-cam 3.6-liter 6-cylinder with 268 horsepower. All models come with a 4-speed automatic transmission. With prices ranging from about $30,000 to nearly $40,000 (with options), the C220 and C280 are in one of the most competitive segments of the luxury sedan market. Some rivals that are priced near the 4-cylinder C220 have stronger 6-cylinder engines, and the Oldsmobile Aurora has a V-8. However, like all Mercedes, the C-Class sedans are rock-solid and well-engineered. Both engines are quiet and refined, even under hard acceleration. The driving position is comfortable and the control layout is user-friendly, but tall drivers may not have enough leg room or head room. Moving the driver's seat all the way back drastically cuts into rear leg room, which is only adequate in any case. Overall we're impressed with the C-Class and think it deserves a look.

Mercedes-Benz C-Class prices are on page 373.

MERCEDES-BENZ C280

Rating Guide	1	2	3	4	5
Performance					
Acceleration			|||||		
Economy		|||||			
Driveability			|||||		
Ride				|||||	
Steering/handling				|||||	
Braking					|||||
Noise				|||||	
Accommodations					
Driver seating				|||||	
Instruments/controls				|||||	
Visibility			|||||		
Room/comfort			|||||		
Entry/exit			|||||		
Cargo room		|||||			
Workmanship					
Exterior					|||||
Interior				|||||	
Value			|||||		
Total Points					**60**

Rating scale 5=Exceptional; 4=Above average; 3=Average; 2=Below average; 1=Poor

Specifications

Body type ....4-door notchback
Wheelbase (in.) 105.9
Overall length (in.) 177.4
Overall width (in.) 67.7
Overall height (in.) 56.1
Curb weight (lbs.) 3173
Seating capacity 5
Front head room (in.) 37.2
Max. front leg room (in.) 41.5
Rear head room (in.) 37.0
Min. rear leg room (in.) 32.8
Cargo volume (cu. ft.).............13.7

Engine type ....dohc I-6
Engine size (l/cu. in.)..........2.8/173
Horsepower @ rpm ...194 @ 5500
Torque @ rpm ....199 @ 3750
Transmission.................auto/4-sp.
Drive wheels ....rear
Brakes, F/R..........disc/disc (ABS)
Tire size 195/65HR15
Fuel tank capacity (gal.) 16.4
EPA city/highway mpg 19/26
Test mileage (mpg) 19.2

Warranties The entire car (including body perforation rust) is covered for 4 years/50,000 miles.

Built in Germany.

MERCEDES-BENZ E-CLASS
Premium Sedan

RECOMMENDED

Mercedes-Benz E320

A redesigned E-Class sedan has new styling highlighted by four oval headlamps, giving the Mercedes lineup a fresh face. From the windshield back, the styling is more evolutionary yet still distinctive from the old E-Class, sold in the U.S. from 1986 through 1995. The wheelbase has grown 1.3 inches to 111.5 and overall length 2.2 inches to 189.4. The new sedan initially comes in two versions: the E320 with a 217-horsepower 3.2-liter gas 6-cylinder and the E300 Diesel with a 134-horsepower 3.0-liter diesel 6-cylinder. Both engines were used last year and team with a 4-speed automatic transmission. This spring the E420 sedan, powered by a 4.2-liter V-8, will arrive as a 1997 model with a new 5-speed automatic transmission. A 5-door wagon is scheduled to join the lineup in fall 1997 and a coupe based on the E-Class design will follow. All models have dual front air bags, anti-lock brakes, and new side air bags mounted in the front door panels. Other new standard features include traction control, a remote entry system, a programmable garage door opener, a tilt/telescopic steering wheel, and 16-inch wheels and tires (last year's were 15-inch). Because it uses last year's engine and transmission, the new E320 has similar performance. Acceleration is brisk from the smooth 6-cylinder engine and the automatic transmission downshifts promptly to deliver strong passing power. Wind and road noise have been substantially reduced. Larger tires and a new rack-and-pinion steering system help the new E320 feel more athletic. The rear seat is much roomier this year, and leg room is ample instead of barely adequate. The new E320's price is the same as last year's and the E300's is slightly lower. With new features like the side air bags, plus sportier road manners and other improvements, the E-Class is a strong contender among premium sedans.

Mercedes-Benz E-Class prices are on page 374.

MERCEDES-BENZ E320

Rating Guide	1	2	3	4	5
Performance					
Acceleration				▓	
Economy		▓			
Driveability				▓	
Ride				▓	
Steering/handling				▓	
Braking				▓	
Noise				▓	
Accommodations					
Driver seating				▓	
Instruments/controls				▓	
Visibility				▓	
Room/comfort			▓		
Entry/exit				▓	
Cargo room			▓		
Workmanship					
Exterior					▓
Interior					▓
Value				▓	
Total Points					66

Rating scale 5=Exceptional; 4=Above average; 3=Average; 2=Below average; 1=Poor

Specifications

Body type	4-door notchback
Wheelbase (in.)	111.5
Overall length (in.)	189.4
Overall width (in.)	70.8
Overall height (in.)	56.7
Curb weight (lbs.)	3605
Seating capacity	5
Front head room (in.)	37.6
Max. front leg room (in.)	41.3
Rear head room (in.)	37.2
Min. rear leg room (in.)	36.1
Cargo volume (cu. ft.)	18.5
Engine type	dohc I-6
Engine size (l/cu. in.)	3.2/195
Horsepower @ rpm	217 @ 5500
Torque @ rpm	229 @ 3750
Transmission	auto/4-sp.
Drive wheels	rear
Brakes, F/R	disc/disc (ABS)
Tire size	215/55R16
Fuel tank capacity (gal.)	18.5
EPA city/highway mpg	19/26
Test mileage (mpg)	NA

Warranties The entire car (including body perforation rust) is covered for 4 years/50,000 miles.

Built in Germany.

CONSUMER GUIDE®

MERCEDES-BENZ S-CLASS
Premium Sedan/Coupe

Mercedes-Benz S420

An anti-skid system called Electronic Stability Program (ESP), developed jointly with Bosch Corporation, is a new standard feature on V-12 models and a new option for V-8 models in the S-Class line this year. When ESP detects a car is sliding from its intended track, it applies the brakes to individual wheels as needed to help the driver maintain control. The V-8 and V-12 models also have a new 5-speed automatic transmission, which replaces a 4-speed automatic. The S350 Turbodiesel has been dropped, so all S-Class models have gas engines this year. The base model is the S320, which comes with a 228-horsepower 3.2-liter 6-cylinder. The S320 is available in 119.7- and 123.6-inch wheelbases, and the other S-Class sedans come only in the longer wheelbase. A 275-horsepower 4.2-liter V-8 powers the S420 sedan, and the S500 sedan and 2-door coupe use a 315-horsepower 5.0-liter V-8. The S600 sedan and coupe have a 389-horsepower 6.0-liter V-12 engine. All models have dual air bags, anti-lock brakes, and traction control. The automatic climate system has a new "smog sensor" that switches to a recirculation mode if it detects high levels of carbon monoxide. Acceleration among the S-Class models runs from tepid on the S320 to terrific on the S600 (6.3 seconds according to Mercedes). All models have commendable ride and handling, roomy interiors that are isolated from the outside world by double-pane windows, and solid structures. The biggest drawbacks are their high prices and low fuel economy. If the prices are too high and the fuel economy too low for your tastes, you should consider alternatives such as the Cadillac Seville, Lexus LS 400, Oldsmobile Aurora, or the new Mercedes E-Class sedan. The S-Class cars are among the world's best, but those alternatives offer plenty of luxury for thousands less.

Mercedes-Benz S-Class prices are on page 375.

MERCEDES-BENZ S420

Rating Guide	1	2	3	4	5
Performance					
Acceleration				4	
Economy	1				
Driveability			3		
Ride				4	
Steering/handling				4	
Braking				4	
Noise				4	
Accommodations					
Driver seating				4	
Instruments/controls			3		
Visibility			3		
Room/comfort				4	
Entry/exit				4	
Cargo room			3		
Workmanship					
Exterior				4	
Interior				4	
Value			3		
Total Points					65

Rating scale 5=Exceptional; 4=Above average; 3=Average; 2=Below average; 1=Poor

Specifications

Body type ....4-door notchback	Engine type.....................dohc V-8
Wheelbase (in.) 123.6	Engine size (l/cu. in.)..........4.2/256
Overall length (in.)................205.2	Horsepower @ rpm ...275 @ 5700
Overall width (in.) 74.3	Torque @ rpm ....295 @ 3900
Overall height (in.)..................58.9	Transmission.........................auto/5-sp.
Curb weight (lbs.) 4760	Drive wheels ....rear
Seating capacity 5	Brakes, F/R..........disc/disc (ABS)
Front head room (in.) 38.0	Tire size 235/60HR16
Max. front leg room (in.) 41.3	Fuel tank capacity (gal.) 26.4
Rear head room (in.) 38.5	EPA city/highway mpg 15/22
Min. rear leg room (in.)...........39.6	Test mileage (mpg) 15.5
Cargo volume (cu. ft.).............15.6	

Warranties The entire car (including body perforation rust) is covered for 4 years/50,000 miles.

Built in Germany.

CONSUMER GUIDE®

MERCURY SABLE
Mid-Size

✓ **BEST BUY**

Mercury Sable LS 4-door

Like the similar Ford Taurus, the front-drive Sable is redesigned for 1996 and has more rounded contours, a roomier interior, and a new V-6 engine with dual overhead camshafts. As before, sedan and wagon versions are available, and the front and rear styling differs from the Ford versions. Wheelbase grows 2.5 inches to 108.5, and both body styles are nearly six inches longer than last year, though the new Sable is still a mid-size car based on interior volume. The sedan seats five or six people, depending on whether there are two bucket seats or a 3-place front seat, while the wagon seats from five to eight (with the optional 2-place rear seat). The 3-place front seat has a folding center armrest with a flip-out console that contains cup holders and space for coins, cassettes, and a cellular phone. The GS models come with a 145-horsepower 3.0-liter overhead-valve V-6, an updated version of last year's base engine. The more-expensive LS models use the new Duratec 3.0-liter V-6, a 200-horsepower engine with dual overhead camshafts. Both come with a 4-speed automatic transmission. Dual air bags are standard on all models and anti-lock brakes are optional. Because the Sable is so similar to the Taurus, see our report on the Ford version of this car as well. The most obvious improvements on the new models are that they have more interior room, a more contemporary dashboard design, more solid construction, and better performance with the new dual-camshaft V-6 engine in the LS. The dual-cam V-6 is quieter and smoother than the overhead-valve engine in the GS. It also provides more spirited acceleration and stronger passing power. Though this year's prices are higher, there are more standard features and significant design improvements. However, discounts will be much harder to get on the new models.

Mercury Sable prices are on page 382.

MERCURY SABLE LS

Rating Guide	1	2	3	4	5
Performance					
Acceleration			■■■		
Economy		■■			
Driveability			■■■		
Ride			■■■		
Steering/handling			■■■		
Braking				■■■■	
Noise				■■■■	
Accommodations					
Driver seating			■■■		
Instruments/controls			■■■		
Visibility			■■■		
Room/comfort			■■■		
Entry/exit			■■■		
Cargo room			■■■		
Workmanship					
Exterior			■■■		
Interior			■■■		
Value			■■■		
Total Points					62

Rating scale 5=Exceptional; 4=Above average; 3=Average; 2=Below average; 1=Poor

Specifications

Body type	4-door notchback
Wheelbase (in.)	108.5
Overall length (in.)	199.7
Overall width (in.)	73.0
Overall height (in.)	55.4
Curb weight (lbs.)	3388
Seating capacity	5
Front head room (in.)	39.4
Max. front leg room (in.)	42.6
Rear head room (in.)	36.6
Min. rear leg room (in.)	38.9
Cargo volume (cu. ft.)	16.0
Engine type	dohc V-6
Engine size (l/cu. in.)	3.0/181
Horsepower @ rpm	200 @ 5750
Torque @ rpm	200 @ 4500
Transmission	auto/4-sp.
Drive wheels	front
Brakes, F/R	disc/disc (ABS)
Tire size	205/65R15
Fuel tank capacity (gal.)	16.0
EPA city/highway mpg	20/29
Test mileage (mpg)	18.7

Warranties The entire car is covered for 3 years/36,000 miles. Body perforation rust is covered for 5 years/unlimited miles.

Built in Atlanta, Ga., and Chicago, Ill.

CONSUMER GUIDE®

MERCURY VILLAGER **RECOMMENDED**
Minivan

Mercury Villager LS

Mercury's front-drive minivan has a passenger-side air bag as a new standard feature and a fresh face for 1996. The new passenger-side air bag joins one for the driver that has been standard since 1994. New height-adjustable manual front seatbelts replace motorized shoulder belts. The dashboard has been redesigned to a new wraparound look, and new audio systems have larger controls. The light bar that stretched between the headlamps on the 1993-95 models has been replaced by a chrome grille. Other styling changes include new front and rear bumper fascias, headlights, and taillights. Villager is built from the same design as the Nissan Quest (see separate report), which also gets a restyled nose and second air bag this year. Both vehicles were designed by Nissan but are built by Ford Motor Company. A Nissan 151-horsepower 3.0-liter V-6 engine and 4-speed automatic transmission remain the only available powertrain. Anti-lock brakes are standard on all models. Seats for five are standard on the GS, and seats for seven are standard on the LS and Nautica and optional on the GS. A pair of integrated child seats that fold out of the backrest of the middle bench seat is a new option on the GS and LS. The middle seat can be removed and the rear seat moved forward on tracks built into the floor. Villager and Quest are luxury-oriented people movers that stress comfort over towing and heavy-duty work. The 3.0-liter engine can't match the muscle of the larger V-6s in other front-drive minivans, though acceleration is adequate. Head room and leg room are ample for the front seats, and adequate for the middle and rear seats. With all seats in their regular positions, there's only a small cargo area at the rear. Villager and Quest are good choices if you need more than a mid-size station wagon but don't want one of the bigger minivans.

Mercury Villager prices are on page 385.

MERCURY VILLAGER LS

Rating Guide	1	2	3	4	5
Performance					
Acceleration			▓▓▓		
Economy		▓▓▓			
Driveability			▓▓▓		
Ride			▓▓▓		
Steering/handling			▓▓▓		
Braking				▓▓▓	
Noise		▓▓▓			
Accommodations					
Driver seating			▓▓▓		
Instruments/controls		▓▓▓			
Visibility			▓▓▓		
Room/comfort			▓▓▓		
Entry/exit			▓▓▓		
Cargo room				▓▓▓	
Workmanship					
Exterior			▓▓▓		
Interior			▓▓▓		
Value			▓▓▓		
Total Points					61

Rating scale 5=Exceptional; 4=Above average; 3=Average; 2=Below average; 1=Poor

Specifications

Body type	4-door van
Wheelbase (in.)	112.2
Overall length (in.)	189.9
Overall width (in.)	73.7
Overall height (in.)	66.0
Curb weight (lbs.)	3815
Seating capacity	7
Front head room (in.)	39.4
Max. front leg room (in.)	39.9
Rear head room (in.)	39.7
Min. rear leg room (in.)	34.8
Cargo volume (cu. ft.)	126.4
Engine type	ohc V-6
Engine size (l/cu. in.)	3.0/181
Horsepower @ rpm	151 @ 4800
Torque @ rpm	174 @ 4400
Transmission	auto/4-sp.
Drive wheels	front
Brakes, F/R	disc/disc (ABS)
Tire size	205/75R15
Fuel tank capacity (gal.)	20.0
EPA city/highway mpg	17/23
Test mileage (mpg)	NA

Warranties The entire vehicle is covered for 3 years/36,000 miles. Body perforation rust is covered for 5 years/unlimited miles.

Built in Avon Lake, Ohio.

CONSUMER GUIDE®

MITSUBISHI ECLIPSE/ EAGLE TALON
Sports Coupe

Mitsubishi Eclipse GS

Mitsubishi plans to unveil an Eclipse Spyder convertible next spring. There will be two models, both with front-wheel drive and 4-cylinder engines. The Spyder GS uses a Chrysler 140-horsepower 2.0-liter engine, while the GS-T has a turbocharged Mitsubishi 2.0-liter with 210 horsepower. The Spyder has a power top with a glass rear window and electric defroster and power windows and door locks. The Eclipse hatchback coupe, which was redesigned for 1995, returns in RS, GS, GS-T, and GSX form. The similar Talon hatchback returns in ESi, TSi, and TSi AWD. There will not be a convertible version of the Talon. All models have front-wheel drive except the GSX and TSi AWD, which have permanent all-wheel drive. The Eclipse RS and GS and Talon ESi use the 140-horsepower engine, and the GS-T, GSX, and Talon TSi models use the 210-horsepower turbocharged engine. Dual air bags are standard and anti-lock brakes are optional on all models. Both the Eclipse and Talon are built in Illinois at a plant owned by Mitsubishi. The Chrysler-built base engine is smooth but no powerhouse below 3500 rpm, so pickup with the automatic transmission is marginal for freeway on-ramps and in passing sprints. Progress is livelier with the slick-shifting 5-speed manual. Turbo models are decidedly faster (6.9 seconds to 60 mph in our test). All models have nimble handling, good grip, and quick, accurate steering. However the ride becomes choppy on freeways and rough secondary roads, especially on the turbocharged models, and there is lots of road noise. Front seat occupants have adequate head room and seat travel is more than ample for 6-footers. The tiny back seat is strictly a pre-teen environment. Except for the AWD models, the Eclipse and Talon don't have any special qualities.

Mitsubishi Eclipse prices are on page 388.
Eagle Talon prices are on page 311.

MITSUBISHI ECLIPSE GS

Rating Guide	1	2	3	4	5
Performance					
Acceleration				■	
Economy			■		
Driveability			■		
Ride			■		
Steering/handling				■	
Braking				■	
Noise		■			
Accommodations					
Driver seating				■	
Instruments/controls				■	
Visibility		■			
Room/comfort		■			
Entry/exit		■			
Cargo room			■		
Workmanship					
Exterior				■	
Interior				■	
Value			■		
Total Points					**50**

Rating scale 5=Exceptional; 4=Above average; 3=Average; 2=Below average; 1=Poor

Specifications

Body type	3-door hatchback
Wheelbase (in.)	98.8
Overall length (in.)	172.2
Overall width (in.)	68.3
Overall height (in.)	51.0
Curb weight (lbs.)	2723
Seating capacity	4
Front head room (in.)	37.9
Max. front leg room (in.)	43.3
Rear head room (in.)	34.1
Min. rear leg room (in.)	28.4
Cargo volume (cu. ft.)	16.6
Engine type	dohc I-4
Engine size (l/cu. in.)	2.0/122
Horsepower @ rpm	140 @ 6000
Torque @ rpm	130 @ 4800
Transmission	manual/5-sp.
Drive wheels	front
Brakes, F/R	disc/disc (ABS)
Tire size	205/55HR16
Fuel tank capacity (gal.)	15.9
EPA city/highway mpg	22/32
Test mileage (mpg)	23.6

Warranties The entire car is covered for 3 years/36,000 miles. Major powertrain components are covered for 5 years/60,000 miles. Body perforation rust is covered for 7 years/100,000 miles.

Built in Normal, Ill.

MITSUBISHI GALANT
Compact

Mitsubishi Galant LS

The V-6 engine planned for Mitsubishi's front-drive Galant sedan has been cancelled because it would raise the Galant's price too much and complicate production at Mitsubishi's Illinois assembly plant. That means all 1996 models will use the same 141-horsepower 2.4-liter cylinder as last year. The S, ES, and LS models return with several equipment changes. The ES offers a new Premium Package with a power sunroof, fog lamps, 6-speaker sound system with a cassette player, and wider tires on 15-inch alloy wheels. The top-line LS now comes with a power driver's seat, leather interior trim, and automatic climate control. A 5-speed manual transmission is standard on the Galant S and a 4-speed automatic is optional. The ES and LS come only with the automatic. Dual air bags are standard and anti-lock brakes are optional across the board. Most Galants sold in the U.S. are built at the Mitsubishi plant in Illinois, where the Mitsubishi Eclipse and Eagle Talon sports coupes also are built. Last summer Mitsubishi resumed importing some Galants from Japan to meet sales demands. The Galant is roomy, comfortable, and competitively priced against other 4-cylinder compact sedans. We timed a 4-cylinder/automatic at 9.4 seconds to 60 mph, a little quicker than a 4-cylinder Honda Accord. Mitsubishi's automatic transmission shifts smoothly most of the time but downshifts harshly in hard acceleration. There's lots of engine noise in even moderate acceleration. The interior has ample space for four adults, with a rear seat that has generous head and leg room. The roomy trunk has a wide, flat floor and a low liftover for easier loading. Though Galant has several good qualities, it doesn't have any exceptional features to make it stand out from the herd of compact sedans. It still deserves a look.

Mitsubishi Galant prices are on page 389.

MITSUBISHI GALANT LS

Rating Guide	1	2	3	4	5
Performance					
Acceleration				4	
Economy		2			
Driveability			3		
Ride			3		
Steering/handling			3		
Braking				4	
Noise			3		
Accommodations					
Driver seating			3		
Instruments/controls			3		
Visibility			3		
Room/comfort			3		
Entry/exit			3		
Cargo room			3		
Workmanship					
Exterior				4	
Interior				4	
Value			3		
Total Points					**59**

Rating scale 5=Exceptional; 4=Above average; 3=Average; 2=Below average; 1=Poor

Specifications

Body type	4-door notchback
Wheelbase (in.)	103.7
Overall length (in.)	187.0
Overall width (in.)	68.1
Overall height (in.)	53.1
Curb weight (lbs.)	2755
Seating capacity	5
Front head room (in.)	39.4
Max. front leg room (in.)	43.3
Rear head room (in.)	37.5
Min. rear leg room (in.)	35.0
Cargo volume (cu. ft.)	12.5
Engine type	ohc I-4
Engine size (l/cu. in.)	2.4/144
Horsepower @ rpm	141 @ 5500
Torque @ rpm	148 @ 3000
Transmission	auto/4-sp.
Drive wheels	front
Brakes, F/R	disc/disc (ABS)
Tire size	195/60HR15
Fuel tank capacity (gal.)	16.9
EPA city/highway mpg	22/28
Test mileage (mpg)	20.2

Warranties The entire car is covered for 3 years/36,000 miles. Major powertrain components are covered for 5 years/60,000 miles. Body perforation rust is covered for 7 years/100,000 miles.

Built in Normal, Ill., and Japan.

CONSUMER GUIDE®

MITSUBISHI 3000GT/ DODGE STEALTH
Sports and GT

Mitsubishi 3000GT Spyder VR-4

Mitsubishi revived the retractable-hardtop idea with the 3000GT Spyder convertible that went on sale last spring in SL and VR-4 price levels. They're back for 1996, along with base, SL, and VR-4 hatchback coupes, with few changes. Mitsubishi also builds the Dodge Stealth, the 3000GT's fraternal twin. There isn't a Stealth convertible, however, and Dodge has announced that its coupe will be dropped after this year. All 3000GT and Stealth models have "2+2" seating (front buckets and tiny rear seats) and use a 3.0-liter V-6 engine. The base Stealth's V-6 has a single-overhead camshaft and 164 horsepower, an engine that isn't offered in the 3000GT. The base and SL 3000GT and the Stealth R/T have a dual-cam version of this engine with 222 horsepower. All of these models have front-wheel drive and come with a standard 5-speed manual or optional 4-speed automatic transmission. The 3000GT VR-4 and Stealth R/T Turbo have twin turbochargers that boost the dual-cam V-6 to 320 horsepower. They come with permanent all-wheel drive and only a 6-speed manual transmission. Dual air bags are standard across the board, and anti-lock brakes are available on all models except on the base 3000GT coupe. The Spyder is slickly done, impressively solid for a convertible, and, in VR-4 form, a jaw-dropping $64,449. You can save $7000 by buying an SL Spyder instead—if you can find one. Mitsubishi says about 80 percent of the orders have been for the VR-4 models—and they're already sold. Among the coupes, the all-wheel drive models have outstanding performance, but we're turned off by the stiff ride and high prices. The front-drive models aren't as potent but are more liveable as daily transportation and more reasonably priced.

Mitsubishi 3000GT prices are on page 390.
Dodge Stealth prices are on page 309.

MITSUBISHI 3000GT SPYDER VR-4

Rating Guide	1	2	3	4	5
Performance					
Acceleration					▮▮▮▮▮
Economy	▮▮				
Driveability				▮▮▮▮	
Ride			▮▮▮		
Steering/handling				▮▮▮▮	
Braking				▮▮▮▮	
Noise		▮▮			
Accommodations					
Driver seating				▮▮▮▮	
Instruments/controls				▮▮▮▮	
Visibility			▮▮▮		
Room/comfort			▮▮▮		
Entry/exit			▮▮▮		
Cargo room		▮▮			
Workmanship					
Exterior				▮▮▮▮	
Interior				▮▮▮▮	
Value			▮▮▮		
Total Points..**49**					

Rating scale 5=Exceptional; 4=Above average; 3=Average; 2=Below average; 1=Poor

Specifications

Body type ....2-door convertible
Wheelbase (in.) 97.2
Overall length (in.) 179.7
Overall width (in.) 72.4
Overall height (in.) 50.8
Curb weight (lbs.) 3780
Seating capacity 4
Front head room (in.) 37.3
Max. front leg room (in.) 44.2
Rear head room (in.) 34.3
Min. rear leg room (in.) 28.5
Cargo volume (cu. ft.)...............4.4

Engine type ....Turbo dohc V-6
Engine size (l/cu. in.)..........3.0/181
Horsepower @ rpm ...320 @ 6000
Torque @ rpm ....315 @ 2500
Transmission............manual/6-sp.
Drive wheels ....all
Brakes, F/R..........disc/disc (ABS)
Tire size.....................245/45ZR17
Fuel tank capacity (gal.).........19.8
EPA city/highway mpg 18/24
Test mileage (mpg) ....NA

Warranties The entire car is covered for 3 years/36,000 miles. Major powertrain components are covered for 5 years/60,000 miles. Body perforation rust is covered for 7 years/100,000 miles.

Built in Japan.

CONSUMER GUIDE®

NISSAN ALTIMA
Compact

RECOMMENDED

Nissan Altima GXE

The Altima sedan returns nearly unchanged for its fourth season. New wheel covers for the XE and GXE models are the most visible changes to the front-drive Altima. The GXE, the best-selling version, has new cloth seat and door trim. Power door locks, which are standard on the GXE, SE, and GLE models, have been revised so that one turn of the key in the driver's door opens only that door, and a second turn opens the others. All models come with a 2.4-liter 4-cylinder engine with dual overhead camshafts and 150 horsepower. A 5-speed manual is standard on the base XE, GXE, and sporty SE. A 4-speed automatic is standard on the luxury-oriented GLE and optional on the other models. Dual air bags are standard and anti-lock brakes are optional across the line. Main rivals for the Altima include Japanese-brand sedans such as the Mazda 626, Toyota Camry, Subaru Legacy, and Mitsubishi Galant and domestic cars such as the Ford Contour and Pontiac Grand Am. Though it's not the roomiest or most refined compact sedan, Altima comes well-equipped at competitive prices. Acceleration is more than adequate with the automatic transmission (9.4 seconds to 60 mph) and passing response is spirited, though the engine is loud and rather rough at higher speeds. Altima's firm steering and suspension make it feel more like a sports sedan than a family sedan. Though you feel most bumps, there is little harshness because the suspension and rigid body absorb most of the impact. The interior has adequate head room for all seats and enough space for two adults in the rear seat. The trunk has a wide, flat floor that gives Altima adequate cargo room. However, the rear seatback doesn't fold down. Overall, we rate Nissan's compact sedan highly and encourage you to give it a close look.

Nissan Altima prices are on page 391.

NISSAN ALTIMA GXE

Rating Guide	1	2	3	4	5
Performance					
Acceleration			▓▓▓▓		
Economy			▓▓▓		
Driveability			▓▓▓		
Ride			▓▓▓		
Steering/handling			▓▓▓		
Braking				▓▓▓▓	
Noise			▓▓▓		
Accommodations					
Driver seating			▓▓▓		
Instruments/controls			▓▓▓		
Visibility			▓▓▓		
Room/comfort			▓▓▓		
Entry/exit			▓▓▓		
Cargo room			▓▓▓		
Workmanship					
Exterior				▓▓▓▓	
Interior				▓▓▓▓	
Value			▓▓▓		
Total Points..**59**					

Rating scale 5=Exceptional; 4=Above average; 3=Average; 2=Below average; 1=Poor

Specifications

Body type ....4-door notchback
Wheelbase (in.) 103.1
Overall length (in.) 180.5
Overall width (in.) 67.1
Overall height (in.) 55.9
Curb weight (lbs.) 2853
Seating capacity..........................5
Front head room (in.) 39.3
Max. front leg room (in.) 42.6
Rear head room (in.) 37.6
Min. rear leg room (in.)...........34.7
Cargo volume (cu. ft.)..............14.0

Engine type ....dohc I-4
Engine size (l/cu. in.)..........2.4/146
Horsepower @ rpm ...150 @ 5600
Torque @ rpm ....154 @ 4400
Transmission.................auto/4-sp.
Drive wheels ....front
Brakes, F/R..........disc/disc (ABS)
Tire size 205/60R15
Fuel tank capacity (gal.).........15.9
EPA city/highway mpg 21/29
Test mileage (mpg) 20.2

Warranties The entire car is covered for 3 years/36,000 miles. Major powertrain components are covered for 5 years/ 60,000 miles. Body perforation rust is covered for 5 years/unlimited miles.

Built in Smyrna, Tenn.

NISSAN MAXIMA
Premium Sedan

BUDGET BUY

Nissan Maxima SE

The front-drive Maxima was redesigned for the 1995 model year, so it receives only minor equipment changes for this year. Among them, a 4-way power front passenger seat is a new standard feature on the GLE model and a new option on the SE, and a large cup holder has been added to the center console. In addition to the luxury GLE and sporty SE price levels, the Maxima comes in a base GXE price level. All come as 4-door sedans with a 3.0-liter V-6 engine with dual overhead camshafts and 190 horsepower. A 5-speed manual transmission is standard on the GXE and SE and a 4-speed automatic is optional. The GLE comes only with the automatic. Dual air bags are standard on all models and anti-lock brakes are optional except on the GXE with the 5-speed manual transmission, where they aren't available. Maxima's basic design and major mechanical components are used for the Infiniti I30, which went on sale last spring. The two differ mainly in styling and the I30's higher level of standard equipment. Infiniti is Nissan's luxury division. Both cars are positioned as "near-luxury" sedans, though the Maxima is priced lower than the I30. We timed a Maxima GXE with the automatic transmission at 7.9 seconds to 60 mph, an impressive performance that rivals some V-8-powered sedans. Passing power also is impressive. Maxima has a comfortable, stable ride, precise steering, and crisp handling. There's ample room for four adults in the Maxima. Instruments and controls are well placed and easy to see and use while driving. The Maxima is a bargain among premium sedans. It performs as well as some more-expensive rivals and has the refinement and amenities expected on a luxury car. The I30's main advantage is that Infiniti dealers are geared to provide a higher level of customer service than Nissan dealers.

Nissan Maxima prices are on page 392.

NISSAN MAXIMA SE

Rating Guide	1	2	3	4	5
Performance					
Acceleration				▓▓▓▓	
Economy		▓▓▓			
Driveability				▓▓▓▓	
Ride				▓▓▓▓	
Steering/handling				▓▓▓▓	
Braking				▓▓▓▓	
Noise			▓▓▓		
Accommodations					
Driver seating			▓▓▓		
Instruments/controls			▓▓▓		
Visibility				▓▓▓▓	
Room/comfort			▓▓▓		
Entry/exit				▓▓▓▓	
Cargo room			▓▓▓		
Workmanship					
Exterior				▓▓▓▓	
Interior				▓▓▓▓	
Value				▓▓▓▓	
Total Points					**64**

Rating scale 5=Exceptional; 4=Above average; 3=Average; 2=Below average; 1=Poor

Specifications

Body type	4-door notchback
Wheelbase (in.)	106.3
Overall length (in.)	187.7
Overall width (in.)	69.7
Overall height (in.)	55.7
Curb weight (lbs.)	3001
Seating capacity	5
Front head room (in.)	40.1
Max. front leg room (in.)	43.9
Rear head room (in.)	37.4
Min. rear leg room (in.)	34.3
Cargo volume (cu. ft.)	14.5
Engine type	dohc V-6
Engine size (l/cu. in.)	3.0/181
Horsepower @ rpm	190 @ 5600
Torque @ rpm	205 @ 4000
Transmission	auto/4-sp.
Drive wheels	front
Brakes, F/R	disc/disc (ABS)
Tire size	215/60R15
Fuel tank capacity (gal.)	18.5
EPA city/highway mpg	21/28
Test mileage (mpg)	18.2

Warranties The entire car is covered for 3 years/36,000 miles. Major powertrain components are covered for 5 years/60,000 miles. Body perforation rust is covered for 5 years/unlimited miles.

Built in Japan.

NISSAN PATHFINDER
Sport-Utility Vehicle

Nissan Pathfinder SE

Scheduled to go on sale early in 1996, the 1996 Pathfinder represents the first major revision to Nissan's sport-utility since it was introduced 10 years ago. A longer-wheelbase unibody chassis replaces the old body-on-frame design, and the new Pathfinder has dual air bags and a larger V-6 engine. The new version comes in a 5-door wagon body style. Overall length increases 6.7 inches to 178.3, the wheelbase stretches two inches to 106.3, and width grows by 2.2 inches to 68.7. Despite the size increase, weight has been pared by about 200 pounds. Dual air bags and 4-wheel anti-lock brakes are new standard features. Three price levels return: base XE, sport-oriented SE, and luxury-equipped LE. Powering all three is a 3.3-liter V-6, an enlargement of the 3.0-liter engine used in the previous generation. Horsepower increases from 153 to 168. A 5-speed manual transmission is standard on XE and SE Pathfinders, and a 4-speed automatic is standard on the LE and optional on the others. The SE has standard 4-wheel drive, a part-time system (not for use on dry pavement) with shift-on-the-fly capability up to 50 mph. XE and LE models list rear-wheel drive as standard and 4WD as optional. The new Pathfinder has a softer ride, better acceleration, a more modern dashboard, and additional rear seat and cargo room. Its relatively low profile and larger rear doors make entry/exit easier than in many sport-utilities. The 3.3-liter V-6 is stronger and smoother than previous engines. Ride and handling are among the most car-like in the sport-utility field, and the dashboard is one of the most user-friendly on the market. Prices weren't announced in time for this issue, so we can't say how the Pathfinder stacks up in terms of value. Our initial impression is that it's good enough to warrant a serious look.

Nissan Pathfinder standard equipment is on page 393.

NISSAN PATHFINDER SE (Preliminary)

Rating Guide	1	2	3	4	5
Performance					
Acceleration			▌		
Economy		▌			
Driveability			▌		
Ride			▌		
Steering/handling			▌		
Braking			▌		
Noise		▌			
Accommodations					
Driver seating			▌		
Instruments/controls			▌		
Visibility			▌		
Room/comfort			▌		
Entry/exit		▌			
Cargo room			▌		
Workmanship					
Exterior			▌		
Interior			▌		
Value			▌		

Total Points..59

Rating scale 5=Exceptional; 4=Above average; 3=Average; 2=Below average; 1=Poor

Specifications

Body type	5-door wagon
Wheelbase (in.)	106.3
Overall length (in.)	178.3
Overall width (in.)	68.7
Overall height (in.)	67.1
Curb weight (lbs.)	3920
Seating capacity	5
Front head room (in.)	39.5
Max. front leg room (in.)	41.7
Rear head room (in.)	37.5
Min. rear leg room (in.)	31.8
Cargo volume (cu. ft.)	NA
Engine type	ohc V-6
Engine size (l/cu. in.)	3.3/201
Horsepower @ rpm	168 @ 4800
Torque @ rpm	196 @ 2800
Transmission	auto/4-sp.
Drive wheels	rear/all
Brakes, F/R	disc/disc (ABS)
Tire size	265/70R15
Fuel tank capacity (gal.)	21.1
EPA city/highway mpg	15/19
Test mileage (mpg)	NA

Warranties The entire vehicle is covered for 3 years/36,000 miles. Major powertrain components are covered for 5 years/60,000 miles. Body perforation rust is covered for 5 years/unlimited miles.

Built in Japan.

NISSAN QUEST
Minivan

RECOMMENDED

Nissan Quest GXE

Quest, Nissan's front-drive minivan, gets its most extensive changes since it was introduced as a 1993 model, including a passenger-side air bag in a redesigned dashboard. Quest gained a driver-side air bag in 1994. The motorized front seatbelts have been replaced by height-adjustable manual belts. Similar changes have been made on the Mercury Villager (see separate report), which is built from the same design. Quest and Villager were designed by Nissan, and both are built at a plant in Ohio owned by Ford Motor Company. Both use a Nissan 3.0-liter V-6 engine with 151 horsepower and a 4-speed automatic transmission. Anti-lock brakes are standard on the Quest GXE model and optional on the base XE. Both models have seats for seven. Integrated child safety seats are a new option available with the 2-place middle bench seat and cloth upholstery. The middle seats can be removed, and the rear seat then can be slid forward on tracks built into the floor. Styling changes this year include a new grille, headlamps, taillamps, and bumper fascias. Quest is a functional family vehicle that's easy to drive and has flexible seating and luggage accommodations. The engine is powerful enough for light loads, but more power would make it easier to accelerate quickly with a full load of passengers. Quest has a low step-in height that allows easy entry/exit, good visibility, and an ample supply of cup holders and cubbies. The modest size for a minivan limits the amount you can haul, whether it's people or packages. Both the Mercury and Nissan models have the sliding rear seat, which we like, but the middle seats are heavy and difficult to remove or install. Quest and Villager deserve a look if you value family-car finesse over cargo space and towing ability.

Nissan Quest prices are on page 394.

NISSAN QUEST GXE

Rating Guide	1	2	3	4	5

Performance

Acceleration	3
Economy	3
Driveability	3
Ride	3
Steering/handling	3
Braking	4
Noise	3

Accommodations

Driver seating	3
Instruments/controls	3
Visibility	3
Room/comfort	3
Entry/exit	3
Cargo room	4

Workmanship

| Exterior | 4 |
| Interior | 4 |

Value | 3 |

Total Points..61

Rating scale 5=Exceptional; 4=Above average; 3=Average; 2=Below average; 1=Poor

Specifications

Body type	4-door van
Wheelbase (in.)	112.2
Overall length (in.)	189.9
Overall width (in.)	73.7
Overall height (in.)	65.6
Curb weight (lbs.)	3876
Seating capacity	7
Front head room (in.)	39.5
Max. front leg room (in.)	39.9
Rear head room (in.)	39.7
Min. rear leg room (in.)	36.3
Cargo volume (cu. ft.)	114.8
Engine type	ohc V-6
Engine size (l/cu. in.)	3.0/181
Horsepower @ rpm	151 @ 4800
Torque @ rpm	174 @ 4400
Transmission	auto/4-sp.
Drive wheels	front
Brakes, F/R	disc/disc (ABS)
Tire size	205/75R145
Fuel tank capacity (gal.)	20.0
EPA city/highway mpg	17/23
Test mileage (mpg)	NA

Warranties The entire vehicle is covered for 3 years/36,000 miles. Major powertrain components are covered for 5 years/60,000 miles. Body perforation rust is covered for 5 years/unlimited miles.

Built in Avon Lake, Ohio.

NISSAN SENTRA
Subcompact

Nissan Sentra GLE

Nissan redesigned its front-drive subcompact last year, so it is virtually unchanged for 1996. The Sentra, which is built at Nissan's plant in Smyrna, Tennessee, comes only as a 4-door notchback sedan. The previous Sentra also came as a 2-door sedan, but that niche is now filled by the 200SX sports coupe, which also is built at the Smyrna plant (see next report). Sentra comes in four price levels: base, XE, GXE, and GLE. All models have standard dual air bags and door guard beams that meet 1997 federal side-impact standards. All models use a dual-camshaft 1.6-liter 4-cylinder engine with 115 horsepower. A 5-speed manual transmission is standard and a 4-speed automatic is optional on all models. Anti-lock brakes are optional on the GXE and GLE models. The new Sentra ranks near the head of the subcompact class for quietness and solidity. Even over the roughest roads, Sentra feels far more substantial than most small cars, with a supple, well-controlled ride and little road noise. In these areas, the new Sentra seems well ahead of rivals such as the Toyota Tercel, Saturn sedan, and Ford Escort, and on a par with the Toyota Corolla. Sentra's 1.6-liter engine doesn't produce much power at low speeds, so it requires lots of throttle for good pickup. With the automatic transmission, it doesn't have enough muscle to easily merge onto freeways. Though the new automatic shifts much more smoothly than older versions, you still have to floor the throttle at times to induce it to downshift for passing power. The interior was enlarged last year and the rear seat now has adequate leg room and foot room for most adults. Sentra is a solid, refined subcompact that deserves a look.

Nissan Sentra prices are on page 395.

NISSAN SENTRA GLE

Rating Guide	1	2	3	4	5

Performance

Acceleration	3
Economy	4
Driveability	3
Ride	3
Steering/handling	3
Braking	3
Noise	3

Accommodations

Driver seating	4
Instruments/controls	4
Visibility	4
Room/comfort	3
Entry/exit	3
Cargo room	3

Workmanship

Exterior	4
Interior	4

Value

Value	3

Total Points 57

Rating scale 5=Exceptional; 4=Above average; 3=Average; 2=Below average; 1=Poor

Specifications

Body type	4-door notchback
Wheelbase (in.)	99.8
Overall length (in.)	170.1
Overall width (in.)	66.6
Overall height (in.)	54.5
Curb weight (lbs.)	2410
Seating capacity	5
Front head room (in.)	39.1
Max. front leg room (in.)	42.3
Rear head room (in.)	36.5
Min. rear leg room (in.)	32.4
Cargo volume (cu. ft.)	10.7
Engine type	dohc I-4
Engine size (l/cu. in.)	1.6/97
Horsepower @ rpm	115 @ 6000
Torque @ rpm	108 @ 4000
Transmission	auto/4-sp.
Drive wheels	front
Brakes, F/R	disc/drum
Tire size	175/65R14
Fuel tank capacity (gal.)	13.2
EPA city/highway mpg	28/37
Test mileage (mpg)	25.8

Warranties The entire car is covered for 3 years/36,000 miles. Major powertrain components are covered for 5 years/60,000. Body perforation rust is covered for 5 years/unlimited miles.

Built in Smyrna, Tenn.

CONSUMER GUIDE®

NISSAN 200SX
Sports Coupe

Nissan 200SX SE-R

Nissan revived the 200SX name for a new front-drive sports coupe that went on sale last spring. Based on the Sentra sedan, the 200SX comes in base, SE, and sportier SE-R models. Nissan positions the 200SX as a lower-cost alternative to sports coupes such as the Ford Probe, Mazda MX-6, Mitsubishi Eclipse, Toyota Celica, and Nissan's rear-drive 240SX. Other rivals include the Saturn SC1/SC2 and Toyota Paseo. The 200SX shares the Sentra sedan's 99.8-inch wheelbase, front styling, and dashboard but has different semi-fastback 2-door styling. The base 200SX and SE models also share Sentra's 115-horsepower 1.6-liter 4-cylinder engine, while the SE-R comes with a 140-horsepower 2.0-liter 4-cylinder. A 5-speed manual transmission is standard and a 4-speed automatic is optional. Dual air bags are standard on all models, and anti-lock brakes are optional on the SE and SE-R. The 200SX comes in two distinct flavors. We timed a 5-speed SE-R model at a speedy 8.4 seconds to 60 mph, which is quicker than a lot of rivals in the same price range. The 2.0-liter engine has enough torque for swift highway passing. The base and SE models aren't nearly as lively, though they have adequate vigor. The SE-R has above-average grip and modest body lean, which make for safe, enjoyable driving on twisting roads. Ride quality is rather jumpy over rippled freeways and rough pavement, as expected of a firmly sprung sports coupe with fairly aggressive tires. The 200SX offers better-than-average passenger room for a small coupe, especially in back. The dashboard has a functional, ergonomic layout that puts most controls close by. The 200SX is a reasonable alternative to the higher-priced versions of cars such as the Probe and MX-6.

Nissan 200SX prices are on page 396.

NISSAN 200SX SE-R

Rating Guide	1	2	3	4	5
Performance					
Acceleration				4	
Economy			3		
Driveability				4	
Ride			3		
Steering/handling				4	
Braking					5
Noise			3		
Accommodations					
Driver seating				4	
Instruments/controls				4	
Visibility			3		
Room/comfort			3		
Entry/exit			3		
Cargo room			3		
Workmanship					
Exterior				4	
Interior				4	
Value				4	

Total Points 58

Rating scale 5=Exceptional; 4=Above average; 3=Average; 2=Below average; 1=Poor

Specifications

Body type	2-door notchback
Wheelbase (in.)	99.8
Overall length (in.)	170.1
Overall width (in.)	66.6
Overall height (in.)	54.2
Curb weight (lbs.)	2330
Seating capacity	5
Front head room (in.)	39.1
Max. front leg room (in.)	42.3
Rear head room (in.)	35.4
Min. rear leg room (in.)	31.4
Cargo volume (cu. ft.)	10.4
Engine type	dohc I-4
Engine size (l/cu. in.)	2.0/122
Horsepower @ rpm	140 @ 6400
Torque @ rpm	132 @ 4800
Transmission	manual/5-sp.
Drive wheels	front
Brakes, F/R	disc/disc (ABS)
Tire size	195/65R15
Fuel tank capacity (gal.)	13.2
EPA city/highway mpg	23/31
Test mileage (mpg)	28.0

Warranties The entire car is covered for 3 years/36,000 miles. Major powertrain components are covered for 5 years/60,000 miles. Body perforation rust is covered for 5 years/unlimited miles.

Built in Smyrna, Tenn.

CONSUMER GUIDE®

OLDSMOBILE ACHIEVA
Compact

Oldsmobile Achieva SL

Oldsmobile's front-drive compact gets a new interior with a passenger-side air bag, a new standard engine, and air conditioning and daytime running lights as new standard features. The new passenger-side air bag resides in a redesigned dashboard with a new analog instrument cluster and illuminated climate controls. A driver-side air bag has been standard since 1994. New front seatbelts are anchored to the roof pillars rather than the doors and are height adjustable on the 4-door sedan. Anti-lock brakes also are standard. Achieva comes as a 2-door coupe (dubbed SC) and 4-door sedan (SL) in three price levels, labeled Series I, II, and III. A new 150-horsepower 2.4-liter 4-cylinder, called the Twin Cam, is standard on all. It replaces a 2.3-liter 4-cylinder. A 155-horsepower 3.1-liter V-6 is optional on all models except the Series I coupe. Both engines have new 100,000-mile spark plugs and coolant designed to last 5 years/100,000 miles. The 4-cylinder comes with either a 5-speed manual or 4-speed automatic transmission, and the V-6 comes only with the automatic. Traction control is included with the automatic transmission as a new feature this year. Achieva is built from the same design as the Buick Skylark and Pontiac Grand Am. These cars share major mechanical components but have different styling and interior features. The Twin Cam 4-cylinder engine is just as potent as the 2.3-liter engine it replaces and quieter and smoother. The optional V-6 engine has more low-speed power, so it feels quicker initially and in highway passing. However, the 4-cylinder is only a little slower and more economical. Achieva has plenty of head room and leg room in front, and adequate amounts of both for the rear seat. Oldsmobile's value-pricing strategy means the fully equipped Achieva is thousands of dollars less than comparable Japanese rivals.

Oldsmobile Achieva prices are on page 397.

OLDSMOBILE ACHIEVA SL

Rating Guide	1	2	3	4	5
Performance					
Acceleration			▓		
Economy			▓		
Driveability			▓		
Ride			▓		
Steering/handling			▓		
Braking				▓	
Noise			▓		
Accommodations					
Driver seating			▓		
Instruments/controls			▓		
Visibility			▓		
Room/comfort			▓		
Entry/exit			▓		
Cargo room			▓		
Workmanship					
Exterior				▓	
Interior			▓		
Value			▓		

Total Points 56

Rating scale 5=Exceptional; 4=Above average; 3=Average; 2=Below average; 1=Poor

Specifications

Body type ....4-door notchback	Engine type ....dohc I-4
Wheelbase (in.) 103.4	Engine size (l/cu. in.) 2.4/146
Overall length (in.) 187.9	Horsepower @ rpm ...150 @ 6000
Overall width (in.) 68.1	Torque @ rpm ....150 @ 4400
Overall height (in.) 53.4	Transmission ....auto/4-sp.
Curb weight (lbs.) 2813	Drive wheels ....front
Seating capacity 5	Brakes, F/R ....disc/drum (ABS)
Front head room (in.) 37.8	Tire size 195/70R14
Max. front leg room (in.) 43.3	Fuel tank capacity (gal.) 15.2
Rear head room (in.) 37.0	EPA city/highway mpg 22/32
Min. rear leg room (in.) 33.5	Test mileage (mpg) ....NA
Cargo volume (cu. ft.) 14.0	

Warranties The entire car is covered for 3 years/36,000 miles. Body perforation rust is covered for 6 years/100,000 miles.

Built in Lansing, Mich.

CONSUMER GUIDE®

OLDSMOBILE AURORA
Premium Sedan

RECOMMENDED

Oldsmobile Aurora

The Aurora luxury sedan has new daytime running lights, a handful of new options, and a base price of $34,360, which is $1295 more than last year's price. In addition, Oldsmobile says it has eliminated the rear window distortion that Aurora owners have complained about since the car was introduced as an early 1995 model. With the new daytime running lights, the headlamps are illuminated at reduced intensity whenever the ignition is on. Aurora's keyless entry system has been revised and now includes a panic button that sounds the horn and flashes the lights for two minutes. Using the keyless entry system, the driver's seat and outside mirrors can be automatically set to one of two positions; interior and exterior lights can be turned on; and the automatic door locks can be programmed to operate in one of four different modes. Aurora is built on the same front-drive platform as the Buick Riviera but has different styling and interior features. Aurora comes with a 250-horsepower 4.0-liter V-8 engine, while the Riviera is available with V-6s. A 4-speed automatic transmission, dual air bags, and anti-lock brakes are standard. Aurora offers a long list of luxury amenities, sporty performance, and distinctive styling at an attractive price. The V-8 delivers brisk acceleration and ample passing power, and the transmission shifts so smoothly you seldom notice it. Aurora has commendable ride control at high speeds and, though the ride is firmer than the Lexus LS 400's, it's not harsh. The roomy interior has ample space for four adults, and there's ample luggage space. Aurora is competitive with Japanese and European sedans that cost thousands more, so we strongly recommend that you include it on your luxury car shopping list.

Oldsmobile Aurora prices are on page 398.

OLDSMOBILE AURORA

Rating Guide	1	2	3	4	5
Performance					
Acceleration				▓▓▓	
Economy	▓▓				
Driveability				▓▓▓	
Ride				▓▓▓	
Steering/handling				▓▓▓	
Braking				▓▓▓	
Noise			▓▓▓		
Accommodations					
Driver seating			▓▓▓		
Instruments/controls			▓▓▓		
Visibility			▓▓		
Room/comfort			▓▓▓		
Entry/exit			▓▓▓		
Cargo room			▓▓▓		
Workmanship					
Exterior				▓▓▓	
Interior				▓▓▓	
Value				▓▓▓	
Total Points					**61**

Rating scale 5=Exceptional; 4=Above average; 3=Average; 2=Below average; 1=Poor

Specifications

Body type	4-door notchback
Wheelbase (in.)	113.8
Overall length (in.)	205.4
Overall width (in.)	74.4
Overall height (in.)	55.4
Curb weight (lbs.)	3967
Seating capacity	5
Front head room (in.)	38.4
Max. front leg room (in.)	42.6
Rear head room (in.)	36.9
Min. rear leg room (in.)	38.4
Cargo volume (cu. ft.)	16.1
Engine type	dohc V-8
Engine size (l/cu. in.)	4.0/244
Horsepower @ rpm	250 @ 5600
Torque @ rpm	260 @ 4400
Transmission	auto/4-sp.
Drive wheels	front
Brakes, F/R	disc/disc (ABS)
Tire size	235/60R16
Fuel tank capacity (gal.)	20.0
EPA city/highway mpg	17/26
Test mileage (mpg)	16.6

Warranties The entire car is covered for 4 years/50,000 miles. Body perforation rust is covered for 6 years/100,000 miles.

Built in Orion, Mich.

CONSUMER GUIDE®

OLDSMOBILE BRAVADA
Sport-Utility Vehicle

Oldsmobile Bravada

Oldsmobile jumps back into the sport-utility market this year with the Bravada, a spinoff of the 5-door Chevy Blazer/GMC Jimmy. The Blazer and Jimmy were redesigned last year, but there was no 1995 edition of the Bravada. The new Bravada is the luxury leader of this trio. The basic design and 190-horsepower 4.3-liter V-6 engine are shared with Chevy and GMC, but Bravada has its own exterior trim and standard leather upholstery, and it is the only one with wood interior accents. Bravada also comes with standard permanently engaged 4-wheel-drive, called SmartTrak, a system that's optional on Blazer and Jimmy. Power is normally split 35 percent front/65 percent rear, but SmartTrak can change to either 100 percent front or rear if needed to maintain traction. Other standard features include a driver-side air bag, anti-lock brakes, daytime running lights, air conditioning, remote keyless entry, and a HomeLink transmitter that can be programmed to replace conventional garage door openers. The Bravada has a base price of $29,505 and only five options: a 5000-pound trailer towing package; gold trim package; white-letter tires; an engine block heater; and a CD player. Because Bravada is a Blazer/Jimmy with a fancier wardrobe, it has the same plus and minus points. One big minus point is that the Bravada and its twins don't have a passenger-side air bag, and all their major competitors do. Aside from that and the lack of a V-8 engine, Bravada is a close match for the Ford Explorer and Jeep Grand Cherokee. The permanent 4-wheel drive system is a nice feature: You concentrate on driving and a computer figures out how to apportion power among the four wheels. Oldsmobile is trying to copy Saturn in the way it treats customers, so there may be some indirect benefits to buying a Bravada.

Oldsmobile Bravada prices are on page 399.

OLDSMOBILE BRAVADA

Rating Guide	1	2	3	4	5
Performance					
Acceleration			■■■■		
Economy	■■				
Driveability			■■■■		
Ride				■■■■	
Steering/handling			■■■■		
Braking					■■■■
Noise			■■■■		
Accommodations					
Driver seating			■■■■		
Instruments/controls			■■■■		
Visibility			■■■■		
Room/comfort			■■■■		
Entry/exit			■■■■		
Cargo room				■■■■	
Workmanship					
Exterior			■■■■		
Interior			■■■■		
Value			■■■■		

Total Points..60

Rating scale 5=Exceptional; 4=Above average; 3=Average; 2=Below average; 1=Poor

Specifications

Body type ....5-door wagon
Wheelbase (in.) 107.0
Overall length (in.) 180.9
Overall width (in.) 66.5
Overall height (in.) 67.0
Curb weight (lbs.) 4184
Seating capacity 5
Front head room (in.) 39.7
Max. front leg room (in.) 42.4
Rear head room (in.) 38.6
Min. rear leg room (in.) 36.1
Cargo volume (cu. ft.).............74.2

Engine type ....ohv V-6
Engine size (l/cu. in.)........4.3/262
Horsepower @ rpm ...190 @ 4400
Torque @ rpm ....250 @ 2800
Transmission.................auto/4-sp.
Drive wheels ....all
Brakes, F/R ....disc/drum (ABS)
Tire size 205/70R15
Fuel tank capacity (gal.) 19.0
EPA city/highway mpg 16/21
Test mileage (mpg) ....NA

Warranties The entire vehicle is covered for 3 years/36,000 miles. Body perforation rust is covered for 6 years/100,000 miles.

Built in Morain, Ohio.

CONSUMER GUIDE®

OLDSMOBILE CUTLASS CIERA/BUICK CENTURY

Mid-Size

BUDGET BUY

Oldsmobile Cutlass Ciera SL 4-door

The cars that refuse to die are back for their 15th season, and the end of the line appears to be in sight. General Motors plans to replace the Cutlass Ciera and similar Century in 1997 with new compact sedans based on the same design that will be used for the Chevrolet Malibu. Both return for 1996 as 6-passenger sedans and 8-passenger wagons with front-wheel drive and a standard driver-side air bag and anti-lock brakes. The Ciera comes as an SL model in Series I and II price levels for the sedan and the Series I level for the wagon. The Century sedan comes in Special, Custom, and Limited price levels and the wagon only in the Special price level. A 120-horsepower 2.2-liter 4-cylinder engine and 3-speed automatic transmission is the base powertrain for the sedans. A 160-horsepower 3.1-liter V-6 and 4-speed automatic are standard on the wagons and optional on the sedans. Both engines have new coolant designed to last 5 years/100,000 miles and spark plugs designed to last 100,000 miles. When the Cutlass Ciera and Century debuted in 1982, most cars still had carburetors and none had air bags or anti-lock brakes. Despite their age, these cars still offer good utility at reasonable cost. For example, a Cutlass Ciera Series II is $16,455, a good deal for a fully equipped V-6 sedan that holds up to six people. The 4-cylinder engine doesn't have enough power for cars of this size and weight, so we strongly recommend the V-6. It has ample torque at low speeds and provides good acceleration and passing power. Now some bad news: The soft suspension allows too much bouncing on highways and too much body lean in turns, and the steering is too light and vague. Though Ciera and Century are aged and conservatively styled, they are bargains among mid-size cars.

Oldsmobile Cutlass Ciera prices are on page 400.
Buick Century prices are on page 256.

OLDSMOBILE CUTLASS CIERA SL

Rating Guide	1	2	3	4	5
Performance					
Acceleration			▓		
Economy			▓		
Driveability			▓		
Ride			▓		
Steering/handling		▓			
Braking				▓	
Noise			▓		
Accommodations					
Driver seating			▓		
Instruments/controls		▓			
Visibility			▓		
Room/comfort			▓		
Entry/exit			▓		
Cargo room			▓		
Workmanship					
Exterior			▓		
Interior		▓			
Value			▓		
Total Points					58

Rating scale 5=Exceptional; 4=Above average; 3=Average; 2=Below average; 1=Poor

Specifications

Body type ....4-door notchback
Wheelbase (in.) 104.9
Overall length (in.) 193.2
Overall width (in.) 69.4
Overall height (in.) 54.2
Curb weight (lbs.) 2974
Seating capacity.........................6
Front head room (in.) 38.6
Max. front leg room (in.) 42.1
Rear head room (in.) 38.3
Min. rear leg room (in.)...........35.9
Cargo volume (cu. ft.).............15.8

Engine type ....ohv V-6
Engine size (l/cu. in.)..........3.1/191
Horsepower @ rpm ...160 @ 5200
Torque @ rpm ....185 @ 4000
Transmission.................auto/4-sp.
Drive wheels ....front
Brakes, F/R ....disc/drum (ABS)
Tire size 195/75R14
Fuel tank capacity (gal.) 16.5
EPA city/highway mpg 20/29
Test mileage (mpg) ....NA

Warranties The entire car is covered for 3 years/36,000 miles. Body perforation rust is covered for 6 years/100,000 miles.

Built in Oklahoma City, Okla.

CONSUMER GUIDE®

OLDSMOBILE CUTLASS SUPREME

RECOMMENDED

Mid-Size

Oldsmobile Cutlass Supreme SL 2-door

The slow-selling convertible has been dropped, and the mid-size Cutlass Supreme 2-door coupe and 4-door sedan return for 1996 in four price levels instead of two. Under Oldsmobile's "value-pricing" strategy adopted last year, its cars are marketed as well-equipped models with few available options. Dealers are encouraged to sell cars at suggested retail price and eliminate the traditional haggling that turns off many consumers. This year the front-drive Cutlass Supreme comes as an SL model in Series I, II, III, and IV price levels, and the coupe and sedan are identically equipped and priced. A 160-horsepower 3.1-liter V-6 engine and 4-speed automatic transmission are standard on all price levels. A 3.4-liter V-6 with dual overhead camshafts is optional on the Series III and IV, and this year it has 215 horsepower and 220 pounds/feet of torque, five more than last year for both ratings. Both engines have new coolant designed to last 5 years/100,000 miles and spark plugs designed to last 100,000 miles. Dual air bags and anti-lock brakes are standard across the board. The Buick Regal, Chevrolet Lumina, and Pontiac Grand Prix are built from the same design and share major mechanical components, but each has different styling and interior features. The Series I Cutlass Supreme costs $17,455 and comes with a full load of comfort and convenience features, making it a good value among mid-size cars. The standard 3.1-liter V-6 provides adequate acceleration. The optional 3.4-liter engine is stronger but not by that much, so its value is questionable. There's ample leg room and head room for all seats, though the rear cushion is too low and soft for long-distance comfort. The roomy trunk holds lots of luggage.

Oldsmobile Cutlass Supreme prices are on page 400.

OLDSMOBILE CUTLASS SUPREME SL

Rating Guide	1	2	3	4	5
Performance					
Acceleration			3		
Economy		2			
Driveability			3		
Ride			3		
Steering/handling			3		
Braking				4	
Noise			3		
Accommodations					
Driver seating			3		
Instruments/controls			3		
Visibility			3		
Room/comfort			3		
Entry/exit			3		
Cargo room			3		
Workmanship					
Exterior			3		
Interior			3		
Value			3		

Total Points 59

Rating scale 5=Exceptional; 4=Above average; 3=Average; 2=Below average; 1=Poor

Specifications

Body type ....2-door notchback
Wheelbase (in.) 107.5
Overall length (in.) 193.9
Overall width (in.) 71.0
Overall height (in.) 53.3
Curb weight (lbs.) 3286
Seating capacity.........................5
Front head room (in.) 37.8
Max. front leg room (in.) 42.3
Rear head room (in.) 37.0
Min. rear leg room (in.) 34.8
Cargo volume (cu. ft.).............15.5

Engine type ....ohv V-6
Engine size (l/cu. in.) 3.1/191
Horsepower @ rpm ...160 @ 5200
Torque @ rpm ....185 @ 4000
Transmission ....auto/4-sp.
Drive wheels ....front
Brakes, F/R....disc/disc (ABS)
Tire size 215/60R16
Fuel tank capacity (gal.) 16.5
EPA city/highway mpg 20/29
Test mileage (mpg) 20.6

Warranties The entire car is covered for 3 years/36,000 miles. Body perforation rust is covered for 6 years/100,000 miles.

Built in Doraville, Ga.

CONSUMER GUIDE®

OLDSMOBILE EIGHTY EIGHT/BUICK LeSABRE

Full-Size

✓ **BEST BUY**

Oldsmobile Eighty Eight LSS

The front-drive Eighty Eight gets a mild facelift and a more powerful optional engine, while the similar LeSabre gets a new standard engine. The Eighty Eight comes in three models—base, LS, and LSS—and the LeSabre in two—Custom and Limited. Standard on all is a 205-horsepower 3.8-liter V-6 (last year LeSabre had a 170-horsepower version of this engine). Optional on the LSS is the 3800 Series II supercharged version with 240 horsepower, 15 more than last year's supercharged engine. Both engines team with a 4-speed automatic transmission and have new 5-year/100,000-mile coolant and 100,000-mile spark plugs. Dual air bags, anti-lock brakes, and new daytime running lights are standard on all models. Styling changes on the Eighty Eight include a twin-nostril grille and new headlights, taillights, and front fenders. The Eighty Eight and LeSabre are built from the same design as the Pontiac Bonneville (see separate report). They share major mechanical features, but each car has different styling and interior features. Though the Chrysler LH sedans have roomier interiors and more contemporary styling, the Eighty Eight and LeSabre are still excellent choices among full-size cars. Oldsmobile's value-pricing is a good deal for consumers because these cars come loaded with safety and convenience features for less money than some Japanese compacts. The 205-horsepower engine has ample low-speed power for strong takeoffs and sufficient reserve power for safe passing. The optional supercharged engine available on the sporty LSS has stronger acceleration, but fuel economy is lower and it requires premium gas. If you're searching for a big sedan that holds lots of people and cargo, put GM's full-size front-drive cars at the top of your shopping list.

Oldsmobile Eighty Eight prices are on page 401.
Buick LeSabre prices are on page 258.

OLDSMOBILE EIGHTY EIGHT LSS

Rating Guide	1	2	3	4	5
Performance					
Acceleration				▓	
Economy		▓			
Driveability				▓	
Ride			▓		
Steering/handling			▓		
Braking				▓	
Noise			▓		
Accommodations					
Driver seating		▓			
Instruments/controls			▓		
Visibility			▓		
Room/comfort			▓		
Entry/exit			▓		
Cargo room			▓		
Workmanship					
Exterior				▓	
Interior			▓		
Value			▓		
Total Points					63

Rating scale 5=Exceptional; 4=Above average; 3=Average; 2=Below average; 1=Poor

Specifications

Body type ....4-door notchback
Wheelbase (in.) 110.8
Overall length (in.) 201.6
Overall width (in.) 74.7
Overall height (in.) 55.7
Curb weight (lbs.) 3455
Seating capacity.........................5
Front head room (in.) 38.8
Max. front leg room (in.) 42.5
Rear head room (in.) 38.3
Min. rear leg room (in.) 38.7
Cargo volume (cu. ft.).............17.5

Engine type......................ohv V-6
Engine size (l/cu. in.).........3.8/231
Horsepower @ rpm ...205 @ 5200
Torque @ rpm ....230 @ 4000
Transmission..................auto/4-sp.
Drive wheels ....front
Brakes, F/R ....disc/drum (ABS)
Tire size 225/60R16
Fuel tank capacity (gal.).........18.0
EPA city/highway mpg 19/30
Test mileage (mpg) 17.2

Warranties The entire car is covered for 3 years/36,000 miles. Body perforation rust is covered for 6 years/100,000 miles.

Built in Flint, Mich.

CONSUMER GUIDE®

PLYMOUTH VOYAGER ✓ BEST BUY
Minivan

Plymouth Voyager SE

Plymouth introduced a redesigned Voyager last spring as an early 1996 model. Only long-wheelbase versions were offered at first; standard-wheelbase models were added in the fall. The Voyager is nearly identical to the Dodge Caravan and Chrysler Town & Country, which differ only in styling details and equipment levels. Among the new features are an optional driver-side sliding door and built-in rollers for the removable bench seats, two minivan firsts. All models have a sliding door on the passenger side and a one-piece rear liftgate. Both the standard-wheelbase (113.3 inches) and long-wheelbase (119.3 inches) versions hold as many as seven people. All models currently have front-wheel drive; all-wheel drive versions will be added during 1996. Dual air bags are standard on all models, and anti-lock brakes are standard on the SE models and optional on the base versions. Voyager's base engine is a new dual-camshaft 150-horsepower 2.4-liter 4-cylinder. Three V-6s are also available, all reruns from last year: a 150-horsepower 3.0-liter; a 158-horsepower 3.3-liter; and a 166-horsepower 3.8-liter. The 4-cylinder and the 3.0-liter V-6 team with a 3-speed automatic, and the two larger V-6s team with a 4-speed automatic. We're highly impressed with Chrysler's 1996 minivans. They are a clear step ahead of the 1995s, which were our Best Buys among minivans last year. Voyager drives more like a car than a van. The steering is precise, and the suspension provides stable cornering with modest body lean. The ride is on the soft side, and the suspension easily irons out smaller rough spots. The new Voyager is roomier and has easier entry/exit because the door sills are 1.4 inches lower. The new driver-side sliding door is well worth its $450 price for the added convenience it provides.

Plymouth Voyager prices are on page 404.

PLYMOUTH VOYAGER SE

Rating Guide	1	2	3	4	5
Performance					
Acceleration			▓		
Economy			▓		
Driveability			▓		
Ride			▓		
Steering/handling			▓		
Braking				▓	
Noise			▓		
Accommodations					
Driver seating			▓		
Instruments/controls			▓		
Visibility			▓		
Room/comfort				▓	
Entry/exit			▓		
Cargo room				▓	
Workmanship					
Exterior			▓		
Interior			▓		
Value			▓		
Total Points					64

Rating scale 5=Exceptional; 4=Above average; 3=Average; 2=Below average; 1=Poor

Specifications

Body type ....4-door van	Engine type......................ohv V-6
Wheelbase (in.) 113.3	Engine size (l/cu. in.)..........3.3/201
Overall length (in.).................186.3	Horsepower @ rpm ...158 @ 4850
Overall width (in.) 75.6	Torque @ rpm ....203 @ 3250
Overall height (in.).................68.5	Transmission..................auto/4-sp.
Curb weight (lbs.) 3528	Drive wheels ....front
Seating capacity............................7	Brakes, F/R..........disc/disc (ABS)
Front head room (in.) 39.8	Tire size 215/65R15
Max. front leg room (in.) 41.2	Fuel tank capacity (gal.)..........20.0
Rear head room (in.) 41.0	EPA city/highway mpg 18/24
Min. rear leg room (in.)...........42.3	Test mileage (mpg) 22.8
Cargo volume (cu. ft.)............146.2	

Warranties The entire vehicle is covered for 3 years/36,000 miles. Body perforation rust is covered for 7 years/100,000 miles.

Built in St. Louis, Mo., and Canada.

PONTIAC BONNEVILLE
Full-Size

✓ **BEST BUY**

Pontiac Bonneville SLE

Revised styling and more power for the available supercharged engine are the key changes to this front-drive sedan. Bonneville shares its basic design with the Buick LeSabre and Oldsmobile Eighty Eight but has different styling. Base SE and performance-oriented SSE models are offered, with major option packages available on both: the Sport Luxury Edition (SLE) for the SE, and the SSEi Supercharger Package for the SSE. Dual air bags and anti-lock brakes are standard on all. The front end has a new fascia, grille, fenders, and headlamps. In back, the taillamps, fascia, and trunk lid are new. New daytime running lights automatically illuminate the headlamps whenever the ignition is on. The standard engine is a 205-horsepower 3.8-liter V-6. Optional with the SLE package and included in the SSEi package is a supercharged version of the V-6 that now has 240 horsepower, 15 more than last year. Both engines have new spark plugs designed to last 100,000 miles and new coolant designed for 5 years/100,000 miles. A 4-speed automatic is the only transmission. Bonneville is much sportier than the similar LeSabre or Eighty Eight but just as functional. There's ample room for four adults, and as many as six in a pinch. The trunk is wide and has a flat floor that extends well forward. We enjoy the strong acceleration of the supercharged engine. However, it uses more gas (around 15-16 mpg in urban driving and 23-24 on the highway) and requires premium. The base engine is strong enough for most needs and uses less gas (about 17-18 mpg in town and 25 or so on the highway)—and less-expensive regular to boot. Though the Chrysler LH sedans are roomier and have more daring styling, Bonneville and its General Motors cousins are high-quality cars that can be tailored to suit a variety of desires.

Pontiac Bonneville prices are on page 407.

PONTIAC BONNEVILLE SLE

Rating Guide	1	2	3	4	5

Performance

Acceleration	4
Economy	2
Driveability	4
Ride	3
Steering/handling	3
Braking	3
Noise	3

Accommodations

Driver seating	4
Instruments/controls	3
Visibility	3
Room/comfort	4
Entry/exit	3
Cargo room	3

Workmanship

Exterior	5
Interior	3

Value

3

Total Points **63**

Rating scale 5=Exceptional; 4=Above average; 3=Average; 2=Below average; 1=Poor

Specifications

Body type	4-door notchback	Engine	Supercharged ohv V-6
Wheelbase (in.)	110.8	Engine size (l/cu. in.)	3.8/231
Overall length (in.)	201.2	Horsepower @ rpm	240 @ 5200
Overall width (in.)	74.5	Torque @ rpm	280 @ 3200
Overall height (in.)	55.7	Transmission	auto/4-sp.
Curb weight (lbs.)	3449	Drive wheels	front
Seating capacity	5	Brakes, F/R	disc/drum (ABS)
Front head room (in.)	39.0	Tire size	225/60R16
Max. front leg room (in.)	43.0	Fuel tank capacity (gal.)	18.0
Rear head room (in.)	38.3	EPA city/highway mpg	17/26
Min. rear leg room (in.)	38.0	Test mileage (mpg)	16.7
Cargo volume (cu. ft.)	18.0		

Warranties The entire car is covered for 3 years/30,000 miles. Body perforation rust is covered for 6 years/100,000 miles.

Built in Flint, Mich.

CONSUMER GUIDE®

PONTIAC GRAND AM
Compact

Pontiac Grand Am SE 2-door

A new base engine, revised styling, and a passenger-side air bag are the major additions for the front-drive Grand Am, which returns as a 2-door coupe and 4-door sedan in base SE and sporty GT price levels. New front and rear fascias, grille, hood, headlamps, taillamps, and other details give the exterior a fresh look. The new passenger-side air bag is contained in a redesigned dashboard. A driver-side air bag already was standard, along with anti-lock brakes. A new dual-camshaft 4-cylinder engine called the 2.4-liter Twin Cam is standard on both models. It is derived from the Quad 4, a 2.3-liter dual-cam 4-cylinder that was standard last year. Horsepower is unchanged at 150, but torque has increased five pounds/feet to 150. A 155-horsepower 3.1-liter V-6 is optional on both models. Both engines have new 100,000-mile spark plugs and coolant designed to last 5 years/100,000 miles. A 5-speed manual transmission is standard with the 4-cylinder. A 4-speed automatic is optional with the 4-cylinder and required with the V-6. Traction control is a new feature included with the automatic transmission. Grand Am is built from the same design as the Buick Skylark and Oldsmobile Achieva but has different styling. In previous years we strongly recommended the V-6 engine over General Motors' noisy 4-cylinder engines. The Twin Cam 4-cylinder is much quieter (though hardly silent) and smoother than the earlier versions, so test drive one before you order the V-6. The 4-cylinder will be more economical and provide acceleration that's nearly as quick. With standard dual air bags and anti-lock brakes, sporty looks, and reasonable prices, Grand Am has some attractions. However, the Grand Am and its siblings are noisier and feel rather crude compared to newer rivals such as the Ford Contour and Mercury Mystique.

Pontiac Grand Am prices are on page 413.

PONTIAC GRAND AM SE

Rating Guide	1	2	3	4	5
Performance					
Acceleration			▓▓▓		
Economy			▓▓▓		
Driveability			▓▓▓		
Ride			▓▓▓		
Steering/handling				▓▓▓	
Braking				▓▓▓	
Noise		▓▓▓			
Accommodations					
Driver seating			▓▓▓		
Instruments/controls			▓▓▓		
Visibility			▓▓▓		
Room/comfort			▓▓▓		
Entry/exit		▓▓▓			
Cargo room			▓▓▓		
Workmanship					
Exterior			▓▓▓		
Interior			▓▓▓		
Value			▓▓▓		
Total Points					57

Rating scale 5=Exceptional; 4=Above average; 3=Average; 2=Below average; 1=Poor

Specifications

Body type	2-door notchback
Wheelbase (in.)	103.4
Overall length (in.)	186.9
Overall width (in.)	68.7
Overall height (in.)	53.2
Curb weight (lbs.)	2881
Seating capacity	5
Front head room (in.)	37.8
Max. front leg room (in.)	43.3
Rear head room (in.)	36.5
Min. rear leg room (in.)	33.9
Cargo volume (cu. ft.)	13.2
Engine type	dohc I-4
Engine size (l/cu. in.)	2.4/146
Horsepower @ rpm	150 @ 6000
Torque @ rpm	150 @ 4400
Transmission	auto/4-sp.
Drive wheels	front
Brakes, F/R	disc/drum (ABS)
Tire size	195/65R15
Fuel tank capacity (gal.)	15.2
EPA city/highway mpg	22/32
Test mileage (mpg)	21.2

Warranties The entire car is covered for 3 years/36,000 miles. Body perforation rust is covered for 6 years/100,000 miles.

Built in Lansing, Mich.

CONSUMER GUIDE®

PONTIAC GRAND PRIX
Mid-Size

RECOMMENDED

Pontiac Grand Prix SE 2-door

The front-drive Grand Prix gets detail changes for its final season before a redesigned model with more curvaceous styling bows late this spring as an early 1997. Grand Prix returns as a 2-door coupe and 4-door sedan in a single SE price series. The previously optional Special Edition Coupe package is now standard on the 2-door. It includes aero body trim, 16-inch alloy wheels, a sport suspension, and monochrome paint. The standard engine is a 160-horsepower 3.1-liter V-6. A dual-camshaft 3.4-liter V-6 is available as part of two major option packages, the GTP package on the coupe and the GT package on the sedan. The 3.4-liter V-6 has 215 horsepower, five more than last year. Dual air bags are standard. Anti-lock brakes are optional (and included in the GT and GTP packages). A 4-speed automatic is the only transmission. Grand Prix shares its basic design with the Buick Regal, Oldsmobile Cutlass Supreme, and Chevrolet Lumina and Monte Carlo, though styling and interior features differ. With a base price of $17,089, the Grand Prix sedan is good deal considering all that's standard: dual air bags, air conditioning, power windows and locks, and a stereo radio. Add anti-lock brakes and a basic option package and the price will climb to about $18,300, which is still below a comparably equipped Ford Taurus. The standard 3.1-liter engine is smooth and delivers enough acceleration to satisfy most needs. The 3.4-liter V-6 is quicker—though not by much—and also louder. The interior has ample room for four adults, though the rear seat is too low and uncomfortable. Though the dashboard has convenient controls that are easy to reach and use, it also has a lot of flimsy plastic that looks and feels cheap. We rate the new Taurus and Mercury Sable and the Honda Accord higher overall, but Grand Prix and the similar General Motors mid-size cars are also good choices.

Pontiac Grand Prix prices are on page 415.

PONTIAC GRAND PRIX SE

Rating Guide	1	2	3	4	5
Performance					
Acceleration			▓▓▓		
Economy		▓▓▓			
Driveability			▓▓▓		
Ride			▓▓▓		
Steering/handling			▓▓▓		
Braking				▓▓▓	
Noise					▓▓▓
Accommodations					
Driver seating				▓▓▓	
Instruments/controls				▓▓▓	
Visibility			▓▓▓		
Room/comfort			▓▓▓		
Entry/exit		▓▓▓			
Cargo room			▓▓▓		
Workmanship					
Exterior			▓▓▓		
Interior			▓▓▓		
Value			▓▓▓		
Total Points					**59**

Rating scale 5=Exceptional; 4=Above average; 3=Average; 2=Below average; 1=Poor

Specifications

Body type	2-door notchback
Wheelbase (in.)	107.5
Overall length (in.)	194.8
Overall width (in.)	71.9
Overall height (in.)	52.8
Curb weight (lbs.)	3275
Seating capacity	5
Front head room (in.)	37.8
Max. front leg room (in.)	42.3
Rear head room (in.)	36.6
Min. rear leg room (in.)	34.8
Cargo volume (cu. ft.)	14.9
Engine type	dohc V-6
Engine size (l/cu. in.)	3.4/207
Horsepower @ rpm	215 @ 5200
Torque @ rpm	215 @ 4000
Transmission	auto/4-sp.
Drive wheels	front
Brakes, F/R	disc/disc (ABS)
Tire size	225/60R16
Fuel tank capacity (gal.)	17.1
EPA city/highway mpg	17/26
Test mileage (mpg)	NA

Warranties The entire car is covered for 3 years/36,000 miles. Body perforation rust is covered for 6 years/100,000 miles.

Built in Kansas City, Mo.

PONTIAC SUNFIRE `RECOMMENDED`
Subcompact

Pontiac Sunfire SE 4-door

Pontiac replaced the Sunbird last year with a new front-drive subcompact called Sunfire. This year Sunfire gets a new dual-camshaft 4-cylinder engine, available traction control, and daytime running lights. Sunfire shares its front-drive chassis and mechanical components with the Chevrolet Cavalier, which has different styling. Two-door coupe, convertible, and 4-door sedan body styles are offered, all with standard dual air bags and anti-lock brakes. The coupe, sedan, and convertible come in SE trim, and the coupe also is available as a sporty GT model. The convertible has a power top. Standard on SE models is a 2.2-liter overhead-valve 4-cylinder with 120 horsepower. Standard on the GT and optional on the SE coupe and convertible is the new 150-horsepower 2.4-liter Twin Cam. It is derived from General Motors' 2.3-liter Quad 4 engine, a similar dual-cam 4-cylinder that has been discontinued. Both engines have new 5-year/100,000-mile coolant and 100,000-mile spark plugs. A 5-speed manual transmission is standard with both engines. A 3-speed automatic is optional with the 2.2-liter engine, and a 4-speed automatic is optional with both engines. Traction control is a new feature included with the 4-speed automatic this year. Daytime running lamps, in which the headlights are illuminated automatically whenever the ignition is on, are now standard. Sunfire takes a somewhat sportier stance than the similar Cavalier but is the same basic car, so it has the same virtues and vices. The base engine is somewhat coarse under hard throttle, but acceleration is adequate. The Twin Cam engine has a lot more zest, and it's smoother and quieter than the base engine. Interior space is adequate for four adults. The Sunfire is a good choice among subcompacts because it comes well equipped at reasonable prices.

Pontiac Sunfire prices are on page 418.

PONTIAC SUNFIRE SE

Rating Guide	1	2	3	4	5
Performance					
Acceleration			▓		
Economy			▓		
Driveability		▓			
Ride			▓		
Steering/handling		▓			
Braking			▓		
Noise		▓			
Accommodations					
Driver seating			▓		
Instruments/controls			▓		
Visibility				▓	
Room/comfort			▓		
Entry/exit			▓		
Cargo room			▓		
Workmanship					
Exterior			▓		
Interior			▓		
Value			▓		
Total Points					58

Rating scale 5=Exceptional; 4=Above average; 3=Average; 2=Below average; 1=Poor

Specifications

Body type	4-door notchback
Wheelbase (in.)	104.1
Overall length (in.)	181.7
Overall width (in.)	67.4
Overall height (in.)	54.8
Curb weight (lbs.)	2723
Seating capacity	5
Front head room (in.)	38.9
Max. front leg room (in.)	42.4
Rear head room (in.)	37.2
Min. rear leg room (in.)	34.4
Cargo volume (cu. ft.)	13.1
Engine type	ohv I-4
Engine size (l/cu. in.)	2.2/133
Horsepower @ rpm	120 @ 5200
Torque @ rpm	130 @ 4000
Transmission	auto/3-sp.
Drive wheels	front
Brakes, F/R	disc/drum (ABS)
Tire size	195/70R14
Fuel tank capacity (gal.)	15.2
EPA city/highway mpg	24/31
Test mileage (mpg)	24.5

Warranties The entire car is covered for 3 years/36,000 miles. Body perforation rust is covered for 6 years/100,000 miles.

Built in Lansing, Mich., and Lordstown, Ohio.

RANGE ROVER 4.0 SE/ 4.6 HSE
Sport-Utility Vehicle

Range Rover 4.6 HSE

Range Rover has a new lineup this year. The Range Rover Classic, whose styling dated to the 1970s, has been dropped. Added to the line is a new flagship model, the 4.6 HSE. Based on the 4.0 SE that was introduced last year, the newcomer has a 4.6-liter V-8 that produces 225 horsepower and 18-inch alloy wheels, features not available on the other model. The 4.0 SE uses a 190 horsepower 4.0-liter V-8. The Range Rovers are imported by Land Rover North America, which also sells the Land Rover Discovery and Defender 90. Both Range Rovers come as 5-door wagons with a 108.1-inch wheelbase. Standard features on both include a 4-speed automatic transmission, permanent 4-wheel drive, traction control, dual air bags, anti-lock brakes, and an electronic suspension. The interiors have leather upholstery and wood trim. Both models can tow trailers weighing up to 7700 pounds. If you ever have to go off-road, the Range Rover models not only are extremely capable but also highly accommodating, with a well-cushioned ride, plush leather seats, premium audio systems, and a lavish array of convenience features. Most sport-utility owners never go off-road, so most of the Range Rovers' capabilities won't be enjoyed by the people who own them. However, the 4.0 SE and 4.6 HSE perform well on-road. Ride quality is excellent. The suspension easily absorbs bumps and ruts and allows only a little bouncing on wavy surfaces. There's noticeable body lean in turns, but these vehicles corner with good grip and reassuring stability. The 4.0 SE's V-8 is smooth, quiet, and provides adequate power. The 4.6 HSE's engine feels a little stronger in all situations. Fuel economy is low with either engine. With base prices of $62,000 for the 4.6 HSE and $55,000 for the 4.0 SE, neither is a bargain.

Range Rover 4.0 SE/4.6 HSE prices are on page 422.

RANGE ROVER 4.0 SE

Rating Guide	1	2	3	4	5
Performance					
Acceleration			▓▓▓		
Economy	▓▓				
Driveability			▓▓▓		
Ride				▓▓▓▓	
Steering/handling			▓▓▓		
Braking				▓▓▓▓	
Noise			▓▓▓		
Accommodations					
Driver seating					▓▓▓▓▓
Instruments/controls				▓▓▓▓	
Visibility			▓▓▓		
Room/comfort			▓▓▓		
Entry/exit		▓▓			
Cargo room			▓▓▓		
Workmanship					
Exterior					▓▓▓▓▓
Interior				▓▓▓▓	
Value			▓▓▓		
Total Points					59

Rating scale 5=Exceptional; 4=Above average; 3=Average; 2=Below average; 1=Poor

Specifications

Body type	5-door wagon
Wheelbase (in.)	108.1
Overall length (in.)	185.6
Overall width (in.)	74.4
Overall height (in.)	71.6
Curb weight (lbs.)	4960
Seating capacity	5
Front head room (in.)	38.1
Max. front leg room (in.)	42.6
Rear head room (in.)	38.2
Min. rear leg room (in.)	36.5
Cargo volume (cu. ft.)	58.0
Engine type	ohv V-8
Engine size (l/cu. in.)	4.0/241
Horsepower @ rpm	190 @ 4750
Torque @ rpm	236 @ 3000
Transmission	auto/4-sp.
Drive wheels	all
Brakes, F/R	disc/disc (ABS)
Tire size	225/65HR16
Fuel tank capacity (gal.)	24.6
EPA city/highway mpg	13/17
Test mileage (mpg)	13.2

Warranties The entire vehicle is covered for 3 years/42,000 miles. Body perforation rust is covered for 6 years/unlimited miles.

Built in England.

CONSUMER GUIDE®

SAAB 900
Premium Sedan

Saab 900 SE 5-door

The turbocharged 4-cylinder engine is available on the 5-door hatchback this year, and a 4-speed automatic transmission will become optional on Turbo models in the spring as the biggest changes for the front-drive 900 line. Previously, the turbocharged 2.0-liter 4-cylinder engine was available only on the 3-door hatchback and convertible—and only with a 5-speed manual transmission. The turbocharged engine produces 185 horsepower. All three body styles come in base S and deluxe SE price levels. A 150-horsepower 2.3-liter 4-cylinder, available with both transmissions, is standard on the S models. The turbocharged 2.0-liter 4-cylinder is standard on the SE models, and a 170-horsepower 2.5-liter V-6 is optional. The V-6 comes only with the automatic transmission. Dual air bags and anti-lock brakes are standard on all 900s. A new feature immobilizes the engine so it can't be started unless the alarm system is deactivated with the standard remote control system. The 900 has generous head and leg room and enormous cargo space for a compact-sized car, but the traditional Saab styling and hatchback design won't appeal to many buyers. Saab loyalists will appreciate having the ignition lock on the floor between the seats and the upright, utilitarian hatchback design. To us, the location of the ignition lock is disorienting and the styling is out of fashion. The base 4-cylinder has adequate power with the manual transmission but feels weak with automatic. The V-6 is strong and smooth and works well with the automatic, while the turbocharged SE models have excellent acceleration. All versions have precise steering and a taut suspension that provides sporty handling. Road noise is moderate, but the upright design results in a lot of wind noise at highway speeds. The 900 deserves a look by those who value function over form.

Saab 900 prices are on page 423.

SAAB 900 SE

Rating Guide	1	2	3	4	5
Performance					
Acceleration			|||||		
Economy		|||||			
Driveability			|||||		
Ride			|||||		
Steering/handling			|||||		
Braking			|||||		
Noise		|||||			
Accommodations					
Driver seating			|||||		
Instruments/controls			|||||		
Visibility		|||||			
Room/comfort			|||||		
Entry/exit			|||||		
Cargo room			|||||		
Workmanship					
Exterior			|||||		
Interior			|||||		
Value			|||||		

Total Points 59

Rating scale 5=Exceptional; 4=Above average; 3=Average; 2=Below average; 1=Poor

Specifications

Body type ....5-door hatchback
Wheelbase (in.) 102.4
Overall length (in.) 182.6
Overall width (in.) 67.4
Overall height (in.) 56.5
Curb weight (lbs.) 2980
Seating capacity 5
Front head room (in.) 39.3
Max. front leg room (in.) 42.3
Rear head room (in.) 37.8
Min. rear leg room (in.) 36.0
Cargo volume (cu. ft.).............49.8

Engine ....Turbocharged dohc I-4
Engine size (l/cu. in.).........2.0/129
Horsepower @ rpm ...185 @ 5500
Torque @ rpm ....194 @ 2100
Transmission ....manual/5-sp.
Drive wheels ....front
Brakes, F/R............disc/disc (ABS)
Tire size....................205/50ZR16
Fuel tank capacity (gal.) 18.0
EPA city/highway mpg 21/28
Test mileage (mpg) ....NA

Warranties The entire car is covered for 4 years/50,000 miles. Body perforation rust is covered for 6 years/unlimited miles.

Built in Sweden and Finland.

CONSUMER GUIDE®

SAAB 9000
Premium Sedan

Saab 9000 CSE

All 9000 models this year come in a 5-door hatchback body style. The CDE model, which was the only 4-door notchback sedan in the 9000 lineup last year, has been dropped. The 9000 CDE also came with a 210-horsepower 3.0-liter V-6 engine. While the 4-door body is gone, the V-6 lives on as an option on the CSE model and is available only with a 4-speed automatic transmission. This year's lineup starts with the 9000 CS, which uses a turbocharged 2.3-liter 4-cylinder with 170 horsepower. Saab calls this a "light-pressure" turbo engine because it develops turbo boost at lower engine manifold pressure and maintains it for a longer duration than usual. There are two other versions of the turbocharged engine. The CSE model comes with a 200-horsepower version, and the high-performance Aero model has 225 horsepower with the 5-speed manual transmission. With the optional 4-speed automatic, the Aero gets the 200-horsepower engine. All models have front-wheel drive, dual air bags, and anti-lock brakes. A new feature immobilizes the engine unless the alarm system is deactivated with the standard remote control system. The V-6 was expected to generate more interest in the 9000 line, but most Saab buyers prefer the turbocharged 4-cylinder engines. Though Saab's V-6 is smooth and quiet, it doesn't have much gusto. Step hard on the throttle and there's steady progress but not much spirit either in acceleration or passing. The turbocharged 4-cylinders have stronger acceleration, and turbo boost arrives pronto when you step on the throttle, but they aren't as quiet or refined as the V-6. All 9000 models have capable handling, but most models ride stiffly because they have high-performance V-rated tires or Z-rated tires. All models have roomy, comfortable interiors and generous cargo space. Saab dealers should be discounting the 9000.

Saab 9000 prices are on page 424.

SAAB 9000 CSE

Rating Guide

	1	2	3	4	5
Performance					
Acceleration					■
Economy	■				
Driveability				■	
Ride			■		
Steering/handling				■	
Braking					■
Noise			■		
Accommodations					
Driver seating		■			
Instruments/controls		■			
Visibility		■			
Room/comfort			■		
Entry/exit			■		
Cargo room					■
Workmanship					
Exterior			■		
Interior		■			
Value		■			
Total Points					**59**

Rating scale 5=Exceptional; 4=Above average; 3=Average; 2=Below average; 1=Poor

Specifications

Body type	5-door hatchback
Wheelbase (in.)	105.2
Overall length (in.)	187.4
Overall width (in.)	70.0
Overall height (in.)	55.9
Curb weight (lbs.)	3110
Seating capacity	5
Front head room (in.)	38.5
Max. front leg room (in.)	41.5
Rear head room (in.)	37.4
Min. rear leg room (in.)	39.0
Cargo volume (cu. ft.)	56.5
Engine type	Turbocharged dohc I-4
Engine size (l/cu. in.)	2.3/140
Horsepower @ rpm	200 @ 5500
Torque @ rpm	238 @ 1800
Transmission	auto/4-sp.
Drive wheels	front
Brakes, F/R	disc/disc (ABS)
Tire size	195/65VR15
Fuel tank capacity (gal.)	17.4
EPA city/highway mpg	17/25
Test mileage (mpg)	NA

Warranties The entire car is covered for 4 years/50,000 miles. Body perforation rust is covered for 6 years/unlimited miles.

Built in Sweden.

SATURN COUPE

Sports Coupe

BUDGET BUY

Saturn SC1

While the Saturn sedan and wagon are restyled this year, the 2-door coupe returns for one more season in the original shape that debuted for 1990. The coupe will be restyled next year. For 1996 the electronic 4-speed automatic transmission has a new adaptive shift program that changes based on how the car is driven. The other big change this year is that traction control, previously included with the optional anti-lock brakes only with the automatic transmission, now also is included when the anti-lock feature is ordered with the 5-speed manual transmission. Dual air bags are standard. Two models are available. The SC1 uses a 100-horsepower 1.9-liter 4-cylinder with a single overhead camshaft. The SC2 has a dual-camshaft 1.9-liter engine with 124 horsepower. Remote keyless entry is a new feature for models with the optional power locks, and the center console bin on the SC2 can now be locked. The SC1 rides on new standard 175/70R14 tires. On the SC2, last year's 195/60R15 tires have been replaced by "touring" tires of the same size. Though the SC1 and SC2 are noisy and unrefined compared to some rival sports coupes, they have compiled impressive records for quality and customer satisfaction. Saturn's no-haggle price policy means that the buying experience is relatively painless—even enjoyable. The SC1 offers most of the virtues of the SC2 at lower cost. The single-cam engine performs well with the smooth-shifting 5-speed manual transmission, but acceleration is tepid with the automatic. The more powerful twin-cam engine in the SC2 performs well with either transmission. Both engines are too noisy at higher speeds, and road noise is prominent as well. Rear seat room is limited, but there's plenty of space in front for tall people.

Saturn Coupe prices are on page 425.

SATURN SC1

Rating Guide	1	2	3	4	5
Performance					
Acceleration			▮		
Economy				▮	
Driveability			▮		
Ride			▮		
Steering/handling			▮		
Braking				▮	
Noise		▮			
Accommodations					
Driver seating				▮	
Instruments/controls				▮	
Visibility			▮		
Room/comfort		▮			
Entry/exit		▮			
Cargo room		▮			
Workmanship					
Exterior			▮		
Interior			▮		
Value				▮	
Total Points					56

Rating scale 5=Exceptional; 4=Above average; 3=Average; 2=Below average; 1=Poor

Specifications

Body type ....2-door notchback
Wheelbase (in.) 99.2
Overall length (in.)................173.2
Overall width (in.) 67.5
Overall height (in.) 50.6
Curb weight (lbs.) 2284
Seating capacity..........................4
Front head room (in.) 37.6
Max. front leg room (in.) 42.6
Rear head room (in.) 35.0
Min. rear leg room (in.) 26.4
Cargo volume (cu. ft.)..............10.9

Engine type ....ohc I-4
Engine size (l/cu. in.)..........1.9/116
Horsepower @ rpm ...100 @ 5000
Torque @ rpm ....114 @ 2400
Transmission ....manual/5-sp.
Drive wheels ....front
Brakes, F/R............disc/disc (ABS)
Tire size 175/70R14
Fuel tank capacity (gal.) 12.8
EPA city/highway mpg 27/37
Test mileage (mpg) 31.9

Warranties The entire car is covered for 3 years/36,000 miles. Body perforation rust is covered for 6 years/100,000 miles.

Built in Spring Hill, Tenn.

CONSUMER GUIDE®

SATURN SEDAN/ WAGON

RECOMMENDED

Subcompact

Saturn SL2

The front-drive Saturn sedan and wagon have a new look for 1996, the first major styling change since these cars debuted for 1990. Dual air bags return as standard, and the sedan and wagon now meet 1997 federal side-impact standards. Front and rear styling on the sedan echo themes from previous years, but the sedan has a more rounded roof that creates more head room for the front and rear seats. Like the previous generation, all vertical panels (doors, fenders, and front and rear facias) are made of plastic-like polymer material that resists dings and rust. The roof, hood, and trunk are made of steel. The wheelbase is unchanged at 102.4 inches, but the new bodies are slightly longer and narrower. Engine choices are unchanged: A 100-horsepower single-camshaft 1.9-liter 4-cylinder is used in the SL and SL1 sedans and the SW1 wagon. A 124-horsepower dual-camshaft version of that engine is used in the SL2 sedan and SW2 wagon. Order the optional anti-lock brakes this year and you'll get traction control whether the car has a 4-speed automatic or 5-speed manual transmission. Last year, traction control was limited to models with the automatic. The automatic transmission has a new adaptive shift program that changes based on how the car is driven. Acceleration is lively in the SL2 and SW2 models with either transmission, and it is adequate in the other models. Engine and road noise have been reduced this year, yet these cars aren't at the head of the subcompact class for refinement. The new Honda Civic and the Toyota Corolla are still quieter. Though the Saturn sedan and wagon aren't perfect, they're pretty good in many key areas. In addition, Saturn leads the subcompact league in customer satisfaction (and ranks just behind Lexus and Infiniti) because of its no-hassle sales policy and excellent customer service.

Saturn Sedan/Wagon prices are on page 426.

SATURN SL2

Rating Guide	1	2	3	4	5
Performance					
Acceleration			▓▓▓		
Economy			▓▓▓		
Driveability			▓▓▓		
Ride			▓▓▓		
Steering/handling			▓▓▓		
Braking				▓▓▓	
Noise		▓▓▓			
Accommodations					
Driver seating			▓▓▓		
Instruments/controls			▓▓▓		
Visibility			▓▓▓		
Room/comfort		▓▓▓			
Entry/exit		▓▓▓			
Cargo room		▓▓▓			
Workmanship					
Exterior			▓▓▓		
Interior			▓▓▓		
Value			▓▓▓		
Total Points					**59**

Rating scale 5=Exceptional; 4=Above average; 3=Average; 2=Below average; 1=Poor

Specifications

Body type ....4-door notchback
Wheelbase (in.) 102.4
Overall length (in.) 176.8
Overall width (in.) 66.7
Overall height (in.) 52.5
Curb weight (lbs.) 2348
Seating capacity 5
Front head room (in.) 39.3
Max. front leg room (in.) 42.5
Rear head room (in.) 38.0
Min. rear leg room (in.) 32.8
Cargo volume (cu. ft.).............11.9

Engine type ....dohc I-4
Engine size (l/cu. in.).........1.9/116
Horsepower @ rpm ...124 @ 5600
Torque @ rpm ....122 @ 4800
Transmission ....auto/4-sp.
Drive wheels ....front
Brakes, F/R...........disc/disc (ABS)
Tire size 185/65R15
Fuel tank capacity (gal.) 12.8
EPA city/highway mpg 24/34
Test mileage (mpg) ....NA

Warranties The entire car is covered for 3 years/36,000 miles. Body perforation rust is covered for 6 years/100,000 miles.

Built in Spring Hill, Tenn.

CONSUMER GUIDE®

SUBARU LEGACY
Compact

Subaru Legacy Outback

Legacy, which was redesigned last year, emphasizes wagons and all-wheel drive (AWD) for 1996. Front-drive Legacys are thinned to just an L 4-door sedan and 5-door wagon. This year's featured attraction is the AWD Outback wagon with a higher roof (to increase head room), a new grille, and a raised suspension that lifts ground clearance to 7.3 inches (vs. 6.1 on other Legacys). Subaru calls it "America's first sport-utility wagon"—as opposed to truck-based sport-utility vehicles. Models include L and LS sedans and wagons and a budget-priced Brighton wagon, all with AWD and a 135-horsepower 2.2-liter 4-cylinder engine with "flat," or horizontally opposed, cylinders. The top-shelf AWD LSi sedan and wagon get a new 2.5-liter flat 4-cylinder engine with 155-horsepower and a standard 4-speed automatic transmission. The same powertrain is used on the new AWD 2.5GT sedan and wagon, which also have a firmer suspension, front and rear spoilers, and other sporty touches. Outback's base powertrain is the 2.2-liter engine and a 5-speed manual transmission. The new 2.5-liter engine and automatic are optional. Dual air bags are standard on all Legacys. Anti-lock brakes are standard on the LSi and GT and optional on other AWD models. Legacy's 2.2-liter engine is adequate for most circumstances, but it throbs and feels strained in hard acceleration and in hilly country. The new 2.5-liter engine is quieter and smoother than the 2.2-liter, and it has better pull at low speeds and stronger passing power. The Outback wagon, with its higher ground clearance, is a good substitute for a sport-utility vehicle. It can crawl over most of the same terrain as an SUV while providing all the comfort and driving ease of a passenger car. If you desire AWD but don't want a truck-based SUV, take a look at the Legacy.

Subaru Legacy prices are on page 428.

SUBARU LEGACY OUTBACK

Rating Guide	1	2	3	4	5
Performance					
Acceleration			3		
Economy			3		
Driveability			3		
Ride			3		
Steering/handling			3		
Braking				4	
Noise			3		
Accommodations					
Driver seating			3		
Instruments/controls				4	
Visibility				4	
Room/comfort			3		
Entry/exit			3		
Cargo room				4	
Workmanship					
Exterior			3		
Interior			3		
Value			3		
Total Points					**60**

Rating scale 5=Exceptional; 4=Above average; 3=Average; 2=Below average; 1=Poor

Specifications

Body type	5-door wagon
Wheelbase (in.)	103.5
Overall length (in.)	183.9
Overall width (in.)	67.5
Overall height (in.)	62.2
Curb weight (lbs.)	3230
Seating capacity	5
Front head room (in.)	39.5
Max. front leg room (in.)	43.3
Rear head room (in.)	38.8
Min. rear leg room (in.)	34.8
Cargo volume (cu. ft.)	73.6
Engine type	ohc flat-4
Engine size (l/cu. in.)	2.5/150
Horsepower @ rpm	155 @ 5600
Torque @ rpm	155 @ 2800
Transmission	auto/4-sp.
Drive wheels	all
Brakes, F/R	disc/disc (ABS)
Tire size	205/70R15
Fuel tank capacity (gal.)	15.9
EPA city/highway mpg	20/26
Test mileage (mpg)	NA

Warranties The entire car is covered for 3 years/36,000 miles. Body perforation rust is covered for 5 years/unlimited miles.

Built in Lafayette, Ind.

SUZUKI ESTEEM/SWIFT
Subcompact

Suzuki Esteem GLX

Air conditioning is standard this year on all three versions of the Esteem, a subcompact 4-door sedan introduced last spring. The front-drive Esteem rides a 97.6-inch wheelbase, 4.5 inches longer than the Suzuki Swift, a 3-door hatchback that is similar to the Geo Metro (see separate report). The Esteem is nearly 16 inches longer overall than the Swift. The three versions of the Esteem are base GL, upscale GLX, and top-of-the-line GLX with anti-lock brakes and cruise control. Esteem has standard dual air bags and a 98-horsepower 1.6-liter 4-cylinder engine. A 5-speed manual transmission is standard and a 4-speed automatic is optional. Power steering is standard across the board. The Swift comes in a single price level with standard dual air bags and a 70-horsepower 1.3-liter 4-cylinder engine. A 5-speed manual transmission is standard and a 3-speed automatic is optional. Anti-lock brakes also are optional. The Esteem is more substantial than the Swift or Metro, yet the body panels feel tinny. Noise levels are lower as well, but there's still lots of road noise and tire thumping, and a loud coarse growl from the engine. The suspension doesn't absorb bumps well, so the ride is rough on bumpy pavement. A GLX we tested with the automatic transmission had adequate acceleration, but the transmission shifted harshly. We averaged 24.2 mpg, which is unimpressive for a small sedan. The Esteem has ample head room for the front seats and adequate room for two people in back. The Esteem GLX is the most desirable model because it has anti-lock brakes, but it is more than $15,000. At that price there are several good alternatives, including the new Honda Civic, the Geo Prizm, and the Dodge/Plymouth Neon.

Suzuki Esteem prices are on page 429.
Suzuki Swift prices are on page 430.

SUZUKI ESTEEM GLX

Rating Guide	1	2	3	4	5
Performance					
Acceleration			▮		
Economy				▮	
Driveability			▮		
Ride			▮		
Steering/handling			▮		
Braking				▮	
Noise				▮	
Accommodations					
Driver seating				▮	
Instruments/controls				▮	
Visibility			▮		
Room/comfort			▮		
Entry/exit			▮		
Cargo room			▮		
Workmanship					
Exterior				▮	
Interior				▮	
Value				▮	
Total Points					**55**

Rating scale 5=Exceptional; 4=Above average; 3=Average; 2=Below average; 1=Poor

Specifications

Body type	4-door notchback
Wheelbase (in.)	97.6
Overall length (in.)	165.2
Overall width (in.)	65.7
Overall height (in.)	53.9
Curb weight (lbs.)	2183
Seating capacity	5
Front head room (in.)	39.1
Max. front leg room (in.)	42.3
Rear head room (in.)	37.2
Min. rear leg room (in.)	34.1
Cargo volume (cu. ft.)	12.0
Engine type	ohc I-4
Engine size (l/cu. in.)	1.6/97
Horsepower @ rpm	98 @ 6000
Torque @ rpm	94 @ 3200
Transmission	auto/4-sp.
Drive wheels	front
Brakes, F/R	disc/drum (ABS)
Tire size	175/70R13
Fuel tank capacity (gal.)	13.5
EPA city/highway mpg	27/34
Test mileage (mpg)	24.2

Warranties The entire car is covered for 3 years/36,000 miles. Body perforation rust is covered for 3 years/unlimited miles.

Built in Japan.

CONSUMER GUIDE®

SUZUKI SIDEKICK
Sport-Utility Vehicle

Suzuki Sidekick Sport

Dual air bags are a new standard feature on all versions of the Sidekick this year and 4-wheel anti-lock brakes are a new option. Sidekick comes as a 2-door convertible and larger 5-door wagon, and there is a new Sport version of the wagon. The Sport model has a 120-horsepower 1.8-liter 4-cylinder with dual overhead camshafts, while the other models use a 95-horsepower 1.6-liter 4-cylinder with a single overhead camshaft. The Sport also has a longer nose, fender flares, 2-tone paint, 16-inch wheels and tires (versus 14-inch on the others), and a wider stance. The other 5-door Sidekicks and the convertible (which is 15 inches shorter than the wagon) return with the new air bags and a redesigned dashboard. Four-wheel anti-lock brakes that work in both 2- and 4-wheel drive are a new option for all models. Last year all models came with a standard anti-lock feature for the rear wheels that worked only when the vehicle was in 2WD. The rear anti-lock feature has been dropped. The Sidekick shares its design and major features with the Geo Tracker (see separate report), which is sold by Chevrolet dealers. The Sport model's stronger engine produces a healthy performance boost, though 120 horsepower doesn't make it a hot rod. The 95-horsepower 1.6-liter engine struggles to provide any zip with the automatic transmission, but it's adequate with the 5-speed manual. On all versions there's lots of engine and road noise, plus abundant wind noise at highway speeds. There's plenty of head room and adequate rear leg room in the 5-door, but the narrow interior lacks shoulder room. The 5-door is much more practical than the convertible for daily use, though the more-expensive versions are priced in the same range as the Jeep Cherokee, a much more substantial vehicle.

Suzuki Sidekick prices are on page 429.

SUZUKI SIDEKICK SPORT

Rating Guide

	1	2	3	4	5
Performance					
Acceleration			▬		
Economy			▬		
Driveability			▬		
Ride			▬		
Steering/handling			▬		
Braking				▬	
Noise			▬		
Accommodations					
Driver seating			▬		
Instruments/controls			▬		
Visibility			▬		
Room/comfort			▬		
Entry/exit			▬		
Cargo room			▬		
Workmanship					
Exterior			▬		
Interior			▬		
Value			▬		

Total Points..**53**

Rating scale 5=Exceptional; 4=Above average; 3=Average; 2=Below average; 1=Poor

Specifications

Body type	5-door wagon
Wheelbase (in.)	97.6
Overall length (in.)	162.4
Overall width (in.)	66.7
Overall height (in.)	66.3
Curb weight (lbs.)	2917
Seating capacity	4
Front head room (in.)	40.6
Max. front leg room (in.)	42.1
Rear head room (in.)	38.6
Min. rear leg room (in.)	32.7
Cargo volume (cu. ft.)	45.0
Engine type	dohc I-4
Engine size (l/cu. in.)	1.8/112
Horsepower @ rpm	120 @ 6500
Torque @ rpm	114 @ 3500
Transmission	auto/4-sp.
Drive wheels	rear/all
Brakes, F/R	disc/drum (ABS)
Tire size	215/65R16
Fuel tank capacity (gal.)	18.5
EPA city/highway mpg	21/24
Test mileage (mpg)	NA

Warranties The entire car is covered for 3 years/36,000 miles. Body perforation rust is covered for 3 years/unlimited miles.

Built in Canada and Japan.

CONSUMER GUIDE®

TOYOTA AVALON
Full-Size

RECOMMENDED

Toyota Avalon XLS

Avalon, Toyota's answer to big American family sedans, returns virtually unchanged for its second season. Avalon was designed strictly for the U.S., so it's built only at Toyota's Georgetown, Kentucky, plant where the compact Camry is built. Avalon uses the same basic front-drive platform but has a 4-inch longer wheelbase and different styling. Camry also lends its 3.0-liter V-6 engine to the Avalon, where it makes 192 horsepower instead of 188, and 4-speed automatic transmission. The base XL model comes with dual air bags, air conditioning, power windows and door locks, and a choice of dual bucket seats or a 3-place front bench that gives the Avalon 6-passenger capacity. The XLS adds standard anti-lock brakes (they're optional on the XL), alloy wheels, automatic climate control, a remote keyless entry system, and other features. The XLS also is available with front buckets or a 3-place bench seat that provides 6-passenger capacity. Avalon is conservatively styled but pleasant to drive and well made. There's a negligible weight difference between the Avalon and the V-6 Camry, so there's no discernible difference in acceleration or passing ability. The interior has ample room for four adults. Six can fit, though everyone will be cramped because the interior isn't wide enough to easily accommodate that many. Leg room is generous in the rear seat, and the rear doors open wide for easy entry and exit. The trunk is wide and deep and has a long, flat floor, and a low liftover makes it easier to load and unload. Avalon's base price is $23,418 and once you add a few options the price can easily top $25,000—more than most comparably equipped domestic full-size cars. A loaded XLS is more than $30,000. If the price isn't too high for your budget, this is a competent, roomy sedan with little excitement but few faults.

Toyota Avalon prices are on page 431.

TOYOTA AVALON XLS

Rating Guide	1	2	3	4	5
Performance					
Acceleration				▓	
Economy			▓		
Driveability				▓	
Ride				▓	
Steering/handling			▓		
Braking				▓	
Noise				▓	
Accommodations					
Driver seating			▓		
Instruments/controls			▓		
Visibility			▓		
Room/comfort				▓	
Entry/exit				▓	
Cargo room				▓	
Workmanship					
Exterior				▓	
Interior				▓	
Value				▓	
Total Points					**62**

Rating scale 5=Exceptional; 4=Above average; 3=Average; 2=Below average; 1=Poor

Specifications

Body type	4-door notchback
Wheelbase (in.)	107.1
Overall length (in.)	190.2
Overall width (in.)	70.3
Overall height (in.)	56.1
Curb weight (lbs.)	3263
Seating capacity	6
Front head room (in.)	39.1
Max. front leg room (in.)	44.1
Rear head room (in.)	37.8
Min. rear leg room (in.)	38.3
Cargo volume (cu. ft.)	15.4
Engine type	dohc V-6
Engine size (l/cu. in.)	3.0/180
Horsepower @ rpm	192 @ 5200
Torque @ rpm	210 @ 4400
Transmission	auto/4-sp.
Drive wheels	front
Brakes, F/R	disc/disc (ABS)
Tire size	205/65HR15
Fuel tank capacity (gal.)	18.5
EPA city/highway mpg	20/29
Test mileage (mpg)	19.4

Warranties The entire car is covered for 3 years/36,000 miles. Major powertrain components are covered for 5 years/60,000 miles. Body perforation rust is covered for 5 years/unlimited miles.

Built in Georgetown, Ky.

CONSUMER GUIDE®

TOYOTA CAMRY
Compact

✓ **BEST BUY**

Toyota Camry XLE

This popular front-drive family car now offers optional leather upholstery on the LE, the highest-volume Camry model, and a power driver's seat is a new option for the station wagon. Camry comes in 4-door sedan, 2-door coupe, and 5-door wagon body styles. The 4-door comes in base DX, LE, luxury XLE, and sporty SE trim. Also back are DX, LE, and SE coupes and the LE 5-door wagon, which seats seven with the optional third seat. A 188-horsepower 3.0-liter V-6 is standard on the SE and optional on the LE and XLE models. The base 2.2-liter 4-cylinder has 125 horsepower. Both engines team with a standard 4-speed automatic transmission except on the DX coupe and sedan, where a 5-speed manual is standard and the automatic is optional. Dual air bags are standard on all Camrys. Anti-lock brakes are standard on the XLE and optional on the others. The current Camry debuted as a 1992 model, so this should be its last year. A redesigned Camry is expected next summer as an early 1997 model. Camry's basic design is also used for the Lexus ES 300, a "near-luxury" sedan with different styling and more standard features. There's a lot of the ES 300 in the Camry, which sets the standard for refinement among mid-size and compact family cars. It's smoother, quieter, and built with higher quality than some luxury sedans that cost thousands more. The 4-cylinder engine gives the Camry sedan adequate acceleration and passing power with the automatic transmission. The V-6 is much quicker but uses more gas and requires premium. Though the 103.1-inch wheelbase is smaller than some compact sedans', Camry has more interior room than some mid-size cars. Cars this good don't come cheaply. The LE sedan starts at $20,168, though strong competition means that Toyota dealers should be discounting Camry.

Toyota Camry prices are on page 432.

TOYOTA CAMRY XLE

Rating Guide	1	2	3	4	5
Performance					
Acceleration			▮▮▮		
Economy			▮▮▮		
Driveability				▮▮▮	
Ride				▮▮▮	
Steering/handling			▮▮▮		
Braking				▮▮▮	
Noise			▮▮▮		
Accommodations					
Driver seating				▮▮▮	
Instruments/controls				▮▮▮	
Visibility				▮▮▮	
Room/comfort			▮▮▮		
Entry/exit				▮▮▮	
Cargo room			▮▮▮		
Workmanship					
Exterior				▮▮▮	
Interior				▮▮▮	
Value				▮▮▮	
Total Points					63

Rating scale 5=Exceptional; 4=Above average; 3=Average; 2=Below average; 1=Poor

Specifications

Body type	4-door notchback
Wheelbase (in.)	103.1
Overall length (in.)	187.8
Overall width (in.)	69.7
Overall height (in.)	55.1
Curb weight (lbs.)	2932
Seating capacity	5
Front head room (in.)	38.4
Max. front leg room (in.)	43.5
Rear head room (in.)	37.1
Min. rear leg room (in.)	35.0
Cargo volume (cu. ft.)	14.9
Engine type	dohc I-4
Engine size (l/cu. in.)	2.2/132
Horsepower @ rpm	125 @ 5400
Torque @ rpm	145 @ 4400
Transmission	auto/4-sp.
Drive wheels	front
Brakes, F/R	disc/disc (ABS)
Tire size	195/70HR14
Fuel tank capacity (gal.)	18.5
EPA city/highway mpg	21/27
Test mileage (mpg)	20.9

Warranties The entire car is covered for 3 years/36,000 miles. Major powertrain components are covered for 5 years/60,000 miles. Body perforation rust is covered for 5 years/unlimited miles.

Built in Georgetown, Ky., and Japan.

CONSUMER GUIDE®

TOYOTA CELICA
Sports Coupe

Toyota Celica GT 3-door

This front-drive sports coupe returns with minor changes and the same lineup as last year. This year's offerings include 2-door notchback and 3-door Liftback (hatchback) coupes in ST and upscale GT guise and a GT convertible. All sport subtle styling changes to the nose and tail (you may need to look twice), and all models have additional sound insulation. Celica has a choice of two 4-cylinder engines, both with dual overhead camshafts. The ST uses a 1.8-liter engine with 105 horsepower. The GT has a 2.2-liter with 130 horsepower. A 5-speed manual transmission is standard and a 4-speed automatic is optional on all models. Dual air bags are standard across the board, and anti-lock brakes are optional on models with cruise control. The convertible has a power soft top with a glass rear window and electric defroster. There are distinct differences between the ST and GT. The 1.8-liter engine in the ST is smooth and fairly quiet except when worked hard. However, it's weak on low-speed torque, so it can't pull with any gusto with the optional automatic transmission. The GT's 2.2-liter packs a pretty good punch with the automatic, but it's too loud in hard acceleration and never sounds refined. All models handle well. The firmer suspension included in the optional Sport Package delivers a little extra cornering precision in exchange for a stiffer, choppier ride. Celica's interior is typical of small coupes, with little room in the rear seat for adults and, with the optional sunroof, marginal head room for 6-footers. The dashboard design is modern and convenient. Though the Celica GT performs well, it's more expensive than V-6 rivals like the Ford Probe and Mazda MX-6. Toyota's reputation for quality and high resale value are two compensating factors.

Toyota Celica prices are on page 434.

TOYOTA CELICA GT

Rating Guide	1	2	3	4	5
Performance					
Acceleration				▓▓▓▓	
Economy			▓▓▓		
Driveability				▓▓▓▓	
Ride			▓▓▓		
Steering/handling				▓▓▓▓	
Braking					▓▓▓▓▓
Noise		▓▓			
Accommodations					
Driver seating				▓▓▓▓	
Instruments/controls				▓▓▓▓	
Visibility			▓▓▓		
Room/comfort		▓▓			
Entry/exit		▓▓			
Cargo room			▓▓▓		
Workmanship					
Exterior				▓▓▓▓	
Interior				▓▓▓▓	
Value				▓▓▓▓	
Total Points					55

Rating scale 5=Exceptional; 4=Above average; 3=Average; 2=Below average; 1=Poor

Specifications

Body type ....3-door hatchback	Engine type ....dohc I-4
Wheelbase (in.) 99.9	Engine size (l/cu. in.).........2.2/132
Overall length (in.)................174.0	Horsepower @ rpm ...130 @ 5400
Overall width (in.) 68.9	Torque @ rpm ....145 @ 4400
Overall height (in.) 50.8	Transmission ....manual/5-sp.
Curb weight (lbs.) 2560	Drive wheels ....front
Seating capacity..........................4	Brakes, F/R............disc/disc (ABS)
Front head room (in.) 34.3	Tire size.....................205/55VR15
Max. front leg room (in.) 44.2	Fuel tank capacity (gal.) 15.9
Rear head room (in.) 29.2	EPA city/highway mpg 22/29
Min. rear leg room (in.)..........26.6	Test mileage (mpg) 25.7
Cargo volume (cu. ft.)............16.2	

Warranties The entire car is covered for 3 years/36,000 miles. Major powertrain components are covered for 5 years/60,000 miles. Body perforation rust is covered for 5 years/unlimited miles.

Built in Japan.

CONSUMER GUIDE®

TOYOTA COROLLA
Subcompact

✓ **BEST BUY**

Toyota Corolla DX 4-door

Last year's highest-priced Corolla, the LE sedan, has been dropped because it was too expensive in the hotly contested subcompact segment. A loaded 1995 LE could exceed $19,000. That leaves base and DX sedans and a 5-door DX wagon to carry on with minor changes, the most obvious one a smaller grille. A built-in child safety seat that folds out of the right side of the rear backrest is a new option for the DX sedan. Corolla's front-drive design is also used for the Geo Prizm, a sedan sold through Chevrolet dealers (see separate report). Prizm uses the same engines and major mechanical components but has different styling. The base Corolla's 1.6-liter 4-cylinder engine has been revised for lower emissions, and horsepower drops by five to 100, while torque increases by five pounds/feet to 105. The DX models use a 1.8-liter 4-cylinder with 105 horsepower. A 5-speed manual transmission is standard across the board. A 3-speed automatic is optional on the base sedan and a 4-speed automatic is optional on the DX. All Corollas have standard dual air-bags and optional anti-lock brakes. Corolla sets the standard for refinement among small sedans. It's quieter and rides more comfortably than most rivals, and it has commendable assembly quality. Acceleration is adequate with either engine, and Corolla's suspension provides a stable highway ride and absorbs bumps better than some larger cars. There's more interior room than in most rivals. The rear seat, however, is tight for two adults. Corolla is more expensive than most subcompact rivals. A DX sedan with the Value Package and anti-lock brakes runs about $17,600— about the same as some larger compact sedans. Reliability and high resale value will compensate somewhat for the high initial cost. The best alternatives are the similar Prizm and the new Honda Civic.

Toyota Corolla prices are on page 435.

TOYOTA COROLLA DX

Rating Guide	1	2	3	4	5
Performance					
Acceleration			▓▓▓		
Economy				▓▓▓	
Driveability			▓▓▓		
Ride				▓▓▓	
Steering/handling			▓▓▓		
Braking					▓▓▓
Noise				▓▓▓	
Accommodations					
Driver seating				▓▓▓	
Instruments/controls				▓▓▓	
Visibility				▓▓▓	
Room/comfort			▓▓▓		
Entry/exit			▓▓▓		
Cargo room			▓▓▓		
Workmanship					
Exterior				▓▓▓	
Interior				▓▓▓	
Value				▓▓▓	

Total Points..**60**

Rating scale 5=Exceptional; 4=Above average; 3=Average; 2=Below average; 1=Poor

Specifications

Body type	4-door notchback
Wheelbase (in.)	97.0
Overall length (in.)	172.0
Overall width (in.)	66.3
Overall height (in.)	54.3
Curb weight (lbs.)	2447
Seating capacity	5
Front head room (in.)	38.8
Max. front leg room (in.)	42.4
Rear head room (in.)	37.1
Min. rear leg room (in.)	33.0
Cargo volume (cu. ft.)	12.7
Engine type	dohc I-4
Engine size (l/cu. in.)	1.8/110
Horsepower @ rpm	105 @ 5200
Torque @ rpm	117 @ 2800
Transmission	auto/4-sp.
Drive wheels	front
Brakes, F/R	disc/disc (ABS)
Tire size	185/65R14
Fuel tank capacity (gal.)	13.2
EPA city/highway mpg	27/34
Test mileage (mpg)	30.1

Warranties The entire car is covered for 3 years/36,000 miles. Major powertrain components are covered for 5 years/60,000 miles. Body perforation rust is covered for 5 years/unlimited miles.

Built in Fremont, Calif., Canada, and Japan.

CONSUMER GUIDE®

TOYOTA LAND CRUISER/ LEXUS LX 450
Sport-Utility Vehicle

Toyota Land Cruiser

Toyota's full-size sport-utility vehicle was updated last spring with a new dashboard, dual air bags, standard anti-lock brakes (formerly optional), and a restyled front end with a new grille and bumper. A more luxurious version of this vehicle will arrive this spring as the Lexus LX 450. Lexus, Toyota's luxury division, wants to cash in on growing demand for expensive sport-utilities. The LX 450 will have a different grille, headlamps, wheels, and exterior trim than the Land Cruiser, along with standard leather upholstery and wood interior trim. LX 450 prices weren't announced in time for this issue. Land Cruiser comes as a 5-door wagon with a 212-horsepower 4.5-liter 6-cylinder engine (the same engine will be used in the LX 450). A 4-speed automatic transmission and permanent 4-wheel-drive system are standard. Seats for five are standard: dual front buckets and a 3-place split bench that double-folds for extra cargo space. A 3-person third seat is available for 8-passenger capacity. It's also split 50/50 but folds up against the sides of the interior. Land Cruiser is an enormously capable vehicle that has bountiful passenger and cargo room and excellent assembly quality. Other strong points include a reputation for ruggedness and durability. The permanent 4WD system provides great traction without any input from the driver. The suspension provides a firm, almost stiff, ride that becomes tiring on long drives. You might also get tired of climbing in and out of this vehicle, which sits high off the ground. Despite the good points, you can still get most or all of what Land Cruiser offers for less money on a Ford Explorer or Jeep Grand Cherokee.

Toyota Land Cruiser prices are on page 437.

TOYOTA LAND CRUISER

Rating Guide	1	2	3	4	5
Performance					
Acceleration			3		
Economy		2			
Driveability				4	
Ride			3		
Steering/handling			3		
Braking				4	
Noise			3		
Accommodations					
Driver seating				4	
Instruments/controls				4	
Visibility			3		
Room/comfort				4	
Entry/exit			3		
Cargo room				4	
Workmanship					
Exterior				4	
Interior				4	
Value			3		
Total Points					**58**

Rating scale 5=Exceptional; 4=Above average; 3=Average; 2=Below average; 1=Poor

Specifications

Body type ....5-door wagon
Wheelbase (in.) 112.2
Overall length (in.) 189.8
Overall width (in.) 76.0
Overall height (in.) 73.2
Curb weight (lbs.) 4834
Seating capacity...........................8
Front head room (in.) 40.3
Max. front leg room (in.) 42.2
Rear head room (in.) 40.0
Min. rear leg room (in.) 33.6
Cargo volume (cu. ft.)..............90.9

Engine type ....dohc I-6
Engine size (l/cu. in.)..........4.5/275
Horsepower @ rpm ...212 @ 4600
Torque @ rpm ....275 @ 3200
Transmission.................auto/4-sp.
Drive wheels ....all
Brakes, F/R..........disc/disc (ABS)
Tire size 275/70R16
Fuel tank capacity (gal.).........25.1
EPA city/highway mpg 13/15
Test mileage (mpg) 13.1

Warranties The entire vehicle is covered for 3 years/36,000 miles. Major powertrain components are covered for 5 years/60,000 miles. Body perforation rust is covered for 5 years/unlimited miles.

Built in Japan.

TOYOTA PASEO
Sports Coupe

Toyota Paseo

Paseo, Toyota's entry-level sports coupe, is based on the front-drive Tercel subcompact. Because Tercel was updated last year, it was predictable that Paseo would follow this year with similar changes. The big surprise is that Toyota cut base prices by $1000 this year. Styling changes include a smoother nose, larger rear side windows, and a more shapely tail. Interior dimensions are unchanged, but the dashboard is a new design, like the Tercel's, with a passenger-side air bag (Paseo already had a driver-side air bag). Last year's automatic shoulder belt and manual lap belt for the front passenger are history. Instead, there is now a manual 3-point seatbelt, same as for the driver. The new Paseo also meets federal 1997 side-impact standards. The only engine is 1.5-liter 4-cylinder engine with dual overhead camshafts and 93 horsepower, which was used last year. Transmission choices are a standard 5-speed manual and optional 4-speed automatic. Anti-lock brakes are optional. With its lower price compared to the Toyota Celica sports coupe, Paseo is designed to appeal to younger buyers with smaller budgets. This year's Paseo is much like last year's, though the 1996 model feels more solid and is a little quieter. There's still a lot of road noise in this car, however, and the engine is noisy even in moderate acceleration. The 1.5-liter engine produces adequate acceleration with either transmission but feels somewhat livelier with the 5-speed manual. Like most sports coupes, Paseo is a "2+2"—which means the back seat is too small except for toddlers or groceries. Paseo isn't exciting to drive and its styling doesn't stir much emotion. Toyota's reputation for durability and high resale value are two good reasons to keep it on your shopping list.

Toyota Paseo prices are on page 438.

TOYOTA PASEO

Rating Guide	1	2	3	4	5
Performance					
Acceleration			▬▬		
Economy				▬▬	
Driveability				▬▬	
Ride			▬▬		
Steering/handling			▬▬		
Braking			▬▬		
Noise		▬▬			
Accommodations					
Driver seating				▬▬	
Instruments/controls				▬▬	
Visibility			▬▬		
Room/comfort	▬▬				
Entry/exit		▬▬			
Cargo room		▬▬			
Workmanship					
Exterior				▬▬	
Interior				▬▬	
Value				▬▬	
Total Points					**53**

Rating scale 5=Exceptional; 4=Above average; 3=Average; 2=Below average; 1=Poor

Specifications

Body type ....2-door notchback
Wheelbase (in.) 93.7
Overall length (in.) 163.6
Overall width (in.) 65.4
Overall height (in.) 51.0
Curb weight (lbs.) 2025
Seating capacity 4
Front head room (in.) 37.8
Max. front leg room (in.) 41.2
Rear head room (in.) 32.0
Min. rear leg room (in.) 30.0
Cargo volume (cu. ft.) 7.5

Engine type ....dohc I-4
Engine size (l/cu. in.) 1.5/90
Horsepower @ rpm .....93 @ 5400
Torque @ rpm ....100 @ 4400
Transmission ....manual/5-sp.
Drive wheels ....front
Brakes, F/R...................disc/drum
Tire size 185/60R14
Fuel tank capacity (gal.) 11.9
EPA city/highway mpg 30/35
Test mileage (mpg) ....NA

Warranties The entire car is covered for 3 years/36,000 miles. Major powertrain components are covered for 5 years/60,000 miles. Body perforation rust is covered for 5 years/unlimited miles.

Built in Japan.

TOYOTA PREVIA
Minivan

Toyota Previa LE

Toyota's egg-shaped minivan is now sold only with the supercharged engine that was a $500 option last year. The naturally-aspirated 2.4-liter 4-cylinder, which produced 138 horsepower, is gone. All models now come with the 161-horsepower supercharged version. With that, Previa model choices shrink by half to four, divided among DX and upscale LE models with either rear-wheel drive or All-Trac permanent all-wheel drive. The only transmission is a 4-speed automatic with a steering-column shift lever. Dual air bags are standard and anti-lock brakes are optional on all models. All Previas have standard 7-passenger seating in a 2-2-3 layout. The rear seat is a 50/50 split bench that can't be removed but folds up against the sides of the interior for extra cargo space. Previa has one sliding door, on the passenger side, and a rear liftgate. Toyota is planning a new U.S.-built minivan that will be based on the front-drive Camry and introduced in 1997 or 1998. Making the supercharged engine standard doesn't move the Previa into the fast lane among minivans, but it does make this minivan more responsive, particularly in passing situations. Previa has a roomy interior with adult-size room for all seats, plus adequate cargo space at the rear with all seats in place. Folding the rear seat against the sides of the vehicle is a clever alternative to removable seats, though that blocks the driver's view over the right shoulder. Previa's base prices range from $24,318 to $32,198, much higher than the rivals from Chrysler Corporation and Ford, which have comparable safety features and stronger V-6 engines. In addition, Previa's standard rear-wheel drive is harder to sell than front-wheel drive in many parts of the country.

Toyota Previa prices are on page 439.

TOYOTA PREVIA LE

Rating Guide	1	2	3	4	5

Performance

Acceleration	3
Economy	2
Driveability	4
Ride	3
Steering/handling	3
Braking	3
Noise	3

Accommodations

Driver seating	3
Instruments/controls	3
Visibility	3
Room/comfort	4
Entry/exit	4
Cargo room	5

Workmanship

Exterior	3
Interior	3

Value

Value	3

Total Points..57

Rating scale 5=Exceptional; 4=Above average; 3=Average; 2=Below average; 1=Poor

Specifications

Body type	4-door van
Wheelbase (in.)	112.8
Overall length (in.)	187.0
Overall width (in.)	70.8
Overall height (in.)	68.7
Curb weight (lbs.)	3755
Seating capacity	7
Front head room (in.)	39.4
Max. front leg room (in.)	40.1
Rear head room (in.)	38.9
Min. rear leg room (in.)	36.6
Cargo volume (cu. ft.)	152.3
Engine	Supercharged dohc I-4
Engine size (l/cu. in.)	2.4/149
Horsepower @ rpm	161 @ 5000
Torque @ rpm	201 @ 3600
Transmission	auto/4-sp.
Drive wheels	rear
Brakes, F/R	disc/disc (ABS)
Tire size	215/65R15
Fuel tank capacity (gal.)	19.8
EPA city/highway mpg	18/22
Test mileage (mpg)	NA

Warranties The entire vehicle is covered for 3 years/36,000 miles. Major powertrain components are covered for 5 years/60,000 miles. Body perforation rust is covered for 5 years/unlimited miles.

Built In Japan.

CONSUMER GUIDE®

TOYOTA RAV4
Sport-Utility Vehicle

Toyota RAV4 3-door

Toyota's new mini sport-utility vehicle is coming to the U.S. in early 1996. Called RAV4 (Recreational Active Vehicle with 4WD), it's sized to compete with the Geo Tracker/Suzuki Sidekick and Kia Sportage. The 4-wheel-drive models will have a permanently engaged system and the 2-wheel-drive models will have front-wheel drive instead of the more typical rear-wheel drive. Prices will be announced closer to the on-sale date. Toyota hints base prices will be in the $13,000-$20,000 range. Toyota claims the RAV4 combines "passenger-car elements with features of a light off-road vehicle." It is based on the Toyota Celica platform and stands apart from its rivals with 4-wheel independent suspension and unibody construction (versus body-on-frame). Three- and 5-door versions will be available. The 5-door, designed especially for the U.S., rides an 8.3-inch longer wheelbase and is 16.1 inches longer overall. All models use a 2.0-liter 4-cylinder engine with 120 horsepower. A 5-speed manual transmission is standard and a 4-speed automatic is optional on the 5-door. The RAV4 has dual air bags, side-impact door beams, power steering, and alloy wheels with 215/70R16 tires. Anti-lock brakes are optional. The RAV4 has stable, car-like cornering and feels solid on rough roads. The RAV4 feels quicker than the Tracker/Sidekick or Sportage, though acceleration borders on sluggish with automatic. The 5-door has about the same passenger and cargo space as the comparable Sportage and Tracker/Sidekick, but less rear leg room than the Sportage. The 3-door is even tighter in the rear. Overall, the RAV4 strikes us as the best small sport-utility vehicle yet. With Toyota's reputation for reliability and durability, if you're in the market for a small SUV, you just can't ignore this one.

Toyota RAV4 standard equipment is on page 440.

TOYOTA RAV4 (Preliminary)

Rating Guide	1	2	3	4	5

Performance

Acceleration	▮▮▮ (3)
Economy	▮▮▮ (3)
Driveability	▮▮▮ (3)
Ride	▮▮▮ (3)
Steering/handling	▮▮▮▮ (4)
Braking	▮▮▮▮ (4)
Noise	▮▮▮ (3)

Accommodations

Driver seating	▮▮▮▮ (4)
Instruments/controls	▮▮▮▮ (4)
Visibility	▮▮▮▮ (4)
Room/comfort	▮▮ (2)
Entry/exit	▮▮▮ (3)
Cargo room	▮▮▮ (3)

Workmanship

Exterior	▮▮▮▮ (4)
Interior	▮▮▮▮ (4)

Value

▮▮▮ (3)

Total Points..54

Rating scale 5=Exceptional; 4=Above average; 3=Average; 2=Below average; 1=Poor

Specifications

Body type	3-door wagon
Wheelbase (in.)	86.6
Overall length (in.)	145.9
Overall width (in.)	66.7
Overall height (in.)	65.2
Curb weight (lbs.)	2634
Seating capacity	4
Front head room (in.)	40.0
Max. front leg room (in.)	40.4
Rear head room (in.)	38.6
Min. rear leg room (in.)	30.1
Cargo volume (cu. ft.)	34.7
Engine type	dohc I-4
Engine size (l/cu. in.)	2.0/122
Horsepower @ rpm	120 @ 5400
Torque @ rpm	125 @ 4600
Transmission	manual/5-sp.
Drive wheels	front/all
Brakes, F/R	disc/drum (ABS)
Tire size	215/70R16
Fuel tank capacity (gal.)	15.3
EPA city/highway mpg	22/27
Test mileage (mpg)	NA

Warranties The entire vehicle is covered for 3 years/36,000 miles. Major powertrain components are covered for 5 years/60,000 miles. Body perforation rust is covered for 5 years/unlimited miles.

Built in Japan.

CONSUMER GUIDE®

TOYOTA TERCEL
Subcompact

Toyota Tercel DX 2-door

There's little news in the 1996 edition of Toyota's entry-level subcompact. That's partly because the front-drive Tercel was revamped last year with crisper styling, more power, optional anti-lock brakes, standard dual air bags, and modifications to meet 1997 side-impact regulations. Three models continue this year. The base 2-door now can be ordered with power steering like the upscale 2- and 4-door DX models. Cloth seat trim also is a new option on the price-leader 2-door, which comes with standard vinyl. Among the DX models, the optional Power Package (which includes power windows and door locks) is now available on the 2-door as well as the 4-door. Tercel returns with a 1.5-liter 4-cylinder engine with dual overhead camshafts and 93 horsepower. The base 2-door has a standard 4-speed manual transmission and an optional 3-speed automatic. On the DX models, a 5-speed manual is standard and a 4-speed automatic is optional. Anti-lock brakes are optional on all models. Though it's a well-made, thrifty subcompact that should be reliable, Tercel doesn't rate as highly overall as the class leaders—the Honda Civic, Geo Prizm, Dodge and Plymouth Neon, and Toyota Corolla. The engine produces adequate acceleration but is noisy, and the automatic transmissions are rather slow to downshift to deliver highway passing power. The suspension allows lots of bouncing on wavy roads and the ride becomes choppy on rough surfaces. In addition, there's abundant road noise. Adults have ample room in front, but the rear seat is tight for anyone over 5-foot-10. Tercel isn't as plush or substantial as the Corolla and some other subcompacts, but it's a good choice as basic transportation for those on a tight budget.

Toyota Tercel prices are on page 441.

TOYOTA TERCEL DX

Rating Guide	1	2	3	4	5
Performance					
Acceleration			███		
Economy				███	
Driveability			███		
Ride			███		
Steering/handling			███		
Braking			███		
Noise		███			
Accommodations					
Driver seating			███		
Instruments/controls			███		
Visibility				███	
Room/comfort			███▍		
Entry/exit			███		
Cargo room			███		
Workmanship					
Exterior				███	
Interior				███	
Value				███	
Total Points					54

Rating scale 5=Exceptional; 4=Above average; 3=Average; 2=Below average; 1=Poor

Specifications

Body type	2-door notchback
Wheelbase (in.)	93.7
Overall length (in.)	161.8
Overall width (in.)	64.8
Overall height (in.)	53.2
Curb weight (lbs.)	1950
Seating capacity	5
Front head room (in.)	38.6
Max. front leg room (in.)	41.2
Rear head room (in.)	36.5
Min. rear leg room (in.)	31.9
Cargo volume (cu. ft.)	9.3
Engine type	dohc I-4
Engine size (l/cu. in.)	1.5/90
Horsepower @ rpm	93 @ 5400
Torque @ rpm	100 @ 4400
Transmission	auto/4-sp.
Drive wheels	front
Brakes, F/R	disc/drum
Tire size	155/80SR13
Fuel tank capacity (gal.)	11.9
EPA city/highway mpg	30/39
Test mileage (mpg)	29.9

Warranties The entire car is covered for 3 years/36,000 miles. Major powertrain components are covered for 5 years/60,000 miles. Body perforation rust is covered for 5 years/unlimited miles.

Built in Japan.

CONSUMER GUIDE®

TOYOTA 4RUNNER
Sport-Utility Vehicle

Toyota 4Runner Limited

Scheduled to go on sale in March, the 1996 4Runner shares its powertrains and some chassis elements with the Tacoma pickup, but it has its own front styling, wheelbase, rear suspension, interior design with dual air bags, and standard 4-wheel anti-lock brakes and side-impact door beams. Last year's 4Runner had neither air bags nor door beams, and a 4-wheel anti-lock feature was optional only on V-6 models. A 2-inch longer wheelbase allows wider doors and adds three inches of rear leg room. The 4Runner comes as a 5-door wagon with 2- or 4-wheel drive in base and sportier SR5 price levels, plus a top-line 4WD Limited. The base engine is the Tacoma's 2.7-liter 4-cylinder, rated at 150 horsepower. Standard on the Limited and optional on the other models is Tacoma's 3.4-liter V-6, rated at 183 horsepower. All 4x4s except the Limited use Toyota's part-time 4WDemand system that's not for use on dry pavement. Exclusive to the Limited is Toyota's electronic One-Touch Hi-4 feature, basically a button on the transfer-case lever for shifting between 2WD and 4WD High. All 4Runners have seats for five (two front buckets and a 3-place rear bench that folds for extra cargo room). A removable 2-passenger third seat is optional on the SR5 and Limited. The new 4Runner is much roomier, with a big gain in rear leg room. However, the interior step-in height is still steep compared to the Ford Explorer and Chevrolet Blazer, and cargo space still lags behind that of most other compact SUVs. With less weight and stronger engines, the new 4Runner charges up hills that winded the old one. The new suspension delivers a comfortable ride on almost any surface and more stable cornering. The steering is car-like and precise. Though the price was the big unknown when this was written, the new 4Runner merits a close look.

Toyota 4Runner standard equipment is on page 442.

TOYOTA 4RUNNER (Preliminary)

Rating Guide	1	2	3	4	5
Performance					
Acceleration			▓		
Economy		▓			
Driveability			▓		
Ride			▓		
Steering/handling			▓		
Braking			▓		
Noise			▓		
Accommodations					
Driver seating			▓		
Instruments/controls			▓		
Visibility			▓		
Room/comfort			▓		
Entry/exit		▓			
Cargo room			▓		
Workmanship					
Exterior			▓		
Interior			▓		
Value			▓		

Total Points..**58**

Rating scale 5=Exceptional; 4=Above average; 3=Average; 2=Below average; 1=Poor

Specifications

Body type ....5-door wagon	Engine type......................dohc V-6
Wheelbase (in.) 105.3	Engine size (l/cu. in.).........3.4/207
Overall length (in.)................178.7	Horsepower @ rpm ...183 @ 4800
Overall width (in.) 66.5	Torque @ rpm ....217 @ 3600
Overall height (in.) 68.7	Transmission.................auto/4-sp.
Curb weight (lbs.) 3880	Drive wheels........................rear/all
Seating capacity..........................5	Brakes, F/R ....disc/drum (ABS)
Front head room (in.) 39.2	Tire size 265/70R16
Max. front leg room (in.) 43.1	Fuel tank capacity (gal.) 18.5
Rear head room (in.) 38.7	EPA city/highway mpg ....NA
Min. rear leg room (in.) 34.9	Test mileage (mpg) ....NA
Cargo volume (cu. ft.).............79.7	

Warranties The entire vehicle is covered for 3 years/36,000 miles. Major powertrain components are covered for 5 years/60,000 miles. Body perforation rust is covered for 5 years/unlimited miles.

Built in Japan.

CONSUMER GUIDE®

VOLKSWAGEN JETTA/GOLF
Subcompact

Volkswagen Golf GL

Volkswagen's new Turbo Direct Injection (TDI) diesel engine will be available on the Jetta sedan and Golf hatchback this year. VW claims the TDI engine, a 90-horsepower 1.9-liter 4-cylinder, has the performance of a gasoline engine and extraordinary fuel economy. Initially, it will team only with a 5-speed manual transmission. Among other changes for the front-drive Jetta and Golf, a dashboard-mounted glovebox, absent since it was displaced by a passenger-side air bag during the 1994 model year, returns on all models. A new dashboard switch for the central locking system can lock or unlock all doors and the trunk. Jetta comes as a 4-door sedan in GL and GLS price levels with a 115-horsepower 2.0-liter gas 4-cylinder engine. The Jetta GLX has a 172-horsepower 2.8-liter V-6. In the Golf lineup, the GL 5-door hatchback and new GTI 3-door hatchback use the 2.0-liter 4-cylinder. The GTI, called the Golf Sport last year, is not to be confused with the GTI VR6, which also comes as a 3-door hatchback but is powered by the V-6 engine. Leather seats are a new option for the GTI VR6. Dual air bags are standard on all models. Anti-lock brakes are standard on the GLX, GTI VR6, and GTI and optional on the others. The Jetta and Golf are conservatively styled but fun to drive and competitively priced against other subcompact and compact cars. In addition, Volkswagen provides a 10-year powertrain warranty that makes these cars good choices for the long haul. Four-cylinder models have adequate acceleration from a standing start and pretty good passing power with either transmission. Both body styles have adequate room for four people and ample cargo space. Volkswagen has been offering big discounts and subsidized leases that make these cars more attractive.

Volkswagen Jetta/Golf prices are on page 442.

VOLKSWAGEN GOLF GL

Rating Guide	1	2	3	4	5

Performance

Acceleration	3
Economy	3
Driveability	3
Ride	3
Steering/handling	4
Braking	4
Noise	3

Accommodations

Driver seating	3
Instruments/controls	3
Visibility	3
Room/comfort	3
Entry/exit	3
Cargo room	4

Workmanship

Exterior	4
Interior	4

Value — 4

Total Points..57

Rating scale 5=Exceptional; 4=Above average; 3=Average; 2=Below average; 1=Poor

Specifications

Body type ....5-door hatchback
Wheelbase (in.) 97.4
Overall length (in.) 160.5
Overall width (in.) 66.7
Overall height (in.) 56.2
Curb weight (lbs.) 2577
Seating capacity 5
Front head room (in.) 39.2
Max. front leg room (in.) 42.3
Rear head room (in.) 37.3
Min. rear leg room (in.) 31.6
Cargo volume (cu. ft.) 16.9

Engine type ....ohc I-4
Engine size (l/cu. in.) 2.0/121
Horsepower @ rpm ...115 @ 5400
Torque @ rpm ....122 @ 3200
Transmission ....manual/5-sp.
Drive wheels ....front
Brakes, F/R ....disc/drum (ABS)
Tire size 185/60HR14
Fuel tank capacity (gal.) 14.5
EPA city/highway mpg 23/30
Test mileage (mpg) 27.2

Warranties The entire car is covered for 2 years/24,000 miles. Major powertrain components are covered for 10 years/100,000 miles. Body perforation rust is covered for 6 years/unlimited miles.

Built in Mexico.

CONSUMER GUIDE®

VOLKSWAGEN PASSAT
Compact

Volkswagen Passat GLX 4-door

A GLS sedan with a 2.0-liter gas 4-cylinder engine was added to the Passat line late in the 1995 model year. For 1996 Volkswagen will offer its 1.9-liter Turbo Direct Injection (TDI) diesel engine in both the Passat sedan and wagon. The TDI engine is a turbocharged 1.9-liter 4-cylinder with 90 horsepower, and Volkswagen says it has the performance of a gasoline engine and the fuel economy of a diesel. Initially it will be available only with a 5-speed manual transmission. The front-drive Passat, which was revamped last year, comes in five models for 1996: the GLS sedan with the 115-horsepower 4-cylinder; the diesel-powered TDI sedan and wagon; and the GLX sedan and wagon, which use a 2.8-liter gas V-6. A 5-speed manual transmission is standard on the gas models and a 4-speed automatic is optional. Dual air bags are standard on all Passats. Anti-lock brakes are standard on the GLX models and optional on the GLS and TDI models. New standard features include daytime running lights (the headlights automatically illuminate at reduced intensity whenever the ignition is on). Passat's V-6 engine isn't as strong or smooth as those in the Toyota Camry or Nissan Maxima, but it delivers more than adequate power over a broad range of speeds. The 4-cylinder GLS is slower in both acceleration and highway passing but still adequate. We haven't driven the new TDI engine, so we can't comment on its performance. The interior is exceptionally roomy, especially in back, where there's ample leg room and enough head room for 6-footers. The sedan's trunk has a flat floor and a bumper-height opening, while the wagon has a flat, wide cargo area that provides generous luggage space. Passat is a roomy, sporty, well-equipped car that should be available at discounts.

Volkswagen Passat prices are on page 443.

VOLKSWAGEN PASSAT GLX

Rating Guide	1	2	3	4	5

Performance

Acceleration	3
Economy	2
Driveability	3
Ride	3
Steering/handling	3
Braking	5
Noise	3

Accommodations

Driver seating	4
Instruments/controls	3
Visibility	3
Room/comfort	3
Entry/exit	3
Cargo room	3

Workmanship

Exterior	3
Interior	3
Value	3

Total Points 61

Rating scale 5=Exceptional; 4=Above average; 3=Average; 2=Below average; 1=Poor

Specifications

Body type	4-door notchback	Engine type	ohc V-6
Wheelbase (in.)	103.3	Engine size (l/cu. in.)	2.8/170
Overall length (in.)	180.0	Horsepower @ rpm	172 @ 5800
Overall width (in.)	67.5	Torque @ rpm	177 @ 4200
Overall height (in.)	56.4	Transmission	auto/4-sp.
Curb weight (lbs.)	3140	Drive wheels	front
Seating capacity	5	Brakes, F/R	disc/disc (ABS)
Front head room (in.)	39.3	Tire size	215/50HR15
Max. front leg room (in.)	41.5	Fuel tank capacity (gal.)	18.5
Rear head room (in.)	36.6	EPA city/highway mpg	18/25
Min. rear leg room (in.)	37.0	Test mileage (mpg)	NA
Cargo volume (cu. ft.)	14.4		

Warranties The entire car is covered for 2 years/24,000 miles. Major powertrain components are covered for 10 years/100,000 miles. Body perforation rust is covered for 6 years/unlimited miles.

Built in Germany.

VOLVO 850
Premium Sedan

Volvo 850 Platinum Limited Edition wagon

New Platinum Limited Edition versions of the sedan and wagon are the major additions this year for the front-drive 850, which last year became the first car sold in North America with standard side air bags. Volvo introduced sporty versions of the sedan and wagon last spring called the T-5R. Only about 1000 units were imported, and the T-5R, along with its 240-horsepower turbocharged 5-cylinder engine, is gone. In its place is the Limited Edition, which has a 222-horsepower turbocharged engine, 16-inch alloy wheels, leather seats, and "pearl white platinum" paint. Next spring Volvo will add a high-performance model similar to the T-5R, though it hasn't released the name or details. The 850 sedan and wagon also come in base and GLT price levels with a 168-horsepower 2.4-liter 5-cylinder engine and in a Turbo price level with the 222-horsepower 2.3-liter 5-cylinder engine. The base and GLT models come with a standard 5-speed manual or optional 4-speed automatic transmission. Turbocharged models come only with the automatic. In addition to the side air bags, which are mounted on the outboard sides of the front seatbacks, all models have dual front air bags and anti-lock brakes. Volvo scored a coup with the side air bags last year, which are a welcome addition because they give occupants even better protection from injuries. In other areas, the 850 also has more going for it than some rivals in the same price range. It looks much like Volvo's larger 960 models, but its trimmer size gives it better maneuverability and more athletic cornering ability. There's plenty of head and leg room for four adults in the 850. The sedan's spacious trunk has a flat floor and a bumper-height opening, and the wagon has a long, flat cargo area when the rear seat is folded down.

Volvo 850 prices are on page 444.

VOLVO 850 TURBO

Rating Guide	1	2	3	4	5
Performance					
Acceleration				▊	
Economy		▊			
Driveability				▊	
Ride			▊		
Steering/handling				▊	
Braking				▊	
Noise			▊		
Accommodations					
Driver seating				▊	
Instruments/controls				▊	
Visibility			▊		
Room/comfort			▊		
Entry/exit			▊		
Cargo room				▊	
Workmanship					
Exterior			▊		
Interior			▊		
Value			▊		

Total Points 61

Rating scale 5=Exceptional; 4=Above average; 3=Average; 2=Below average; 1=Poor

Specifications

Body type .... 5-door wagon	Engine type .... Turbo dohc I-5
Wheelbase (in.) 104.9	Engine size (l/cu. in.) 2.3/141
Overall length (in.) 185.4	Horsepower @ rpm ... 222 @ 5200
Overall width (in.) 69.3	Torque @ rpm .... 221 @ 2100
Overall height (in.) 56.9	Transmission .... auto/4-sp.
Curb weight (lbs.) 3342	Drive wheels .... front
Seating capacity 5	Brakes, F/R .... disc/disc (ABS)
Front head room (in.) 39.1	Tire size 205/50ZR16
Max. front leg room (in.) 41.4	Fuel tank capacity (gal.) 19.3
Rear head room (in.) 37.8	EPA city/highway mpg 19/26
Min. rear leg room (in.) 35.3	Test mileage (mpg) 22.5
Cargo volume (cu. ft.) 67.0	

Warranties The entire car is covered for 4 years/50,000 miles. Body perforation rust is covered for 5 years/unlimited miles.

Built in Belgium.

CONSUMER GUIDE®

VOLVO 960
Premium Sedan

Volvo 960 4-door

Volvo's rear-drive 900 Series, which listed six models last year, has just two for 1996. The naturally aspirated and turbocharged 4-cylinder versions have been dropped, leaving only the 6-cylinder 960 sedan and station wagon. Both have side air bags as a new standard feature. Volvo introduced the side air bags last year on its front-drive 850 line. The side air bags, which are mounted in the outboard sides of the front seatbacks, deploy in a side impact to protect the chest area of front-seat occupants. Dual front air bags and anti-lock brakes also are standard. The 960 sedan and wagon are powered by a 181-horsepower 2.9-liter inline 6-cylinder engine that comes with a 4-speed automatic transmission. A new remote entry system standard on both models unlocks the driver's door with one tap of the remote transmitter and unlocks the other doors and the trunk with a second tap. On paper the 960's 6-cylinder engine doesn't look like it can cut much mustard. On the road, it performs better than we expected. We timed a 1995 sedan at a brisk 8.6 seconds to 60 mph. The 960 sedan rides on stiff 16-inch tires rated for speeds up to 149 mph that make the ride harsh and lumpy except on glass-smooth pavement and generate lots of road noise. These tires improve the sedan's cornering ability a little, but the harsher ride makes the wagon a clear choice for comfort seekers. The wagon has softer 15-inch tires rated for speeds up to 129 mph. Both body styles have a roomy, functional interior that can hold four adults comfortably and five with a little squeezing. We rate the 960 highly in most areas, but there are good alternatives in the same price range with similar features—except for the new side air bags, which are a commendable addition.

Volvo 960 prices are on page 446.

VOLVO 960

Rating Guide	1	2	3	4	5
Performance					
Acceleration				▮	
Economy		▮			
Driveability			▮		
Ride				▮	
Steering/handling			▮		
Braking			▮		
Noise			▮		
Accommodations					
Driver seating			▮		
Instruments/controls			▮		
Visibility			▮		
Room/comfort			▮		
Entry/exit			▮		
Cargo room			▮		
Workmanship					
Exterior			▮		
Interior			▮		
Value		▮			

Total Points 60

Rating scale 5=Exceptional; 4=Above average; 3=Average; 2=Below average; 1=Poor

Specifications

Body type ....4-door notchback
Wheelbase (in.) 109.1
Overall length (in.) 191.8
Overall width (in.) 68.9
Overall height (in.) 55.5
Curb weight (lbs.) 3461
Seating capacity..........................5
Front head room (in.) 38.6
Max. front leg room (in.) 41.0
Rear head room (in.) 37.1
Min. rear leg room (in.) 34.7
Cargo volume (cu. ft.).............16.6

Engine type ....dohc I-6
Engine size (l/cu. in.) 2.9/178
Horsepower @ rpm ...181 @ 5200
Torque @ rpm ....199 @ 4100
Transmission.................auto/4-sp.
Drive wheels ....rear
Brakes, F/R..........disc/disc (ABS)
Tire size....................205/55VR16
Fuel tank capacity (gal.) 19.8
EPA city/highway mpg 18/26
Test mileage (mpg) 17.8

Warranties The entire car is covered for 4 years/50,000 miles. Body perforation rust is covered for 5 years/unlimited miles.

Built in Sweden and Canada.

CONSUMER GUIDE®

ACURA

PRICES

ACURA

Acura Integra

	Retail Price	Dealer Invoice	Fair Price
RS 3-door hatchback, 5-speed	$16100	14144	14944
RS 3-door hatchback, automatic	16900	14847	15647
LS 3-door hatchback, 5-speed	18850	16560	17360
LS 3-door hatchback, automatic	19650	17263	18063
Special Edition 3-door hatchback, 5-speed	20600	18097	18897
Special Edition 3-door hatchback, automatic	21400	18800	19600
GS-R 3-door hatchback, 5-speed	21100	18536	19336
GS-R 3-door hatchback w/leather, 5-speed	21900	19239	20039
RS 4-door notchback, 5-speed	16860	14811	15611
RS 4-door notchback, automatic	17660	15514	16314
LS 4-door notchback, 5-speed	19650	17263	18063
LS 4-door notchback, automatic	20450	17965	18765
Special Edition 4-door notchback, 5-speed	21150	18581	19381
Special Edition 4-door notchback, automatic	21950	19283	20083
GS-R 4-door notchback, 5-speed	21400	18800	19600
GS-R 4-door notchback w/leather, 5-speed	22200	19503	20303
Destination charge	420	420	420

Standard Equipment:

RS: 1.8-liter DOHC 4-cylinder engine, 5-speed manual or 4-speed automatic transmission, 4-wheel disc brakes, driver- and passenger-side air bags, variable-assist power steering, cloth reclining front bucket seats with driver-side lumbar support adjustment, center console with armrest, 50/50 split folding rear seat (hatchback), one-piece folding rear seat (notchback), power windows and mirrors, power door locks (notchback), AM/FM/cassette player with four speakers, power antenna, tinted glass, remote fuel door and decklid/hatch releases, fog lamps, rear defogger, rear wiper/washer (hatchback), tachometer, coolant temperature gauge, tilt steering column, intermittent wipers, door pockets, cargo cover (hatchback), 195/60HR14 tires, wheel covers. **LS** adds: anti-lock brakes, air conditioning, power door locks (hatchback), power moonroof, cruise control, map lights (hatchback), Michelin 195/60HR14 all-season tires. **Special Edition** adds:

ACURA

leather upholstery, rear spoiler (hatchback), wood-pattern console trim (notchback), color-keyed bodyside moldings, Michelin 195/55VR15 tires, alloy wheels. **GS-R** adds to LS: 1.8-liter DOHC VTEC engine, rear spoiler (hatchback), AM/FM/cassette with six speakers, map lights (notchback), Michelin 195/55VR15 all-season tires, alloy wheels.

Options are available as dealer-installed accessories.

Acura SLX
Prices not available at time of publication.

Standard Equipment:
3.2-liter V-6 engine, 4-speed automatic transmission, anti-lock brakes, driver- and passenger-side air bags, variable-assist power steering, air conditioning, cruise control, cloth reclining front bucket seats with folding armrests, 60/40 split folding rear seats, AM/FM/cassette with six speakers, power antenna, tilt steering column, power door locks and windows, power heated mirrors, rear defogger, tachometer, coolant temperature and oil pressure gauges, voltmeter, trip odometer, digital clock, tinted windows, leather-wrapped steering wheel, tilt steering column, theft deterrent system, center storage console with cup holders, cornering lights, rear storage compartment, cargo lights, map lights, front and rear stabilizer bars, skid plates, rear step bumper, rear air deflector, mud guards, 245/70R16 all season tires, 5-spoke alloy wheels, full-size spare tire. **Premium Pkg.** adds: heated power front seats, leather upholstery, power moonroof, power fold-in outside mirrors, simulated woodgrain interior trim, integrated fog lamps, 6-spoke alloy wheels.

Acura TL Sedan	Retail Price	Dealer Invoice	Fair Price
2.5TL 4-door notchback	$27900	$24228	—
2.5TL 4-door notchback w/Premium Pkg.	29950	26009	—
3.2TL 4-door notchback	32950	28614	—
3.2TL 4-door notchback w/Premium Pkg.	35500	30828	—
Destination charge	420	420	420

Fair price not available at time of publication.

Standard Equipment:
2.5: 2.5-liter 5-cylinder engine, 4-speed automatic transmission, driver- and passenger-side air bags, anti-lock 4-wheel disc brakes, variable-assist power steering, automatic climate control, cloth reclining front bucket seats, 8-way power driver's seat with lumbar support adjuster, console with armrest, rear seat center armrest, tilt steering column, cruise control, tinted glass, rear defogger, power windows and door locks, AM/FM/cassette/CD player, theft-deterrent system, leather-wrapped steering wheel, power mirrors, map lights, visor mirrors, color-keyed bumpers and bodyside mold-

Prices are accurate at time of publication; subject to manufacturer's change.

ACURA • AUDI

ings, fog lights, 205/60HR15 tires, alloy wheels. **Premium Pkg.** adds: power moonroof, leather upholstery, leather door-trim panels. **3.2** deletes power moonroof and adds: 3.2-liter V-6 engine, remote keyless entry, 205/65VR15 tires. **Premium Pkg.** adds: traction control, power moonroof, heated front seats, 4-way power passenger seat, heated mirrors.

Options are available as dealer-installed accessories.

AUDI

Audi A4	Retail Price	Dealer Invoice	Fair Price
4-door notchback	$26500	$23300	—
Destination charge	475	475	475

Fair price not available at time of publication.

Standard Equipment:

2.8-liter V-6 engine, 5-speed manual transmission, driver- and passenger-side air bags, anti-lock 4-wheel disc brakes, Electronic Differential Lock, engine and transmission oil cooler, automatic air conditioning, power steering, leather-wrapped steering wheel, AM/FM/cassette, cloth reclining front seats with height adjustment, 60/40 split folding rear seat, power driver's seat, front and rear fold-down armrests, power windows and door locks, cruise control, tilt/telescopic steering wheel, tinted glass, headlight washers, alarm system, fog lights, rear defogger, analog clock, center storage console, remote decklid and fuel door releases, heated power mirrors, exterior temperature gauge, front seatback map pockets, intermittent wipers, tachometer, oil pressure, oil temperature, and coolant temperature gauges, trip odometer, reading lights, lighted visor mirrors, polished walnut trim, color-keyed body-side moldings, floormats, 205/55HR16 tires, alloy wheels.

Optional Equipment:

5-speed automatic transmission	930	880	—
Quattro all-wheel drive system	1500	1500	1500
All-Weather Package	450	392	—
Includes heated front door locks, heated front seats, heated windshield washer nozzles.			
Audi/Bose 8-speaker sound system	640	557	—
Leather upholstery	1280	1114	—
Leatherette upholstery	NC	NC	—
Remote keyless entry	190	165	—
Power sunroof	990	861	—
Leather-wrapped steering wheel	150	131	—
Expandable ski/storage sack	160	139	—

AUDI

Audi A6/S6

	Retail Price	Dealer Invoice	Fair Price
A6 4-door notchback	$32300	$28417	—
A6 5-door wagon	34000	29896	—
1995 S6 4-door notchback	46400	40613	—
1995 S6 5-door wagon	47940	41953	—
Destination charge	475	475	475

Fair price not available at time of publication.

Standard Equipment:

A6: 2.8-liter V-6 engine, 4-speed automatic transmission, anti-lock 4-wheel disc brakes w/Electronic Differential Lock, driver- and passenger-side air bags, automatic climate control, speed-sensitive power steering, tilt and telescoping steering column, engine and transmission oil cooler, velour reclining front bucket seats with height and lumbar adjustments, 8-way power driver's seat, front folding storage armrest, rear folding armrest with ski sack, center storage console with cup holders, exterior temperature gauge, tachometer, oil pressure gauge, coolant temperature gauge, trip odometer, Active Auto Check System, power windows and door locks, cruise control, heated power mirrors, power sunroof, remote fuel door and decklid releases, AM/FM/cassette with diversity antenna, seatback pockets, leather-wrapped steering wheel, reading lamps, lighted visor mirrors, anti-theft alarm, tinted glass, rear defogger, intermittent wipers, analog clock, front and rear fog lights, floormats, burled walnut trim, color-keyed bumpers and bodyside moldings, 195/65HR15 all-season tires, alloy wheels. **S6** deletes 4-speed automatic transmission, engine and transmission oil cooler; and adds: 2.2-liter turbocharged DOHC 5-cylinder engine, 5-speed manual transmission, Quattro all-wheel drive system, voice-activated cellular telephone, voltmeter, leather upholstery, heated front and rear seats, power passenger's seat, 4-way memory driver's seat, Audi/Bose audio system, leather-wrapped manual shift knob, remote keyless entry, power glass moonroof, heated windshield washer nozzles, headlight washers, fender flares, 225/50ZR16 tires. **Wagons** delete diversity antenna and remote decklid release, and add: 60/40 split folding seat, 2-place rear child seat, roof-mounted antenna, rear wiper/washer, retractable rear window sunshade, luggage rack, cargo area cover and net.

Optional Equipment:

Quattro all-wheel drive system, A6	1550	1550	1550
Comfort and Convenience Pkg., A6	1030	896	—

Power front passenger's seat, memory driver's seat and mirrors, remote keyless entry, power glass moonroof.

All-Weather Pkg., A6	500	435	—

Heated front seats, heated windshield washer nozzles, heated front door locks (NA Comfort and Convenience Pkg.), headlight washers.

Leather seats, A6	1500	1305	—

Prices are accurate at time of publication; subject to manufacturer's change.

AUDI • BMW

	Retail Price	Dealer Invoice	Fair Price
Audi/Bose audio system, A6	$640	$557	—
Pearlescent metallic paint	550	497	—
6-spoke alloy wheels, S6	NC	NC	NC

Includes 215/60VR15 all-season tires.

BMW

1995 BMW 5-Series	Retail Price	Dealer Invoice	Fair Price
525i 4-door notchback	$36500	$30810	—
525i Touring 5-door wagon	38900	32820	—
530i 4-door notchback	43400	36515	—
530i Touring 5-door wagon	48600	41015	—
540i 4-door notchback, automatic	49000	41260	—
540i 4-door notchback, 6-speed	49900	42055	—
Destination charge	570	570	570
Gas Guzzler Tax,			
530i with manual transmission	1000	1000	1000
540i with manual transmission	1300	1300	1300

Fair price not available at time of publication.

Standard Equipment:

525i: 2.5-liter DOHC 6-cylinder engine, 5-speed manual transmission, variable-assist power steering, anti-lock 4-wheel disc brakes, driver- and passenger-side air bags, cruise control, air conditioning with dual climate controls, 10-way power front seats with power lumbar support adjusters, leather-wrapped steering wheel, folding center armrests, rear center storage armrest, anti-theft AM/FM stereo cassette, diversity antenna, telescopic steering column, power windows and locks, heated power mirrors, fog lights, tinted glass, tachometer, map lights, intermittent wipers, heated windshield-washer jets, heated driver-side door lock, rear defogger, seatback pockets, trip odometer, power sunroof, Service Interval Indicator, Active Check Control system, fuel economy indicator, lighted visor mirrors, tool kit, 205/65HR15 tires, alloy wheels. **525i Touring** deletes diversity antenna and power sunroof and adds: 4-speed automatic transmission, split folding rear seat, rear wiper/washer, cargo area tiedowns and cover, 225/60HR15 tires. **530i** adds to 525i: 3.0-liter DOHC V-8 engine, outside temperature display, automatic ventilation system, onboard computer, remote keyless entry, leather seats, 225/60HR15 tires. **530i Touring** adds to 525i Touring: 3.0-liter DOHC V-8 engine, 5-speed automatic transmission, ASC+T traction control, automatic ventilation system, twin-panel power sunroof, onboard computer, remote keyless entry, leather seats. **540i** adds to 530i: 4.0-liter DOHC V-8 engine, 5-speed automatic transmission, power tele-

BMW

scopic steering wheel, 3-position driver's-seat memory. **540i 6-speed** adds: 6-speed manual transmission, sport suspension, 12-way power front seats.

Optional Equipment:

	Retail Price	Dealer Invoice	Fair Price
4-speed automatic transmission, 525i	$975	$800	—
5-speed automatic transmission, 530i	1200	980	—
Premium Package, 525i	3450	2830	—
Onboard computer, leather seats and door handles, wood interior trim, remote keyless entry and alarm, cross-spoke alloy wheels.			
Premium Package, 525i Touring	4625	3795	—
Onboard computer, leather seats and door handles, wood interior trim, power sunroof, remote keyless entry and alarm, cross-spoke alloy wheels.			
ASC+T traction control,			
525i and 525i Touring	1100	900	—
530i and 540i automatic	1500	1230	—
Twin-panel power sunroof, 525i Touring	1400	1150	—
Heated front seats	400	330	—
Luggage net, Touring models	260	215	—
Metallic paint	NC	NC	NC

1995 BMW 7-Series

	Retail Price	Dealer Invoice	Fair Price
740i 4-door notchback	$59900	$49975	—
740iL 4-door notchback	61900	51630	—
750iL 4-door notchback	89900	75780	—
Destination charge	570	570	570
Gas Guzzler Tax, 740i, 740iL	1000	1000	1000
750iL	1700	1700	1700

Fair price not available at time of publication.

Standard Equipment:

740i: 4.0-liter DOHC V-8 engine, 5-speed automatic transmission, anti-lock 4-wheel disc brakes, variable-assist power steering, driver- and passenger-side air bags, automatic climate control system with dual controls, 14-way power front seats with driver-side memory system, 4-way driver-seat lumbar support adjustment, power tilt/telescopic steering wheel with memory, leather and walnut interior trim, door pockets, power windows and door locks, heated power mirrors with 3-position memory, remote keyless entry, variable intermittent wipers, heated windshield-washer jets, heated driver-side door lock, cruise control, rear head rests, rear armrest with storage, automatic dimming mirror, front and rear reading lamps, tinted glass, lighted visor mirrors, tachometer, trip odometer, Service Interval Indicator, Active Check Control system, onboard computer, rear defogger, interior air filtration system, power sunroof, fog lamps, 10-speaker AM/FM/cassette

BMW • BUICK

with diversity antenna and steering wheel controls, luggage net, toolkit, 235/60HR16 tires, alloy wheels, full-size spare tire. **740iL** adds: self-leveling rear suspension. **750iL** adds: 5.4-liter V-12 engine, ASC+T traction control with Dynamic Stability Control, Electronic Damping Control, heated seats, 2-way power upper backrest adjustment, power rear seats with power lumbar adjustment, power rear headrests, cellular telephone, 14-speaker audio system, 6-disc CD changer, power rear sunshade, parking distance control, headlight washers, ski sack.

Optional Equipment:

	Retail Price	Dealer Invoice	Fair Price
Cold Weather Pkg., 740i, 740iL	$1000	$805	—
Heated front seats, headlight washers, ski sack.			
14-speaker audio system w/6-disc CD changer, 740i, 740iL	2100	1690	—
ASC+T traction control, 740i, 740iL	1500	1230	—
Power upper backrest adjusters, 740i, 740iL	1200	965	—
Power rear sunshade, 740iL	740	590	—
Parking distance control, 740iL	900	720	—

BUICK

Buick Century

	Retail Price	Dealer Invoice	Fair Price
Special 4-door notchback	$16720	$15633	$15933
Special 5-door wagon	18135	16956	17256
Destination charge	540	540	540

Additional "value-priced" models may be available in California.

Standard Equipment:

Special: 2.2-liter 4-cylinder engine, 3-speed automatic transmission, anti-lock brakes, driver-side air bag, door-mounted automatic front seatbelts, power steering, air conditioning, automatic power door locks, power windows, tilt steering wheel, intermittent wipers, left remote and right manual mirrors, tinted glass, coolant temperature gauge, trip odometer, map lights, reading lights, 55/45 cloth seats, front storage armrest with cup holders, power front seatback recliners, AM/FM radio, digital clock, rear defogger, remote decklid release, visor mirrors, body-color bodyside molding, 185/75R14 tires, wheel covers. **Wagon** adds: 3.1-liter V-6 engine, 4-speed automatic transmission, remote tailgate release, split folding rear seatback, cargo-area light, cargo-area storage compartments, black bodyside moldings, rear air deflector.

BUICK

Optional Equipment:

	Retail Price	Dealer Invoice	Fair Price
3.1-liter V-6 engine, Special 4-door	$610	$525	$555
Requires 4-speed automatic transmission.			
4-speed automatic transmission, Special 4-door	200	172	182
Requires 3.1-liter V-6 engine.			
Premium Pkg. SC, wagon	253	218	225
Front and rear floormats, cassette player with premium speakers, whitewall tires.			
Custom Pkg. SK, 4-door	1663	1430	1480
3.1-liter V-6 engine, 4-speed automatic transmission, cruise control, cassette player with premium speakers, upgraded cloth upholstery, cargo net, front and rear floormats, Custom exterior badging, 195/75R14 whitewall tires, styled wheel covers.			
Limited Pkg. SL, 4-door	2686	2310	2391
Pkg. SK plus remote keyless entry, power mirrors, 6-way power driver's seat, leather upholstery, Limited exterior badging, wire wheel covers.			
Cruise control, Special	225	194	205
Remote keyless entry, Special, Custom	135	116	123
Cassette player, Special	140	120	127
Premium speakers, Special 4-door	70	60	64
Requires cassette player.			
Automatic power antenna	85	73	77
Power mirrors, Special, Custom	78	67	71
6-way power driver's seat, Special, Custom	305	262	278
Body-side stripes	45	39	41
Body-side woodgrain trim, wagons	380	327	346
Includes door edge guards.			
Rear wiper/washer, wagon	85	73	77
Deletes air deflector.			
Third seat, wagon	215	185	191
Includes rear swing-out vent windows.			
Cargo cover, wagon	69	59	61
Cargo net, Special 4-door	30	26	27
Door-edge guards	25	22	23
Heavy-duty engine and transmission cooling	40	34	36
Requires 3.1-liter V-6 engine.			
Engine-block heater	18	15	16
Roof rack, wagon	115	99	102
Locking wire-wheel covers, Special	240	206	218
Custom	205	176	182
Styled steel wheels, Special	115	99	105
Custom	80	69	71

Prices are accurate at time of publication; subject to manufacturer's change.

CONSUMER GUIDE®

BUICK

	Retail Price	Dealer Invoice	Fair Price
Chrome wheel covers, Special	$35	$30	$32
Alloy wheels, Special	295	254	268
Custom	260	224	231
Limited	55	47	50
185/75R14 whitewall tires, Special	68	58	62
195/75R14 tires, wagon	40	34	36
wagon with Pkg. SC (credit)	(28)	(24)	(24)
Custom, Limited (credit)	(68)	(58)	(58)
195/75R14 whitewall tires, wagon	108	93	98
wagon with Pkg. SC	40	34	36
Floormats	45	39	41

Buick LeSabre

	Retail Price	Dealer Invoice	Fair Price
Custom 4-door notchback	$21380	$19563	$20063
Limited 4-door notchback	25385	23227	23727
Destination charge	590	590	590

Additional "value-priced" models may be available in California.

Standard Equipment:

Custom: 3.8-liter V-6 engine, 4-speed automatic transmission, anti-lock brakes, driver- and passenger-side air bags, power steering, air conditioning, power door locks, power windows, AM/FM radio with clock, tilt steering wheel, intermittent wipers, Pass-Key theft-deterrent system, color-keyed left remote and right manual mirrors, solar-control tinted glass, rear defogger, instrument panel courtesy lights, trip odometer, 55/45 cloth seats, front storage armrest with cup holders, manual front seatback recliners, visor mirrors, 205/70R15 all-season tires, and wheel covers. **Limited** adds: automatic climate control with dual temperature controls, cruise control, remote keyless entry, memory door locks, remote decklid release, 6-way power seats, voltmeter, tachometer, oil pressure and coolant temperature gauges, cassette player, Concert Sound II speakers, power mirrors, automatic day/night mirror, Twilight Sentinel headlamp control, rear armrest, lighted visor mirrors, front- and rear-door courtesy lights, front and rear reading lights, floormats, trunk net, 205/70R15 all-season whitewall tires, and alloy wheels.

Optional Equipment:

Traction control system, Custom w/Pkg. SE, Limited	175	151	159
Cruise control, Custom	225	194	200
Luxury Pkg. SD, Custom	941	809	837

Includes cruise control, cassette player, cargo net, floormats, striping, 205/70R15 all-season whitewall tires, and alloy wheels.

BUICK

	Retail Price	Dealer Invoice	Fair Price
Prestige Pkg. SE, Custom	$1918	$1649	$1707

Pkg. SD plus 6-way power driver's seat, memory door locks, remote keyless entry, voltmeter, tachometer, oil-pressure and coolant-temperature gauges, power mirrors, remote decklid release, Concert Sound II speakers, lighted visor mirrors, and door-edge guards.

Prestige Pkg. SE, Limited	609	524	542

Includes automatic level control, automatic day/night left outside rearview mirror, theft-deterrent system, cassette player with automatic tone control, steering-wheel radio controls, and cornering lamps.

Gran Touring Pkg., Custom w/Pkg. SE,

Limited	512	440	456
Limited w/Pkg. SE	337	290	300

Includes variable-assist power steering, Gran Touring Suspension, 3:06 axle ratio, automatic level control, leather-wrapped steering wheel, 215/60R16 touring tires, and alloy wheels. Requires traction control.

Leather upholstery, Custom	995	856	905
Limited	550	473	501

Custom requires option pkg. Custom with Pkg. SD requires power mirrors, 6-way power driver's seat, remote keyless entry, memory door locks, remote decklid release.

Automatic level control, Custom w/Pkg. SE,

Limited	175	151	156
6-way power driver's seat, Custom	305	262	278

Requires power mirrors and cruise control. With Pkg. SD, requires power mirrors, remote keyless entry, memory door locks, remote decklid release.

6-way power passenger seat,

Custom w/Pkg. SE	305	262	278
Power mirrors, Custom	78	67	71

Requires 6-way power driver's seat and cruise control. With Pkg. SD, requires 6-way power driver's seat, remote keyless entry, memory door locks, and remote decklid release.

Remote decklid release,

Custom w/Pkg. SD	60	52	55

Requires remote keyless entry, 6-way power driver's seat, power mirrors, and memory door locks.

Remote keyless entry, Custom w/Pkg. SD	135	116	123

Requires remote decklid release, 6-way power driver's seat, power mirrors, and memory door locks.

Memory door locks, Custom w/Pkg. SD	25	22	23

Requires remote decklid release, remote keyless entry, 6-way power driver's seat, and power mirrors.

UN6 audio system, Custom	195	168	174

Includes cassette player with clock.

Prices are accurate at time of publication; subject to manufacturer's change.

BUICK

	Retail Price	Dealer Invoice	Fair Price
UL0 audio system, Custom w/Pkg. SE, Limited	$150	$129	$137

Includes cassette player with clock, automatic tone control, and steering-wheel radio controls.

	Retail Price	Dealer Invoice	Fair Price
UN0 audio system, Custom w/Pkg. SE, Limited	250	215	228
Limited w/Pkg. SE	100	86	89

Includes CD player with clock, automatic tone control, and steering-wheel radio controls.

	Retail Price	Dealer Invoice	Fair Price
UP0 audio system, Custom w/Pkg. SE, Limited	350	301	319
Limited w/Pkg. SE	200	172	182

UN0 audio system plus cassette player.

	Retail Price	Dealer Invoice	Fair Price
Twilight Sentinel headlamp control, Custom w/Pkg. SE	60	52	53

Requires 6-way power passenger seat.

	Retail Price	Dealer Invoice	Fair Price
Floormats, Custom	45	39	40
Engine block heater	18	15	16
Alloy wheels, Custom	325	280	296
Locking wire wheel covers, Custom w/option pkg., Limited	NC	NC	NC

NA with Gran Touring Pkg.

	Retail Price	Dealer Invoice	Fair Price
205/70R15 whitewall tires, Custom	76	65	69

NA with Gran Touring Pkg.

	Retail Price	Dealer Invoice	Fair Price
205/70R15 tires, Custom w/option pkg., Limited (credit)	(76)	(65)	(65)

NA with Gran Touring Pkg.

	Retail Price	Dealer Invoice	Fair Price
205/70R15 self-sealing whitewall tires, Custom	226	194	206
Custom w/option pkg., Limited	150	129	137

Buick Park Avenue

	Retail Price	Dealer Invoice	Fair Price
4-door notchback	$28205	$25243	$25843
Ultra 4-door notchback	32820	29374	29974
Destination charge	640	640	640

Additional "value-priced" models may be available in California.

Standard Equipment:

3.8-liter V-6 engine, 4-speed automatic transmission, anti-lock brakes, driver- and passenger-side air bags, air conditioning, 55/45 cloth reclining front seat with storage armrest and cup holders, 6-way power driver's seat, automatic level control, power windows with driver-side express down and pas-

BUICK

senger lockout, power door locks, power mirrors, overhead console, cruise control, rear defogger, tilt steering wheel, AM/FM/cassette player, power antenna, solar-control tinted glass, Pass-Key theft-deterrent system, remote decklid and fuel-door releases, front and rear reading and courtesy lights, lighted visor mirrors, intermittent wipers, analog gauge cluster w/trip odometer, 205/70R15 tires, and alloy wheels. **Ultra** adds: supercharged 3.8-liter V-6 engine, variable-assist power steering, automatic climate control with dual temperature controls, rear-seat climate controls, 6-way power front seats with power recliners, leather upholstery, leather-wrapped steering wheel, rear head restraints, remote keyless entry (with perimeter lighting, instant alarm, security feedback functions, and central unlocking), illuminated entry system with retained accessory power, Twilight Sentinel headlamp control, lamp monitors, analog gauge cluster (including tachometer, trip odometer, and oil-life moniter), power antenna, power decklid pulldown, automatic programmable power door locks, Reminder Pkg. (includes low-washer-fluid, low-coolant, and door-ajar indicators), theft-deterrent system with starter interrupt, cargo net, cornering lamps, automatic day/night inside rearview mirror, Concert Sound II speakers, lighted driver-side visor mirror, rear lighted vanity mirrors, 4-note horn, and 215/70R15 all-season whitewall tires.

Optional Equipment:

	Retail Price	Dealer Invoice	Fair Price
Automatic day/night rearview mirror w/compass, base w/Pkg.SD	$150	$129	$134
Ultra w/option pkg.	70	60	62
Base w/Pkg. SD	1678	1443	1493

Includes power passenger seat with power recliner, illuminated entry with retained accessory power, remote keyless entry (w/perimeter lighting, instant alarm, and security feedback functions), automatic air conditioning, theft-deterrent system with central unlocking and starter interrupt, automatic programmable door locks, power decklid pulldown, automatic day/night rearview mirror, analog gauge cluster (including tachometer, trip odometer, and oil-life monitor), lamp monitors, Twilight Sentinel headlamp control, Concert Sound II speakers, cornering lamps, Reminder Pkg. (includes low-washer-fluid, low-coolant, and door-ajar indicators), door-edge guards, cargo net, 4-note horn, and 205/70R15 whitewall tires.

Base w/Pkg. SE	2503	2153	2228

Base w/Pkg. SD plus cassette player with automatic tone control and steering-wheel radio controls, rear-seat air conditioning, heated remote sideview mirrors w/automatic day/night left mirror, programmable 6-way power driver's seat w/memory mirrors and electric seat-back recliner, rear-seat storage armrest, automatic day/night rearview mirror with compass, self-sealing tires, and trunk mat.

Ultra w/Pkg. SD	705	606	627

Includes automatic ride control, traction control system, and cassette player with automatic tone control and steering-wheel radio controls.

Prices are accurate at time of publication; subject to manufacturer's change.

BUICK

	Retail Price	Dealer Invoice	Fair Price
Ultra w/Pkg. SE	$1465	$1260	$1304

Ultra w/Pkg. SD plus heated remote sideview mirrors with automatic day/night left mirror, heated front seats, programmable 6-way power driver's seat w/memory mirrors, automatic day/night rearview mirror w/compass, self-sealing tires, and trunk mat.

UL0 audio system, base w/Pkg. SD,
base Ultra Pkg.	150	129	134

Includes AM/FM/cassette player with clock, seek and scan, automatic tone control, and steering-wheel radio controls.

UN0 audio system, base w/Pkg. SD,
base Ultra	250	215	223
base w/Pkg. SE, Ultra w/option pkg.	100	86	89

Includes AM/FM/CD player with clock, seek and scan, automatic tone control, and steering-wheel radio controls.

UP0 audio system, base w/Pkg. SD,
base Ultra	350	301	312
base w/Pkg. SE, Ultra w/option pkg.	200	172	178

UN0 audio system plus cassette player.

Electric sliding sunroof, base w/Pkg. SE
	918	789	817
Ultra w/option pkg.	802	690	714

Deletes lamp monitors. Deletes rear lighted vanity mirrors from Ultra.

Rear-seat air conditioning,
base w/Pkg. SD	45	39	40

Trailering Pkg.,
base w/option pkg.	177	152	158
Ultra w/option pkg. (credit)	(203)	(175)	(175)

Includes auxiliary transmission oil and engine oil cooling, Gran Touring suspension, and 3:06 axle ratio. Requires traction control system. NA with automatic level control.

Gran Touring Pkg., base w/option pkg.
	317	273	282
base Ultra	261	224	232
Ultra w/option pkg., (credit)	(294)	(253)	(253)

Includes Gran Touring suspension, aluminum wheels, and 215/60R16 touring tires. Base w/option pkg. also includes 3:06 axle ratio, leather-wrapped steering wheel, and variable-assist power steering. Base Ultra also includes traction-control system. Base SA requires traction control.

Automatic ride control, base w/Pkg. SE
	473	407	421

Includes variable-assist steering. Requires traction control system. NA with Gran Touring or Trailer Towing Pkgs.

Traction-control system,
base w/option pkg., Ultra w/Pkg. SD	175	151	156

Leather/vinyl 55/45 seat w/storage armrest,
base w/Pkg. SD	650	559	579
base w/Pkg. SE	600	516	534

BUICK

	Retail Price	Dealer Invoice	Fair Price
Heated front seats, base w/Pkg. SE, Ultra w/Pkg. SD	$225	$194	$200
Engine-block heater	18	15	16
Solid paint color, Ultra	NC	NC	NC
Beige exterior lower-accent color, Ultra	195	168	174
205/70R15 self-sealing whitewall tires, base SA	226	194	201
base w/Pkg. SD	150	129	134
205/70R15 whitewall tires, base SA	76	65	68
205/70R15 tires, base w/Pkg. SD (credit)	(76)	(65)	(65)
base w/Pkg. SE (credit)	(226)	(194)	(194)
8NA with Gran Touring Pkg.			
215/70R15 self-sealing whitewall tires, Ultra, Ultra w/Pkg. SD (credit)	150	129	134
15-inch wire wheel covers, base	NC	NC	NC
NA with Gran Touring Pkg. or Ultra.			

Buick Regal

	Retail Price	Dealer Invoice	Fair Price
Custom 2-door notchback	$19445	$17792	$18292
Custom 4-door notchback	19740	18062	18562
Limited 4-door notchback	21195	19393	19893
Gran Sport 4-door notchback	21800	19947	20447
Destination charge	540	540	540

Additional "value-priced" models may be available in California.

Standard Equipment:

Custom: 3.1-liter V-6 engine, 4-speed automatic transmission, driver- and passenger-side air bags, anti-lock 4-wheel disc brakes, power steering, automatic air conditioning with driver/passenger climate controls, cruise control, automatic power door locks, remote trunk release, power windows with driver-side express down and passenger lockout, tilt steering wheel, tachometer, voltmeter, oil pressure and engine coolant temperature gauges, cloth reclining 55/45 front seat with storage armrest and cup holders, front seatback recliners, tinted glass, intermittent wipers, Pass-Key theft-deterrent system, remote sideview mirrors, rear defogger, courtesy/reading lights with inside rearview mirror, visor mirrors, AM/FM/cassette player with clock, 205/70R15 tires, wheel covers. **Limited** adds: 3.8-liter V-6 engine, dual exhaust outlets, 4-way manual driver's seat and 2-way manual passenger's seat, overhead courtesy/reading lights, seatback map pockets, Concert Sound II speakers, power antenna, floormats. **Gran Sport** adds: Gran Touring suspension, variable-assist power steering, leather-wrapped steering wheel, cloth reclining bucket seats with 6-way power driver's seat,

Prices are accurate at time of publication; subject to manufacturer's change.

BUICK

auxiliary power receptacle, storage console with armrest and cup holders, argent lower body accent paint, color-keyed grille, 225/60R16 all-season tires, alloy wheels.

Optional Equipment:

	Retail Price	Dealer Invoice	Fair Price
3.8-liter V-6 engine, Custom	$395	$340	$352
Luxury Pkg. SD, Custom	185	159	165

Power antenna, front overhead console with courtesy/reading lights, rear courtesy/reading lights, and floormats.

Prestige Pkg. SE, Custom 4-door	655	563	583

Pkg. SD plus remote keyless entry system, 6-way power driver's seat, and cargo net.

Gran Sport Pkg. SK, Custom 2-door	1895	1630	1687

Pkg. SD plus 3.8-liter V-6 engine, Gran Touring suspension, variable-assist power steering, cloth bucket seats with console and 6-way power driver's seat, Concert Sound II speakers, leather-wrapped steering wheel, body-color grille, alloy wheels, 225/60R16 tires.

Prestige Pkg. SE, Limited, Gran Sport	677	582	603

6-way power driver's seat, remote keyless entry, cassette player with automatic tone control and steering-wheel-mounted controls, power mirrors, and cargo net.

Gran Touring Pkg., Custom 4-door w/option pkg., Limited	745	641	663

3.8-liter V-6 engine, Gran Touring suspension, leather-wrapped steering wheel, variable-assist power steering, 225/60R16 tires, alloy wheels.

UL0 audio system	25	22	23

Includes cassette player with clock and automatic tone control. Requires Concert Sound II speakers.

UN0 audio system, Custom w/option pkg., base SA Limited/Gran Sport	125	108	111
Limited/Gran Sport w/option pkg.	100	86	89

Includes CD player with clock and automatic tone control. Requires Concert Sound II speakers.

UP0 audio system, Custom w/option pkg., base SA Limited/Gran Sport	225	194	200
Limited/Gran Sport w/option pkg.	200	172	178

Includes CD/cassette player with clock and automatic tone control. Requires Concert Sound II speakers.

Steering-wheel radio control	125	108	111

NA with base Custom. NA with standard-equipment audio system.

Concert Sound II speakers, Custom	70	60	62
Power antenna, Custom	85	73	76
Power sunroof	695	598	619

Includes mirror reading lights. NA with base SA models or Custom 4-door w/Pkg. SD. Custom 2-door requires 6-way power seat(s).

BUICK

	Retail Price	Dealer Invoice	Fair Price
Remote keyless entry, Limited, Gran Sport, Custom w/option pkg.	$135	$116	$120
6-way power driver's seat,			
Custom w/Pkg. SD	305	262	271
Limited, Gran Sport	270	232	240
Dual 6-way power front seats, Custom 2-door w/Pkg. SK, Limited/Gran Sport w/option pkg.	305	262	271
Leather 55/45 front seat w/storage armrest, Custom 4-door w/option pkg., Limited	550	473	490

Custom 4-door requires Concert Sound II speakers or 6-way power seat. Limited requires 6-way power seat(s).

Leather bucket seats with console, Custom/Limited w/option pkg., Gran Sport	550	473	490

Customs require 6-way power seat(s) and Concert Sound II speakers. Limited and Gran Sport require 6-way power seat(s).

Cloth bucket seats with console, Custom	NC	NC	NC
Lighted visor mirrors, Custom w/option pkg.	92	79	82
Decklid luggage rack (black), Custom 2-door w/option pkg.	115	99	102
Decklid luggage rack (chrome), SE Pkgs.	115	99	102
Monotone paint, Gran Sport	NC	NC	NC
Engine block heater	18	15	16
Floormats, Custom	45	39	40
Cargo net, Custom w/option pkg.	30	26	27
15-inch alloy wheels, Custom, Limited	325	280	289

NA with Gran Touring Pkg. or Custom w/SK Pkg.

16-inch chrome wheels, Custom w/SK Pkg., Gran Sport	650	559	579
205/70R15 whitewall tires, Custom, Limited	76	65	68

NA with Gran Touring Pkg. or Custom w/SK Pkg.

Buick Riviera

	Retail Price	Dealer Invoice	Fair Price
2-door notchback	$29475	$26380	—
Destination charge	640	640	640

Fair price not available at time of publication.

Prices are accurate at time of publication; subject to manufacturer's change.

BUICK

Standard Equipment:

3.8-liter V-6 engine, 4-speed automatic transmission, anti-lock 4-wheel disc brakes, driver- and passenger-side air bags, variable-assist power steering, automatic air conditioning with dual climate controls, rear-seat heating vents, cruise control, cloth 6-way power 55/45 split bench front seat with power recliners, front storage armrest with cup holders, rear-seat armrest, power windows and mirrors, automatic power door locks w/delayed locking and lockout protection, remote keyless entry system (w/perimeter lighting, security feedback, and instant alarm), Pass-Key II theft-deterrent system, automatic level control, tachometer, coolant temperature gauge, trip odometer, lighted passenger-side visor mirror, power remote fuel door and decklid releases, solar-control tinted glass, AM/FM/cassette/CD player with clock, automatic power antenna, intermittent wipers, rear defogger, tilt steering wheel, leather-wrapped steering wheel, front reading and courtesy lights, trunk and rear courtesy lights, door floodlights, supplemental and extendable sunshades, cargo net, 225/60R16 all-season tires, and alloy wheels.

Optional Equipment:

	Retail Price	Dealer Invoice	Fair Price
3.8-liter supercharged V-6 engine	$1100	$946	—
Includes 225/60R16 touring tires and specific alloy wheels.			
SE Prestige Pkg.	1092	939	—
Twilight Sentinel, driver-side lighted visor mirror, programmable automatic door locks, theft-deterrent system, cornering lights, accent striping, 3-function remote universal transmitter, automatic day/night mirrors, steering-wheel-mounted radio controls, driver's seat power lumbar adjustment, and traction-control system.			
Power sunroof with sunshade	995	856	—
Memory/heated driver's seat w/memory outside mirrors	310	267	—
Power leather front bucket seats with operating console	750	645	—
Leather 55/45 split bench seats	600	516	—
Bright white diamond paint	395	340	—
Engine block heater	18	15	—
Chrome wheels	695	598	—
Requires supercharged engine.			

Buick Roadmaster

	Retail Price	Dealer Invoice	Fair Price
4-door notchback	$25560	$23387	$23887
Estate 5-door wagon	27575	25231	25731
Limited 4-door notchback	27490	25153	25653
Destination charge	590	590	590

Additional "value-priced" models may be available in California.

BUICK

Standard Equipment:

5.7-liter V-8 engine, 4-speed automatic transmission, anti-lock brakes, driver- and passenger-side air bags, power steering, cruise control, air conditioning with automatic climate control, power windows with driver-side express down and passenger lockout, power door locks, Pass-Key theft-deterrent system with starter interrupt, AM/FM/cassette with clock and automatic tone control, Concert Sound II speakers, cloth 55/45 seats with storage armrest and cup holders (sedan), manual seatback recliners, front seatback map pockets, tilt steering wheel, remote decklid release, inside day/night mirror with reading lights, left remote and right manual mirrors, delayed illuminated entry, tinted glass, rear defogger, intermittent wipers, analog gauge cluster with coolant temperature and oil pressure gauges, trip odometer, low-fuel warning light, windshield washer fluid, oil, voltage, and coolant level indicators, oil life monitor, visor mirrors, 4-note horn (2-note on wagon), cargo net, floormats (not standard on wagon), collector's-edition hood ornament, 235/70R15 all-season whitewall tires, wheel covers.
Estate Wagon adds: variable-assist steering, power antenna, front-center armrest, tailgate-ajar indicator luggage rack, solar-control windshield, rear-window wiper/washer, vista roof with shade, third rear-facing vinyl seat, cargo cover, door-edge guards, woodgrain trim, 225/75R15 tires, 15-inch alloy wheels. **Limited** adds: variable-assist steering, automatic climate control, power antenna, remote keyless entry, automatic door locks, automatic day/night rearview mirror, lighted visor mirrors, leather-wrapped steering wheel, 6-way power front seats with power recliners and lumbar supports.

Optional Equipment:

	Retail Price	Dealer Invoice	Fair Price
Luxury Pkg. SD, base 4-door	$703	$605	$626

6-way power driver's seat, remote heated sideview mirrors, power antenna, and CD/cassette player with automatic tone control.

Luxury Pkg. SD, wagon	613	527	546

6-way power driver's seat, automatic day/night rearview mirror with reading lights, power heated sideview mirrors, storage armrest with cup holders, and floormats.

Prestige Pkg. SE, base 4-door	1340	1152	1193

Pkg. SD plus 6-way power passenger seat, automatic programmable door locks, remote keyless entry, automatic day/night rearview mirror with reading lights, and lighted visor mirrors.

Prestige Pkg. SE, Limited	945	813	841

Power decklid pull-down, Twilight Sentinel headlamp control, cornering lamps, CD/cassette player with automatic tone control, heated front seats with memory driver's seat, and self-sealing tires.

Prestige Pkg. SE, wagon	1290	1109	1148

Pkg. SD plus 6-way power passenger seat, remote keyless entry, automatic programmable door locks, Twilight Sentinel headlamp control, lighted visor mirrors, and cornering lamps.

Prices are accurate at time of publication; subject to manufacturer's change.

CONSUMER GUIDE®

BUICK

	Retail Price	Dealer Invoice	Fair Price
Limited Wagon Pkg.	$1870	$1608	$1664

Includes 6-way power front seats with power recliners, lumbar supports, storage armrest and cup holders, 6-way headrests, exterior Limited badges, floormats, leather-wrapped steering wheel, remote keyless entry, automatic programmable locks, remote heated power mirrors, automatic day/night mirror with reading lamps, lighted visor mirrors, Twilight Sentinel headlight control, and cornering lamps.

Gran Touring/Trailer Towing Pkg., wagon	325	280	289
base 4-door, Limited	375	323	334
Limited w/Pkg. SE	225	194	200

Includes 2.93 axle ratio, heavy-duty engine cooling, automatic level control, engine oil cooler, gran-touring suspension (4-doors), and solar-control windshield (4-doors). NA with Cooling Pkg. 4-doors require limited-slip differential.

Limited-slip differential, base 4-door/wagon w/option pkg., Limited	100	86	89

Wagon requires Trailer Towing Pkg.

Cooling Pkg., base 4-door w/Pkg. SD or SE, Limited	200	172	178
wagon w/option pkg.	150	129	134

Includes solar control windshield (4-doors), engine oil cooler, higher-output fans, and increased capacity air conditioner. NA with Gran Touring/Trailer Towing Pkg.

Automatic level control, base 4-door/wagon w/option pkg., Limited	175	151	156
Leather 55/45 seats, base 4-door w/option pkg., Limited, wagon w/SD or SE Option Pkg.........	775	667	690
wagon w/Limited Wagon Pkg.	685	589	610

Includes leather-wrapped steering wheel.

UP0 audio system, 4-doors	200	172	178

Includes AM/FM/cassette/CD player with clock and automatic tone control.

Heated front seats with memory driver's seat, Limited, wagon w/Limited Wagon Pkg.	395	340	352
6-way power passenger's seat, base 4-door w/Pkg. SJ	305	262	271
Automatic door locks, Pkg. SD	25	22	23

Requires remote keyless entry.

Remote keyless entry, Pkg. SD	135	116	120

Requires automatic door locks.

Third seat delete (credit), wagon	(215)	(185)	(185)

NA with Pkg. SE or Limited Wagon Pkg.

Vinyl landau roof, base 4-door w/Pkg. SD or Pkg. SE, Limited	695	598	619

BUICK

	Retail Price	Dealer Invoice	Fair Price
Woodgrain trim delete, wagon	NC	NC	NC
Includes body-side stripe.			
Engine block heater	$18	$15	$16
15-inch wire wheel covers, 4-doors	240	206	214
wagon	NC	NC	NC
Alloy wheels, 4-doors	325	280	289
235/70R15 self-sealing whitewall tires 4-doors	150	129	134
NA with Gran Touring/Trailer Towing Pkg.			
225/75R15 self-sealing whitewall tires, wagon	150	129	134
Full-size spare tire,			
4-door, wagon, or Limited w/wire wheel covers and w/o self-sealing tires	75	65	67
4-door, wagon, or Limited w/wire wheel covers and self-sealing tires	125	108	111
4-door or Limited w/alloy wheels and w/o self-sealing tires	125	108	111
4-door or Limited w/alloy wheels and self-sealing tires	175	151	156
4-door or Limited w/o alloy wheels, wire wheel covers, and self-sealing tires	75	65	67
4-door or Limited w/o alloy wheels or wire wheel covers, w/self-sealing tires	125	108	111
wagon w/o alloy wheels or wire wheel covers, w/self-sealing tires	175	151	156
wagon w/o wire wheel covers and self-sealing tires	125	108	111

Buick Skylark

	Retail Price	Dealer Invoice	Fair Price
Custom 2-door notchback	$15495	$14798	$15098
Custom 4-door notchback	15495	14798	15098
Destination charge	500	500	500

Additional "value-priced" models may be available in California.

Standard Equipment:

Custom: 2.4-liter DOHC 4-cylinder engine, 4-speed automatic transmission, driver- and passenger-side air bags, anti-lock brakes, traction control, air conditioning, power steering, tilt steering wheel, cloth 55/45 split bench seat with seatback recliners, trip odometer, coolant-temperature gauge, AM/FM radio with clock, tinted glass, intermittent wipers, rear defogger, automatic power door locks, Passlock theft-deterrent system, remote fuel door and decklid releases, remote mirrors, front and rear courtesy lights, vanity mirrors, floormats, 195/70R14 tires, and wheel covers.

Prices are accurate at time of publication; subject to manufacturer's change.

BUICK

Optional Equipment:

	Retail Price	Dealer Invoice	Fair Price
3.1-liter V-6 engine	$395	$340	$352
Limited Pkg. SK	1131	973	1007
Without standard 55/45 bench seat	1023	880	910

Cruise control, power rearview mirrors (black), power windows, cassette player, front storage armrest with cupholders, 4-way manual driver's seat, cargo net, polycast wheels.

Gran Sport Pkg. SL	2206	1897	1963

Pkg. SK plus 3.1-liter V-6, bucket seats with full console and driver-side lumbar support, analog gauge cluster including tachometer, voltmeter, and oil-pressure gauge, body color grille, blackout taillamps, black window trim, sport suspension, 205/55R16 tires, alloy wheels.

Cruise control, Custom	225	194	200
6-way power driver's seat, Limited, Gran Sport	270	232	240
Custom	305	262	271

Requires rear-window antenna. Custom also requires power windows and mirrors.

Bucket seats with full console	160	138	142

Custom requires cruise control and 4-way manual driver's seat or 6-way power driver's seat. Custom and Limited require analog gauge cluster.

Bucket seats with full console and driver-side lumbar support	175	151	156

NA with Custom Pkg. Limited requires analog gauge cluster.

4-way manual driver's seat, Custom	35	30	31
Leather/cloth trim, Limited	620	533	552
Gran Sport	495	426	441

Includes leather-wrapped steering wheel and shifter. Limited includes analog gauge cluster.

Front storage armrest with cupholders	108	93	96

Included in Limited Pkg. NA with bucket seats.

Analog gauge cluster	126	108	112

Includes tachometer, trip odometer, voltmeter, oil pressure and coolant temperature gauges. Requires bucket seats.

Deluxe headliner pkg.	135	116	120

Includes assist handles, lighted visor vanity mirrors, extendable sunshade, reading lamps. NA with power sunroof.

Power windows, 2-doors, Custom	290	249	258
4-doors, Custom	355	305	316
Power sunroof	595	512	530

Includes covered vanity mirrors, extendable sunshades, and reading lamps.

Power rearview mirrors (black), Custom	78	67	69

Requires power windows.

Remote keyless entry system	135	116	120

Requires rear-window antenna, power windows, and remote rearview mirrors.

BUICK • CADILLAC

	Retail Price	Dealer Invoice	Fair Price
Cassette player, Custom	$195	$168	$174
Cassette player with auto tone control			
Limited, Gran Sport	25	22	23
Custom	220	189	196
Requires Concert Sound II speakers.			
CD player,			
Limited, Gran Sport	125	108	111
Custom	320	275	285
Requires Concert Sound II speakers.			
CD/cassette player,			
Limited, Gran Sport	225	194	200
Custom	420	361	374
Requires Concert Sound II speakers.			
Concert Sound II speakers	45	39	40
NA with with base radio.			
Steering-wheel-mounted radio controls	125	108	111
Requires cassette player with auto tone control or CD player.			
Rear-window antenna	22	19	20
Requires power windows.			
Engine block heater	18	15	16
15-inch styled wheel covers,			
Custom	28	24	25
Limited	(75)	(65)	(75)
Requires 195/65R15 tires.			
14-inch polycast wheels, Custom	115	99	102
NA with optional tires.			
195/65R15 tires, Custom, Limited	131	113	117
Requires 15-inch styled wheel covers.			
195/70R14 whitewall tires, Custom	72	62	64
NA with 14-inch polycast wheels or 15-inch styled wheel covers.			

CADILLAC

Cadillac De Ville/Concours

	Retail Price	Dealer Invoice	Fair Price
Sedan De Ville 4-door notchback	$35995	$32935	$33735
Concours 4-door notchback	40495	37053	37853
Destination charge	640	640	640

Standard Equipment:

Sedan De Ville: 4.6-liter DOHC V-8 engine (275 horsepower), 4-speed automatic transmission, anti-lock 4-wheel disc brakes, traction control,

Prices are accurate at time of publication; subject to manufacturer's change.

CADILLAC

driver- and passenger-side air bags, variable-assist power steering, Road-Sensing Suspension, cloth reclining power front seats with storage armrest, automatic climate control, outside temperature readout, power windows, programmable power locks w/valet lockout, remote keyless entry system, illuminated entry, heated power mirrors, cruise control, AM/FM/cassette with six speakers, power antenna, steering wheel radio and climate controls, power decklid pulldown, automatic parking-brake release, Twilight Sentinel headlamp control, wiper-activated headlights, tinted glass, driver's-side visor storage, automatic level control, intermittent wipers, Driver Information Center, electronic gearshift indicator, trip odometer, tilt steering wheel, leather-wrapped steering wheel, power decklid release and pulldown, remote fuel door release, rear defogger, Pass-Key II anti-theft system, automatic day/night inside rear-view mirror, Integrated Chassis Control System, cornering lamps, daytime running lamps, battery-run-down protection, accent stripe, trunk mat and cargo net, floormats, 225/60R16 all-season whitewall tires, alloy wheels. **Concours** adds: 4.6-liter DOHC V-8 engine (300 horsepower), Magnasteer variable-assist steering, continuously variable Road-Sensing Suspension, dual exhaust, leather seats, Zebrano wood trim, power front-seat recliners, remote memory driver's seat, 4-way power lumbar-support front seats, rear center storage armrest, Active Audio System with cassette and 11 speakers, automatic windshield wipers, automatic day/night driver-side mirror, front and rear lighted visor mirrors and maplights, 225/60HR16 blackwall tires.

Optional Equipment:

	Retail Price	Dealer Invoice	Fair Price
Option Pkg. 1SB, De Ville	$530	$451	$472
Automatic day/night driver-side mirror, lighted visor mirrors, and power front seat recliners.			
Heated windshield system	377	320	336
De Ville requires Option Pkg. 1SB.			
Memory driver's seat, De Ville w/Pkg. 1SB	235	200	209
Heated front seats	225	191	200
De Ville requires Option Pkg. 1SB and leather seats.			
Leather seats, De Ville	785	667	699
Astroroof, Concours, De Ville w/Pkg. 1SB	1550	1318	1380
De Ville	1700	1445	1513
Includes lighted visor mirrors and rear reading lamps on De Ville without Pkg. 1SB.			
Theft-deterrent system	295	251	263
De Ville requires Option Pkg. 1SB.			
Electronic compass	100	85	89
De Ville requires Option Pkg. 1SB.			
Programmable garage door opener	107	91	95
Active Audio Sound System, De Ville w/Pkg. 1SB	274	233	244
Includes AM/FM/cassette with 11 speakers.			

CADILLAC

	Retail Price	Dealer Invoice	Fair Price
Active Audio Sound System, Concours,			
De Ville w/Pkg. 1SB	$869	$739	$773
Concours	595	506	530
Includes AM/FM/cassette/CD with 12-disc CD changer and 11 speakers.			
Active Audio Sound System, Concours,			
De Ville w/Pkg. 1SB	1064	904	947
Concours	790	672	703
Includes AM/FM/cassette/CD with 12-disc CD changer, digital signal processing, and 11 speakers.			
Chrome wheels	1195	523	1064
3000-lb. Trailer Towing Pkg.	110	94	98
White diamond or pearl red paint	500	425	445
Accent striping delete	NC	NC	NC

Cadillac Eldorado

	Retail Price	Dealer Invoice	Fair Price
2-door notchback	$39595	$34250	$35050
Touring Coupe 2-door notchback	42995	37191	37991
Destination charge	640	640	640

Standard Equipment:

4.6-liter DOHC V-8 engine (275 horsepower), 4-speed automatic transmission, anti-lock 4-wheel disc brakes, driver- and passenger-side air bags, variable-assist power steering, Integrated Chassis Control System, automatic parking-brake release, Road-Sensing Suspension, automatic level control, traction control, dual exhaust, battery-run-down protection, automatic climate control, cloth power front bucket seats with power recliners, center console with armrest and storage bins, overhead console, power windows, automatic power locks, remote keyless entry system, cruise control, heated power mirrors, rear defogger, solar-control tinted glass, automatic day/night rearview mirror, AM/FM/cassette player with 6 speakers, power antenna, remote fuel door release, power decklid release and pull-down, electronic gearshift indicator, trip odometer, Driver Information Center, Zebrano wood trim, front-seatback and door pockets, driver's-side visor storage flap, intermittent wipers, leather-wrapped steering wheel with controls for radio and climate control, tilt steering wheel, valet lockout, Pass-Key II theft-deterrent system, Twilight Sentinel headlamp control, daytime running lamps, wiper-activated headlights, fog lamps, cornering lamps, illuminated entry, reading lights, lighted visor mirrors, floormats, trunk mat and cargo net, 225/60R16 tires, and alloy wheels. **Touring Coupe** adds: high-output 4.6-liter DOHC V-8 engine (300 horsepower), continuously variable Road-Sensing Suspension, Magnasteer variable-assist steering, tachometer, coolant-temperature gauge, remote memory driver's seat,

Prices are accurate at time of publication; subject to manufacturer's change.

CADILLAC

power lumbar adjusters, leather seats, center rear-seat storage armrest with cup holders, automatic windshield wiper system, automatic day/night driver-side mirror, theft-deterrent system, and 225/60HR16 tires.

Optional Equipment:

	Retail Price	Dealer Invoice	Fair Price
Sport Interior Pkg., base	$146	$124	$130
Analog instruments and floor console with leather-wrapped shift knob.			
Astroroof	1550	1318	1380
Heated windshield	377	320	336
Leather upholstery, base	785	667	699
Heated front seats	225	191	200
Base requires leather upholstery.			
Memory driver's seat, base	235	200	209
Requires leather upholstery.			
Power lumbar support, base	292	248	260
Requires leather upholstery.			
Automatic driver's-side day/night rearview mirror, base	87	74	77
Electronic compass	100	85	89
Base requires automatic day/night rearview mirror.			
Theft-deterrent system, base	295	251	263
Bose sound system	723	615	643
Includes AM/FM/cassette player with four Bose amplified speakers.			
Bose sound system	1318	1120	1173
Includes AM/FM/cassette/CD player with 12-disc changer and four Bose amplified speakers.			
Bose sound system	1513	1286	1347
Includes AM/FM/cassette/CD player with 12-disc changer, digital signal processing, and four Bose amplified speakers.			
Programmable garage door opener	107	91	95
White diamond or red pearl paint	500	425	445
Striping, base	75	64	67
225/60R16 whitewall tires, base	76	65	68
225/60ZR16 tires, Touring Coupe	250	213	223
Chrome wheels	1195	523	1064

Cadillac Fleetwood

	Retail Price	Dealer Invoice	Fair Price
4-door notchback	$36995	$33850	$34650
Destination charge	640	640	640

Standard Equipment:

5.7-liter V-8 engine, 4-speed automatic transmission, anti-lock brakes, driver- and passenger-side air bags, variable-assist power steering, traction control,

CADILLAC

power 55/45 front seat with power recliners and storage armrest with cup holders, automatic climate control, outside-temperature readout, power windows, automatic power locks, illuminated entry, cruise control, heated power mirrors, lighted vanity mirrors, automatic day/night rearview mirror, map lights, remote keyless entry, Pass-Key II anti-theft deterrent system, AM/FM/cassette with auto tone control and six speakers, power antenna, automatic level control, leather-wrapped tilt steering wheel, trip odometer, cornering lamps, automatic parking brake release, tinted glass, intermittent wipers, rear defogger, floormats, door-edge guards, Twilight Sentinel headlamp control, daytime running lights, power decklid pulldown and release, trunk mat and cargo net, 235/70R15 whitewall tires, and alloy wheels.

Optional Equipment:

	Retail Price	Dealer Invoice	Fair Price
Security Pkg.	$360	$306	$320
Includes remote fuel-door release and theft-deterrent system.			
7000-lb. Trailer Towing Pkg.	215	183	191
Performance axle ratio (2.93:1), base	NC	NC	NC
NA with Trailer Towing Pkg.			
Astroroof	1550	1318	1380
Fleetwood Brougham Pkg. with cloth trim	1680	1428	1495
with leather trim	2465	2095	2194
Heated front seats, 2-position driver's seat memory feature, power lumbar adjustment, articulating front headrests, rear seat storage armrest with cup holders, rear lighted vanity mirrors, fully padded roof, unique trim and alloy wheels, and 2.93:1 rear-axle ratio.			
Leather upholstery, base	785	667	699
Sungate windshield	50	43	45
CD/cassette player	200	170	178
Includes auto tone control and six speakers.			
Programmable garage-door opener	107	91	95
Full padded vinyl roof delete, Brougham	NC	NC	NC
Full padded vinyl roof, base	925	786	823
Chrome wheels	1195	523	1064
NA with full-size spare tire.			
Full-size spare tire	95	81	85
NA with chrome wheels.			

Cadillac Seville

	Retail Price	Dealer Invoice	Fair Price
SLS 4-door notchback	$42995	$37191	$37991
STS 4-door notchback	47495	41083	41883
Destination charge	640	640	640

Standard Equipment:

SLS: 4.6-liter DOHC V-8 engine (275 horsepower), 4-speed automatic

Prices are accurate at time of publication; subject to manufacturer's change.

CADILLAC

transmission, anti-lock 4-wheel disc brakes, driver- and passenger-side air bags, variable-assist power steering, Road-Sensing Suspension, traction control, automatic level control, cloth power front seats with articulating headrests and power recliners, center console with armrest and storage bins, overhead console, driver's-side visor storage flap, dual zone automatic climate control with outside temperature display, Zebrano wood trim, power windows, programmable power door locks, valet lockout, cruise control, heated power mirrors, automatic day/night rearview mirror, AM/FM/cassette with six speakers, power antenna, remote fuel door and decklid releases, power decklid pull-down, Driver Information Center, on-board diagnostics, Pass-Key II theft-deterrent system, remote keyless entry, leather-wrapped tilt steering wheel with controls for radio and climate system, intermittent wipers, wiper-activated headlights, rear defogger, solar-control tinted glass, floormats, decklid liner, trunk mat and cargo net, battery-run-down protection, Twilight Sentinel headlamp control, cornering lamps, daytime running lamps, reading lights, lighted visor mirrors, illuminated entry, trip odometer, automatic parking-brake release, 225/60R16 tires, and alloy wheels. **STS** adds: 4.6-liter V-8 DOHC engine (300 horsepower), continuously variable Road-Sensing Suspension, Magnasteer variable-assist steering, leather upholstery, rear-seat center storage armrest, front-seat power lumbar adjustment, memory driver's seat, automatic windshield wipers, analog instruments with tachometer, full console, driver-side automatic day/night outside mirror, theft-deterrent system, fog lamps, and 225/60HR16 tires.

Optional Equipment:

	Retail Price	Dealer Invoice	Fair Price
Sport Interior Pkg., SLS	$146	$124	$130
Analog instruments and full center console with shift lever.			
Astroroof	1550	1318	1380
Anti-theft alarm, SLS	295	251	266
Heated windshield	377	320	336
Leather upholstery, SLS	785	667	699
Programmable garage door opener	107	91	95
White diamond or red pearl paint	500	425	445
Heated front seats	225	191	200
SLS requires leather upholstery.			
Memory driver's seat, SLS	235	200	209
Requires leather upholstery.			
Power lumbar adjustment, SLS	292	248	260
Requires leather upholstery.			
Driver-side automatic day/night sideview mirror, SLS	87	74	77
Electronic compass	100	85	89
Base requires driver-side automatic day/night sideview mirror.			
Bose Sound System	723	615	643
Includes AM/FM/cassette with four Bose amplified speakers.			

CADILLAC • CHEVROLET

	Retail Price	Dealer Invoice	Fair Price
Bose Sound System	$1318	$1120	$1173

Includes AM/FM/cassette/CD player with 12-disc CD changer and four Bose amplified speakers.

Bose Sound System	1513	1286	1347

Includes AM/FM/cassette/CD player with 12-disc CD changer, digital signal processing, and four Bose amplified speakers.

Striping, SLS	75	64	67
Chrome wheels	1195	523	1064
225/60ZR16 tires, STS	250	213	223

CHEVROLET

Chevrolet Beretta

	Retail Price	Dealer Invoice	Fair Price
2-door notchback	$13490	$12208	$12508
Special Value 2-door notchback (Pkg. 1SK)	13295	12335	—
Special Value 2-door notchback (Pkg. 1SL)	13895	12890	—
Special Value 2-door notchback (Pkg. 1SM)	14395	13353	—
Z26 2-door notchback	16690	15104	15404
Z26 Special Value 2-door notchback	17295	16035	—
Destination charge	500	500	500

Special Value models' fair price not available at time of publication. Special Value models include destination charge. Additional "value-priced" models may be available in California.

Standard Equipment:

Base: 2.2-liter 4-cylinder engine, 5-speed manual transmission, anti-lock brakes, driver-side air bag, power steering, air conditioning, automatic door locks, cloth reclining front bucket seats with 4-way manual driver's seat, center shift console with armrest and storage compartment, cup holders, dual remote mirrors, door map pockets, passenger-side visor mirror, tinted glass, daytime running lights, AM/FM radio, digital clock, battery rundown protection, 195/70R14 tires, wheel covers. **Special Value Pkg. 1SK** adds: rear defogger, intermittent wipers, day/night rearview mirror with reading lights, driver-side visor mirror, trunk net, floormats. **Special Value Pkg. 1SL** adds: 3-speed automatic transmission, cassette player. **Special Value Pkg. 1SM** adds: 3.1-liter V-6 engine, 4-speed automatic transmission, tilt steering wheel. **Z26** adds to base: 3.1-liter V-6 engine, 4-speed automatic transmission, Level II Sport suspension, 4-way manual passenger seat, front seat lumbar supports, split folding rear seat, body-color grille and mirrors, front and rear spoilers, fog lamps, intermittent wipers, Gauge Pkg. with tachometer and trip odometer, cassette player, day/night rearview mirror with reading lamps,

Prices are accurate at time of publication; subject to manufacturer's change.

CHEVROLET

visor mirrors, trunk net, 205/60R15 tires. **Z26 Special Value** adds: rear defogger, tilt steering wheel, power windows, power decklid release, cruise control, floormats, 205/55R16 tires, alloy wheels.

Optional Equipment:

	Retail Price	Dealer Invoice	Fair Price
3.1-liter V-6 engine, base	$1275	$1097	$1122
Includes 4-speed automatic transmission.			
3-speed automatic transmission, base	555	477	488
NA with 3.1-liter V-6 engine.			
Preferred Equipment Group 1	165	142	145
Intermittent wipers, reading lamps, visor mirrors, trunk net, floormats.			
Preferred Group 2	745	641	656
Group 1 plus cruise control, tilt steering wheel, power decklid release, split folding rear seat.			
Preferred Equipment Group 1, Z26	463	398	407
Cruise control, tilt steering wheel, power decklid release, floormats.			
Cassette player, base	140	120	123
CD player, base	396	341	348
Z26	256	220	225
Rear defogger, base, Z26	170	146	150
Gauge Pkg., base	111	95	98
Includes tachometer, trip odometer.			
Rear spoiler, base	110	95	97
Power windows, base, Z26	275	237	242
Engine block heater	20	17	18
205/60R15 tires, base	175	151	154
Includes Level II Sport suspension, front and rear stabilizer bars.			
205/55R16 tires, Z26	372	320	327
Includes alloy wheels, Level III performance suspension.			

Chevrolet Blazer

	Retail Price	Dealer Invoice	Fair Price
3-door wagon, 2WD	$19444	$17597	—
3-door wagon, 4WD	21204	19190	—
5-door wagon, 2WD	21150	19141	—
5-door wagon, 4WD	23252	21043	—
Destination charge	490	490	490

Fair price not available at time of publication.

Standard Equipment:

2WD: 4.3-liter V-6 engine, 4-speed automatic transmission, anti-lock

CHEVROLET

brakes, driver-side air bag, power steering, air conditioning, front and rear stabilizer bars, solar-control tinted glass, coolant temperature and oil pressure gauges, voltmeter, AM/FM radio, digital clock, dual outside mirrors, trip odometer, front bucket seats with manual lumbar adjustment and console (3-door), 60/40 reclining cloth front bench seat with storage armrest (5-door), cup holders, door map pockets, floormats, cargo-area tiedown hooks, daytime running lights, intermittent wipers, day/night rearview mirror, passenger-side visor mirror, color-keyed bumpers, 7-lead trailer wiring harness, 205/75R15 tires, full-size spare tire. **4WD** adds: Insta-Trac part-time 4WD with manual transfer case, split folding rear bench seat (5-door), tow hooks, dark gray bumpers.

Optional Equipment:

5-speed manual transmission, 3-door (credit)	($890)	($765)	($765)
Locking differential	252	217	—
Electronic shift transfer case, 4WD	123	106	—

Base requires Group 2.

All-wheel drive, 5-door 4WD	200	172	—

Requires LT Decor, premium ride suspension. NA with Shield Pkg.

Off-road suspension, 3-door 4WD	555	477	—
3-door 4WD with option group	166	143	—

Includes gas shock absorbers, uprated torsion bar, jounce stabilizer bar. Requires 235/75R15 on-off road white outline letter tires.

Preferred Equipment Group 2, 3-door	1742	1498	—
5-door, 2WD	1917	1649	—
5-door, 4WD	1442	1240	—

ZQ3 convenience group (includes tilt steering wheel, cruise control), ZQ6 convenience group (includes power windows, door locks and mirrors), luggage rack, cassette player, bucket seats with power lumbar adjuster (5-door), folding rear bench seat, premium (5-door) or touring (3-door) suspension pkg. (includes gas shock absorbers), 235/70R15 tires.

LS Preferred Equipment Group 3, 3-door	2496	2147	—
5-door, 2WD	2760	2374	—
5-door, 4WD	2285	1965	—

Group 2 plus LS Decor Group (luggage rack, deep-tinted glass, chrome grille, rear window wiper/washer, cargo net, additional cup holders, power remote tailgate release, rear defogger, map lights, power outlets, upgraded cloth seat and door trim, rear compartment shade [5-door], leather-wrapped steering wheel, lighted visor mirrors, alloy wheels).

LS Preferred Equipment Group 4, 3-door	3018	2595	—
5-door, 2WD	3443	2961	—
5-door, 4WD	2968	2552	—

Group 3 plus overhead console, remote keyless entry, bucket seats with console, 6-way power driver's seat.

LT Preferred Equipment Group 5, 5-door 2WD	5161	4438	—

Prices are accurate at time of publication; subject to manufacturer's change.

CHEVROLET

	Retail Price	Dealer Invoice	Fair Price
4WD	$4694	$4037	—

LT Decor Group (LS Decor Group plus remote keyless entry, upper body pinstriping, simulated leather door panel trim, leather bucket seats with 4-way adjustable headrest and console, 6-way power driver's seat), ZQ3 and ZQ6 convenience groups, luggage rack, rear folding bench seat (2WD), premium suspension pkg., overhead console, air dam with fog lamps (2WD), electronic transfer case (4WD), tachometer, 235/70R15 tires.

	Retail Price	Dealer Invoice	Fair Price
Exterior Appearance Pkg., 5-door with LS Decor Group	346	298	—

Front bumper rub strip, composite headlights, bodyside and wheel lip moldings.

Folding cloth rear seat, base 3-door and 5-door 2WD	475	409	—
Cloth highback reclining bucket seats with console, 5-door with Group 3	161	138	—
6-way power driver's seat, with LS Decor Group	240	206	—

Requires remote keyless entry.

Driver Convenience Pkg. ZQ3, base	395	340	—

Includes cruise control and tilt steering wheel.

Driver Convenience Pkg. ZQ6, base 3-door	535	460	—
5-door	710	611	—

Includes power windows, door locks, and mirrors.

Driver Convenience Pkg. ZM8, base, base with Group 2	322	277	—

Includes rear defogger, remote tailgate release and rear wiper/washer.

Remote keyless entry system, LS Group 3	135	116	—

Requires 6-way power driver's seat.

Air dam with fog lamps, 2WD	115	99	—

NA base, base with Group 2.

Heavy duty battery	56	48	—
Exterior spare wheel and tire carrier, 3-door 4WD	159	137	—
Cold Climate Pkg.	89	77	—

Includes heavy duty battery, engine block heater.

Overhead console, LS Group 3	147	126	—
Luggage rack, base	126	108	—
Tachometer	59	51	—
Radio delete (credit)	(226)	(194)	(194)

NA with LS and LT Decor Groups.

Cassette player, base	122	105	—
Cassette player with equalizer, base	327	281	—
base with Group 2, LS Decor Group	205	176	—
CD player, with LS Decor Group	329	283	—

CHEVROLET

	Retail Price	Dealer Invoice	Fair Price
with LT Decor Group	$124	$107	—
Shield Pkg., 4WD	126	108	—
Includes transfer case and front differential skid plates, fuel tank and steering linkage shields.			
Smooth ride suspension, 5-door with option group, (credit)	(275)	(237)	(237)
Solid/smooth ride suspension, 3-door with option group, (credit)	(275)	(237)	(237)
Touring suspension, base	197	169	—
Includes gas shock absorbers.			
Premium ride suspension, base 5-door	197	169	—
Includes gas shock absorbers.			
Trailering Special Equipment (heavy duty)	210	181	—
Includes platform hitch, heavy duty flasher. NA 2WD models with 5-speed manual transmission.			
Sport 2-tone paint	172	148	—
Requires LS Decor Group.			
Rear compartment shade, 3-door 4WD with LS Decor Group	69	59	—
Requires exterior spare tire carrier.			
Argent alloy wheels, base 2WD, base 2WD with Group 2	248	213	—
Cast alloy wheels, base 4WD, base 4WD with Group 2	280	241	—
Gray-accent alloy wheels, 3-door 4WD with LS Decor Group	NC	NC	NC
Special cast alloy wheels, 4WD with LS Decor Group	NC	NC	NC
205/75R15 all-season white letter tires	121	104	—
235/70R15 all-season white outline letter tires with touring suspension	335	288	—
with option group	133	114	—
235/70R15 all-season tires, base 5-door	192	165	—
235/75R15 on/off road white outline letter tires, 4WD	335	288	—
4WD with option group	143	123	—
Requires off-road or touring suspension. Includes exterior spare tire carrier with LS 3-door 4WD.			

Chevrolet Camaro

	Retail Price	Dealer Invoice	Fair Price
3-door hatchback	$14990	$13716	$14216
2-door convertible	21270	19462	20270
Z28 3-door hatchback	19390	17742	18390

Prices are accurate at time of publication; subject to manufacturer's change.

CHEVROLET

	Retail Price	Dealer Invoice	Fair Price
Z28 convertible	$24490	$22408	$23490
Destination charge	505	505	505

Standard Equipment:

3.8-liter V-6 engine, 5-speed manual transmission, anti-lock brakes, driver- and passenger-side air bags, power steering, cloth reclining front bucket seats with 4-way adjustable driver's seat, center console with cup holders and lighted storage compartment, folding rear seatback, solar-control tinted glass, color-keyed left remote and right manual sport mirrors, tilt steering wheel, intermittent wipers, AM/FM/cassette, digital clock, day/night rearview mirror with dual reading lights, Pass-Key theft-deterrent system, tachometer, voltmeter, oil pressure and temperature gauges, trip odometer, low oil level indicator system, covered visor mirrors, door map pockets, rear spoiler, front floormats, 215/60R16 all-season tires, wheel covers. **Z28** adds: 5.7-liter V-8 engine, 6-speed manual transmission, 4-wheel disc brakes, limited-slip differential, performance ride and handling suspension, air conditioning, black roof and mirrors, low coolant indicator system, 235/55R16 all-season tires, alloy wheels. **Base and Z28 convertibles** add: air conditioning, rear defogger, power folding top, 3-piece hard boot with storage bag, color-keyed mirrors (Z28), 4-way adjustable driver's seat (Z28).

Optional Equipment:

4-speed automatic transmission	790	679	727
Base hatchback requires air conditioning.			
Traction control, Z28	450	387	414
Requires option group. NA with Performance Pkg.			
Air conditioning, base hatchback	895	770	823
Rear defogger, hatchbacks	170	146	156
Base Preferred Equipment Group 1, hatchback	1240	1066	1104
convertible	565	486	503
Air conditioning, power door locks (convertible), cruise control, remote hatch/decklid release, fog lights.			
Base Preferred Equipment Group 2, hatchback	2126	1828	1956
convertible	1231	1059	1133
Group 1 plus power windows with driver-side express down, power door locks (hatchback) and mirrors, remote illuminated entry, leather-wrapped steering wheel, theft-deterrent alarm.			
Z28 Preferred Equipment Group 1, hatchback	600	516	552
convertible	565	486	520
Cruise control, power door locks, remote hatch/decklid release, fog lights, 4-way manual seat adjuster (hatchback).			
Z28 Preferred Equipment Group 2, hatchback	1266	1089	1165

CHEVROLET

	Retail Price	Dealer Invoice	Fair Price
convertible	$1231	$1059	$1133

Group 1 plus power windows with driver-side express down, power mirrors, remote illuminated entry, leather-wrapped steering wheel, theft-deterrent alarm.

Performance Pkg., base	400	344	368

Limited-slip differential, 4-wheel disc brakes, sport steering ratio, dual outlet exhaust, 3.42 rear axle ratio (with automatic transmission). Requires option group, 235/55R16 tires, alloy or chrome wheels.

Performance Pkg., Z28 hatchback	310	267	285

Special Handling Suspension System (includes larger stabilizer bars, stiffer adjustable shock absorbers and bushings), engine oil cooler. Requires performance axle ration (when ordered with automatic transmission), 245/50ZR16 tires. NA with option groups, power seat or removable roof panels.

6-way power driver's seat	270	232	248

Z28 hatchback requires option group. NA Performance Pkg.

Leather bucket seats	499	429	459

Z28 hatchback requires option group.

Performance axle ratio, Z28	250	215	230

Requires 4-speed automatic transmission and 245/50ZR16 tires.

Power door locks, base hatchback	220	189	202

Requires Preferred Group 1.

Removable roof panels	970	834	892

Includes locks and storage provisions. NA Performance Pkg.

Hatch roof sunshades, hatchbacks	25	22	23
Color-keyed roof and mirrors, base with removable roof panels, Z28	NC	NC	NC
Delco/Bose AM/FM/cassette player, hatchbacks	350	301	322

Requires option group.

Delco/Bose AM/FM/CD player, hatchbacks	606	521	558

Requires option group.

AM/FM/CD player, convertibles	226	194	208
Color-keyed bodyside moldings	60	52	55
Rear floormats	15	13	14
235/55R16 tires, base	132	114	121

Requires alloy or chrome wheels.

245/50ZR16 tires, Z28	225	194	207
245/50ZR16 all-season tires, Z28	225	194	207
Alloy wheels, base	275	237	253

Requires 235/55R16 tires.

Chrome wheels, base	775	667	713
Z28	500	430	460

Base requires 235/55R16 tires.

Prices are accurate at time of publication; subject to manufacturer's change.

CHEVROLET

Chevrolet Caprice/Impala SS

	Retail Price	Dealer Invoice	Fair Price
Classic 4-door notchback (Pkg. 1SA)	$19905	$18213	$18713
Classic 4-door notchback (Pkg. 1SB)	20905	19128	19628
Classic 4-door notchback (Pkg. 1SC)	21905	20043	20543
Classic 5-door wagon	22405	20501	21001
Impala SS 4-door notchback	24405	22331	—
Destination charge	590	590	590

Impala SS fair price not available at time of publication. Additional "value-priced" models may be available in California.

Standard Equipment:

Classic with Pkg. 1SA: 4.3-liter V-8 engine, 4-speed automatic transmission, anti-lock brakes, driver- and passenger-side air bags, power steering, air conditioning, cruise control, power windows and door locks, cloth 55/45 seats with recliners and seatback pockets, front and rear armrests, tilt steering wheel, AM/FM/cassette with automatic tone control, power antenna, digital clock, Pass-Key theft-deterrent system, tinted glass, voltmeter and oil pressure gauge, trip odometer, oil change monitor, intermittent wipers, rear defogger, door pockets, front door courtesy lamps, automatic day/night mirror, front and rear reading lights, heated power mirrors, power decklid release, passenger-side visor mirror, cup holders, floormats, 215/75R15 whitewall tires, wheel covers, conventional spare tire. **Wagon** adds: 5.7-liter V-8 engine, automatic leveling suspension, Custom Interior Pkg. (upgraded door trim panels, driver-side visor mirror, cargo net), upgraded cloth upholstery, power front seats, vinyl rear-facing third seat, heat-reflective windshield, luggage rack, 2-way tailgate, rear wiper/washer, power tailgate window release, deluxe rear compartment trim, lighted passenger-side visor mirror, 225/75R15 whitewall tires, wire wheel covers. **Classic with Pkg. 1SB** adds to notchback with Pkg. 1SA: power front seats, cornering lamps, lighted passenger-side visor mirror, alloy wheels. **Classic with Pkg. 1SC** adds: Twilight Sentinel, remote keyless entry system, CD player, Custom Interior Pkg., heat-reflective windshield. **Impala SS** deletes automatic day/night mirror and front reading lights, and adds to Classic with Pkg. 1SA: 5.7-liter V-8 engine, 4-wheel disc brakes, extra capacity engine cooling, transmission oil cooler, special ride and handling suspension, limited-slip differential, gas shock absorbers, remote keyless entry system, rear spoiler, tachometer, leather-wrapped steering wheel, 45/45 leather seats with recliners, power driver's seat, console, driver-side visor mirror, color-keyed grille and moldings, black-out exterior trim, cargo net, 5-spoke alloy wheels, 255/50ZR17 tires.

Optional Equipment:

5.7-liter V-8 engine, Classic notchback	550	473	490
Includes transmission oil cooler. Requires sport suspension.			
CD player	155	133	138

CHEVROLET

	Retail Price	Dealer Invoice	Fair Price
Limited-slip differential,			
Classic notchback with standard engine	$250	$215	$223
Classic wagon	100	86	89

Notchback includes 3.23 rear axle ratio, extra capacity engine cooling, engine oil cooler. Wagon requires Trailering Pkg.

Preferred Equipment Group 1, Impala SS	490	421	436

6-way power passenger seat, automatic day/night mirror with front reading lights, Twilight Sentinel, passenger-side lighted visor mirror.

Sport suspension, Classic notchback	508	437	452

Limited slip differential, leather-wrapped steering wheel, Trailering Pkg., 235/70R15 tires. Requires 5.7-liter V-8 engine.

Trailering Pkg., Classic wagon	21	18	19

Includes heavy duty cooling, 2.93 rear axle ratio.

Leather 55/45 seat, Classic notchback with Pkg. 1SC	775	667	574
Heat-reflective windshield, Impala SS	52	45	46
Woodgrain exterior trim, Classic wagon	595	512	530

NA wagon with pinstriping.

Pinstriping, Classic	61	52	54

NA wagon with woodgrain exterior trim.

Wire wheel covers, Classic notchback	215	185	191
Alloy wheels, Classic notchback with Pkg. 1SA	250	215	223
235/70R15 all-season whitewall tires, Classic notchback	90	77	80

Requires 5.7-liter V-8 engine.

Engine block heater	20	17	18

Chevrolet Cavalier

	Retail Price	Dealer Invoice	Fair Price
2-door notchback	$10500	$9923	—
4-door notchback	10700	10112	—
LS 4-door notchback	12900	11933	—
LS 2-door convertible	17500	16188	—
Z24 2-door notchback	14200	12993	—
Destination charge	495	495	495

Fair price not available at time of publication. Additional "value-priced" models may be available in California.

Standard Equipment:

Base: 2.2-liter 4-cylinder engine, 5-speed manual transmission, anti-lock brakes, driver- and passenger-side air bags, power steering, tinted glass, cloth reclining front bucket seats, folding rear seat, battery rundown protec-

Prices are accurate at time of publication; subject to manufacturer's change.

CHEVROLET

tion, floor console with armrest, daytime running lights, theft-deterrent system, left remote and right manual mirrors, 195/70R14 tires, wheel covers. **LS** adds: 4-speed automatic transmission, traction control, air conditioning, AM/FM radio, digital clock, tachometer, trip odometer, dual reading lamps, visor mirrors, remote decklid release, power top (convertible), color-keyed fascias and bodyside moldings, rear decklid spoiler (convertible), front mud guards (notchback), trunk net, floormats, 195/65R15 tires. **Z24** deletes 4-speed automatic transmission and mud guards, and adds to LS notchback: 2.4-liter DOHC 4-cylinder engine, 5-speed manual transmission, sport suspension, tilt steering wheel, cassette player, rear decklid spoiler, fog lights, 205/55R16 tires, alloy wheels.

Optional Equipment:

	Retail Price	Dealer Invoice	Fair Price
2.4-liter DOHC 4-cylinder engine, LS	$395	$352	—
3-speed automatic transmission, base	550	490	—
4-speed automatic transmission, base, Z24	795	708	—
Includes traction control.			
5-speed manual transmission, convertible (credit)	(795)	(708)	(708)
Air conditioning, base	795	708	—
Preferred Equipment Group 1, base 2-door	240	214	—
base 4-door	223	198	—
Remote decklid release, intermittent wipers, visor mirrors, charcoal bodyside moldings, trunk net, front mud guards, floormats. 2-door adds easy-entry front passenger seat.			
Preferred Equipment Group 2, base 2-door	696	619	—
base 4-door	593	528	—
Group 1 plus cruise control, tilt steering wheel, power mirrors (2-door).			
Preferred Equipment Group 3, base 2-door	1295	1153	—
Group 2 plus power windows and door locks, remote keyless entry. Requires Exterior Appearance Pkg.			
Preferred Equipment Group 1, LS	435	387	—
Tilt steering wheel, intermittent wipers, cruise control.			
Preferred Equipment Group 2, LS 4-door	1225	1090	—
convertible	1120	997	—
Group 1 plus power mirrors, power windows and door locks, remote keyless entry.			
Preferred Equipment Group 1, Z24	290	258	—
Intermittent wipers, cruise control.			
Preferred Equipment Group 2, Z24	975	868	—
Group 1 plus power mirrors, power windows and door locks, remote keyless entry.			
Exterior Appearance Pkg., base	255	227	—
Color-keyed fascias and bodyside molding, 195/65R15 tires, 15-inch wheel covers. Requires option group.			

CHEVROLET

	Retail Price	Dealer Invoice	Fair Price
Rear defogger	$170	$151	—
Power sunroof, base 2-door, Z24	670	596	—
Includes mirror-mounted front map light. Requires option group.			
Power door locks, 2-doors	210	187	—
4-doors	250	223	—
AM/FM radio, base	332	295	—
AM/FM/cassette, base	497	442	—
LS	165	147	—
AM/FM/cassette with automatic tone control,			
base	552	491	—
LS	220	196	—
Z24	55	49	—
AM/FM/CD player with automatic			
tone control, base	652	580	—
LS	320	285	—
Z24	155	138	—
Engine block heater	20	18	—
Alloy wheels, LS	295	263	—

Chevrolet Corsica

	Retail Price	Dealer Invoice	Fair Price
4-door notchback	$14385	$13018	$13318
Special Value 4-door notchback (Pkg. 1SP)	13995	12983	—
Special Value 4-door notchback (Pkg. 1SQ)	14995	13908	—
Destination charge	500	500	500

Special Value models' fair price not available at time of publication. Special Value models include destination charge. Additional "value-priced" models may be available in California.

Standard Equipment:

Base: 2.2-liter 4-cylinder engine, 3-speed automatic transmission, anti-lock brakes, driver-side air bag, door-mounted automatic front seatbelts, power steering, air conditioning, automatic power door locks, cloth reclining front bucket seats, 4-way manual driver's seat, center console with cup holders and storage, AM/FM radio, digital clock, daytime running lights, color-keyed remote manual mirrors, color-keyed grille and bodyside moldings, tinted glass, passenger-side visor mirror, front door pockets, 195/70R14 tires, full wheel covers. **Special Value Pkg. 1SP** adds: intermittent wipers, rear defogger, day/night rearview mirror with reading lamps, visor mirrors, trunk net, floormats. **Special Value Pkg. 1SQ** adds: 3.1-liter V-6 engine, 4-speed automatic transmission, cassette player, tilt steering wheel.

Prices are accurate at time of publication; subject to manufacturer's change.

CHEVROLET

Optional Equipment:

	Retail Price	Dealer Invoice	Fair Price
3.1-liter V-6, base	$720	$619	$634
Includes 4-speed automatic transmission.			
Preferred Equipment Group 1, base	165	142	145
Intermittent wipers, reading lights, driver- and passenger-side covered visor mirrors, trunk net, floormats.			
Preferred Equipment Group 2, base	745	641	656
Group 1 plus cruise control, tilt steering wheel, power decklid release, split folding rear seat with armrest.			
Power windows, base	340	292	299
Rear defogger, base	170	146	150
Cassette player, base	140	120	123
CD player, base	396	341	348
Styled steel wheels, base	56	48	49
195/70R14 whitewall tires, base	68	58	60
Engine block heater, base	20	17	18

Chevrolet Corvette

	Retail Price	Dealer Invoice	Fair Price
3-door hatchback	$37225	$31827	$32827
2-door convertible	45060	38526	39726
Destination charge	565	565	565

Standard Equipment:

5.7-liter V-8 engine, 4-speed automatic transmission, heavy duty anti-lock 4-wheel disc brakes, driver- and passenger-side air bags, power steering, Acceleration Slip Regulation traction control, Pass-Key theft-deterrent system, remote keyless entry with remote hatch release, air conditioning, liquid-crystal gauges with analog and digital display, AM/FM/cassette, power antenna, digital clock, cruise control, rear defogger, reclining leather bucket seats, center console with coin tray and cassette/CD storage, armrest with lockable storage compartment, leather-wrapped tilt steering wheel, solar-control tinted glass, heated power mirrors, power windows with driver-side express down, power door locks, intermittent wipers, removable roof panel (hatchback), day/night rearview mirror with reading lights, fog lamps, lighted visor mirrors, door armrest storage compartment, cargo cover (hatchback), Goodyear Eagle GS-C tires (255/45ZR17 front, 285/40ZR17 rear), alloy wheels. **Convertible** adds: manual folding top.

Optional Equipment:

LT4 5.7-liter V-8 engine	1450	1218	1291
Includes 6-speed manual transmission.			
Preferred Equipment Group 1	1333	1120	1186
Automatic climate control, Delco/Bose audio system, 6-way power driver's seat.			

CHEVROLET

	Retail Price	Dealer Invoice	Fair Price
Collector Edition Pkg.	$1250	$1050	$1125

Sebring silver metallic paint, chrome emblems, 6-way power leather sport bucket seats, silver-painted 5-spoke alloy wheels. Requires Group 1.

Grand Sport Pkg., hatchback	3250	2730	2925
convertible	2880	2419	2592

LT4 5.7-liter V-8 engine, 6-speed manual transmission, admiral blue paint with white center stripe, 6-way power leather sport bucket seats, rear wheel flares (hatchback), black floormats, 275/40ZR17 front and 315/35ZR17 rear tires (hatchback), black-painted 5-spoke alloy wheels. Requires Group 1. NA with optional roofs, spare tire delete, Extended Mobility Tires (hatchback).

Z51 Performance Handling Pkg., hatchback	350	294	315

Sport suspension, Bilstein shock absorbers, stiffer springs, stabilizer bars and bushings, 275/40ZR17 front tires and 285/40ZR17 rear tires. Requires power seats; 4-speed automatic transmission requires performance axle ratio. NA with Extended Mobility tires, F45 Selective Real Time Damping Suspension.

F45 Selective Real Time Damping Suspension	1695	1424	1526

Requires power seats. NA with Performance Handling Pkg.

Adjustable sport bucket seats	625	525	556

Requires driver's and passenger's 6-way power seats.

6-way power seats, each	305	256	271

Power passenger's seat requires power driver's seat.

Delco/Bose audio system with cassette and CD player	396	333	352

Requires Group 1.

Performance axle ratio	50	42	45

NA with LT4 5.7-liter V-8 engine.

Low-tire-pressure warning indicator	325	273	289
Transparent blue- or bronze-tint removable roof panel, hatchback	650	546	579

NA with Grand Sport Pkg. Deletes standard solid removable roof panel.

Roof Pkg., hatchback	950	798	846

Standard solid removable roof panel and transparent blue- or bronze-tint roof panel. NA with Grand Sport Pkg.

Removable hardtop, convertible	1995	1676	1776

Includes rear defogger. NA with Grand Sport Pkg.

Extended Mobility Tires	70	59	62

Front 255/45ZR17 and rear 285/40ZR17 tires. Requires low-tire-pressure warning indicator. NA hatchback with Grand Sport or Performance Handling Pkg.

Spare tire delete (credit)	(100)	(84)	(84)

Requires Extended Mobility Tires and low-tire-pressure warning indicator. NA Grand Sport Pkg.

Prices are accurate at time of publication; subject to manufacturer's change.

CHEVROLET

Chevrolet Lumina Minivan

	Retail Price	Dealer Invoice	Fair Price
4-door van	$19890	$18000	$18500
Destination charge	545	545	545

Additional "value-priced" models may be available in California.

Standard Equipment:

3.4-liter V-6 engine, 4-speed automatic transmission, anti-lock brakes, driver-side air bag, power steering, front air conditioning, cloth reclining front bucket seats, 4-way manual driver's seat, five folding modular rear seats, tinted glass with solar-control windshield, lockable center console, cup holders, overhead console, power sliding door, front and rear reading lights, rear auxiliary power outlet, left remote and right manual mirrors, AM/FM radio, digital clock, intermittent wipers, rear wiper/washer, reading and courtesy lights, cargo light, floormats, 205/70R15 tires, wheel covers.

Optional Equipment:

Front and rear air conditioning	450	387	405
Requires Preferred Equipment Group 2.			
Preferred Equipment Group 1	NC	NC	NC
Cruise control, tilt steering wheel, power door/tailgate locks with side door delay, power mirrors.			
Preferred Equipment Group 2	878	755	790
Group 1 plus cassette player, power windows with driver-side express down, rear defogger, remote keyless entry, deep-tinted glass, luggage rack, cargo area net.			
Trailering Pkg.	320	275	288
Includes load leveling suspension.			
Custom cloth bucket seats	125	108	113
Luggage rack	145	125	131
Rear defogger	170	146	153
Deep-tinted glass	20	18	19
Requires Group 2.			
Power door/tailgate locks	300	258	270
Power windows	275	237	248
Includes driver-side express down.			
6-way power driver's seat	270	232	243
Integrated child safety seats, dual	225	194	203
single	125	108	113
Power sliding side door	350	301	315

CHEVROLET

	Retail Price	Dealer Invoice	Fair Price
Load leveling suspension	$205	$176	$185
Includes 205/70R15 touring tires.			
Cruise control	225	194	203
Tilt steering wheel	145	125	131
Cassette player	140	120	126
CD player	396	341	356
with Group 2	256	220	230
Custom 2-tone paint	148	127	133
Alloy wheels	275	237	248
Engine block heater	20	17	19

Chevrolet Lumina/Monte Carlo

	Retail Price	Dealer Invoice	Fair Price
Lumina 4-door notchback	$16355	$14801	$15855
Lumina LS 4-door notchback	18055	16340	17555
Monte Carlo LS 2-door notchback	17255	15616	16755
Monte Carlo Z34 2-door notchback	19455	17607	18955
Destination charge	540	540	540

Standard Equipment:

Lumina: 3.1-liter V-6 engine, 4-speed automatic transmission, driver- and passenger-side air bags, power steering, air conditioning, power door locks, 60/40 cloth reclining front seat with center armrest and 4-way manual driver-side adjustment, seatback storage pocket, cup holder, tilt steering wheel, AM/FM radio with digital clock, visor mirrors, reading lights, Pass-Key theft-deterrent system, trip odometer, tinted glass, left remote and right manual mirrors, intermittent wipers, color-keyed grille, bodyside moldings, wheel covers, 205/70R15 tires. **Lumina LS/Monte Carlo LS** add: anti-lock brakes, power windows, custom cloth 60/40 reclining front seat with center armrest and 4-way manual driver-side adjustment, split fold-down rear seat (Monte Carlo LS), tachometer, cassette player with automatic tone control, power mirrors, lighted passenger-side visor mirror, chrome grille (Monte Carlo LS), lower body accent paint, floormats (Monte Carlo LS), trunk net (Lumina LS), deluxe wheel covers. **Monte Carlo Z34** adds to Monte Carlo LS: 3.4-liter DOHC V-6 engine, 4-wheel disc brakes, ride and handling suspension, custom cloth front bucket seats with center console, cruise control, leather-wrapped steering wheel with auxiliary radio controls, power decklid release, remote keyless entry, trunk net, alloy wheels, 225/60R16 tires.

Prices are accurate at time of publication; subject to manufacturer's change.

CHEVROLET

Optional Equipment:

	Retail Price	Dealer Invoice	Fair Price
3.4-liter DOHC V-6 engine, Lumina LS	$1095	$975	$1040

Includes 4-wheel disc brakes. Requires bucket seats, Group1, 225/60R16 tires and alloy wheels.

	Retail Price	Dealer Invoice	Fair Price
Anti-lock brakes, base Lumina	575	512	546
Preferred Equipment Group 1, base Lumina	736	655	699

Power windows and mirrors, cruise control, power decklid release, trunk net, floormats.

	Retail Price	Dealer Invoice	Fair Price
Preferred Equipment Group 1, Lumina LS	625	556	594
Monte Carlo LS	403	359	383

Remote keyless entry (Lumina LS), cruise control, dual heater/air conditioner controls, power decklid release, floormats (Lumina LS), trunk net (Monte Carlo LS).

	Retail Price	Dealer Invoice	Fair Price
Dual heater/air conditioner controls	100	89	95
Rear defogger	170	151	162
Remote keyless entry, base Lumina, Monte Carlo LS	220	196	209

Requires Group 1.

	Retail Price	Dealer Invoice	Fair Price
Premium cassette player, base Lumina	232	206	220
Premium CD player, base Lumina	325	289	309
Lumina LS, Monte Carlo	93	83	88
Steering wheel-mounted radio controls, Monte Carlo LS	171	152	162
Power driver's seat	300	267	285
Integrated child safety seat, Lumina LS	195	174	185
Custom cloth front bucket seats w/center console, Lumina LS, Monte Carlo LS	48	43	46

Lumina LS requires Group 1.

	Retail Price	Dealer Invoice	Fair Price
Custom cloth 60/40 seat, base Lumina	150	134	143
Monte Carlo Z34	NC	NC	NC
Leather 60/40 seat, Lumina LS	627	558	596

Requires integrated child safety seat.

CHEVROLET • CHRYSLER

	Retail Price	Dealer Invoice	Fair Price
Leather front bucket seats,			
Monte Carlo LS	$675	$601	$641
Monte Carlo Z34	627	558	596
Monte Carlo Z34 requires front bucket seats.			
Cruise control (std. Monte Carlo Z34)	217	193	205
Front floormats, Lumina	15	13	14
Rear floormats, Lumina	15	13	14
Deluxe wheel covers, base Lumina	100	89	95
Alloy wheels (std. Monte Carlo Z34)	300	267	285
Requires 225/60R16 tires.			
225/60R16 tires, Lumina LS	190	169	181
Requires alloy wheels.			
225/60R16 touring tires			
(NA Monte Carlo Z34)	175	156	166
Requires alloy wheels.			
Engine block heater	19	17	18

CHRYSLER

Chrysler Cirrus

	Retail Price	Dealer Invoice	Fair Price
LX 4-door notchback	$17560	$16098	—
LXi 4-door notchback	20430	18653	—
Destination charge	535	535	535

Fair price not available at time of publication.

Standard Equipment:

LX: 2.4-liter DOHC 4-cylinder engine, 4-speed automatic transmission, anti-lock brakes, driver- and passenger-side air bags, variable-assist power steering, air conditioning, cloth reclining front bucket seats with driver's-side manual height and lumbar adjusters, front seat back map pockets, console, folding rear bench seat, AM/FM/cassette, digital clock, trip odometer, oil pressure and coolant temperature gauges, voltmeter, tachometer, cruise control, tilt steering column, rear defogger, power windows and door locks, tinted glass with solar-control windshield, heated power mirrors, speed-sensitive intermittent wipers, illuminated entry, remote decklid release, universal garage-door opener, reading lights, auxiliary power outlet, color-keyed bodyside moldings, lighted visor mirrors, fog lights, floormats, trunk net, 195/65R15 tires, wheel covers. **LXi** adds: 2.5-liter V-6 engine, sport suspension, leather upholstery, leather-wrapped steering wheel and shift lever, 8-way power driver's seat, remote keyless entry w/security alarm, 8-speaker cassette player, power antenna, alloy wheels, 195/65HR15 touring tires.

CHRYSLER

Optional Equipment:

	Retail Price	Dealer Invoice	Fair Price
2.5-liter V-6 engine, LX	$800	$712	—
Power driver's seat, LX	380	338	—
Integrated child safety seat, LX	100	89	—
Includes fixed rear seatback. Requires cloth upholstery.			
Premium cassette player, LX	370	329	—
Includes eight speakers and power amplifier.			
CD player, LX	495	441	—
LXi	125	111	—
Includes eight speakers and power amplifier.			
Power sunroof	580	516	—
Remote keyless entry w/security alarm, LX	150	134	—
Extra-cost paint	100	89	—
Metallic candy apple red paint	150	134	—
Full-size spare tire	95	85	—
Engine block and battery heater	30	27	—
Smokers Pkg.	15	13	—

Chrysler Concorde

	Retail Price	Dealer Invoice	Fair Price
LX 4-door notchback w/Pkg. 22B	$19445	$17836	$18636
Destination charge	550	550	550

Standard Equipment:

LX: 3.3-liter V-6 engine, 4-speed automatic transmission, anti-lock 4-wheel disc brakes, driver- and passenger-side air bags, touring suspension, power steering, air conditioning, tinted glass with solar-control front and rear windows, cloth front bucket seats, lumbar support adjuster, front console with armrest, power windows and door locks, tachometer, trip odometer, coolant temperature gauge, AM/FM/cassette with six speakers, rear defogger, intermittent wipers, heated power mirrors, tilt steering wheel, cruise control, power decklid release, reading lights, trunk floormats, 225/60R16 tires, wheel covers.

Optional Equipment:

3.5-liter V-6 engine	725	645	689
Requires LXi Pkg.			
Traction control, Pkg. 22C	175	156	166
Pkg. 22C	1620	1442	1539

Automatic temperature control, variable-assist power steering, power driver's seat, eight speakers, illuminated/remote entry systems, overhead console (trip computer, compass, outside temperature readout, automatic day/night mirror, lighted visor mirrors), illuminated visor mirrors, automatic day/night rearview mirror, cargo net.

CHRYSLER

	Retail Price	Dealer Invoice	Fair Price
LXi Pkg.	$3930	$3498	$3734

Pkg. 22C plus Infinity cassette system, traction control, power passenger seat, leather front bucket seats, leather-wrapped steering wheel and shifter, security alarm, sparkle-gold alloy wheels. Requires 3.5-liter engine.

Integrated child seat	100	89	95

NA LXi Pkg.

Power driver's and front passenger's seats

Pkg. 22C	380	338	361
Cloth 50/50 split bench front seat, LX	NC	NC	NC
Pkg. 22C (credit)	(155)	(138)	(138)

Overhead console is deleted when ordered with Pkg. 22C.

Power moonroof, Pkg. 22C	1100	979	1045
w/LXi Pkg.	720	641	684

Includes mini overhead console. Mini console replaces full overhead console.

Security alarm, Pkg. 22C	150	134	143

Chrysler/Infinity cassette system,

w/LXi Pkg. 22C	300	267	285

Includes equalizer, 11 speakers, amplifier, power antenna.

Chrysler/Infinity cassette/CD system,

w/Pkg. 22C	600	534	570
w/LXi Pkg.	300	267	285

Includes equalizer, 11 speakers, amplifier, power antenna.

Alloy wheels, Pkg. 22C	365	325	347
Full-size spare tire	95	85	90

Requires option pkg.

Extra cost paint	100	89	95
Bright platinum metallic paint	200	178	190
Engine block heater	20	18	19

Chrysler LHS/New Yorker

	Retail Price	Dealer Invoice	Fair Price
New Yorker 4-door notchback	$27300	$24992	$25792
LHS 4-door notchback	30255	27702	28502
Destination charge	595	595	595

Standard Equipment:

New Yorker: 3.5-liter V-6 engine, 4-speed automatic transmission, anti-lock 4-wheel disc brakes, driver- and passenger-side air bags, variable-assist power steering, automatic air conditioning, 50/50 cloth front seat with center armrests, 8-way power driver's seat with manual lumbar adjustment, tilt steering wheel, cruise control, power windows and locks, heated power mirrors, automatic day/night rearview mirror, speed-sensitive intermittent

CHRYSLER

wipers, rear defogger, mini overhead console with compass and outside temperature readout, trip computer, solar control tinted glass, tachometer, trip odometer, coolant temperature gauge, Chrysler/Infinity AM/FM/cassette system with equalizer and 11 speakers, integrated antenna, power decklid release, automatic headlights, universal garage-door opener, remote keyless illuminated entry system, theft security alarm, lighted visor mirrors, reading lights, floormats, trunk cargo net, touring suspension, 225/60R16 touring tires, alloy wheels. **LHS** adds: traction control, leather upholstery, 8-way power passenger seat, front bucket seats with power recliners, center storage console with cup holders and rear heat/AC ducts, leather-wrapped steering wheel and shift knob, fog lamps, conventional spare tire.

Optional Equipment:

	Retail Price	Dealer Invoice	Fair Price
New Yorker Pkg. 26C	$1135	$1010	$1078
8-way power passenger seat, traction control, leather upholstery, leather-wrapped steering wheel, conventional spare tire.			
8-way power front seats, New Yorker	380	338	361
Leather seats, New Yorker	1080	961	1026
Includes leather-wrapped steering wheel.			
Traction control, New Yorker	175	156	166
Power moonroof	795	708	755
Chrysler/Infinity cassette/CD system	300	267	285
Includes equalizer and 11 speakers.			
Extra-cost paint	100	89	95
Bright platinum or candy apple red metallic paint	200	178	190
Conventional spare tire, New Yorker	95	85	90
Engine block heater	20	18	19

Chrysler Sebring

	Retail Price	Dealer Invoice	Fair Price
LX 2-door notchback	$16441	$15102	—
LXi 2-door notchback	20150	18404	—
Destination charge	535	535	535

Fair price not available at time of publication.

Standard Equipment:

LX: 2.0-liter DOHC 4-cylinder engine, 5-speed manual transmission, driver- and passenger-side air bags, anti-lock brakes, variable-assist power steering, air conditioning, cloth front bucket seats, console with storage armrest and auxiliary power outlet, split folding rear seat, rear headrests, tinted glass, rear defogger, tilt steering column, AM/FM radio, trip odometer, oil pressure and coolant temperature gauges, tachometer, variable intermittent wipers, remote fuel door and decklid releases, dual remote mirrors, map

CHRYSLER

lights, color-keyed front and rear fascias, fog lights, visor mirrors, floormats, 195/70R14 tires, wheel covers. **LXi** adds: 2.5-liter V-6 engine, 4-speed automatic transmission, 4-wheel disc brakes, power windows and door locks, heated power mirrors, upgraded cloth upholstery and driver's seat lumbar support adjuster, leather-wrapped steering wheel, 8-speaker Infinity audio system with cassette player and equalizer, cruise control, remote keyless entry system w/security alarm, lighted visor mirrors, universal garage-door opener, trunk net, 205/55HR16 tires, alloy wheels.

Optional Equipment:

	Retail Price	Dealer Invoice	Fair Price
2.5-liter V-6 engine, LX	$830	$739	—
Includes 4-wheel disc brakes, upgraded suspension, 205/55HR16 tires. Requires 4-speed automatic transmission.			
4-speed automatic transmission, LX	683	608	—
Pkg. 21H/22H/24H, LX	759	676	—
Cruise control, power windows, door locks, and mirrors, lighted visor mirrors, trunk net. Pkg. 22H requires 4-speed automatic transmission. Pkg. 24H requires 2.5-liter V-6 engine and 4-speed automatic transmission.			
Pkg. 24K, LXi	1266	1127	—
Power driver's seat, leather and vinyl upholstery, power sunroof.			
Power driver's seat	203	181	—
LX requires option pkg.			
Power sunroof	640	570	—
LX requires option pkg.			
Cassette player with eight Infinity speakers and equalizer, LX w/option pkg.	550	490	—
CD/cassette player with eight Infinity speakers and equalizer, LX w/option pkg.	842	759	—
LXi	292	260	—
Remote keyless entry w/security alarm, LX w/option pkg.	272	242	—
Ashtray and cigarette lighter	15	13	—
Universal garage-door opener, LX w/option pkg.	108	96	—

Chrysler Town & Country

	Retail Price	Dealer Invoice	Fair Price
Base 4-door van	$24415	$22200	—
LX 4-door van, SWB	24400	22187	—
LXi 5-door van	30045	27155	—
Destination charge	560	560	560

Fair price not available at time of publication. SWB denotes standard wheelbase.

Prices are accurate at time of publication; subject to manufacturer's change.

CHRYSLER

Standard Equipment:

Base: 3.3-liter V-6 engine, 4-speed automatic transmission, driver- and passenger-side air bags, anti-lock brakes, power steering, air conditioning with dual controls, cruise control, tinted glass, tilt steering column, cloth reclining front bucket seats, folding 2-passenger middle bench seat, folding 3-passenger rear bench seat, passenger-side underseat storage drawer, leather-wrapped steering wheel, overhead console with compass and trip computer, AM/FM/cassette, digital clock, tachometer, coolant temperature gauge, trip odometer, power windows and door locks, power rear quarter windows, heated power mirrors, variable intermittent wipers, variable intermittent rear wiper/washer, windshield wiper de-icer, rear defogger, reading lights, fog lights, front and rear auxiliary power outlets, lighted visor mirrors, floormats, 215/65R15 tires, wheel covers. **LX** adds: striping, 215/65R16 tires, alloy wheels. **LXi** deletes middle bench seat and adds: 3.8-liter V-6 engine, rear air conditioning, sunscreen/solar tinted windshield, rear privacy glass, dual sliding side doors, 8-way power front bucket seats with driver-side memory, dual folding and reclining middle bucket seats, leather upholstery, Infinity Acoustic 10 audio system with CD player and equalizer, automatic day/night mirror, exterior memory mirrors, remote keyless entry, security alarm, front door map pockets, rear reading lights, roof rack, full-size spare tire.

Optional Equipment:

	Retail Price	Dealer Invoice	Fair Price
Pkg. 28R/29R base, 28H/29H LX	$530	$451	—

Sunscreen/solar glass, headlight-off delay, illuminated entry, remote keyless entry, 10-speaker sound system, 8-way power driver's seat. Pkg. 29R and 29H require 3.8-liter V-6 engine.

3.8-liter V-6, base, LX	305	259	—

Requires option pkg.

Seating Group 1, base, LX	225	191	—
LXi	NC	NC	NC

Deluxe 7-passenger Seating Group (includes middle- and rear-seat recliners and headrests) with integrated child seats in middle bench. Base/LX require option pkg. NA base with leather upholstery.

Seating Group 2, base, LX	625	531	—

Reclining and folding middle bucket seats, rear-seat recliner and headrests. Requires option pkg.

Climate Group 1, base	405	344	—

Rear heater and air conditioning. Requires option pkg.

Convenience/Security Group 1, base	150	128	—

Security alarm. Requires option pkg.

Loading & Towing Group 1, base, LX	110	94	—

Conventional spare tire. Requires option pkg.

Loading & Towing Group 1, LXi	270	230	—

Heavy Duty Trailer Tow Group (heavy duty battery, brakes, suspension, and radiator, heavy-duty transmission oil cooler, trailer wiring harness).

CHRYSLER • DODGE

	Retail Price	Dealer Invoice	Fair Price
Loading & Towing Group 2, base, LX	$180	$153	—
with Wheel/Handling Group 2	145	123	—
Base Group 1 plus heavy load/firm ride suspension. Requires option pkg.			
Loading & Towing Group 3, base, LX	380	323	—
with Wheel/Handling Group 2	345	293	—
Group 2 plus Heavy Duty Trailer Tow Group. Requires option pkg.			
Wheel/Handling Group 2, base, LX	470	400	—
Touring Handling Group (touring suspension, upgraded front struts and rear shock absorbers, rear stabilizer bar), alloy wheels, 215/65R16 tires. Requires option pkg.			
Sliding driver's-side door, base, LX	500	425	—
Requires option pkg.			
Leather bucket seats, base, LX	890	757	—
Requires Seating Group 2.			
10-speaker CD/cassette player with equalizer, base, LX	395	336	—
Requires option pkg.			
Roof rack, base, LX	175	149	—
Requires option pkg.			
Extra-cost paint	100	85	—
candy apple red metallic, base	200	170	—
white pearl, LX, LXi	200	170	—
Engine block heater	35	30	—
Smoker's Group	15	13	—
Cigarette lighter, ashtrays.			
Alloy wheels, base with option pkg.	410	349	—

DODGE

Dodge Avenger

	Retail Price	Dealer Invoice	Fair Price
2-door notchback	$14040	$12946	—
ES 2-door notchback	18121	16578	—
Destination charge	535	535	535

Fair price not available at time of publication.

Standard Equipment:

Base: 2.0-liter DOHC 4-cylinder engine, 5-speed manual transmission, driver- and passenger-side air bags, variable-assist power steering, cloth reclining front bucket seats, console with storage armrest and auxiliary power outlet, split folding rear seat, rear headrests, tinted glass, rear defogger, tilt steering column, AM/FM radio, trip odometer, oil pressure and coolant tem-

DODGE

perature gauges, tachometer, intermittent wipers, dual remote mirrors, map lights, color-keyed front and rear fascias, visor mirrors, 195/70HR14 tires, wheel covers. **ES** adds: 2.5-liter V-6 engine, 4-speed automatic transmission, anti-lock 4-wheel disc brakes, air conditioning, upgraded cloth upholstery and driver's seat lumbar support adjuster, cassette player, cruise control, handling suspension, cargo nets and hooks, decklid spoiler, fog lights, floormats, 205/55HR16 tires, alloy wheels.

Optional Equipment:

	Retail Price	Dealer Invoice	Fair Price
2.0-liter DOHC 4-cylinder engine, ES (credit)	($609)	($542)	($542)
Requires 5-speed manual transmission.			
4-speed automatic transmission, base	683	608	—
5-speed manual transmission, ES (credit)	(683)	(608)	(608)
Requires 2.0-liter DOHC 4-cylinder engine.			
Pkg. 21B/22B, base	1216	1082	—
Air conditioning, cruise control, cassette player, floormats. Pkg. 22B requires 4-speed automatic transmission.			
Pkg. 21C/22C, base	1750	1558	—
Pkg. 21B/22B plus power windows and door locks, power mirrors, trunk net. Pkg. 22C requires 4-speed automatic transmission.			
Pkg. 21E/24E, ES	534	475	—
Power windows and door locks, power mirrors, lighted visor mirrors. Pkg. 21E requires 2.0-liter DOHC 4-cylinder engine and 5-speed manual transmission.			
Pkg. 21F/24F, ES	2309	2055	—
Pkg. 24E plus cassette player with equalizer and Infinity speakers, power driver's seat, security alarm, universal garage-door opener, remote keyless entry system, power sunroof. Pkg. 21F requires 2.0-liter DOHC 4-cylinder engine and 5-speed manual transmission.			
Anti-lock brakes, base	599	533	—
Air conditioning, base	788	701	—
Leather upholstery, ES	423	376	—
Requires option pkg. and power driver's seat.			
Power driver's seat, base w/Pkg. 21C/22C, ES w/Pkg. 21E/24E	203	181	—
Cassette player, base	174	155	—
Cassette player with eight Infinity speakers and equalizer	550	490	—
Base requires option pkg.			
CD/cassette player with eight Infinity speakers and equalizer	842	749	—
ES w/Pkg. 21F/24F	292	260	—
Base requires option pkg.			
Power sunroof	640	570	—
Requires option pkg.			

DODGE

	Retail Price	Dealer Invoice	Fair Price
Security alarm, base w/Pkg. 21C/22C, ES w/Pkg. 21E/24E	$274	$244	—
Includes remote keyless entry system.			
Universal garage-door opener	108	96	—
Requires option pkg.			
Ashtray and cigarette lighter	15	13	—
Alloy wheels, base w/option pkg	464	413	—
Includes 205/55HR16 all-season tires.			

Dodge Caravan

	Retail Price	Dealer Invoice	Fair Price
Base 4-door van, SWB	$16575	$15096	—
Base Grand 4-door van	17825	16221	—
SE 4-door van, SWB	19270	17468	—
Grand SE 4-door van	20010	18144	—
LE 4-door van, SWB	23620	21296	—
Grand LE 4-door van	24110	21752	—
ES 4-door van, SWB	24210	21815	—
Grand ES 4-door van	24700	22271	—
Destination charge	560	560	560

Fair prices not available at time of publication. SWB denotes standard wheelbase.

Standard Equipment:

Base: 2.4-liter DOHC 4-cylinder engine, 3-speed automatic transmission, driver- and passenger-side air bags, power steering, cloth reclining front bucket seats, 3-passenger rear bench seat (short wheelbase), 2-passenger middle bench seat (Grand), folding 3-passenger rear bench seat (Grand), cup holders, tinted glass, variable intermittent wipers, variable intermittent rear wiper/washer, coolant-temperature gauge, trip odometer, AM/FM radio, digital clock, dual exterior mirrors, visor mirrors, auxiliary power outlet, 205/75R14 tires, wheel covers. **SE** adds: 4-speed automatic transmission, anti-lock brakes, cruise control, tilt steering column, passenger-side underseat storage drawer, heated power mirrors, tachometer, cassette player, 215/65R15 tires. **LE** adds: 3.3-liter V-6 engine, air conditioning, computer with compass, temperature, and travel displays, overhead storage console with map/reading lights, CD/cassette storage, upgraded cloth upholstery, power windows and door locks, power rear quarter vent and front-door windows, oil pressure gauge, voltmeter, windshield wiper de-icer, rear defogger, ignition-switch light, liftgate lights, reading lights, striping, lighted visor mirrors, rear auxiliary power outlet, deluxe sound insulation, floormats. **ES** adds: ES Decor Group (color-keyed fascias, bodyside moldings, and lower bodyside appliqués, leather-wrapped steering wheel, striping, fog lights, alloy wheels, 215/65R16 tires.)

Prices are accurate at time of publication; subject to manufacturer's change.

DODGE

Optional Equipment:

	Retail Price	Dealer Invoice	Fair Price
Anti-lock brakes, base	$415	$353	—
3.0-liter V-6 engine, base, SWB SE	770	655	—

Requires 3-speed automatic transmission. Base requires option pkg. NA with SWB SE Sport pkgs.

3.3-liter V-6 engine, SE	890	757	—

Requires option pkg. 28B, 28C, 28D, or 28E.

3.8-liter V-6 engine, LE, ES	305	259	—

Requires option pkg.

3-speed automatic transmission (credit), SWB SE	(250)	(213)	(213)

Requires 3.0-liter engine. NA with SWB SE Sport Pkgs.

Pkg. 22T/24T, base SWB	605	514	—
Base Grand	255	217	—

Air conditioning, 7-passenger seating (SWB), front passenger underseat storage drawer, Light Group (interior courtesy lights, map/reading lights, illuminated ignition, auxiliary power outlet), dual horns, rear-floor sound insulation. Pkg. 24T requires 3.0-liter V-6 engine.

Pkg. 23B/24B, base SE, 23B/28B Grand SE	470	400	—

Air conditioning, Deluxe 7-passenger Seating Group (includes middle- and rear-seat recliners and headrests), Light Group (interior courtesy lights, map/reading lights, illuminated ignition, auxiliary power outlet), rear defogger. Pkg. 24B requires 3.0-liter V-6 engine. Pkg. 28B requires 3.3-liter V-6 engine.

Pkg. 28C (Sport), SWB SE	1630	1386	—

Pkg. 23B/24B plus Sport decor group (touring suspension, leather-wrapped steering wheel, Sport decals, sunscreen/solar glass, body-color door handles, fascias, luggage rack, and bodyside moldings, fog lights, white alloy wheels, 215/65R16 touring tires). Requires 3.3-liter V-6 engine.

Pkg. 24D/28D, SWB SE, 28D Grand SE	1205	1024	—

Pkg. 23B/28B plus power windows and door locks, power rear quarter vent windows, lighted visor mirrors, added sound insulation, floormats. Pkg. 24D requires 3.0-liter V-6 engine. Pkg. 28D requires 3.3-liter V-6 engine.

Pkg. 28E (Sport), SWB SE	2365	2010	—

Pkg. 24D/28D plus Sport decor group (touring suspension, leather-wrapped steering wheel, Sport decals, sunscreen/solar glass, body-color door handles, fascias, luggage rack, and bodyside moldings, fog lights, white alloy wheels, 215/65R16 touring tires). Requires 3.3-liter V-6 engine.

Pkg. 28K/29K, SWB/Grand LE	690	587	—

Air conditioning with dual controls, 8-way power driver's seat, solar-control glass, headlight-off delay, illuminated entry, 10-speaker cassette player, remote keyless entry, Deluxe 7-passenger seating group. Pkg. 29K requires 3.8-liter V-6 engine.

CONSUMER GUIDE®

DODGE

	Retail Price	Dealer Invoice	Fair Price
Pkg. 28M/29M, SWB ES	$835	$710	—
Grand ES	1335	1135	—

Pkg. 28K/29K plus sliding driver's-side door (Grand), Touring Handling Group (touring suspension, upgraded front struts and rear shock absorbers, rear stabilizer bar), automatic day/night mirror. Pkg. 29M requires 3.8-liter V-6 engine.

7-passenger seating, base SWB	350	298	—

2-passenger middle bench seat, 3-passenger rear bench seat.

7-passenger seating w/integrated child seat, base	285	242	—

2-passenger reclining middle bench seat with headrest and integrated child seats, 3-passenger rear bench seat. Requires option pkg.

Deluxe 7-passenger seating w/integrated child seats, SE, LE, ES	225	191	—

Premium cloth 2-passenger reclining middle bench seat with headrests and integrated child seats, 3-passenger reclining rear bench seat. Requires option pkg.

Deluxe 7-passenger seating w/quad bucket seats, SE	745	633	—
LE, ES	625	531	—

Premium cloth reclining middle bucket seats, 3-passenger reclining rear bench seat with headrests. LE requires option pkg. SE requires Pkg. 24D, 28D, or 28E.

Sliding driver's-side door	500	425	—

Requires option pkg.

Air conditioning, base, SE	860	731	—
Rear heater/air conditioning, Grand LE	470	400	—
Grand ES	405	344	—

Requires option pkg.

Rear heater/air conditioning w/overhead console, Grand SE w/Pkg. 23B/28B	1130	961	—
w/Pkg. 28D	1020	867	—
w/Pkg. 28D and Trailer Tow Group	955	812	—
Sunscreen/solar glass, base, SE	450	383	—

Requires option pkg.

Convenience/Security Group 1, base	435	370	—

Cruise control, tilt steering column, power mirrors. Requires option pkg.

Convenience/Security Group 2, base	750	638	—

Group 1 plus power door locks. Requires option pkg.

Convenience/Security Group 2, SE	315	268	—

Power door locks. Requires option pkg.

Convenience/Security Group 3, SE	685	582	—

SE Group 2 plus power windows and rear quarter vent windows. Requires option pkg.

Prices are accurate at time of publication; subject to manufacturer's change.

DODGE

	Retail Price	Dealer Invoice	Fair Price
Convenience/Security Group 4, SE	$235	$200	—
Group 3 plus remote keyless entry, illuminated entry, headlamp-off delay. Requires Pkg. 24D, 28D, or 28E.			
Convenience/Security Group 5, SE	385	327	—
Group 4 plus security alarm. Requires Pkg. 24D, 28D, or 28E.			
Convenience/Security Group 5, Grand LE, Grand ES	150	128	—
Security alarm. Requires option pkg.			
Loading & Towing Group 1	110	94	—
Full-size spare tire. Requires option pkg.			
Loading & Towing Group 2, SE, LE	180	153	—
LE with Wheel/Handling Group 2, ES	145	123	—
Group 1 plus heavy load/firm ride suspension. Requires option pkg. NA with SWB Sport Pkg. 28C or 28E.			
Loading & Towing Group 3, Grand SE, LE	445	378	—
LE with Wheel/Handling Group 2	410	349	—
ES	345	293	—
Group 2 plus Heavy Duty Trailer Tow Group (heavy duty battery alternator, brakes, and radiator, heavy duty transmission oil cooler, trailer wiring harness). LE and ES require option pkg. Grand SE requires Pkg. 28D.			
Wheel/Handling Group 2, LE	470	400	—
Touring Handling Group, alloy wheels, 215/65R16 tires. Requires option pkg.			
Rear defogger, SE	230	196	—
base	195	166	—
base w/Convenience/Security Group 1 or 2	230	196	—
Includes windshield wiper de-icer.			
Leather bucket seats, LE, ES	890	757	—
Requires option pkg.			
Cassette player, base	170	145	—
Requires option pkg.			
10-speaker cassette player with equalizer, SE	335	285	—
Requires Pkg. 24D, 28D, or 28E.			
10-speaker CD player with equalizer, SE	730	621	—
LE, ES	395	336	—
LE and ES require option pkg. SE requires Pkg. 24D, 28D, or 28E.			
Roof rack	175	149	—
Requires option pkg.			
Extra-cost paint	100	85	—
candy apple red metallic, LE, ES	200	170	—
white pearl, ES	200	170	—
Engine block heater	35	30	—
Smoker's Group	15	13	—
Cigarette lighter, ash trays.			
Alloy wheels, Grand SE with option pkg.	415	353	—

DODGE

	Retail Price	Dealer Invoice	Fair Price
SWB SE w/Sport Pkg.	NC	NC	NC
LE with option pkg.	$410	$349	—

Dodge Intrepid

	Retail Price	Dealer Invoice	Fair Price
4-door notchback	$18445	$16946	$17746
ES 4-door notchback	22260	20341	21141
Destination charge	550	550	550

Standard Equipment:

3.3-liter V-6 engine, 4-speed automatic transmission, driver- and passenger-side air bags, power steering, air conditioning, cruise control, cloth front bucket seats, console with armrest and cupholders, solar-control glass, heated power mirrors, power windows and door locks, rear defogger, tilt steering column, intermittent wipers, AM/FM cassette with six speakers, tachometer, coolant temperature gauge, headlamp shut-off delay, trip odometer, AM/FM radio, reading lights, visor mirrors, remote decklid release, touring suspension, fog lamps, floormats, 225/60R16 touring tires, wheel covers. **ES** adds: 3.5-liter OHC V-6 engine, anti-lock 4-wheel disc brakes, variable-assist power steering, premium cloth front bucket seats with lumbar support adjustment, power driver's seat, leather-wrapped steering wheel, eight speakers, Message Center, illuminated visor mirrors, alloy wheels.

Optional Equipment:

Pkg. 22C/24C, base	723	633	687
Pkg. 22D, base	1235	1099	1173

4-wheel disc brakes, variable-assist power steering, power driver's seat, Remote/Illuminated Entry Group, Message Center, eight speakers, lighted visor mirrors.

Pkg. 26M, ES	1125	1001	1069

Traction control, automatic temperature control, overhead console with compass and thermometer, Chrysler/Infinity cassette system, security alarm, cargo net, conventional spare tire.

Anti-lock 4-wheel disc brakes, base	625	556	594
base w/Pkg. 22D	600	534	570
Traction control, ES	175	156	166
Automatic temperature control, ES	155	138	147
Overhead console, ES	385	343	366

Compass/temperature/traveler displays, front and rear reading lamps, storage compartment, automatic day/night mirror, illuminated visor mirrors. NA with power sunroof.

AM/FM/cassette, base	350	312	333

Includes eight speakers.

Prices are accurate at time of publication; subject to manufacturer's change.

DODGE

	Retail Price	Dealer Invoice	Fair Price
Chrysler/Infinity Spatial Imaging Cassette Sound System, ES	$300	$267	$285

AM/FM cassette with equalizer, amplifier, 11 Infinity speakers, power antenna.

Chrysler/Infinity Spatial Imaging Cassette/Compact Disc Sound System, ES w/Pkg. 26L	600	534	570
ES w/Pkg. 26M	300	267	285

AM/FM stereo, compact disc player, equalizer, amplifier, power antenna.

Power moonroof, base w/Pkg. 22D	1015	903	964
ES	1100	979	1045
ES w/Pkg. 26M	720	641	684

Includes mini overhead console.

Integrated child seat	100	89	95

Not available with leather seats.

Cloth 50/50 front bench seat, base	NC	NC	NC
Power passenger's seat, ES	380	338	361
Leather front bucket seats, ES	1015	903	964

Includes power front seats, leather-wrapped shift knob. NA with integrated child seat.

Security alarm, ES	150	134	143

Requires automatic temperature control.

Performance Handling Group, ES	220	196	209

Performance suspension, 225/60R16 performance tires.

Conventional spare tire	95	85	90
Extra-cost paint	100	89	95
Bright platinum metallic paint	200	178	190
Engine block heater	20	18	19
Polycast wheel, base	NC	NC	NC
Base w/Pkg. 22D	105	93	100

Dodge/Plymouth Neon

	Retail Price	Dealer Invoice	Fair Price
Base 4-door notchback	$9995	$9390	$9495
Base 2-door notchback	9495	8930	8995
Highline 4-door notchback	11500	10545	11000
Highline 2-door notchback	11300	10365	10800
Sport 4-door notchback	12700	11625	12200
Sport 2-door notchback	12500	11445	12000
Destination charge	500	500	500

Standard Equipment:

Base: 2.0-liter 4-cylinder engine, 5-speed manual transmission, driver- and passenger-side air bags, 18:1 ratio power steering, touring suspension, cloth reclining bucket seats, tinted glass, floor storage console with dual

DODGE

cup holders and coin holder, left remote outside mirror, passenger-side visor mirror, variable intermittent wipers, trip odometer, 185/65R14 all-season touring tires. **Highline** adds: 60/40 split folding rear seat, dual remote mirrors, driver-side visor mirror, AM/FM radio with four speakers, remote decklid release, bodyside moldings, wheel covers. **Sport 4-door** adds: power mirrors and door locks, padded covered floor storage console with tissue pack holder, dual cup holders, and cassette/CD holders, rear defogger, tilt steering wheel, tachometer w/low-fuel light, fog lights, power bulge hood, Sport wheel covers. **Sport 2-door** adds: 16:1 ratio power steering, performance-tuned suspension, 185/65R14 all-season performance tires.

Optional Equipment:

	Retail Price	Dealer Invoice	Fair Price
2.0-liter DOHC 4-cylinder engine, Sport	$150	$134	$143
Included with 2-door Competition Pkg. NA 4-door Competition Pkg.			
3-speed automatic transmission	600	534	570
Anti-lock 4-wheel brakes	565	503	537
NA with Competition Pkg.			
Competition Pkg., Base 2-door	1745	1605	1658
Base 4-door	1575	1449	1496
2.0-liter DOHC 4-cylinder engine (2-door), 5-speed manual performance transmission, 4-wheel disc brakes, dual remote mirrors, heavy duty radiator, 16:1 ratio power steering, competition suspension, tachometer with low fuel light, 175/65HR14 tires (4-door) or 185/60HR 14 tires (2-door), alloy wheels.			
Highline Pkg. 21D/22D	735	654	698
Air conditioning, rear defogger, floor storage console. Pkg. 22D requires 3-speed automatic transmission.			
Highline Expresso Pkg. 21G/22G	935	832	888
Pkg 21D/22D plus tachometer with low fuel light, flash decor cloth upholstery, Expresso graphics, power bulge hood, rear spoiler. Pkg. 22G requires 3-speed automatic transmission.			
Sport Pkg. 21K/22K/23K/24K	965	859	917
Air conditioning, premium AM/FM/cassette with CD changer controls, front and rear floormats. Pkg. 22K/24K requires 3-speed automatic transmission. Pkg 23K/24K requires 2.0-liter DOHC 4-cylinder engine.			
Deluxe Convenience Group,			
Highline w/option pkg.	350	312	333
Cruise control, tilt steering.			
Power Convenience Group,			
Highline 4-door	300	267	285
Highline 2-door	260	231	247
Power mirrors and door locks. Requires option pkg.			
Light Group, Highline, Sport w/option pkg.	130	116	124
Illuminated visor mirrors, courtesy/reading lights.			

Prices are accurate at time of publication; subject to manufacturer's change.

DODGE

	Retail Price	Dealer Invoice	Fair Price
Air conditioning, Base	$900	$801	$855
Power moonroof, Highline w/Pkg. 21D/22D, Sport w/option pkg.	595	530	565
Rear defogger, Base, Highline	175	156	166
Remote keyless entry, Highline W/Pkg. 21D/22D, Sport w/option pkg.	155	138	147
Highline requires Power Convenience Group.			
Bodyside moldings, Base	30	27	29
NA with Competition Pkg.			
Dual manual remote mirrors, Base	70	62	67
NA with Competition Pkg.			
AM/FM radio with four speakers, Base	335	298	318
AM/FM/cassette with six speakers, Base	585	521	556
Highline, Sport	250	223	238
NA with Competition Pkg.			
Premium AM/FM/cassette w/six speakers, Highline w/option pkg.	300	367	285
Includes CD changer controls.			
Premium AM/FM/CD player w/six speakers, Highline w/option pkg., Sport	480	427	456
Sport w/option pkg.	180	160	171
Flash decor cloth upholstery, Sport w/option pkg.	120	107	114
NA with integrated child seat.			
Integrated child seat, Highline w/Pkg. 21D/22D, Sport w/option pkg.	100	89	95
Includes fixed rear seat back. NA with flash decor cloth upholstery on Sport.			
Cruise control, Sport w/option pkg.	225	200	214
Tilt steering wheel	150	134	143
NA with Competition Pkg.			
Power front door windows, Highline w/Pkg. 21D/22D, Sport w/option pkg.	265	236	252
Tachometer with low fuel light, Highline w/Pkg. 21D/22D	95	85	90
Front and rear floormats, Highline, Sport	50	45	48
Extra-cost paint, Base, Highline	100	89	95
Alloy wheels, Sport w/option pkg.	355	316	337

DODGE

Dodge Stealth

	Retail Price	Dealer Invoice	Fair Price
3-door hatchback	$24461	$22166	$22666
R/T 3-door hatchback	27755	25064	26064
R/T Turbo 3-door hatchback	34820	31282	32782
Destination charge	535	535	535

Standard Equipment:

3.0-liter V-6 engine, 5-speed manual transmission, 4-wheel disc brakes, power steering, driver- and passenger-side air bags, air conditioning, cloth reclining front bucket seats, front seat height adjusters, storage console with armrest, tachometer, coolant temperature and oil pressure gauges, trip odometer, tinted glass, rear defogger, intermittent wipers, remote fuel door and hatch releases, power mirrors, auto-off headlights, AM/FM/cassette with equalizer and six speakers, tilt steering column, leather-wrapped steering wheel, fog lamps, rear spoiler, tonneau cover, visor mirrors, 205/65HR15 tires, wheel covers. **R/T** adds: DOHC engine, floormats, 225/55VR16 tires, alloy wheels with locking lug nuts. **R/T Turbo** adds: turbocharged engine, 6-speed manual transmission, permanent 4-wheel drive, cruise control, turbo boost gauge, heated power mirrors, power windows and locks, remote keyless entry system, rear wiper/washer, 245/45ZR17 tires.

Optional Equipment:

Pkg. 21C/22C, base	655	563	590

Power windows and door locks, cruise control, floormats. Pkg. 22C requires automatic transmission.

Pkg. 21D/22D, base	1306	1123	1175

Remote keyless entry system, eight Infinity speakers, rear wiper/washer. Pkg. 22D requires automatic transmission.

Pkg. 23H/24H, R/T	917	789	825

Cruise control, power windows and door locks, remote keyless entry system, rear wiper/washer. Pkg. 24H requires automatic transmission.

Pkg. 23M/24M, R/T	2780	2391	2502

Pkg. 23H/24H plus anti-lock brakes, security alarm, trunk-mounted CD changer, eight Infinity speakers. Pkg. 24M requires automatic transmission.

Pkg. 25W, R/T Turbo AWD	2525	2172	2273

Anti-lock brakes, power driver's seat, eight Infinity speakers, leather upholstery, security alarm.

Pkg. 25Y, R/T Turbo AWD	4612	3966	4151

Pkg. 25W plus sunroof, trunk-mounted CD changer, 245/40ZR18 tires, chrome wheels.

4-speed automatic transmission, base, R/T	883	759	795
Anti-lock brakes, base, R/T	799	687	719

Prices are accurate at time of publication; subject to manufacturer's change.

DODGE

	Retail Price	Dealer Invoice	Fair Price
Leather/vinyl seats, base w/Pkg. 21D/22D., R/T w/option pkg., R/T Turbo AWD w/option pkg.	$843	$725	$759
Trunk-mounted CD changer	542	466	488
Sunroof	633	544	570
Base, R/T require option pkg.			
Wheel Group, R/T Turbo AWD	912	784	821
245/40ZR18 tires, chrome wheels.			
White pearlescent paint	205	176	185
NA base.			

Dodge Stratus

	Retail Price	Dealer Invoice	Fair Price
4-door notchback	$14460	$13299	—
ES 4-door notchback	16110	14768	—
Destination charge	535	535	535

Fair price not available at time of publication.

Standard Equipment:

Base: 2.0-liter 4-cylinder engine, 5-speed manual transmission, driver- and passenger-side air bags, power steering, air conditioning, cloth reclining front bucket seats, console, folding rear bench seat, AM/FM/cassette, digital clock, trip odometer, oil pressure and coolant temperature gauges, tachometer, voltmeter, cruise control, tilt steering column, rear defogger, tinted glass with solar-control windshield, dual remote mirrors, color-keyed bodyside moldings, intermittent wipers, remote decklid release, visor mirrors, floormats, 195/70R14 tires, wheel covers. **ES** adds: anti-lock brakes, touring suspension, variable-assist power steering, manual driver's seat height and lumbar support adjusters, power windows and door locks, heated power mirrors, reading lights, fog lights, lighted visor mirrors, alloy wheels, 195/65HR15 touring tires.

Optional Equipment:

2.4-liter DOHC 4-cylinder engine	450	401	—
Requires 4-speed automatic transmission. NA ES w/Pkg. 26K.			
2.5-liter V-6 engine, ES	1250	1113	—
Requires 4-speed automatic transmission.			
4-speed automatic transmission	825	734	—
Requires 2.4-liter DOHC 4-cylinder engine or 2.5-liter V-6 engine.			
Anti-lock brakes, Base	565	503	—
Pkg. 21B/24B, Base	655	583	—

Power windows and door locks, heated power mirrors, power driver's seat height adjuster. Pkg. 24B requires 2.4-liter DOHC 4-cylinder engine and 4-speed automatic transmission.

DODGE • EAGLE

	Retail Price	Dealer Invoice	Fair Price
Pkg. 26K, ES	$1920	$1709	—

Premium cassette player, power antenna, Personal Security Group, anti-theft alarm, 8-way power driver's seat, leather upholstery, leather-wrapped steering wheel, trunk net. Requires 2.5-liter V-6 engine.

Personal Security Group	170	151	—

Remote keyless entry, illuminated entry, panic alarm. Base requires Pkg. 21B/24B.

Power sunroof, Base w/Pkg. 21B/24B	695	619	—
ES	580	516	—

Base includes illuminated visor mirrors, map lights.

Anti-theft alarm, ES	150	134	—

Requires Personal Security Group.

Integrated child safety seat	100	89	—

Includes fixed rear seatback. NA ES w/Pkg. 26K.

Premium cassette player	370	329	—

Includes eight speakers and power amplifier.

CD player	495	441	—
ES with Pkg. 26K	125	111	—

Includes eight speakers and power amplifier.

Extra-cost paint	100	89	—
Candy apple red metallic paint	150	134	—
Full-size spare tire	95	85	—
Engine block and battery heater	30	27	—
Smokers Group	15	13	—

Ash tray, lighter.

EAGLE

Eagle Talon

	Retail Price	Dealer Invoice	Fair Price
ESi 3-door hatchback	$14830	$13767	—
TSi 3-door hatchback	18015	16663	—
TSi AWD 3-door hatchback	20271	18714	—
Destination charge	535	535	535

Fair price not available at time of publication.

Standard Equipment:

ESi: 2.0-liter DOHC 4-cylinder engine, 5-speed manual transmission, 4-wheel disc brakes, driver- and passenger-side air bags, variable-assist power steering, cloth reclining front bucket seats, folding rear seat, front console with storage and armrest, tinted glass, tachometer, coolant temperature gauge, trip odometer, map lights, dual remote mirrors, visor mirrors,

Prices are accurate at time of publication; subject to manufacturer's change.

EAGLE

AM/FM radio, digital clock, remote fuel door and hatch releases, tilt steering column, intermittent wipers, rear wiper/washer, rear spoiler, color-keyed bodyside moldings, 195/70R14 tires, wheel covers. **TSi** adds: turbocharged engine, sport-tuned exhaust system, upgraded suspension, driver's seat lumbar support adjustment, split folding rear seat, leather-wrapped steering wheel and manual gearshift handle, power mirrors, turbo boost and oil pressure gauges, cassette player, lighted visor mirrors, rear defogger, cargo-area cover, cargo net, lower bodyside cladding, fog lamps, 205/55R16 tires, alloy wheels. **TSi AWD** adds: permanent 4-wheel drive, cruise control, power door locks and windows, 215/55VR16 tires.

Optional Equipment:

	Retail Price	Dealer Invoice	Fair Price
Pkg. 21B/22B, ESi	$1664	$1414	—

Air conditioning, cruise control, rear defogger, power mirrors, cassette player, cargo area cover, front floormats. Pkg. 22B requires 4-speed automatic transmission.

Pkg. 21C/22C, ESi	2198	1868	—

Pkg. 21B/22B plus power windows and door locks, cargo net, upgraded interior trim. Pkg. 22C requires 4-speed automatic transmission.

Pkg. 23P/24P, TSi	1590	1351	—

Air conditioning, cruise control, power windows and door locks, front floormats. Pkg. 24P requires automatic transmission.

Pkg. 25S/26S, TSi AWD	889	756	—

Air conditioning, front floormats. Pkg. 26S requires automatic transmission.

Pkg. 25L/26L, TSi AWD	3535	3005	—

Pkg. 25S/26S plus power driver's seat, leather/vinyl front upholstery, CD/cassette player with graphic equalizer, power sunroof, remote keyless entry with security alarm. Pkg. 26L requires automatic transmission.

4-speed automatic transmission, ESi	745	633	—
TSi	891	757	—
TSi AWD	861	732	—

TSi AWD includes 205/55VR16 tires.

Air conditioning	860	731	—
Remote keyless entry with security alarm, ESi w/Pkg. 21C/22C, TSi w/option pkg., TSi AWD w/Pkg. 25S/26S	334	284	—
Rear defogger, ESi	162	138	—
Cassette/CD player, ESi w/Pkg. 21C/22C, TSi w/option pkg., TSi AWD w/Pkg. 25S/26S	390	332	—
TSi AWD w/Pkg. 25L/26L (credit)	(403)	(343)	(343)
Cassette/CD player with graphic equalizer, TSi w/option pkg., TSi AWD w/Pkg. 25S/26S	793	674	—

Includes eight Infinity speakers.

EAGLE

	Retail Price	Dealer Invoice	Fair Price
Power sunroof, ESi w/Pkg. 21C/22C, TSi w/option pkg., TSi AWD w/Pkg. 25S/26S	$730	$621	—
Leather/vinyl upholstery, TSi w/option pkg., TSi AWD w/Pkg. 25S/26S	457	388	—
Anti-lock brakes	649	552	—
Limited-slip differential, TSi AWD	266	226	—
Power driver's seat, TSi w/option pkg., TSi AWD w/Pkg. 25S/26S	332	282	—
Universal garage-door opener, ... *Requires option pkg.*	113	96	—
Alloy wheels, ESi w/option pkg. .... *Includes 205/55HR16 tires.*	489	416	—

Eagle Vision

	Retail Price	Dealer Invoice	Fair Price
ESi 4-door notchback	$19245	$17648	$18248
TSi 4-door notchback	23835	21768	21368
Destination charge	550	550	550

Standard Equipment:

ESi: 3.3-liter V-6 engine, 4-speed automatic transmission, 4-wheel disc brakes, driver- and passenger-side air bags, power steering, air conditioning, reclining front bucket seats with lumbar support adjustment, floor console, remote decklid release, rear defogger, intermittent wipers, power windows and door locks, power mirrors, AM/FM/cassette with six speakers, tilt steering wheel, cruise control, touring suspension, dual visor mirrors, reading lights, floormats, 225/60R16 touring tires, polycast wheels. **TSi** adds: 3.5-liter V-6 engine, Autostick 4-speed automatic transmission, anti-lock brakes, traction control, variable-assist power steering, automatic temperature control, power driver's seat, overhead console, illuminated/remote keyless entry system, AM/FM/cassette with eight speakers, trip computer, leather-wrapped steering wheel, lighted visor mirrors, fog lamps, 225/60R16 tires, alloy wheels.

Optional Equipment:

Pkg. 22C, ESi	705	627	670
Power driver's seat, variable-assist power steering, illuminated/remote keyless entry system, lighted visor mirrors.			
Pkg. 26M, TSi	1050	935	998
Pkg. 26L plus Chrysler/Infinity cassette system, leather/vinyl bucket seats, cargo net, conventional spare tire.			
Anti-lock brakes, ESi	600	534	570
Power moonroof, ESi w/Pkg. 22C	1015	903	964

Prices are accurate at time of publication; subject to manufacturer's change.

EAGLE • FORD

	Retail Price	Dealer Invoice	Fair Price
TSi	$720	$641	$684
Mini overhead console replaces full console (TSi).			
Integrated child seat	100	89	95
Not available with leather seats.			
Leather/vinyl bucket seats, TSi	620	552	589
Performance Handling Group, TSi w/Pkg. 26M	220	196	209
Performance suspension, 225/60VR16 performance tires. Requires conventional spare tire.			
AM/FM/cassette with eight speakers, ESi	350	312	333
Chrysler/Infinity cassette system, ESi	650	534	570
TSi	300	267	285
Includes equalizer, amplifier, 11 speakers, power antenna. ESi requires Pkg. 22C.			
Chrysler/Infinity CD system, TSi	600	534	570
TSi w/Pkg. 26M	300	267	285
Includes equalizer, amplifier, 11 speakers, power antenna.			
Security alarm, TSi	150	134	143
Conventional spare tire	95	85	90
Extra-cost paint	100	89	95
Bright platinum metallic paint	200	178	190
Engine block heater	20	18	19

FORD

Ford Aspire

	Retail Price	Dealer Invoice	Fair Price
3-door hatchback	$8790	$8239	$8539
5-door hatchback	9405	8798	9098
Destination charge	310	310	310

Standard Equipment:

1.3-liter 4-cylinder engine, 5-speed manual transmission, driver- and passenger-side air bags, reclining front seats, folding rear bench seat, cloth and vinyl upholstery, trip odometer, radio prep pkg., body-color bumpers and grille, dual outside mirrors, front storage console with cup holders, 165/70R13 all-season tires.

Optional Equipment:

3-speed automatic transmission	660	588	601
5-door requires power steering.			
Anti-lock brakes	570	507	519

FORD

	Retail Price	Dealer Invoice	Fair Price
Air conditioning	$825	$735	$743
Includes tinted glass.			
Power steering	250	223	228
Interior Decor and Convenience Group	265	236	241
Intermittent wipers, manual remote mirrors, upgraded upholstery and door trim, split folding rear seat, cargo area cover, door map pockets.			
Rear defogger	170	151	155
AM/FM radio with clock	300	267	270
AM/FM/cassette with clock	465	414	419

Ford Contour

	Retail Price	Dealer Invoice	Fair Price
GL 4-door notchback	$13785	$12649	—
LX 4-door notchback	14470	13258	—
SE 4-door notchback	16170	14771	—
Destination charge	510	510	510

Fair price not available at time of publication.

Standard Equipment:

GL: 2.0-liter DOHC 4-cylinder engine, 5-speed manual transmission, driver- and passenger-side air bags, power steering, solar-control tinted glass, cloth reclining front bucket seats, console, dual remote mirrors, digital clock, trip odometer, coolant temperature gauge, variable intermittent wipers, visor mirrors, AM/FM radio, remote decklid releases, passenger compartment air filtration system, color-keyed bodyside moldings, 185/70R14 tires, wheel covers. **LX** adds: fog lamps, heated power mirrors, console with armrest and cup holders, lumbar support adjusters, split folding rear seat, tachometer, illuminated entry, cassette player. **SE** adds: 2.5-liter DOHC V-6 engine, 4-wheel disc brakes, sport suspension, leather-wrapped steering wheel, rear spoiler, 205/60R15 tires, alloy wheels.

Optional Equipment:

2.5-liter DOHC V-6 engine, GL	1080	961	—
LX	1045	930	—
Includes 4-wheel disc brakes, tachometer (GL), sport suspension, 195/65R14 tires. Requires Groups 1 and 2 on GL, Groups 2 and 3 on LX.			
4-speed automatic transmission	815	725	—
Requires option group.			
Traction control	805	716	—
Includes anti-lock brakes.			
Cruise control	215	191	—
Anti-lock brakes	570	507	—
Air conditioning	780	694	—

Prices are accurate at time of publication; subject to manufacturer's change.

FORD

	Retail Price	Dealer Invoice	Fair Price
Preferred Pkg. 235A, GL	$870	$774	—

Console with armrest and cup holders, cassette player, air conditioning, rear defogger, heated power mirrors.

Preferred Pkg. 236A, GL	1330	1184	—

Pkg. 235A plus cruise control, power door locks, and light group.

Preferred Pkg. 240A, GL	3365	2995	—

Pkg. 236A plus 2.5-liter DOHC V-6 engine, automatic transmission, power windows.

Preferred Pkg. 238A, LX	3060	2724	—

2.5-liter V-6 engine, automatic transmission, air conditioning, rear defogger, light group, power door locks and windows, heated power mirrors, cruise control.

Preferred Pkg. 239A, SE	1370	1219	—

Air conditioning, rear defogger, heated power mirrors, light group, power door locks and windows, cruise control.

Option Group 1, GL	220	196	—

Console with armrest and cup holders, cassette player.

Option Group 2, GL	1050	935	—
LX, SE	970	863	—

Heated power mirrors (GL), air conditioning, rear defogger.

Option Group 3/power door locks and light group	345	307	—

Light group includes lighted passenger-side visor, front map light, trunk light, illuminated door handles, courtesy lights.

Leather upholstery, LX	645	574	—
SE	595	530	—

Requires power windows and power driver's seat. LX includes leather-wrapped steering wheel.

10-way power driver's seat, LX, SE	330	294	—

Requires Group 3 and power windows.

Split folding rear seat, GL	205	182	—
Rear defogger	170	151	—
Cassette player with Premium Sound, GL	295	263	—
GL with Group 1, LX, SE	130	116	—

Includes amplifier.

CD player and Premium Sound, GL	435	387	—
GL with Group 1, LX, SE	270	240	—

Includes amplifier.

Remote keyless entry	190	169	—

Requires power locks and light group, power windows, Group 1.

Alloy wheels, GL, LX	425	379	—

Includes 205/60R15 tires. Requires option group.

Power windows, GL with Pkg. 236A	340	302	—

Requires power locks and light group, rear defogger.

FORD

	Retail Price	Dealer Invoice	Fair Price
Power moonroof	$595	$530	—
Requires power locks and light group. NA on GL with Pkg. 235A.			
Floormats	45	40	—
Engine block heater	20	18	—

Ford Crown Victoria

	Retail Price	Dealer Invoice	Fair Price
4-door notchback	$20955	$19598	$20098
LX 4-door notchback	22675	21149	21649
Destination charge	580	580	580

Standard Equipment:

4.6-liter V-8 engine, 4-speed automatic transmission, 4-wheel disc brakes, variable-assist power steering, driver- and passenger-side air bags, air conditioning, cloth reclining split bench seat, map pockets, digital clock, power windows and mirrors, voltmeter, oil pressure and coolant temperature gauges, trip odometer, tilt steering wheel, solar-control tinted glass, automatic parking brake release, rear defogger, intermittent wipers, AM/FM radio, utility power outlet, 215/70R15 all-season tires, wheel covers. **LX** adds: upgraded interior trim, power driver's seat with power recliner and power lumbar support, carpeted spare tire cover.

Optional Equipment:

4.6-liter natural gas V-8, base	6165	5485	5549
Anti-lock brakes with Traction Assist	670	596	603
Automatic air conditioning, LX	175	156	158
Preferred Equipment Pkg. 111A, base	(840)	(747)	(747)
Group 1 plus front and rear floormats, radial-spoke wheel covers.			
Preferred Equipment Pkg. 113A, LX	(360)	(321)	(321)
Pkg. 111A plus Group 2.			
Preferred Equipment Pkg. 114A, LX	2335	2077	2102
Pkg. 113A plus Group 3.			
Group 1, base	620	552	558
LX	600	534	540
Power Lock Group, cruise control, illuminated entry, spare tire cover (base).			
Group 2, LX	995	886	896
Cassette player, Light/Decor Group, leather-wrapped steering wheel, cornering lamps, 12-spoke alloy wheels.			
Group 3, LX	2795	2488	2516

Automatic air conditioning, anti-lock brakes with Traction Assist, high-level audio system, electronic instruments, automatic day/night mirror, rear air suspension, remote keyless entry, 6-way power passenger seat, driver memory seat.

Prices are accurate at time of publication; subject to manufacturer's change.

CONSUMER GUIDE®

FORD

	Retail Price	Dealer Invoice	Fair Price
Keyless remote entry, LX	$240	$213	$216
Requires Group 1.			
Rear air suspension, LX	270	240	243
Leather upholstery, LX	645	574	581
Requires power front passenger seat.			
6-way power passenger seat, LX	360	321	324
6-way power driver's seat, base	360	321	324
Power memory driver's seat, LX	175	156	158
Requires remote keyless entry, Group 1, power passenger seat.			
Light/Decor Group	225	201	203
Includes illuminated visor mirrors, map and dome lights, bodyside paint stripes, secondary visors.			
Handling and Performance Pkg.	1100	979	990
LX with Group 2	680	605	612
LX with Group 3	830	739	747
LX with Pkg. 114A	410	365	369
Includes performance springs, shocks and stabilizer bars, alloy wheels, anti-lock brakes with Traction Assist, dual exhaust, 3.27 axle ratio, power steering cooler, rear air suspension, 225/60R16 tires.			
Cassette player	185	165	167
High-level audio system, LX	545	485	491
with Group 2 or Pkg. 113A	360	321	324
Cassette player, upgraded amplifier and speakers. Requires automatic air conditioning.			
215/70R15 whitewall tires	80	71	72
Full-size spare tire	80	71	72
with Handling and Performance Pkg.	260	232	234
Floormats, front	25	23	24
Floormats, front with preferred equipment pkg. (credit)	(25)	(23)	(23)
Floormats, rear	20	18	19
Floormats, rear with preferred equipment pkg. (credit)	(20)	(18)	(18)
Engine block heater	25	23	24

Ford Escort

	Retail Price	Dealer Invoice	Fair Price
3-door hatchback	$10065	$9454	$9654
LX 3-door hatchback	10910	10232	10432
LX 4-door notchback	11515	10782	10982
LX 5-door hatchback	11345	10627	10827
LX 5-door wagon	11900	11133	11333
GT 3-door hatchback	13205	12311	12511
Destination charge	390	390	390

FORD

Standard Equipment:

1.9-liter 4-cylinder engine, 5-speed manual transmission, driver- and passenger-side air bags, motorized front shoulder belts, cloth and vinyl reclining bucket seats, folding rear seat, center console with cup holders, tinted glass, trip odometer, intermittent wipers, flip-out quarter window (3-door), cargo cover (hatchback), door pockets, right visor mirror, 175/70R13 all-season tires. **LX** adds: upgraded upholstery and door trim panels, 60/40 split rear seatback, AM/FM radio, digital clock, bodyside molding, full wheel covers, 175/65R14 all-season tires. **GT** adds: 1.8-liter DOHC 4-cyclinder engine, power steering, 4-wheel disc brakes, sport suspension, tachometer, cloth sport seats, cassette player, Light Group, lighted visor mirrors, removable cup holder tray, power mirrors, lighted visor mirrors, fog lamps, rear spoiler, rocker panel cladding, 185/60HR15 all-season tires, alloy wheels.

Optional Equipment:

	Retail Price	Dealer Invoice	Fair Price
4-speed automatic transmission	$815	$725	$734
LX requires power steering.			
Anti-lock brakes, GT	570	507	513
Air conditioning	785	699	707
Requires power steering. NA on base model.			
Power steering, LX	250	223	225
Power moonroof, LX, GT	525	468	473
LX requires Light/Convenience Group, power steering. NA on wagon.			
Comfort Group, base	860	766	774
Air conditioning, power steering.			
Preferred Pkg. 320M, LX 5-speed	200	178	180
LX 3-door 5-speed	250	222	225
Power steering, Light/Convenience Group, Sport Appearance Group (3-, 4-, and 5-door), rear defogger.			
Preferred Pkg. 330A, GT	445	396	401
Rear defogger, air conditioning.			
Light/Convenience Group, LX	160	143	144
Light Group, power mirrors, removable cup holder tray.			
One Price Pkg. 321M (5-speed)			
and 322M (automatic):LX 3-door, 5-speed	1195	1064	—
LX 3-door, automatic	2010	1789	—
LX 4-door, 5-speed	590	525	—
LX 4-door, automatic	1405	1251	—
LX 5-door, 5-speed	760	676	—
LX 5-door, automatic	1575	1402	—
LX wagon, 5-speed	205	182	—
LX wagon, automatic	1020	908	—

Air conditioning, power steering, Light/Convenience Group, rear defogger, rear spoiler, alloy wheels. 3-door includes AM/FM/cassette. Wagon adds Wagon Group. 3-, 4-, and 5-door add Sport Appearance Group.

Prices are accurate at time of publication; subject to manufacturer's change.

FORD

	Retail Price	Dealer Invoice	Fair Price
Sport Appearance Group,			
LX 3-door without Preferred Pkg.	$720	$641	$648
LX 4- and 5-door without Preferred Pkg.	615	547	554
Tachometer and rear cladding (3-door only), liftgate spoiler, clearcoat paint, alloy wheels. Liftgate-spoiler delete optional for 4- and 5-door.			
Rear defogger	170	151	153
Light Group, LX	65	58	59
Removable cup-holder tray, dual map lights, cargo-area light, headlights-on warning chime, lighted visor mirrors.			
Power mirrors	95	85	86
Luxury Convenience Group,			
LX 3-door, LX 4-door, LX 5-door	465	414	419
LX wagon, LX 3-door with Sport			
Appearance Group	410	365	369
GT	460	410	414
Tilt steering column, cruise control, tachometer, remote decklid release (except wagon), leather-wrapped steering wheel (GT only). Requires power steering.			
Power Equipment Group,			
LX 4-door, LX 5-door, and wagon	575	512	518
LX 4-door/LX 5-door/wagon with Luxury			
Convenience Group	520	463	468
LX 3-door	515	458	464
GT, LX 3-door with Luxury Convenience			
Group or Sport Appearance Group	460	410	414
Power windows and door locks, tachometer.			
Integrated child seat, LX	135	120	122
AM/FM radio, base	300	267	270
AM/FM/cassette, base	465	414	419
LX	165	147	149
AM/FM/CD player, base	625	557	563
LX with Preferred Pkg. 320M, LX 4/5-door, wagon	325	290	293
GT, LX 3-door with One Price Pkg.	160	143	144
Includes premium sound system.			
Premium sound system	60	54	55
Requires AM/FM/cassette.			
Radio delete (credit), GT	(465)	(414)	(414)
Wagon Group, wagon	240	213	216
Luggage rack, rear wiper/washer. Requires Light/Convenience Group.			
Clearcoat paint	85	76	77
with LX Preferred Pkgs., Sport			
Appearance Group	NC	NC	NC
Engine block heater	20	18	19

FORD

Ford Explorer

	Retail Price	Dealer Invoice	Fair Price
XL 3-door wagon, 2WD	$19570	$17822	—
XL 3-door wagon, 4WD	21535	19551	—
XL 5-door wagon, 2WD	20970	19054	—
XL 5-door wagon, 4WD	22890	20744	—
Sport 3-door wagon, 2WD	20750	18861	—
Sport 3-door wagon, 4WD	22580	20470	—
XLT 5-door wagon, 2WD	23705	21460	—
XLT 5-door wagon, 4WD	25710	23225	—
Eddie Bauer 5-door wagon, 2WD	28210	25425	—
Eddie Bauer 5-door wagon, 4WD	30215	27189	—
Limited 5-door wagon, 2WD	31835	28615	—
Limited 5-door wagon, 4WD	34750	31181	—
Destination charge	500	500	500

Fair price not available at time of publication.

Standard Equipment:

XL: 4.0-liter V-6 engine, 5-speed manual transmission, anti-lock 4-wheel disc brakes, driver- and passenger-side air bags, power steering, air conditioning, vinyl front bucket seats, split folding rear bench seat with headrests, solar control tinted windshield, intermittent wipers, auxiliary power outlet, illuminated entry, trip odometer, tachometer, AM/FM radio with digital clock, map light, cargo hooks, chrome bumpers, passenger-side visor mirror, 3.27 ratio axle, 225/70R15 tires, full-size spare tire. **Sport and XLT** add: Power Equipment Group, speed-sensitive intermittent wipers, cloth front captain's chairs (XLT), console (XLT), rear privacy glass, rear wiper/washer and defogger, power rear-liftgate lock, power mirrors, leather-wrapped steering wheel, color-keyed grille (Sport), color-keyed bodyside moldings, black painted bumpers (Sport), cruise control, tilt steering wheel, striping (XLT), cargo cover (Sport), lighted visor mirrors, alloy wheels. **Eddie Bauer** adds: 4-speed automatic transmission, 6-way power sport cloth front bucket seats with power lumbar adjusters, roof rack, cassette player, 2-tone paint, cargo cover, floormats, 4.10 ratio axle, 255/70R16 tires, chrome wheels. **Limited** deletes 2-tone paint, 4.10 ratio axle, chrome wheels, and adds to Eddie Bauer: automatic air conditioning, Automatic Ride Control levelling system (4WD), Electronics Group, leather upholstery and door trim, reclining rear 60/40 seats, Ford JBL Audio System with cassette player, power antenna, console with rear climate and radio controls, systems message center, overhead console with electronic compass and outside temperature readout, heated power mirrors, running boards, automatic day/night rearview mirror, automatic headlights, fog lights, color-keyed grille and bumpers, 235/75R15 tires. **4WD** models have Control Trac part-time 4WD, 3.55 axle ratio (5-doors), transfer-case skid plate.

Prices are accurate at time of publication; subject to manufacturer's change.

FORD

Optional Equipment:	Retail Price	Dealer Invoice	Fair Price
5.0-liter V-8 engine, 2WD XLT	$760	$646	—

Requires 235/75R15 all-terrain outline white-letter tires, cassette player, limited-slip 3.73 ratio axle with Trailer Towing Pkg.

4-speed automatic transmission, XL, Sport, XLT	945	803	—
Limited-slip axle (3.27 ratio), 3-door XL, XLT	255	217	—
Limited-slip axle (3.73 ratio) w/Trailer Tow Pkg.	350	298	—

NA with Eddie Bauer.

Limited-slip axle (4.10 ratio) w/Trailer Tow Pkg. Sport w/Pkg. 934A, Eddie Bauer	305	259	—
Preferred Equipment Pkg. 931A, Sport	145	123	—

Cloth front captain's chairs, premium cassette player, 235/75R15 all-terrain outline white-letter tires.

Preferred Equipment Pkg. 934A, Sport	2160	1836	—

4-speed automatic transmission, 6-way power sport cloth bucket seats with power lumbar adjusters, console with rear climate and radio controls, overhead console with electronic compass and outside temperature readout, Electronics Group, fog lights, premium cassette player, floormats, 235/75R15 all-terrain outline white-letter tires.

Preferred Equipment Pkg. 941A, XLT	NC	NC	NC

Roof rack, cassette player.

Preferred Equipment Pkg. 945A, XLT	2010	1710	—

Pkg. 941A plus 4-speed automatic transmission, 6-way power sport cloth bucket seats with power lumbar adjusters, console with rear climate and radio controls, overhead console with electronic compass and outside temperature readout, Electronics Group, fog lights, cargo cover, floormats.

Preferred Equipment Pkg. 942A, Eddie Bauer	NC	NC	NC

6-way power leather bucket seats with power lumbar adjusters and rear seat recliner. Requires Ford JBL Audio System.

Preferred Equipment Pkg. 946A, Eddie Bauer	1815	1543	—

Pkg. 942A plus Ford JBL Audio System, automatic temperature control, systems message center, console with rear climate and radio controls, overhead console with electronic compass and outside temperature readout, Electronics Group, fog lights.

Decor Group, XL	370	314	—

Privacy glass, bodyside molding. Requires rear wiper/washer and defogger.

Power Equipment Group, XL 3-door	685	583	—
XL 5-door	1020	867	—

Power window, door, and liftgate locks, power mirrors, upgraded door-panel trim, delayed-off accessory power. Requires cruise control, and rear wiper/washer and defogger.

FORD

	Retail Price	Dealer Invoice	Fair Price
Electronics Group, Eddie Bauer	$370	$314	—

Remote keyless entry, anti-theft system, automatic locks, door keypad.

Premium Sport Pkg., Sport w/Pkg. 934A	2925	2487	—

Includes 4.10 ratio axle, medium-graphite bumpers, moldings, and side-step bar, roof rack, rear tow hook, chrome wheels, 255/70R16 all-terrain outline white-letter tires.

Cloth captain's chairs, XL	280	238	—

Includes console.

Cloth 60/40 bench seat, XL 5-door	285	243	—
XLT w/Pkg. 941A	10	8	—

Includes storage consolette. Requires automatic transmission.

6-way power cloth bucket seats, Sport	1020	867	—
XLT w/Pkg. 941A	955	812	—

Includes power lumbar adjusters and console. Requires Premium Sound stereo.

6-way power leather bucket seats, Sport w/Pkg. 934A, XLT w/Pkg. 945A	625	532	—

Includes floor console (XLT), rear seat recliner (Sport, XLT).

Integrated rear child seat, 5-door	200	170	—

NA with vinyl bucket seats.

Console with rear climate and radio controls, Eddie Bauer	390	332	—

Requires Electronics Group.

Rear wiper/washer and defogger, XL	280	238	—

Includes speed-sensitive front wipers. Requires cruise control.

Automatic day/night mirror, Sport w/Pkg. 934A, XLT w/Pkg. 945A, Eddie Bauer w/Pkg. 946A	185	158	—

Includes automatic headlights.

Cruise control and leather-wrapped tilt steering wheel, XL	385	328	—

Requires rear wiper/washer and defogger.

Power moonroof, Sport w/Pkg. 934A, XLT w/Pkg.945A, Eddie Bauer w/Pkg. 946A, Limited	800	680	—

Includes front overhead console with rear reading lamps. Sport requires roof rack.

Side step bar, Sport	295	251	—
Cellular telephone, Eddie Bauer w/Pkg. 946A, Limited	690	587	—
Roof rack, XL, Sport	140	119	—
Running boards, XLT, Eddie Bauer	395	336	—
Cassette player w/Premium Sound, XL	210	178	—

Includes amp. Requires rear wiper/washer and defogger, cruise control.

Prices are accurate at time of publication; subject to manufacturer's change.

CONSUMER GUIDE®

FORD

	Retail Price	Dealer Invoice	Fair Price
Ford JBL Audio System with cassette, Sport w/Pkg. 934A, XLT w/Pkg. 945A, Eddie Bauer	$830	$706	—

Includes sub-woofer, digital signal processor, and power antenna. Eddie Bauer and XLT require console with rear climate and radio controls, Electronics Group.

CD changer, Sport w/Pkg. 934A, XLT w/Pkg. 945A, Eddie Bauer, Limited	370	314	—

Sport requires cassette player. Eddie Bauer and XLT require console with rear climate and radio controls.

2-tone paint, XLT	120	102	—
Floormats and cargo cover, XLT	125	107	—
Floormats, Sport with Pkg. 931A	45	38	—
Deep-dish alloy wheels, XLT	NC	NC	NC
235/75R15 all-terrain outline white-letter tires, XLT	230	196	—

Ford Mustang

	Retail Price	Dealer Invoice	Fair Price
2-door notchback	$15180	$13965	—
2-door convertible	21060	19199	—
GT 2-door notchback	17610	16128	—
GT 2-door convertible	23495	21366	—
Cobra 2-door notchback	24810	—	—
Cobra 2-door convertible	—	—	—
Destination charge	500	500	500

Cobra convertible and fair prices not available at time of publication.

Standard Equipment:

3.8-liter V-6 engine, 5-speed manual transmission, driver- and passenger-side air bags, 4-wheel disc brakes, variable-effort power steering, reclining cloth bucket seats, split folding rear seat (notchback), armrest storage console with cup holder and CD/cassette storage, power mirrors, AM/FM radio, digital clock, visor mirrors, tachometer, trip odometer, coolant-temperature and oil-pressure gauges, tilt steering wheel, intermittent wipers, tinted glass, 205/65R15 all-season tires, wheel covers. **Convertible** adds: power convertible top, power door locks, remote decklid release, power windows, illuminated visor mirrors. **GT** adds to base: 4.6-liter OHC V-8 engine, split folding rear seat (notchback), GT Suspension Pkg., dual exhaust, passive anti-theft system, 225/55ZR16 all-season tires, alloy wheels. **GT Convertible** adds: GT sport seats with 4-way head restraint and power lumbar support, leather-wrapped steering wheel, lighted visor mirrors, fog lamps, rear decklid spoiler. **Cobra** adds: 4.6-liter DOHC V-8 engine, cruise control, cassette player with Premium Sound.

FORD

Optional Equipment:	Retail Price	Dealer Invoice	Fair Price
4-speed automatic transmission	$815	$725	$774
Requires air conditioning.			
Anti-lock brakes	570	507	542
Air conditioning	855	761	812
Cruise control	215	191	204
NA on base with Pkg. 241A.			
Preferred Pkg. 241A, base notchback	640	570	608
Air conditioning, cassette player.			
Preferred Pkg. 243A, base notchback	1990	1771	1891
base convertible	1560	1389	1482
Air conditioning, Groups 1 and 2, power driver's seat, illuminated visor mirrors, remote keyless entry.			
Preferred Pkg. 248A, GT notchback	640	570	608
Air conditioning, cassette player.			
Preferred Pkg. 249A, GT notchback	2815	2505	2674
GT convertible	1620	1442	1539
Anti-lock brakes, air conditioning, Groups 1, 2, and 3, power driver's seat.			
Preferred Pkg. 250A, Cobra	1335	—	—
Leather upholstery, Mach 460 cassette/CD player, anti-theft system.			
Group 1, GT notchback w/ Pkg 248A	505	449	480
Power windows and door locks, remote decklid release.			
Group 2, base	775	690	736
GT	510	454	485
Cruise control, cassette player with Premium Sound, alloy wheels (base).			
Group 3, GT notchback with Pkg. 248A	690	614	656
GT sport seats, leather-wrapped steering wheel, illuminated visor mirrors, fog lamps, rear spoiler.			
Power driver's seat	175	156	166
Leather upholstery, base convertible with Pkg. 243A, GT with Pkg. 249A	500	445	475
Rear defogger	170	151	162
Cassette player	165	147	157
NA on base with Pkg. 241A.			
Premium Sound cassette player,	295	263	280
with base cassette player	130	116	124
Mach 460 cassette player, with Group 2	395	352	375
without Group 2	690	614	656
Includes 460 watts peak power, AM/FM stereo, 60-watt equalizer, CD-changer compatibility, soft-touch tape controls, 10 speakers. Requires Group 1. NA on base with Pkg. 241A or GT with Pkg. 248A.			
CD player	295	263	280
Requires cassette player (in Group 2) and Group 1. NA on base with Pkg. 241A.			

Prices are accurate at time of publication; subject to manufacturer's change.

FORD

	Retail Price	Dealer Invoice	Fair Price
Anti-theft system	$145	$129	$138
Requires Group 1 and remote keyless entry. Base requires Pkg. 243A.
Illuminated visor mirrors	95	85	90
Optional axle ratio, GT	100	89	95
Alloy wheels, base	265	236	252
Front floormats	30	27	29
Base requires Pkg. 243A.
| Remote keyless entry | 270 | 240 | 257 |
NA on base with Pkg. 241A. Requires Group 1.
Mystic paint, Cobra	815	—	—
Engine block heater	20	18	19
15-inch alloy wheels, base	265	236	252
17-inch alloy wheels and 245/45ZR17 tires, GT with Pkg. 249A	380	338	361

Ford Probe

	Retail Price	Dealer Invoice	Fair Price
SE 3-door hatchback	$13930	$12788	$13288
GT 3-door hatchback	16450	15031	15831
Destination charge	375	375	375

Standard Equipment:

SE: 2.0-liter DOHC 4-cylinder engine, 5-speed manual transmission, power steering, driver- and passenger-side air bags, velour cloth reclining front bucket seats with memory, split folding rear seat, tachometer, coolant-temperature and oil-pressure gauges, voltmeter, trip odometer, tinted rear and quarter windows, right visor mirror, center console, dual remote mirrors, inside liftgate/fuel-door releases, AM/FM radio, 195/65R14 all-season tires, wheel covers. **GT** adds: 2.5-liter DOHC V-6 engine, 4-wheel disc brakes, handling suspension, full console with storage armrest and cup holders, door pockets, multi-adjustable front seats with driver-side lumbar support and side bolsters, leather-wrapped steering wheel and manual transmission shift knob, fog lights, lower bodyside cladding, 225/50VR16 tires, alloy wheels.

Optional Equipment:

4-speed automatic transmission	815	725	734
GT requires anti-lock brakes.
| Anti-lock brakes, SE | 740 | 658 | 666 |
| GT | 570 | 507 | 513 |
SE includes 4-wheel disc brakes, handling suspension.
| SE Preferred Pkg. 253A | 1120 | 998 | 1008 |
Air conditioning (includes tinted glass), AM/FM/cassette, SE Appearance Group, rear defogger, intermittent wipers.

FORD

	Retail Price	Dealer Invoice	Fair Price
GT Preferred Pkg. 263A	$1905	$1696	$1714

Air conditioning (includes tinted glass), AM/FM/cassette, remote mirrors, power windows and locks, anti-lock brakes, rear defogger, intermittent wipers, rear spoiler.

	Retail Price	Dealer Invoice	Fair Price
Convenience Group, SE	185	166	167
GT	125	112	113

Remote mirrors, full console with storage armrest and cup holders.

	Retail Price	Dealer Invoice	Fair Price
Driver Comfort Group	355	316	320

Tilt steering column, cruise control.

	Retail Price	Dealer Invoice	Fair Price
Power Group	485	432	436

Power windows and locks.

	Retail Price	Dealer Invoice	Fair Price
SE Appearance Group	530	472	477

Handling suspension, GT front fascia without fog lights, SE badging, alloy wheels, 205/55HR15 tires.

	Retail Price	Dealer Invoice	Fair Price
Air Conditioning	895	797	806

Includes tinted glass.

	Retail Price	Dealer Invoice	Fair Price
Intermittent wipers	60	54	55
Rear defogger	170	151	153
Remote keyless entry	270	240	243

Requires Power Group and Convenience Group.

	Retail Price	Dealer Invoice	Fair Price
Power driver's seat, GT	290	258	261
Leather front bucket seats, GT	500	445	450

Requires power driver's seat.

	Retail Price	Dealer Invoice	Fair Price
Cassette player	165	147	149
CD player, GT with Preferred Pkg.	430	383	387
GT without Preferred Pkg.	595	530	536

Includes Premium Sound and subwoofer.

	Retail Price	Dealer Invoice	Fair Price
Rear spoiler	235	209	212
Color-keyed bodyside moldings	50	45	46
Sliding power roof, GT	615	547	554

Includes dome light and map lights.

	Retail Price	Dealer Invoice	Fair Price
Alloy wheels and 205/55HR15 tires, SE	430	383	387

Includes handling suspension.

	Retail Price	Dealer Invoice	Fair Price
Chrome wheels, GT	390	347	351
Floormats	30	27	28
Engine block heater	20	18	19

Ford Taurus

	Retail Price	Dealer Invoice	Fair Price
GL 4-door notchback	$18600	$17019	—
LX 4-door notchback	20980	19137	—
SHO 4-door notchback	—	—	—
GL 4-door wagon	19680	17980	—
LX 4-door wagon	22000	20045	—

Prices are accurate at time of publication; subject to manufacturer's change.

FORD

	Retail Price	Dealer Invoice	Fair Price
Destination charge	$550	$550	$550

SHO price and fair price not available at time of publication.

Standard Equipment:

GL: 3.0-liter V-6 engine, 4-speed automatic transmission, air conditioning, variable-assist power steering, 4-wheel disc brakes (wagon), driver- and passenger-side air bags, 6-passenger seating with front bucket seats and center seating console, 60/40 split/folding rear seat, center console with cup holder, coin holder, and cassette storage, tilt steering wheel, power windows, power mirrors, visor mirrors, solar-tinted glass, intermittent wipers, rear defogger, rear-seat heat ducts, AM/FM radio, power antenna (wagon), digital clock, coolant temperature gauge, trip odometer, tachometer, illuminated entry, remote decklid/liftgate releases, wheel covers, luggage rack (wagon), 205/65R15 tires. **LX** adds to GL: 3.0-liter DOHC V-6 engine, dual exhaust (notchback), rear-seat air conditioning, 5-passenger seating with reclining front bucket seats and floor console, 6-way power driver's seat with power lumbar support, leather-wrapped steering wheel and shifter, Passive Anti-Theft System, power door locks, illuminated visor mirrors, cassette player with six speakers, air-filtration system, automatic on/off clear-lens headlights, bodyside cladding, illuminated entry, reading lights, cargo net (wagon), alloy wheels. **SHO** adds: 3.4-liter DOHC V-8 engine, anti-lock 4-wheel disc brakes, cruise control, leather upholstery, rear spoiler, semi-active handling suspension, aerodynamic wipers, floormats, chrome wheels. 225/55VR16 tires.

Optional Equipment:

Anti-lock 4-wheel disc brakes, GL, LX	570	507	—
Automatic air conditioning, LX, SHO	175	156	—

Notchback requires JBL audio system. Wagon requires Premium Sound.

Cruise control	215	191	—
6-way power driver's seat, GL with Pkg. 204A	290	258	—
Preferred Pkg. 204A, GL	240	213	—

Groups 1 and 2.

Preferred Pkg. 205A, GL, notchback	840	747	—
wagon	880	783	—

Groups 1, 2, and 3.

Preferred Pkg. 208A, LX	150	134	—

Group 1.

Preferred Pkg. 209A, LX	860	766	—

Group 1, anti-lock 4-wheel disc brakes, remote keyless entry with perimeter anti-theft.

FORD

	Retail Price	Dealer Invoice	Fair Price
Preferred Pkg. 210A, LX notchback	$1915	$1704	—
LX wagon	1730	1540	—

Group 1, anti-lock 4-wheel disc brakes, remote keyless entry with perimeter anti-theft, automatic air conditioning, Ford JBL audio system (sedan), Premium Sound (wagon), power antenna, chrome wheels.

Group 1, GL	260	232	—

Includes cruise control, floormats.

Group 1A, GL	350	312	—

Includes cruise control, floormats, leather-wrapped steering wheel.

Group 2, GL	480	427	—

Cassette player, power door locks, air-filtration system.

Group 3, GL notchback	700	623	—
GL wagon	740	658	—

Power driver's seat, alloy wheels, light group (front courtesy reading, map, and dome lights. Moonroof deletes dome light), cargo tie-down net (wagon).

Wagon group, wagon	255	227	—

Rear wiper/washer, cargo area cover. Requires power door locks. NA on GL with Pkg. 201A.

Cloth bucket seats w/center seating console, LX	NC	NC	NC
Leather upholstery, LX	990	881	—
Rear-facing third seat, wagon	340	302	—
Integrated child seat, wagon	135	120	—
Cassette player, GL with Pkg. 201A	175	156	—
Cassette player with Premium Sound, LX wagon	315	280	—

Requires automatic air conditioning.

Ford JBL Audio System, LX, SHO	500	445	—

Requires automatic air conditioning. Includes power antenna. NA on wagon.

6-disc CD changer, LX, SHO	595	530	—

Notchback requires JBL sound system. Wagon requires Premium Sound.

Air-filtration system, GL with Pkg. 201A	30	27	—
Cellular telephone	650	579	—
Remote keyless entry, GL	190	169	—

NA with Pkg. 201A. May not be available on first production run.

Remote keyless entry with perimeter anti-theft, LX, SHO	440	391	—
Power moonroof, LX, SHO	740	658	—

Includes overhead map lights.

Daytime running lights	40	35	—

Includes heavy-duty battery.

Reading lights, GL	45	41	—
Rear spoiler	270	240	—

Prices are accurate at time of publication; subject to manufacturer's change.

CONSUMER GUIDE®

FORD

	Retail Price	Dealer Invoice	Fair Price
Alloy wheels, GL with Pkg. 204A	$315	$280	—
Chrome wheels, LX	580	516	—
Full-size spare tire	125	112	—
NA on wagon or SHO.			
Heavy duty suspension, GL wagon	25	23	—
Engine block heater	35	31	—
Floormats	45	40	—

Ford Thunderbird

	Retail Price	Dealer Invoice	Fair Price
LX 2-door notchback	$17485	$15982	$16482
Destination charge	510	510	510

Standard Equipment:

3.8-liter V-6 engine, 4-speed automatic transmission, driver- and passenger-side air bags, power steering, air conditioning, cruise control, cloth front bucket seats, center storage console with cup holders, rear seat center armrest, rear-seat heat ducts, remote mirrors, visor mirrors, solar-control tinted glass, coolant-temperature gauge, tachometer, voltmeter, tilt steering wheel, trip odometer, AM/FM/cassette, digital clock, power windows and door locks, leather-wrapped shift knob, remote fuel door and decklid releases, intermittent wipers, map/dome lights, lower bodyside cladding with integral bodyside molding, 205/70R15 tires, wheel covers.

Optional Equipment:

4.6-liter V-8 engine	1130	1006	1017
Includes variable-assist power steering and heavy-duty battery. NA with Pkg. 155A.			
Anti-lock 4-wheel disc brakes	570	507	513
6-way power driver's seat, Pkg. 155A	290	258	261
Preferred Pkg. 155A	NC	NC	NC
Group 1.			
Preferred Pkg. 157A	835	745	752
4.6-liter V-8 engine, Groups 1 and 2, variable-assist steering.			
Group 1	380	338	342
Rear defroster, alloy wheels, 215/70R15 tires.			
Group 2	455	407	410
6-way power driver's seat, illuminated entry, leather-wrapped steering wheel.			
Luxury/Lighting Group	495	445	446
Semi-automatic air conditioning, autolamp system, power antenna, footwell courtesy light, engine-compartment light, integrated warning lamp module, illuminated visor mirrors. Requires Preferred Pkg.			

FORD

	Retail Price	Dealer Invoice	Fair Price
Sport Option, Pkg. 157A	$210	$187	$189
Performance suspension, alloy wheels, 225/65R16 touring tires.			
Leather upholstery	490	436	441
Requires Preferred Pkg.			
Traction-Assist	210	187	189
Requires anti-lock brakes and Luxury/Lighting Group. NA with Traction-Lok axle.			
Traction-Lok axle	95	85	86
Premium Sound cassette player	290	258	261
Premium Sound CD player	430	383	387
Remote keyless entry/Illuminated entry,			
Pkg. 155A	270	240	243
Pkg. 157A	190	169	171
Power moonroof	740	658	666
Requires Preferred Pkg. and Luxury/Lighting Group.			
Anti-theft system	145	129	131
Requires remote keyless entry.			
Front floormats	30	27	28
Tri-coat paint	225	201	203
Chrome wheels	580	517	522
Requires alloy wheels (group 1).			
Engine block heater	20	18	19

Ford Windstar

	Retail Price	Dealer Invoice	Fair Price
GL 4-door van	$19590	$17765	$19090
LX 4-door van	24465	22054	23965
Destination charge	555	555	555

Standard Equipment:

GL: 3.0-liter V-6 engine, 4-speed automatic transmission, driver- and passenger-side air bags, height-adjustable front shoulder belts, anti-lock brakes, power steering, 7-passenger seating (high-back front buckets, 2-place middle and 3-place rear bench seats), solar tinted windshield and front door glass, dual outside mirrors, AM/FM radio with digital clock, intermittent wipers, rear wiper/washer, cup holders, front-door map pockets, storage drawer under front passenger seat, coolant temperature gauge, 205/70R15 tires, full wheel covers.
LX adds: 3.8-liter V-6 engine, front air conditioning, power mirrors, power front windows with 30-second delay feature, power rear quarter vent windows, power locks, premium cassette player, Light Group, illuminated entry, illuminated visor vanity mirrors, tilt steering wheel, cruise control, tachometer, low-back bucket seats with power lumbar adjustment, 6-way power driver's seat, map pockets on front seatbacks, 7-inch rear seat travel, bodyside molding, cargo net, 25-gallon fuel tank, 215/70R15 tires, alloy wheels.

Prices are accurate at time of publication; subject to manufacturer's change.

FORD

Optional Equipment:

	Retail Price	Dealer Invoice	Fair Price
Preferred Pkg. 470A, GL	$640	$544	$608

Includes air conditioning and 7-inch rear-seat travel.

Preferred Pkg. 471A, GL	1760	1496	1584

Pkg. 470A plus 3.8-liter V-6 engine, tachometer, Power Convenience Group.

Preferred Pkg. 472A, GL	2150	1826	1935

Pkg. 471A plus premium cassette player, cruise control, and tilt steering wheel, Light Group, rear-window defroster.

Preferred Pkg. 476A, LX	320	271	288

Rear window defroster, cruise control, tilt steering wheel, front and rear floormats, luggage rack, 2-tone paint.

Preferred Pkg. 477A, LX	1300	1150	1143

Pkg. 476A plus quad bucket seats, privacy glass, remote entry.

Air conditioning, GL	855	727	770
Front and rear air conditioning	465	395	442

Includes rear heater. GL requires Power Convenience Group, Light Group. NA with Pkg. 470A.

Load-levelling air suspension, LX	290	247	261

Requires Power Convenience Group.

Rear defogger, GL	170	144	162
Cruise control and tilt steering wheel, GL	370	314	352
Electronic instrument cluster, LX	490	417	466

Includes autolamp feature and electrochromatic mirror. Requires rear defroster.

Floor console	140	119	133

Includes cup holders and covered storage bin. Requires rear air conditioning. NA with Pkg. 470A.

Privacy glass	415	352	394

NA with Pkg. 470A.

Light Group, GL (std. LX)	50	43	48

Front map/dome light and glovebox, instrument panel and engine compartment lights.

Interior Convenience Group, GL w/Pkgs. 471A or 472A	50	43	45

Left rear storage bin, covered center bin, cargo net.

Power Convenience Group, GL w/Pkg. 470A	670	569	603

Power front windows with 30-second delay feature, power rear quarter vent windows, power door locks and mirrors.

Traction Control	365	310	329

NA with Pkg. 470 A.

Trailer Towing Pkg.	435	371	392
with front and rear A/C	410	348	369
with traction control	375	319	338

FORD • GEO

	Retail Price	Dealer Invoice	Fair Price
with front/rear A/C and traction control	$350	$297	$315
NA with Pkg. 470 A. Requires 3.8-liter engine.			
Fog lamps, LX	110	93	105
Requires electronic instrument cluster.			
Luggage rack, GL w/Pkg. 472A	175	149	158
Remote entry, GL w/Pkgs. 471A or 472A, LX w/Pkg. 476A	175	149	158
Remote entry system and illuminated entry. Requires Power Convenience Group.			
Keyless entry pkg., LX	340	289	323
Keyless entry system, anti-theft system, and heated mirrors. Requires remote entry and rear defroster.			
Premium cassette player, GL	170	144	153
Premium AM/FM/CD player, GL w/Pkg. 471A	535	455	482
GL w/Pkg. 472A	325	276	293
LX	170	144	153
Requires cruise control and tilt steering wheel, Light Group.			
JBL Audio System, LX	510	433	485
Requires premium cassette or CD player.			
Seat bed, GL w/Pkg. 472A	615	522	566
Quad bucket seats, GL	695	591	626
LX	600	510	570
Leather upholstery, LX	865	735	779
Requires quad bucket seats.			
Integrated child seats (2)	225	192	214
Replacing quad bucket seats, *Pkg. 477A*	(260)	(221)	(221)
Requires adjustable third-seat track.			
Floormats, GL	90	76	81
2-tone paint, LX w/Pkg. 476A or 477A (credit)	(135)	(115)	(115)
Bodyside molding, GL w/Pkg. 240A	80	68	72
25-gallon fuel tank, GL (std. LX)	30	26	27
NA with Pkg. 470A.			
Engine block heater	35	30	33
Alloy wheels, GL w/Pkg. 472A	415	353	374
Includes 215/70R15 tires.			
Conventional spare tire	110	93	105

GEO

Geo Metro	Retail Price	Dealer Invoice	Fair Price
Base 3-door hatchback	$8380	$7894	—
Base 4-door notchback	9330	8696	—

Prices are accurate at time of publication; subject to manufacturer's change.

GEO

	Retail Price	Dealer Invoice	Fair Price
LSi 3-door hatchback	$8780	$8183	—
LSi 4-door notchback	9730	9068	—
Destination charge	315	315	315

Fair price not available at time of publication. Additional "value-priced" models may be available in California.

Standard Equipment:

Base 3-door: 1.0-liter 3-cylinder engine, 5-speed manual transmission, driver- and passenger-side air bags, daytime running lights, cloth and vinyl reclining front bucket seats, one-piece folding rear seatback, dual exterior mirrors, day/night rearview mirror, coolant temperature gauge, console with cup holders and storage tray, door pockets, 155/80R13 tires. **LSi 3-door** adds: remote hatch release, remote mirrors, intermittent wipers, upgraded cloth and vinyl upholstery, seatback pockets, trip odometer, passenger visor mirror, bodyside moldings, wheel covers. **Base 4-door** adds to base 3-door: 1.3-liter 4-cylinder engine, trip odometer, intermittent wipers, passenger-side visor mirror, bodyside moldings, wheel covers. **LSi 4-door** adds: color-keyed bumpers, remote fuel door and decklid releases, remote mirrors, cloth door trim, seatback pockets, split folding rear seat.

Optional Equipment:

1.3-liter 4-cylinder engine, 3-doors	$360	$320	—
Power door locks, 4-doors	220	196	—
3-speed automatic transmission	500	445	—
Requires 1.3-liter 4-cylinder engine. NA base 3-door.			
Air conditioning	785	699	—
Anti-lock brakes	565	503	—
Preferred Equipment Group 2, base 3-door	207	184	—
Tachometer, bodyside moldings, floormats, wheel covers.			
Preferred Equipment Group 3, base 3-door	1293	1151	—
Group 2 plus air conditioning, AM/FM radio with digital clock.			
Preferred Equipment Group 2, LSi 3-door	391	348	—
Tachometer, AM/FM radio with digital clock, floormats.			
Preferred Equipment Group 3, LSi 3-door	1176	1047	—
Group 2 plus air conditioning.			
Preferred Equipment Group 2, 4-doors	596	530	—
Power steering, AM/FM radio with digital clock, floormats.			
Preferred Equipment Group 3, 4-doors	1381	1229	—
Group 2 plus air conditioning.			
Power steering, 4-doors	260	231	—
AM/FM radio	301	268	—
Includes seek and scan, digital clock, and four speakers.			

GEO

	Retail Price	Dealer Invoice	Fair Price
AM/FM/cassette	$521	$464	—
base 3-door w/Group 3, LSi 3-door w/Group 2 or 3, 4-door w/Group 2 or 3	220	196	—
Includes seek and scan, theft deterrent, tone select, digital clock, and four speakers.			
AM/FM/cassette and CD players	721	642	—
LSi 3-door w/Group 2 or 3, 4-door w/Group 2 or 3	520	463	—
Includes seek and scan, theft deterrent, tone select, digital clock, and four speakers. NA base 3-door.			
Rear defogger	160	142	—
Rear wiper/washer, 3-doors	125	111	—
Requires rear defogger.			
Tachometer	55	49	—
base 3-door	70	62	—
Includes trip odometer.			
Dual remote mirrors, base	20	18	—
Front and rear floormats	35	31	—
Bodyside moldings, base 3-door	50	45	—
Cargo security cover, 3-doors	50	45	—
Wheel covers, base 3-door	52	46	—

Geo Prizm

	Retail Price	Dealer Invoice	Fair Price
4-door notchback	$12495	$11895	$12195
LSi 4-door notchback	13145	12120	12620
Destination charge	380	380	380

Additional "value-priced" models may be available in California.

Standard Equipment:

1.6-liter DOHC 4-cylinder engine, 5-speed manual transmission, driver- and passenger-side air bags, left remote and right manual mirrors, reclining front bucket seats, cloth/vinyl upholstery, center console with storage tray and cup holders, daytime running lights, remote fuel door and decklid releases, tinted glass, rear-seat heating ducts, bodyside moldings, 175/65R14 tires. **LSi** adds: tilt steering column, upgraded full cloth upholstery, center console with storage box, dual front storage pockets, split-folding rear seat, visor mirrors, wheel covers.

Optional Equipment:

1.8-liter 4-cylinder engine, LSi	352	303	308
Includes rear stabilizer bar and 185/65R14 tires. Requires option group.			

Prices are accurate at time of publication; subject to manufacturer's change.

CONSUMER GUIDE®

GEO

	Retail Price	Dealer Invoice	Fair Price
3-speed automatic transmission	$495	$426	$433
Requires 1.6-liter engine and option group.			
4-speed automatic transmission, LSi	800	688	700
Requires 1.8-liter engine.			
Anti-lock brakes	595	512	521
Air conditioning	795	684	696
Preferred Equipment Group 2, base	630	542	561
Power steering, AM/FM radio with digital clock, floormats.			
Preferred Equipment Group 2, LSi	690	593	614
AM/FM radio with digital clock, dual power mirrors, power steering, floormats.			
Preferred Equipment Group 3, LSi	1525	1312	1357
Group 2 plus air conditioning, variable intermittent wipers.			
Convenience Pkg., LSi	695	598	619
Power windows and door locks, cruise control. Requires option group.			
Cruise control, LSi with Group 2	175	151	153
Leather upholstery, LSi	595	512	521
Requires Convenience Pkg.			
Integrated child safety seat, LSi	100	86	89
Rear defogger	170	146	149
Power door locks	220	189	193
Power sunroof, LSi	660	568	578
Includes map light.			
Intermittent wipers	40	34	35
Tachometer	60	52	53
AM/FM radio	330	284	289
Includes seek and scan, digital clock, and four speakers.			
AM/FM/cassette player	550	473	481
with option group	220	189	193
Includes seek and scan, theft deterrent, tone select, digital clock, and four speakers.			
AM/FM radio with CD and cassette players, LSi with option group	420	361	368
Includes seek and scan, theft deterrent, tone select, digital clock, and six speakers.			
Alloy wheels, LSi	335	288	293
Requires option group.			
Wheel covers, base	52	45	46
Front and rear floormats	40	34	35

Geo Tracker

	Retail Price	Dealer Invoice	Fair Price
2-door convertible, 2WD	$12970	$12347	$12547
2-door convertible, 4WD	14450	13756	13956

GEO

	Retail Price	Dealer Invoice	Fair Price
5-door wagon, 2WD	$14570	$13871	$14371
5-door wagon, 4WD	15320	14585	15085
LSi 2-door convertible, 2WD	13870	13204	13404
LSi 2-door convertible, 4WD	14880	14166	14366
LSi 5-door wagon, 2WD	14970	14251	14751
LSi 5-door wagon, 4WD	15710	14956	15456
Destination charge	315	315	315

Standard Equipment:

1.6-liter 4-cylinder engine, 5-speed manual transmission, driver- and passenger-side air bags, power steering (wagon, 4WD convertible), rear defogger (wagon), cloth/vinyl reclining front bucket seats, folding rear bench seat (4WD convertible) or split folding rear bench seat (wagon), center console with storage tray and cup holders, daytime running lights, tachometer, trip odometer, dual mirrors, intermittent wipers, full-size lockable spare tire, spare tire cover, front and rear tow hooks, 195/75R15 tires (2WD) or 205/75R15 tires (4WD), styled steel wheels. **LSi** adds: floormats, upgraded cloth/vinyl upholstery and door trim, adjustable rear bucket seats, color-keyed bumpers, bodyside moldings.

Optional Equipment:

3-speed automatic transmission, convertibles	595	530	538
Base 2WD requires option group.			
4-speed automatic transmission, wagons	800	712	724
Air conditioning	745	663	674
Anti-lock brakes	565	503	511
Preferred Group 2, base 4WD convertible	419	373	379
base 2WD convertible	694	618	628
base wagon	426	379	386
AM/FM radio with digital clock, power steering (2WD convertible), bodyside moldings, floormats.			
Preferred Group 3, base 4WD convertible	1164	1036	1053
base 2WD convertible	1439	1281	1302
base wagon	1171	1042	1060
Group 2 plus air conditioning.			
Preferred Group 2, 2WD LSi convertible	581	517	526
4WD LSi convertible	306	272	277
AM/FM radio with digital clock, power steering (2WD).			
Preferred Group 3, 2WD LSi convertible	1326	1180	1200
4WD LSi convertible	1051	935	951
Group 2 plus air conditioning.			
Preferred Group 2, LSi wagon	1051	935	951
AM/FM radio with digital clock, air conditioning.			

Prices are accurate at time of publication; subject to manufacturer's change.

GEO • GMC

	Retail Price	Dealer Invoice	Fair Price
Preferred Group 3, LSi wagon	$1631	$1452	$1476
Group 2 plus Convenience Pkg.			
Convenience Pkg., LSi wagon	580	516	525
Power windows and door locks, power mirrors.			
Power steering, 2WD convertibles	275	245	249
Cruise control	175	156	158
Automatic locking front hubs, 4WD	200	178	181
AM/FM radio	306	272	277
Includes seek and scan, digital clock, and four speakers.			
AM/FM/cassette	526	468	476
with option group	220	196	199
Includes seek and scan, theft deterrent, tone select, digital clock, and four speakers.			
AM/FM/cassette and CD players	726	646	657
with option group	420	374	380
Includes seek and scan, theft deterrent, tone select, digital clock, and four speakers.			
Rear seat delete, 2WD	NC	NC	NC
Folding rear bench seat, 2WD convertible	445	396	403
Rear wiper/washer, wagons	125	111	113
Transfer case shield, 4WD	75	67	68
Alloy wheels	335	298	303
Floormats, base convertible	28	25	26
base wagon	35	31	32
Bodyside moldings, base	85	76	77
Tan Accent Package, convertibles	130	116	118

GMC

GMC Jimmy

	Retail Price	Dealer Invoice	Fair Price
3-door wagon, 2WD	$19573	$17714	—
3-door wagon, 4WD	21456	19418	—
5-door wagon, 2WD	21279	19258	—
5-door wagon, 4WD	23504	21271	—
Destination charge	490	490	490

Fair price not available at time of publication.

Standard Equipment:

3-door: 4.3-liter V-6 engine, 4-speed automatic transmission, part-time 4WD with electronic transfer case (4WD), anti-lock brakes, driver-side air bag, air conditioning, power steering, tinted glass, coolant temperature and

GMC

oil pressure gauges, tachometer, voltmeter, trip odometer, AM/FM radio, digital clock, dual outside manual mirrors, illuminated entry, front reclining cloth bucket seats with manual lumbar support adjusters, console with storage and cup holders, intermittent wipers, door map pockets, passenger-side visor mirror, floormats, 205/75R15 tires, full-size spare tire, trailering harness, front tow hooks (4WD), wheel trim rings. **5-door** deletes console with storage and cup holders and adds: cloth 60/40 front bench seat with storage armrest, folding rear 3-passenger bench seat.

Option Pkgs., 3-door:

	Retail Price	Dealer Invoice	Fair Price
SL Pkg. 2	$1742	$1498	—

Base plus cassette player, power windows, door locks and mirrors, cruise control, tilt steering wheel, split folding rear 3-passenger bench seat, Euro-Ride Suspension Pkg., roof rack, 235/70R15 tires.

SLS Pkg. 3	2773	2385	—

SL Pkg. 2 contents plus SLS Sport Decor Pkg.

Option Pkgs., 5-door:

SL Pkg. 5, 2WD	1917	1649	—
4WD	1442	1240	—

Base plus cassette player, power windows, door locks and mirrors, cruise control, tilt steering wheel, split folding rear 3-passenger bench seat, Luxury Ride Suspension Pkg., roof rack, 235/70R15 tires.

SLS Pkg. 6, 2WD	3128	2750	—
4WD	2723	2342	—

SL Pkg. 5 contents plus SLS Sport Decor Pkg.

SLE Pkg. 6, 2WD	3500	3010	—
4WD	3025	2602	—

SL Pkg. 5 contents plus SLE Comfort Decor Pkg.

SLT Pkg. 7, 2WD	5150	4429	—
4WD	4675	4021	—

SL Pkg. 5 contents plus SLT Touring Decor Pkg., cassette player with equalizer.

Individual Options:

5-speed manual transmission 3-door (credit)	(890)	(765)	(765)
All-wheel drive, 5-door 4WD	200	172	—

Requires SLT Decor, Luxury Ride Suspension Pkg.

Optional axle ratio	NC	NC	NC
Locking differential	252	217	—
Manual transfer case, 4WD (credit)	(123)	(106)	(106)

Replaces standard electronic push button shift with manual floor mounted shift.

Prices are accurate at time of publication; subject to manufacturer's change.

GMC

	Retail Price	Dealer Invoice	Fair Price
SLS Sport Decor Pkg., 3-door	$2984	$2566	—
5-door 2WD	3409	2932	—
5-door 4WD	2934	2523	—

Adds to standard SL Decor Pkg.: cruise control, front reclining cloth bucket seats with manual lumbar support adjusters (5-door), split folding rear seat, dual auxiliary power outlets, power windows and door locks, power mirrors, cassette player, leather-wrapped steering wheel, lighted visor mirrors, power remote tailgate release, rear defogger, intermittent rear wiper/washer, tilt steering wheel, console with storage and cup holders (5-door), roof rack, striping, deep-tinted glass on rear doors (5-door) and rear quarter windows, cloth door trim panels, reading lamps, cargo cover (5-door), cargo net, alloy wheels.

SLE Comfort Decor Pkg., 5-door 2WD	3711	3191	—
5-door 4WD	3236	2783	—

Adds to standard SL Decor Pkg.: cruise control, front reclining cloth bucket seats with manual lumbar support adjusters (5-door), split folding rear seat, cloth door trim panels, reading lamps, dual auxiliary power outlets, power windows and door locks, power mirrors, cassette player, leather-wrapped steering wheel, lighted visor mirrors, power remote tailgate release, rear defogger, intermittent rear wiper/washer, tilt steering wheel, roof rack, lower body moldings, deep-tinted glass on rear doors and rear quarter windows, cargo cover, cargo net, alloy wheels.

SLT Touring Decor Pkg., 5-door 2WD	5156	4434	—
5-door 4WD	4681	4026	—

Adds to standard SL Decor Pkg.: cruise control, leather front bucket seats with power lumbar support adjusters, 6-way power seat, leather split folding rear seat, power windows and door locks, power mirrors, cassette player, tilt steering wheel, console with storage and cup holders, overhead console with reading lamps, outside temperature gauge and compass, remote keyless entry system, dual auxiliary power outlets, leather-wrapped steering wheel, lighted visor mirrors, power remote tailgate release, rear defogger, intermittent rear wiper/washer, simulated leather door trim panels, roof rack, lower body moldings, deep-tinted glass on rear doors and rear quarter windows, cargo cover, cargo net, alloy wheels.

Split folding rear seat, 3-door	475	409	—
Rear seat delete, SL	NC	NC	NC

NA 5-door 4WD.

Cloth 60/40 front bench seat with storage armrest, 5-door (credit)	(161)	(138)	(138)

NA with SLT Decor Pkg.

6-way power driver's seat and remote keyless entry, SLS, SLE	375	323	—
Cold Climate Pkg.	89	77	—

Heavy duty battery, engine block heater.

GMC

	Retail Price	Dealer Invoice	Fair Price
Overhead console	$147	$126	—
Includes reading lights, outside temperature gauge, and compass. Requires SLS or SLE decor pkgs., bucket seats.			
Heavy duty battery	56	48	—
Convenience Pkg. ZQ3	395	340	—
Cruise control, tilt steering wheel.			
Convenience Pkg. ZM8	322	277	—
Power remote tailgate release, rear defogger, rear wiper/washer.			
Convenience Pkg. ZQ6, 3-door	535	460	—
5-door	710	611	—
Power windows, mirrors, and door locks.			
Air deflector with fog lamps, 2WD	115	99	—
Requires option pkg.			
Roof rack	126	108	—
Cassette player	122	105	—
Cassette player with equalizer	327	281	—
with SLS, SLE, or SLT Decor Pkgs.	205	176	—
CD player with SLS, SLE, or SLT Decor Pkgs.	329	283	—
Radio delete, SL (credit)	(226)	(194)	(194)
Shield Pkg., 4WD	126	108	—
Front differential skid plates, transfer case, steering linkage and fuel tank shields.			
Smooth Ride Suspension Pkg., 5-door with option pkg.	114	98	—
Gas shock absorbers, front and rear stabilizer bars. Requires 205/75R15 tires.			
Luxury Ride Suspension Pkg., 5-door	197	169	—
Gas shock absorbers, urethane jounce bumpers, front and rear stabilizer bars. Requires 235/75R15 tires.			
Solid Smooth Ride Suspension Pkg., 3-door with Pkg. 2 or 3	114	98	—
Gas shock absorbers, urethane jounce bumpers, front and rear stabilizer bars, upgraded rear springs. Requires 205/75R15 tires.			
Euro-Ride Suspension Pkg.	197	169	—
Gas shock absorbers, front and rear stabilizer bars, heavy duty springs.			
Off-road Suspension Pkg., 3-door 4WD	220	189	—
Gas shock absorbers, urethane jounce bumpers, front and rear stabilizer bars, upgraded torsion bars. Requires 235/75R15 on/off-road white letter tires.			
Heavy duty trailering equipment	210	181	—
Weight distributing hitch platform, 7-lead wiring harness, heavy duty flasher.			
Two-tone paint, 5-door	172	148	—
Requires SLE or SLT decor Pkg.			

Prices are accurate at time of publication; subject to manufacturer's change.

GMC • HONDA

	Retail Price	Dealer Invoice	Fair Price
205/75R15 all-season white letter tires	$121	$104	—
235/70R15 all-season tires	192	165	—
235/70R15 all-season white letter tires	325	280	—
235/75R15 on/off-road white letter tires, 4WD	335	288	—
Requires exterior spare tire carrier with 3-door.			
Exterior spare tire carrier, 3-door 4WD	159	137	—
Alloy wheels, 2WD	248	213	—
4WD	280	241	—
Cargo cover, 3-door 4WD with SLS Decor Pkg.	69	59	
Requires exterior spare tire carrier.			

HONDA

Honda Accord	Retail Price	Dealer Invoice	Fair Price
LX 2-door notchback, 5-speed	$17890	$15808	$16308
LX 2-door notchback, automatic	18690	16515	17015
LX 2-door notchback, 5-speed w/ABS	18840	16648	17148
LX 2-door notchback, automatic w/ABS	19640	17355	17855
EX 2-door notchback, 5-speed	20400	18026	18826
EX 2-door notchback, automatic	21200	18733	19533
EX 2-door notchback, 5-speed w/leather	21550	19042	19842
EX 2-door notchback, automatic w/leather	22350	19749	20549
DX 4-door notchback, 5-speed	15100	13343	13843
DX 4-door notchback, automatic	15900	14050	14550
LX 4-door notchback, 5-speed	18090	15985	16489
LX 4-door notchback, automatic	18890	16692	17192
LX 4-door notchback w/ABS, 5-speed	19040	16825	17325
LX 4-door notchback w/ABS, automatic	19840	17531	18031
LX 4-door notchback V-6, automatic	22500	19882	—
EX 4-door notchback, 5-speed	20600	18203	19003
EX 4-door notchback, automatic	21400	18910	19710
EX 4-door notchback w/leather, 5-speed	21750	19219	20019
EX 4-door notchback w/leather, automatic	22550	19926	20729
EX 4-door notchback V-6, automatic	25100	22179	—
LX 5-door wagon, 5-speed	18990	16780	17280
LX 5-door wagon, automatic	19790	17487	17987
EX 5-door wagon, automatic	22430	19820	20620
Destination charge	380	380	380

V-6 models' fair price not available at time of publication.

HONDA

Standard Equipment:

DX: 2.2-liter 4-cylinder engine, 5-speed manual or 4-speed automatic transmission, variable-assist power steering, driver- and passenger-side air bags, cloth reclining front bucket seats, folding rear seatback with cargo pass-through, front console with armrest, tachometer, coolant temperature gauge, trip odometer, digital clock, tinted glass, tilt steering column, cup holder, intermittent wipers, rear defogger, dual remote mirrors, remote fuel door and decklid releases, door pockets, maintenance interval indicator, passenger-side visor mirror, 185/70R14 tires, wheel covers. **Models with ABS** add anti-lock 4-wheel disc brakes. **LX** adds: air conditioning, cruise control, power windows and door locks, power mirrors, AM/FM/cassette, integrated antenna (4-door notchback), power antenna (wagon), rear armrest, lighted visor mirrors; wagon has rear wiper/washer, split folding rear seatback, variable intermittent wipers, cargo cover, 195/60HR15 tires, full-size spare tire. **LX V-6** adds to LX: 2.7-liter V-6 engine, 4-speed automatic transmission, anti-lock 4-wheel disc brakes, 6-way power driver's seat, 205/60R15 tires. **EX** adds to LX: 145-horsepower VTEC engine, anti-lock 4-wheel disc brakes, driver's seat lumbar support and power height adjusters, 6-way power driver's seat (leather models), power moonroof, upgraded audio system, color-keyed bodyside moldings, alloy wheels. **Wagon** adds: remote keyless entry, roof rack. **EX V-6** adds to EX: 2.7-liter V-6 engine, 4-speed automatic transmission, leather upholstery, 8-way power driver's seat, variable intermittent wipers, 205/60R15 tires.

Options are available as dealer-installed accessories.

Honda Civic

	Retail Price	Dealer Invoice	Fair Price
CX 3-door hatchback, 5-speed	$9980	$9362	$9862
CX 3-door hatchback, automatic	10980	10300	10800
DX 3-door hatchback, 5-speed	11250	10094	10994
DX 3-door hatchback, automatic	12250	10991	11891
DX 2-door notchback, 5-speed	11900	10677	11577
DX 2-door notchback, automatic	12900	11574	12474
HX 2-door notchback, 5-speed	13100	11753	12653
HX 2-door notchback, CVT	—	—	—
EX 2-door notchback, 5-speed	14950	13413	14313
EX 2-door notchback, automatic	15750	14131	15031
EX 2-door notchback w/ABS, 5-speed	15550	13951	14851
EX 2-door notchback w/ABS, automatic	16350	14669	15569
DX 4-door notchback, 5-speed	12250	10991	11891
DX 4-door notchback, automatic	13050	11708	12608
LX 4-door notchback, 5-speed	13600	12202	13102
LX 4-door notchback, automatic	14400	12920	13820
LX 4-door notchback with A/C, 5-speed	14450	12719	13619
LX 4-door notchback with A/C, automatic	15250	13437	14337

Prices are accurate at time of publication; subject to manufacturer's change.

CONSUMER GUIDE®

HONDA

	Retail Price	Dealer Invoice	Fair Price
LX 4-door notchback with A/C and ABS, 5-speed	$15050	$13257	$14157
LX 4-door notchback with A/C and ABS, automatic	15850	13975	14875
EX 4-door notchback, 5-speed	16280	14607	15507
EX 4-door notchback, automatic	17080	15325	16225
Destination charge	380	380	380

Standard Equipment:

CX: 1.6-liter 4-cylinder engine (106 horsepower), 5-speed manual or 4-speed automatic transmission, driver- and passenger-side air bags, power steering (requires automatic transmission), reclining cloth front bucket seats, 50/50 split folding rear seats, remote fuel door and hatch releases, tinted glass, rear defogger, dual remote mirrors, cup holder, intermittent wipers, visor mirrors, bodyside molding, 175/70R13 tires. **DX hatchback** adds: rear wiper/washer, AM/FM stereo w/clock, rear map pocket, cargo cover. **DX notchback** adds to CX: power steering (2-door requires automatic transmission), lockable folding rear seat, AM/FM stereo w/clock, tilt steering column, remote trunk release, rear map pocket, wheel covers (2-door). **HX** adds to DX notchback: 1.6-liter 4-cylinder engine (115 horsepower), 5-speed manual or Continuously Variable Transmission (CVT), power steering, power windows and door locks, power mirrors, tachometer, cargo-area light, alloy wheel covers, 185/65R14 tires. **LX** adds to DX notchback: power steering, power mirrors, power windows and door locks, cruise control, tachometer, front console with storage armrest, cargo-area light, 185/65R14 tires, wheel covers. **EX** adds to LX: 1.6-liter 4-cylinder engine (127 horsepower), anti-lock brakes (4-door), air conditioning, power moonroof, six-speakers (2-door), remote keyless entry, color-keyed bodyside molding. **Models with ABS** add anti-lock 4-wheel disc brakes. **Models with A/C** add air conditioning.

Options are available as dealer-installed accessories.

Honda Odyssey

	Retail Price	Dealer Invoice	Fair Price
LX 5-door van, 7-passenger	$23560	—	—
LX 5-door van, 6-passenger	23970	—	—
EX 5-door van	25550	—	—
Destination charge	395	395	395

Dealer invoice and fair price not available at time of publication.

Standard Equipment:

LX: 2.2-liter 4-cylinder engine, 4-speed automatic transmission, anti-lock 4-

HONDA

wheel disc brakes, driver- and passenger-side air bags, variable-assist power steering, front and rear air conditioning, cloth front bucket seats, split folding middle bench seat (7-passenger seating) or removable captain's chairs (6-passenger seating), folding third bench seat, AM/FM/cassette, digital clock, power windows and door locks, power mirrors, cruise control, remote fuel-door release, rear defogger, intermittent wipers, tilt steering column, visor mirrors, cup holders, rear wiper/washer, bodyside moldings, 205/65R15 tires. **EX** adds: power sunroof, 6-passenger seating, driver's seat with power height adjustment, remote keyless entry system, 6-speaker sound system, map lights, color-keyed bodyside moldings, alloy wheels.

Options are available as dealer-installed accessories.

1995 Honda Passport	Retail Price	Dealer Invoice	Fair Price
DX 2WD 5-door wagon, 5-speed	$17630	$15638	$16638
LX 2WD 5-door wagon, 5-speed	20840	18485	19485
LX 2WD 5-door wagon, automatic	21760	19301	20301
LX 4WD 5-door wagon, 5-speed	23520	20862	21862
LX 4WD 5-door wagon with 16-inch Wheel Pkg., 5-speed	24120	21394	22394
LX 4WD 5-door wagon, automatic	24670	21882	22882
LX 4WD 5-door wagon with 16-inch Wheel Pkg., automatic	25270	22414	23414
EX 2WD 5-door wagon, automatic	25600	22707	23707
EX 4WD 5-door wagon, 5-speed	26650	23639	24639
EX 4WD 5-door wagon, automatic	27800	24659	25659
Destination charge	380	380	380

Standard Equipment:

DX: 2.6-liter 4-cylinder engine, 5-speed manual transmission, anti-lock rear brakes, driver- and passenger-side air bags, variable-assist power steering, reclining front bucket seats, center storage console, folding rear seatback, tinted glass, rear defogger, cargo-area light, dual exterior mirrors, fuel tank skid plate, full-size spare tire, outside mounted spare tire carrier, 225/75R15 mud and snow tires, styled steel wheels. **LX 2WD** adds: 3.2-liter V-6 engine, 5-speed manual or 4-speed automatic transmission, 4-wheel disc brakes, cruise control, power windows and door locks, tilt steering column, remote tailgate release, tachometer, 60/40 split folding rear bench seat, upgraded door trim panels, door courtesy lights, AM/FM/cassette, visor mirrors. **LX 4WD** adds to LX 2WD: part-time 4-wheel drive, automatic locking front hubs, air conditioning, 2-speed transfer case, transfer case skid plate, alloy wheels. **16-inch Wheel Pkg.** adds to LX 4WD: flared wheel opening moldings, splash guards, 245/70R16 tires, 16-inch alloy wheels. **EX 2WD** adds to LX 2WD: air conditioning, removable tilt-up moonroof,

Prices are accurate at time of publication; subject to manufacturer's change.

HONDA • HYUNDAI

heated power mirrors, chrome bumpers, rear privacy glass, rear wiper/washer, leather-wrapped steering wheel, intermittent wipers, cargo net, map lights, 16-inch Wheel Pkg. **EX 4WD** adds to EX 2WD: limited-slip differential, part-time 4-wheel drive, automatic locking front hubs, 2-speed transfer case, transfer case skid plate.

Options are available as dealer-installed accessories.

HYUNDAI

Hyundai Accent	Retail Price	Dealer Invoice	Fair Price
L 3-door hatchback, 5-speed	$8285	$7808	—
Base 3-door hatchback, 5-speed	8795	8289	—
Base 3-door hatchback, automatic	9550	8973	NA
Base 4-door notchback, 5-speed	9295	8760	—
Base 4-door notchback, automatic	10050	9444	—
Destination charge	405	405	405

Fair price not available at time of publication.

Standard Equipment:

L: 1.5-liter 4-cylinder engine, 5-speed manual transmission, driver- and passenger-side air bags, cloth reclining front bucket seats, folding rear seat, console with cup holder, coolant temperature gauge, trip odometer, dual exterior remote mirrors, intermittent wipers, rear defogger, remote fuel door release, front door map pockets, passenger-side visor mirror, cargo area cover, color-keyed bumpers, 155/80R13 tires. **Base** adds: 5-speed manual or 4-speed automatic transmission, digital clock, remote hatch (3-door) or decklid (4-door) release, bodyside moldings, 175/70R13 tires, wheel covers. 4-door deletes cargo area cover and rear seat folding feature.

Optional Equipment:

Option Pkg. 4, base	675	559	—
AM/FM/cassette, tinted glass, power steering.			
Option Pkg. 5, base	1570	1329	—
Pkg. 4 plus air conditioning.			
Option Pkg. 6, base	1920	1617	—
Pkg. 5 plus pop-up sunroof.			
Option Pkg. 7, base	2120	1839	—
Pkg. 5 plus anti-lock brakes.			

Hyundai Sonata	Retail Price	Dealer Invoice	Fair Price
4-door notchback, 5-speed	$13999	$12689	$13189
4-door notchback, automatic	14799	13480	13980

346   CONSUMER GUIDE®

HYUNDAI

	Retail Price	Dealer Invoice	Fair Price
GL 4-door notchback, automatic	$15699	$14068	$14568
GL 4-door notchback, V-6 automatic	16699	14853	15353
GLS 4-door notchback, V-6 automatic	17999	15758	16258
Destination charge	405	405	405

Standard Equipment:

2.0-liter DOHC 4-cylinder engine, 5-speed manual or 4-speed automatic transmission, air conditioning, power steering, driver- and passenger-side air bags, cloth reclining front bucket seats with 4-way adjustable driver's seat, center console, tachometer, coolant temperature gauge, trip odometer, AM/FM/cassette, tilt steering column, digital clock, remote fuel door and decklid releases, rear defogger, door pockets, remote outside mirrors, bodyside molding, tinted glass, intermittent wipers, visor mirrors, 195/70R14 tires. **GL** adds: 2.0-liter DOHC 4-cylinder or 3.0-liter V-6 engine, 4-speed automatic transmission, power windows and door locks, power mirrors. **GLS** adds to GL: 3.0-liter V-6 engine, 6-way adjustable driver's seat, 60/40 split folding rear seat with center armrest, dual map lights, power antenna, upgraded cloth upholstery and door trim, upgraded cassette player, lighted passenger-side visor mirror, front seatback pockets, 205/60R15 tires, alloy wheels.

Optional Equipment:

Option Pkg. 2, GL and GL V-6	230	190	202
Cruise control.			
Option Pkg. 3, GL and GL V-6	965	767	849
Cruise control, console armrest, sunroof.			
Option Pkg. 4, GL V-6	1245	1107	1195
Anti-lock brakes, cruise control, console armrest.			
Option Pkg. 10, GLS	600	494	570
Sunroof.			
Option Pkg. 11, GLS	1350	1112	1283
Sunroof, CD player.			
Option Pkg. 12, GLS	1400	1226	1330
CD player, Leather Pkg. (leather upholstery, leather-wrapped steering wheel).			
Option Pkg. 13, GLS	2000	1720	1900
Leather Pkg., CD player, sunroof.			
Option Pkg. 14, GLS	2880	1554	2736
Anti-lock brakes, Leather Pkg., CD player, sunroof.			
Option Pkg. 15, GLS	880	834	845
Anti-lock brakes.			

Prices are accurate at time of publication; subject to manufacturer's change.

INFINITI

Infiniti G20

	Retail Price	Dealer Invoice	Fair Price
4-door notchback, 5-speed	$23800	$20190	$20790
4-door notchback, automatic	24800	21038	21638
G20t with Touring Package, 5-speed	26900	22820	23420
G20t with Touring Package, automatic	27900	23668	24228
Destination charge	480	480	480

Standard Equipment:

2.0-liter DOHC 4-cylinder engine, 5-speed manual or 4-speed automatic transmission, anti-lock 4-wheel disc brakes, power steering, driver- and passenger-side air bags, automatic climate control, cloth reclining front bucket seats, tachometer, coolant temperature gauge, trip odometer, power windows and locks, power mirrors, AM/FM/CD player, power antenna, leather-wrapped steering wheel, remote fuel door and decklid releases, tinted glass, anti-theft device, 195/65R14 all-season tires, alloy wheels. **G20t** adds: Touring Package (limited-slip differential, rear spoiler, fog lamps, Leather Appointment Group, sport bucket seats, split folding rear seat), 195/65HR14 performance tires.

Optional Equipment:

Power glass sunroof, base	1000	848	910
Leather Appointment Group, base	2350	1995	2100

Includes leather upholstery, 4-way power front seats, padded leather center console armrest, remote keyless entry system, power glass sunroof.

Infiniti I30

	Retail Price	Dealer Invoice	Fair Price
4-door notchback, 5-speed	$28420	$24683	—
4-door notchback, automatic	29420	25551	—
Leather-Appointed 4-door notchback, automatic	31120	26399	—
I30t with Touring Package, 5-speed	32720	27757	—
I30t with Touring Package, automatic	33720	28605	—
Destination charge	480	480	480

Fair price not available at time of publication.

Standard Equipment:

Standard: 3.0-liter DOHC V-6 engine, 5-speed manual or 4-speed automatic transmission, anti-lock 4-wheel disc brakes, variable-assist power steering, driver- and passenger-side air bags, cloth power front bucket seats, console

INFINITI

with armrest, automatic climate control, cruise control, tilt steering column, AM/FM/cassette and CD player with six speakers, power antenna, tinted glass, rear defogger, power windows and door locks, power mirrors, remote fuel door and decklid releases, remote keyless entry and anti-theft alarm systems, intermittent wipers, tachometer, coolant temperature gauge, trip odometer, digital clock, leather-wrapped steering wheel, shifter knob, and parking brake handle, rear folding armrest, map pockets, lighted visor mirrors, map lights, fog lights, floormats, 205/65R15 all-season tires, cast alloy wheels. **Leather-Appointed** model adds: 4-speed automatic transmission, leather upholstery, power glass sunroof, HomeLink remote control transmitter, automatic day/night mirror. **I30t** adds: 5-speed manual or 4-speed automatic transmission, limited-slip differential, sport suspension, Heated Seat Pkg., decklid spoiler, 215/60HR15 tires, forged alloy wheels.

Optional Equipment:

	Retail Price	Dealer Invoice	Fair Price
Power glass sunroof, base	$1000	$848	—
Requires 4-speed automatic transmission.			
Heated Seat Pkg., Leather-Appointed	400	339	—
Heated front seats and mirrors, low windshield washer fluid warning light, heavy duty battery.			
Heated Seat Pkg. delete, I30t (credit)	(400)	(339)	(339)
Limited-slip differential, Leather-Appointed	800	679	—
Includes Heated Front Seat Pkg.			

Infiniti J30

	Retail Price	Dealer Invoice	Fair Price
4-door notchback	$39920	$33460	$34260
J30t with Touring Package	41920	35136	35936
Destination charge	480	480	480

Standard Equipment:

3.0-liter DOHC V-6 engine, 4-speed automatic transmission, anti-lock 4-wheel disc brakes, variable-assist power steering, limited-slip differential, driver- and passenger-side air bags, 8-way heated power front bucket seats, driver's seat power lumbar adjuster, leather upholstery, walnut inlays, automatic climate control, cruise control, tilt steering column, AM/FM/cassette and CD player with six speakers, power sunroof, tinted glass, power windows and locks, heated power mirrors, remote fuel door and decklid releases, remote keyless entry and anti-theft alarm systems, intermittent wipers, tachometer, trip odometer, leather-wrapped steering wheel, automatic day/night mirror, rear folding armrest, floormats, 215/60R15 all-season tires, cast alloy wheels. **J30t** adds: Touring Pkg. (rear spoiler, firmer suspension, larger stabilizer bars, forged alloy wheels), 215/60HR15 performance tires.

Options are available as dealer-installed accessories.

Prices are accurate at time of publication; subject to manufacturer's change.

INFINITI • ISUZU

Infiniti Q45

	Retail Price	Dealer Invoice	Fair Price
4-door notchback	$53520	$44860	$45860
Q45t with Touring Pkg.	56970	47752	48752
Destination charge	480	480	480

Standard Equipment:
4.5-liter DOHC V-8 engine, 4-speed automatic transmission, anti-lock 4-wheel disc brakes, power steering, limited-slip differential, driver- and passenger-side air bags, cruise control, automatic climate control, leather reclining front bucket seats (wool is available at no charge), wood interior trim, Nissan/Bose AM/FM/cassette, power antenna, power sunroof, tinted glass, power windows and locks, remote keyless entry system, power driver's seat with 2-position memory (memory includes tilt/telescopic steering column), power passenger seat, heated power mirrors, fog lights, remote fuel door and decklid releases, intermittent wipers, front and rear folding armrests, theft deterrent system, 215/65VR15 tires, alloy wheels. **Q45t** adds to base: Touring Pkg. (Includes rear spoiler, rear stabilizer bar, performance alloy wheels and tires, 10-disc CD changer, heated front seats).

Optional Equipment:
Traction control, base	1950	1635	1800
with Touring Pkg.	1850	1551	1700

Includes traction control system, heated front seats.

ISUZU

1995 Isuzu Rodeo	Retail Price	Dealer Invoice	Fair Price
S 4-cylinder 2WD 5-door wagon, 5-speed	$16990	15971	16771
S V-6 2WD 5-door wagon, 5-speed	19900	18209	19009
S V-6 2WD 5-door wagon, automatic	20820	19051	19851
LS V-6 2WD 5-door wagon, automatic	25190	23049	23849
S V-6 4WD 5-door wagon, 5-speed	21740	19784	20584
S V-6 4WD 5-door wagon, automatic	22890	20830	21630
LS V-6 4WD 5-door wagon, 5-speed	26310	23942	24742
LS V-6 4WD 5-door wagon, automatic	27460	24988	25788
Destination charge	445	445	445

Standard Equipment:
S: 2.6-liter 4-cylinder engine, 5-speed manual transmission, anti-lock rear brakes, driver- and passenger-side air bags, power steering, cloth front bench seat with folding armrest, folding rear seat with headrests, rear

ISUZU

defogger, tinted glass, day/night mirror, oil pressure and coolant temperature gauges, voltmeter, trip odometer, cargo rope hooks, carpet, 225/75R15 all-season tires, styled steel wheels with bright center caps, full-size spare tire. **S V-6** adds: 3.2-liter V-6, 5-speed manual or 4-speed automatic transmission, 4-wheel disc brakes, reclining front bucket seats, center console, tachometer, outside spare tire, wheel trim rings. **LS** adds: air conditioning, tilt steering column, split folding rear seat, power windows and door locks, heated power mirrors, cruise control, AM/FM/cassette, velour upholstery, front door map pockets, map and courtesy lights, intermittent wipers, intermittent rear wiper/washer, visor mirrors, leather-wrapped steering wheel, roof rack, privacy rear quarter and rear side glass, cargo net, carpeted floormats, alloy wheels. **4WD** adds: part-time 4WD, automatic locking hubs, tow hooks, skid plates, 245/70R16 tires (LS), alloy wheels.

Optional Equipment:

	Retail Price	Dealer Invoice	Fair Price
Air conditioning, S	$950	$846	$879
Preferred Equipment Pkg., S	2150	1913	1989

Air conditioning, tilt steering column, power windows and door locks, power mirrors, cruise control, intermittent wipers, intermittent rear wiper/washer, visor mirrors, roof rack, AM/FM/cassette, cargo net, cargo area cover, courtesy lamp, map pocket.

Alloy Wheel Pkg., S 4WD	1080	961	999

16-inch alloy wheels, 245/70R16 tires, limited-slip differential, fender flares, mud flaps.

Exterior Appearance Pkg., S 4-cylinder	349	276	323

Bodyside moldings, striping, roof rack, wheel trim rings.

Limited-slip differential, LS 4WD	280	249	259
Sunroof, LS	350	312	324
Remote keyless entry	230	181	213
S requires Preferred Equipment Pkg.			
Rear wiper/washer, S 4-cylinder	200	178	185
Outside spare tire carrier, S 4-cylinder	275	245	254
Brush/grille guard	305	241	282
CD changer	650	514	601
S requires Preferred Equipment Pkg.			
Premium CD player	550	435	509
S requires Preferred Equipment Pkg.			
CD player, S	500	395	462
Roof rack, S	195	154	180
Sport side step, 4WD	345	273	319
Running boards	335	264	310
Splash guards, S 2WD	40	32	37
Hood protector	68	54	63
Carpeted floormats, S 4-cylinder	55	43	51
Cargo area cover, S	90	71	83

Prices are accurate at time of publication; subject to manufacturer's change.

ISUZU

	Retail Price	Dealer Invoice	Fair Price
Cargo net, S	$22	$17	$20
Alloy wheels, S 2WD	400	356	370

Requires Preferred Equipment Pkg.

1995 Isuzu Trooper

	Retail Price	Dealer Invoice	Fair Price
Base S 4-door 4WD wagon, 5-speed	$22670	$21310	$22110
S 4-door 4WD wagon, 5-speed	24410	22091	22891
S 4-door 4WD wagon, automatic	25560	23131	23931
LS 4-door 4WD wagon, 5-speed	29570	26318	27118
LS 4-door 4WD wagon, automatic	30720	27341	28141
SE 4-door 4WD wagon, automatic	34000	30260	31060
Limited 4-door 4WD wagon, automatic	37720	33571	34371
Destination charge	445	445	445

Standard Equipment:

Base S: 3.2-liter V-6 engine, 5-speed manual transmission, variable-assist power steering, driver- and passenger-side air bags, 4-wheel disc brakes, anti-lock rear brakes, part-time 4WD system with automatic locking front hubs, cloth reclining front bucket seats, folding rear seat, full door trim, AM/FM/cassette, center console, dual outside mirrors, rear defogger, tilt steering column, intermittent wipers, rear wiper/washer, skid plates, tachometer, voltmeter, coolant temperature and oil pressure gauges, trip odometer, visor mirrors, tinted glass, rear step pad, rear air deflector, front and rear tow hooks, mud flaps, 245/70R16 tires, full-size spare tire, wheel trim rings. **S** adds: 5-speed manual transmission or 4-speed automatic transmission, **LS** adds: air conditioning, cruise control, split folding rear seat, bright grille, overfenders with formed mud flap, rocker panel molding, leather-wrapped steering wheel, upgraded cloth upholstery, 6-speaker sound system, power windows and door locks, heated power mirrors, variable intermittent wipers, map light, cargo cover and net, alloy wheels. **SE** adds: 4-speed automatic transmission, anti-lock 4-wheel disc brakes, leather upholstery, power moonroof, color-keyed mud flaps and overfenders. **Limited** adds: DOHC engine, limited-slip differential, power front seats, CD changer, bronze-tint windshield, rear privacy glass, fog light, power antenna, headlight wiper/washer, remote keyless entry, anti-theft alarm, cargo floor rails.

Optional Equipment:

4-wheel anti-lock brakes	1200	1068	1080
S requires Preferred Equipment Pkg. NA Base S.			
Limited-slip differential	290	259	261
S requires Preferred Equipment Pkg. NA Base S.			

ISUZU • JAGUAR

	Retail Price	Dealer Invoice	Fair Price
Air conditioning, Base S	$1000	$890	$900
Split folding rear seat, S	300	267	270
Preferred Equipment Pkg., S	2490	2216	2241

Air conditioning, power windows and door locks, 6-speaker radio, split-folding rear seat, heated power mirrors, cruise control, alloy wheels.

Overfenders, S	550	490	508
CD player, S, LS	550	435	468
CD changer	650	514	585

NA Base S.

Remote keyless entry	350	277	315

S requires Preferred Equipment Pkg. NA Base S.

JAGUAR

Jaguar XJ Sedan

	Retail Price	Dealer Invoice	Fair Price
XJ6 4-door notchback	$56320	—	—
Vanden Plas 4-door notchback	63720	—	—
XJR 4-door notchback	66270	—	—
XJ12 4-door notchback	79370	—	—
Destination charge	580	580	580

Dealer invoice and fair price not available at time of publication.

Standard Equipment:

XJ6: 4.0-liter DOHC 6-cylinder engine, driver- and passenger-side side air bags, 4-speed automatic transmission, anti-lock 4-wheel disc brakes, variable-assist power steering, 12-way power front bucket seats with power lumbar support adjusters, leather upholstery, automatic climate control, driver's seat memory system, power windows and door locks, cruise control, power sunroof, heated power mirrors, heated door locks and windshield washer nozzles, intermittent wipers, trip computer, power tilt steering column, fog lamps, remote entry and alarm system, remote fuel door and decklid releases, rear defogger, AM/FM/cassette, folding rear armrest, lighted visor mirrors, automatic day/night rearview mirror, seatback pockets, console with storage, overhead console, map lights, cellular phone pre-wiring, cup holders, programmable garage-door opener, walnut trim, rear headrests, chrome hood ornament, color-keyed bodyside moldings, floormats, full-size spare tire, 225/60ZR16 tires, alloy wheels. **Vanden Plas** adds: CD changer, wood- and leather-rimmed steering wheel, folding burl walnut picnic tables on front seatbacks, upgraded leather upholstery, storage in rear armrest, rear reading lights. **XJR** deletes seatback picnic tables, walnut trim, and footwell rugs and adds: supercharged engine, traction con-

JAGUAR • JEEP

trol, limited-slip differential, sport suspension, Harman/Kardon audio system, heated front and rear seats, maple interior trim and shifter knob, mesh grille with color-keyed frame, 255/45ZR17 tires. **XJ12** adds to Vanden Plas: 6.0-liter V-12 engine, traction control, Harman/Kardon audio system with CD changer, heated front and rear seats, upgraded leather upholstery, upgraded suspension, walnut shifter knob.

Optional Equipment:

	Retail Price	Dealer Invoice	Fair Price
All-weather Pkg., XJ6, Vanden Plas	$2250	—	—
Traction control, heated front and rear seats.			
Harman/Kardon audio system w/CD changer,			
XJ6	1800	1440	—
Vanden Plas	1000	—	—
Non-standard color/trim option	2000	1600	—
Chrome wheels	1500	1200	—
NA XJR.			
Engine block heater	100	80	—

JEEP

Jeep Cherokee

	Retail Price	Dealer Invoice	Fair Price
SE 3-door 2WD	$14645	$13782	$14032
SE 3-door 4WD	16160	15181	15431
SE 5-door 2WD	15683	14747	15197
SE 5-door 4WD	17194	16142	16592
Sport 3-door 2WD	16999	15414	15664
Sport 3-door 4WD	18511	16765	17015
Sport 5-door 2WD	18033	16344	16794
Sport 5-door 4WD	19545	17695	18145
Country 5-door 2WD	20462	18482	18932
Country 5-door 4WD	21976	19834	20284
Destination charge	500	500	500

Standard Equipment:

SE: 2.5-liter 4-cylinder engine, 5-speed manual transmission, driver-side air bag, power steering, vinyl front wingback-style bucket seats, front armrest, folding rear seat, mini console, AM/FM radio with two speakers, tinted glass, intermittent wipers, dual remote mirrors, 215/75R15 tires; 4WD system is Command-Trac part-time. **Sport** adds: 4.0-liter 6-cylinder engine, cloth reclining front bucket seats, AM/FM stereo with four speakers and sound bar, tachometer, trip odometer, oil pressure and coolant temperature gauges, voltmeter, Sport Decor Group, spare tire cover, cargo tiedown

JEEP

hooks, 225/75R15 outlined white letter all-terrain tires. **Country** adds: 4-speed automatic transmission, front console with armrest and storage, rear-seat heater ducts, Light Group, leather-wrapped steering wheel, roof rack, rear wiper/washer, dual remote break-away mirrors, Country Decor Group, floormats, 225/70R15 tires, lattice-design alloy wheels.

Optional Equipment:

	Retail Price	Dealer Invoice	Fair Price
Pkg. 23B/25B/26B, SE	$155	$132	$136

Cloth highback bucket seats, floor console with armrest, rear wiper/washer. Pkg. 25B requires 4.0-liter 6-cylinder engine. Pkg. 26B requires 4.0-liter 6-cylinder engine and automatic transmission.

Pkg. 25E/26E, Sport	159	135	159

Air conditioning, floor console, roof rack, leather-wrapped tilt steering wheel, rear wiper/washer, floormats. Pkg. 26E requires 4-speed automatic transmission.

Pkg. 26H, Country (credit)	(212)	(181)	(181)

Air conditioning, cruise control, cassette player with four speakers, tilt steering wheel. Pkg. 26H requires automatic transmission.

4.0-liter 6-cylinder engine	812	690	711
4-speed automatic transmission, SE, Sport	897	762	785

Requires 4.0-liter 6-cylinder engine.

Selec-Trac full-time 4WD, Sport, Country	394	335	345

Requires automatic transmission.

Trac-Lok rear differential	285	242	249

Requires conventional spare tire.

Anti-lock brakes	599	509	524

Requires 4.0-liter 6-cylinder engine.

Air conditioning	NC	NC	NC
Rear defogger	161	137	141
Fog lamps, Sport, Country	110	94	96

Requires air conditioning or Heavy Duty Alternator/Battery Group.

Rear wiper/washer	147	125	129
Deep-tinted glass,			
Sport 3-door	305	259	267
Sport and Country 5-doors	144	122	126
Power Windows and Door Locks Group,			
Sport 3-door	437	371	382
Sport and Country 5-doors	582	495	509

Power windows and locks, remote keyless entry.

Dual remote break-away mirrors, SE, Sport	22	19	20
Power mirrors, Country	100	85	88
Sport	122	104	107

Requires floor console (Sport), and Power Windows and Door Locks Group.

Tilt steering wheel	132	112	116

Prices are accurate at time of publication; subject to manufacturer's change.

CONSUMER GUIDE®

JEEP

	Retail Price	Dealer Invoice	Fair Price
Cruise control	$230	$196	$201
Leather-wrapped steering wheel, SE, Sport	48	41	42
Cassette player with four speakers, SE	291	247	255
Sport, Country	201	171	176
Premium speakers (six), Sport, Country	128	109	112 |//
Requires Power Windows and Door Locks Group.
Rear sound bar, SE	140	119	123
Cloth seats, SE	61	52	53
Power driver's seat, Country	296	252	259
Leather seats, Country 5-door	831	706	727 |//
Includes power driver's seat, front-seat map pockets.
Floor console with armrest, SE, Sport	147	125	129
Overhead console, Sport, Country	203	173	178 |//
Includes compass and thermometer, reading lights. Requires Power Windows and Door Locks Group.
Cargo area cover	72	61	63
Roof rack, SE, Sport	139	118	122
Light Group, SE, Sport	195	166	171
with cassette player or rear sound bar	156	133	137 |//
Headlamp-off delay system, lighted visor mirrors, misc. lights. Rear sound bar NA with Sport.
Bright Group, Country	202	172	177 |//
Bright dual power remote mirrors, front and rear bumpers, grille and headlamp bezels, door handles.
Trailer Tow Group	358	304	313
4WD models with Off-Road Suspension	242	206	212 |//
Requires automatic transmission, conventional spare tire.
Up Country Suspension Group, 4WD, SE	1046	889	920
Sport	733	623	645
Country	645	548	568 |//
Trac-Lok rear differential, gas shock absorbers, heavy duty springs, tow hooks, skid plates, auxiliary fan (with 4.0-liter 6-cylinder engine), heavy duty radiator, transmission oil cooler (with automatic transmission and 4.0-liter 6-cylinder engine), 225/75R15 outline white letter tires, conventional spare tire. Requires dual remote break-away mirrors.
Skid Plates Group, 4WD models	144	122	126
225/75R15 outline white letter tires (four), SE	313	266	274 |//
Requires conventional spare tire.
225/75R15 outline white letter conventional spare tire, SE, Sport	116	99	102
215/75R15 conventional spare tire, SE	71	60	62
Conventional (225/70R15) spare tire, Country	140	119	123
10-hole alloy wheels, SE	435	370	381
Sport	245	208	216

JEEP

	Retail Price	Dealer Invoice	Fair Price
Country	$87	$74	$76
Requires conventional spare tire.			
Matching fifth wheel, Sport	26	22	23
Requires conventional spare tire.			
Matching fifth alloy wheel, Sport, Country	87	74	76
Requires conventional spare tire.			
Floormats, SE, Sport	46	39	40
Engine block heater	31	26	27

Jeep Grand Cherokee

	Retail Price	Dealer Invoice	Fair Price
Laredo 5-door 2WD	$24603	$22311	$23111
Laredo 5-door 4WD	26571	24077	24877
Limited 5-door 2WD	30479	27482	28282
Limited 5-door 4WD	32906	29652	30452
Destination charge	500	500	500

Standard Equipment:

Laredo: 4.0-liter 6-cylinder engine, 4-speed automatic transmission, driver- and passenger-side air bags, anti-lock 4-wheel disc brakes, power steering, cloth reclining front bucket seats, split folding rear seat, air conditioning, power windows, remote keyless entry, leather-wrapped tilt steering wheel, cruise control, tachometer, voltage and temperature gauges, trip odometer, illuminated entry system, storage console with armrest and cup holders, AM/FM/cassette, tinted glass, rear defogger, intermittent front and rear wiper/washer, remote keyless entry system, heated power mirrors, map and courtesy lights, lighted visor mirrors, roof rack, floor mats, cargo cover, net and tiedown hooks, 215/75R15 tires, alloy wheels. 4WD system is Selec-Trac full-time 4WD. **Limited** adds: automatic temperature control, leather power memory front seats, variable-assist steering, Luxury Group, remote keyless entry w/memory feature, automatic day/night rearview and driver's-side mirrors, memory outside mirrors, fog lamps, deep-tinted side and rear glass, universal garage-door opener, steering wheel w/radio controls, overhead console (compass, trip computer, map/reading lights), security system, Infinity Gold speakers w/amplifier and graphic equalizer, gold badging and graphics, 225/70R16 outlined white letter tires, gold-accented alloy wheels. 4WD system is Quadra-Trac permanent 4WD.

Optional Equipment:

Pkg. 26X/28X, Laredo	154	131	146

Overhead console (compass, trip computer, map/reading lights), tinted glass, 225/75R15 outlined white-letter tires. Pkg. 28X requires 5.2-liter V-8 engine.

Prices are accurate at time of publication; subject to manufacturer's change.

JEEP

	Retail Price	Dealer Invoice	Fair Price
Pkg. 26F/28F, Laredo	$1475	$1254	$1401

Package 26X/28X plus Luxury Group, security system, cassette player with equalizer. Pkg. 28F requires 5.2-liter V-8 engine.

Pkg. 26K/28K, Limited	1290	1097	1226

Power sunroof, heated front seats, CD player, mini overhead console. Pkg. 28K requires 5.2-liter V-8 engine.

5.2-liter V-8 engine, 4WD Laredo	1311	1114	1245
4WD Limited	867	737	824

Includes Quadra-Trac permanent 4WD, Trailer Tow Prep Group.

Quadra-Trac permanent 4WD, Laredo	444	377	422
Trac-Lok rear differential (4WD)	285	242	271
Luxury Group, Laredo w/Pkg. 26X/28X	962	818	914

Power front seats, automatic day/night rearview mirror, automatic headlamp system.

Trailer Tow Prep Group	101	86	96
Trailer Tow Group III	359	305	341

Includes Trailer Tow Prep Group. NA with 5.2-liter V-8.

Trailer Tow Group IV (4WD only)	242	206	230

Includes Trailer Tow Prep Group. Requires 5.2-liter V-8.

Fog lamps, 2WD Laredo	110	94	105
Fog Lamp/Skid Plate Group (4WD only),			
Laredo	254	216	241
Laredo w/Up Country Suspension Group	110	94	105
Limited with 4.0-liter engine	144	122	137
Up Country Suspension Group (4WD only),			
Laredo	794	675	754
Laredo w/option pkg.	578	491	549

Skid Plate Group, tow hooks, high-pressure gas shocks, 245/70R15 outlined white letter all-terrain tires, conventional spare tire, matching fifth wheel.

Security system, Laredo	149	127	142
Power sunroof, Limited	760	646	722

Limited includes mini overhead console.

Leather seats, Laredo	576	490	547

Requires Luxury Group.

Heat front seats, Limited	250	213	238
Integrated child safety seat	150	128	143
Deep tinted glass, Laredo	226	192	215
Flip-up liftgate glass	90	77	86
AM/FM/cassette with equalizer, Laredo	660	561	627

Includes eight speakers, amplifier, power antenna.

AM/FM with CD and equalizer,			
Laredo Pkg. 26X/28X	770	655	732
Laredo Pkg. 26F/28F	110	94	105

Includes eight speakers, amplifier, power antenna.

JEEP • KIA

	Retail Price	Dealer Invoice	Fair Price
AM/FM with CD, cassette, and equalizer,			
Laredo Pkg. 26X/28X	$940	$799	$893
Laredo Pkg. 26F/28F, Limited	280	238	266
Includes eight speakers, amplifier, power antenna.			
Conventional spare tire,			
Laredo w/Pkg. 26F/28F, Limited	160	136	152
225/75R15 outlined white letter tires,			
Laredo	246	209	234
225/75R15 outlined white letter all-terrain			
tires, Laredo	313	266	297
Laredo w/option pkg.	67	57	64
Engine block heater	31	26	29

KIA

1995 Kia Sportage

	Retail Price	Dealer Invoice	Fair Price
Base 5-door wagon, 2WD	$13495	$12268	—
Base 5-door wagon, 4WD	15295	13779	—
EX 5-door wagon, 4WD	16195	14460	—
Destination charge	400	400	400

Fair price not available at time of publication.

Standard Equipment:

Base: 2.0-liter 4-cylinder engine (2WD), DOHC engine (4WD), 5-speed manual transmission, anti-lock rear brakes, power steering, cloth reclining front bucket seats with driver's-side manual lumbar support adjuster, tilt steering column, front door map pockets, console, split folding rear bench seat, digital clock, tachometer, rear defogger, tinted glass, automatic locking hubs (4WD), intermittent wipers, power windows, power mirrors, remote fuel door release, passenger-side visor mirror, 205/75R15 tires, alloy wheels. **EX** adds to base 4WD: cruise control, power door locks, remote tailgate release, rear wiper/washer, color-keyed mirrors.

Optional Equipment:

4-speed automatic transmission, 4WD	1000	910	—
Air conditioning	900	763	—
AM/FM/cassette	400	305	—
Leather upholstery, EX	1000	865	—
Roof rack	185	142	—
Spare tire carrier with cover	335	274	—
Floormats	60	41	—

Prices are accurate at time of publication; subject to manufacturer's change.

CONSUMER GUIDE®

LEXUS

Lexus ES 300

	Retail Price	Dealer Invoice	Fair Price
4-door notchback	$32400	$27540	$30000
Destination charge	495	495	495

Standard Equipment:
3.0-liter DOHC V-6, 4-speed automatic transmission, anti-lock 4-wheel disc brakes, variable-assist power steering, driver- and passenger-side air bags, tilt steering column, automatic climate control, cruise control, power windows and locks, AM/FM cassette, cloth multi-adjustable power front bucket seats, split folding rear seatback, rear defogger, variable intermittent wipers, lighted visor mirrors, outside temperature indicator, automatic on/off headlamps, remote fuel door and decklid releases, tool kit, first aid kit, cellular phone pre-wiring, remote keyless entry system, theft deterrent system, fog lamps, 205/65VR16 tires, alloy wheels.

Optional Equipment:

Leather Trim Pkg.	1300	1040	1235
SE Luxury Pkg.	2000	1800	1900
Leather Trim Pkg. plus remote 6-CD disc changer, power moonroof.			
SF/SJ Luxury Pkg.	3000	2700	2850
SE Luxury Pkg. plus chrome wheels. SJ Pkg. requires all-season tires.			
Heated front seats	420	336	399
Requires Leather Trim Pkg.			
Power moonroof with sunshade	950	760	903
Remote 6-CD disc changer	1050	788	998
205/65VR16 all-season tires	NC	NC	NC
Chrome wheels	1700	850	1615

Lexus GS 300

	Retail Price	Dealer Invoice	Fair Price
4-door notchback	$45700	$38845	$40345
Destination charge	495	495	495

Standard Equipment:
3.0-liter DOHC 6-cylinder engine, 5-speed automatic transmission, anti-lock 4-wheel disc brakes, driver- and passenger-side air bags, variable-assist power steering, dual power/heated outside mirrors, electronic analog instruments, power tilt/telescopic steering column, cloth power driver and front passenger seats, power windows and door locks, walnut wood trim, automatic climate control, automatic on/off headlamps, remote entry system,

LEXUS

illuminated entry system, rear defogger, variable intermittent wipers, theft-deterrent system, illuminated visor mirrors, remote electric trunk and fuel-filler door releases, Pioneer Audio System with AM/FM/cassette and seven speakers, power diversity antenna, cellular phone pre-wiring, outside temperature indicator, tool kit, first aid kit, 215/60VR16 tires, alloy wheels.

Optional Equipment:

	Retail Price	Dealer Invoice	Fair Price
Traction Control System	$1870	$1496	$1777
Includes heated front seats. Requires Leather Trim Pkg. and all-season tires.			
Leather Trim Pkg.	1300	1040	1235
Lexus/Nakamichi Premium Audio System	1200	900	1140
Requires Leather Trim Pkg. and remote 12-CD auto changer.			
Remote 12-CD auto changer	1050	788	998
Power glass moonroof	950	760	903
All-season tires	NC	NC	NC
Chrome wheels	1700	850	1615

Lexus LS 400

	Retail Price	Dealer Invoice	Fair Price
4-door notchback	$52900	$44436	—
Destination charge	495	495	495

Fair price not available at time of publication.

Standard Equipment:

4.0-liter DOHC V-8 engine, 4-speed automatic transmission, anti-lock 4-wheel disc brakes, driver- and passenger-side air bags, variable-assist power steering, seatbelt pretensioners, air conditioning with automatic climate control, leather upholstery, reclining front bucket seats with 10-way power adjustment, power lumbar support adjusters, power windows and locks, cruise control, remote entry system, walnut wood trim, heated power mirrors, automatic day/night mirrors, tachometer, trip odometer, coolant temperature gauge, outside temperature indicator, remote fuel door and decklid releases, lighted visor mirrors, theft deterrent system, automatic on/off headlamps, power tilt/telescopic steering column, AM/FM/cassette with seven speakers and power diversity antenna, digital clock, intermittent wipers, cellular phone pre-wiring, tool kit, first aid kit, full-size spare tire, 225/60VR16 tires, alloy wheels.

Optional Equipment:

Power moonroof with sunshade	1050	840	—
Traction control with heated front seats	2020	1616	—
Requires memory seats and all-season tires.			

Prices are accurate at time of publication; subject to manufacturer's change.

LEXUS

	Retail Price	Dealer Invoice	Fair Price
Electronic air suspension	$1850	$1480	—
Requires Lexus/Nakamichi Premium Audio System and traction control.			
Seat memory system	800	640	—
Lexus/Nakamichi Premium Audio System	1200	900	—
Requires 6-CD auto changer.			
6-CD auto changer	1050	788	—
Chrome wheels	1700	850	—
All-season tires	NC	NC	NC

Lexus SC 300/400

	Retail Price	Dealer Invoice	Fair Price
300 2-door notchback, 5-speed	$43400	$36890	—
300 2-door notchback, automatic	44300	37655	—
400 2-door notchback	52400	44016	—
Destination charge	495	495	495

Fair price not available at time of publication.

Standard Equipment:

300: 3.0-liter DOHC 6-cylinder engine, 5-speed manual or 4-speed automatic transmission, anti-lock 4-wheel disc brakes, variable-assist power steering, driver- and passenger-side air bags, air conditioning with automatic climate control, tinted glass, power front seats, tilt/telescopic steering column, rear defogger, heated power mirrors, automatic day/night mirrors, power windows and door locks, remote entry system, maple wood trim, illuminated entry system, cruise control, tachometer, outside temperature readout, Pioneer Audio System with AM/FM/cassette with seven speakers and integrated antenna, automatic on/off headlamps, lighted visor mirrors, remote fuel door and decklid releases, variable intermittent wipers, theft-deterrent system, cellular phone pre-wiring, tool kit, first aid kit, 225/55VR16 tires, alloy wheels. **400** adds: 4.0-liter DOHC V-8 engine, 4-speed automatic transmission, power tilt/telescopic steering column, leather upholstery, driver-side seat memory system.

Optional Equipment:

Traction control system with heated front seats	1800	1440	—
Requires automatic transmission, all-season tires. 300 also requires Leather Trim Pkg.			
Remote 12-CD auto changer	1050	788	—
Lexus/Nakamichi Premium Sound System	1200	900	—
Requires remote CD changer; 300 also requires Leather Trim Pkg. with seat memory system.			
Power glass moonroof	950	760	—

LEXUS • LINCOLN

	Retail Price	Dealer Invoice	Fair Price
Leather Trim Pkg. with seat memory system, 300	$1950	$1560	—
Heated front seats, 300 with manual transmission	420	336	—
Requires Leather Trim Pkg.			
Rear spoiler, 400	420	336	—
All-season tires	NC	NC	NC
Chrome wheels	1700	850	—

LINCOLN

Lincoln Continental

	Retail Price	Dealer Invoice	Fair Price
4-door notchback	$41800	$36867	$37867
Destination charge	640	640	640

Standard Equipment:

4.6-liter DOHC V-8 engine, 4-speed automatic transmission, anti-lock 4-wheel disc brakes, driver- and passenger-side air bags, programmable variable-assist power steering, cruise control, automatic climate control, leather upholstery, reclining front bucket seats with power lumbar adjusters, 6-way power front seats, center console, power windows, heated power mirrors, automatic power door locks, automatic headlights, automatic parking brake release, Road Calibrated Suspension System, 2-driver memory system for seat, mirror, radio station, and steering effort/ride settings, automatic load leveling, rear defogger, variable intermittent wipers, solar-control tinted glass, tachometer, coolant temperature gauge, AM/FM/cassette, digital clock, anti-theft alarm system, remote keyless entry, remote fuel filler door and decklid releases, overhead console, systems message center, interior air filtration system, burl walnut interior trim, leather-wrapped tilt steering wheel, reading lights, automatic day/night rearview mirror, lighted visor mirrors, color-keyed bodyside moldings, floormats, trunk net, 225/60R16 tires, alloy wheels.

Optional Equipment:

Touring Pkg.	250	216	225
JBL audio system, traction control, automatic day/night inside/outside mirrors, compass.			
Touring Pkg. w/power moonroof	1395	1200	1256
Diamond Anniversary Edition Pkg.	1750	1506	—
Voice-activated cellular telephone, quarter-window nomenclature, light graphite/cordovan leather seats, cordovan or silver-frost paint, chrome wheels. Requires Touring Pkg.			

Prices are accurate at time of publication; subject to manufacturer's change.
CONSUMER GUIDE®

LINCOLN

	Retail Price	Dealer Invoice	Fair Price
Traction control	$360	$310	$324
Power moonroof	1515	1302	1364
Front split bench seat	NC	NC	NC
Heated seats	290	250	261
Requires traction control.			
Voice-activated cellular telephone	690	594	621
Requires JBL Audio System.			
Automatic day/night inside/outside mirrors	330	284	297
JBL Audio System	565	486	509
Digital signal processing, subwoofer amplifier, additional speakers.			
CD changer	595	512	536
Requires JBL Audio System.			
Trunk cargo organizer	265	228	239
Tri-coat paint	300	258	270
Chrome wheels	845	726	761
Engine block heater	60	52	54

Lincoln Mark VIII

	Retail Price	Dealer Invoice	Fair Price
2-door notchback	$39650	$34970	$35770
Destination charge	640	640	640

Standard Equipment:

4.6-liter DOHC V-8 engine, 4-speed automatic transmission, anti-lock 4-wheel disc brakes, driver- and passenger-side air bags, automatic air conditioning, variable-assist power steering, tilt steering wheel, analog instrumentation with message center and programmable trip functions, tachometer, service interval reminder, console with cup holder and storage bin, leather seat trim, rear armrest, Autoglide dual reclining 6-way power front seats with power lumbar supports and remote driver-side memory, leather-wrapped steering wheel, automatic headlamps, door map pockets, solar-control tinted glass, anti-theft alarm system, cruise control, power windows and locks, heated power mirrors with remote 3-position memory, universal garage-door opener, lighted visor mirrors, rear defogger, remote decklid and fuel door releases, illuminated and remote keyless entry systems, AM/FM/cassette with premium sound system, automatic power antenna, intermittent wipers, cargo net, floormats, 225/60VR16 tires, alloy wheels.

Optional Equipment:

LSC Pkg. — — —
Sport suspension, higher 3.27 axle ratio, Euro perforated leather seats, dual exhaust, monochromatic body-side moldings and fascias.

LINCOLN

	Retail Price	Dealer Invoice	Fair Price
LSC Feature Car	—	—	—
LSC Pkg. plus chrome wheels.			
Diamond Anniversary Edition Pkg.	$1770	$1523	—
with power moonroof	3285	2825	3121

Voice-activated cellular telephone, quarter-window nomenclature, light graphite/cordovan leather seats, cordovan or silver-frost paint, Diamond Anniversary floormats, chrome wheels. Requires Touring Pkg.

Traction Assist	215	184	204
Touring Pkg.	450	385	428

JBL audio system, CD changer, traction control, automatic day/night inside/outside mirrors, compass.

Power moonroof	1515	1302	1439
Voice-activated celluar telephone	690	594	656
Requires JBL Audio System.			
Automatic day/night inside/outside mirrors	215	184	204
JBL Audio System	565	486	537
Amplifier, additional speakers, cellular-phone prewire.			
CD changer	815	700	774
Requires JBL Audio System.			
Tri-coat paint	300	258	285
Cast alloy wheels	50	44	48
Chrome wheels	845	726	803
Engine block heater	60	52	57

Lincoln Town Car

	Retail Price	Dealer Invoice	Fair Price
Executive 4-door notchback	$36910	$32592	$33392
Signature Series 4-door notchback	38960	34356	35156
Cartier Designer Series 4-door notchback	41960	36936	37736
Destination charge	640	640	640

Standard Equipment:

Executive: 4.6-liter V-8, 4-speed automatic transmission, anti-lock 4-wheel disc brakes, adjustable variable-assist power steering, driver- and passenger-side air bags, automatic climate control, 6-way power twin-comfort lounge seats with 2-way front head restraints, front and rear folding armrests, power windows and door locks, tilt steering wheel, leather-wrapped steering wheel, cruise control, automatic parking brake release, heated power mirrors, rear defogger, AM/FM/cassette with premium sound, diversity antenna, coolant temperature gauge, solar-control tinted glass, remote fuel door and decklid releases, power decklid pulldown, illuminated and remote keyless entry systems, automatic headlights, anti-theft alarm system, cornering lamps, intermittent wipers, electronic instruments, digital

LINCOLN

clock, map pockets on front doors, lighted visor mirrors, front and rear floormats, dual exhaust, auxiliary power outlet, trunk net, 215/70R15 whitewall tires, alloy wheels. **Signature Series** adds: dual shade paint, driver's seat position memory and power lumbar support, power front recliners, memory mirrors, dual footwell lights, front seat storage with cup holders, steering wheel radio and climate controls, cellular-phone pre-wire, programmable garage door opener, map pockets on front seatbacks, striping. **Cartier Designer Series** adds: Traction Assist, leather upholstery, heated seats, 4-way front seat headrests, Ford JBL Audio System, compass, automatic day/night mirror, rear-seat vanity mirrors, wood instrument-panel trim, upgraded door trim panels, 225/60R16 tires.

Optional Equipment:

	Retail Price	Dealer Invoice	Fair Price
Traction Assist (std. Cartier)	$215	$184	$194
Leather seat trim (std. Cartier)	570	490	513
Heated front seats, Signature	290	250	261

Requires leather seat trim.

Automatic day/night mirror (std. Cartier)	110	94	99
Power moonroof	1515	1302	1364

NA Executive. Deletes rear-seat vanity mirrors on Cartier.

Ford JBL Audio System (std. Cartier)	565	486	509
Trunk-mounted CD changer	815	700	734

Requires Ford JBL Audio System.

Touring Pkg., Signature	1825	1570	1643

Power moonroof, traction assist, Ride Control Pkg., JBL Audio System, automatic day/night mirror.

Ride Control Pkg., Signature	300	258	270
Cartier	100	86	90

Auxiliary power steering fluid cooler, 3.27 rear axle ratio, 225/60R16 whitewall tires (Signature), 16-inch alloy wheels (Signature). NA with Livery/Heavy Duty Trailer Towing Pkg.

Livery/Heavy Duty Trailer Towing Pkg.	575	494	518

Wiring harness, heavy duty engine cooling, auxiliary power steering and transmission fluid coolers, 3.27 rear axle ratio, heavy duty U-joints and shock absorbers, larger front stabilizer bar, full-size spare tire, heavy duty battery, 5000-lb. towing capacity, heavy duty flasher and turn signals, Y-spoke alloy wheels. NA with Ride Control Pkg.

Diamond Anniversary Edition Pkg., Signature	1565	1346	—

Leather upholstery, voice-activated cellular phone, rear vanity mirrors, wood instrument panel, light graphite interior, cordovan or silver paint with striping, window nomenclature, Diamond Anniversary floormats. Requires Touring Pkg.

Voice activated cellular telephone	690	594	621

NA Executive.

LINCOLN • MAZDA

	Retail Price	Dealer Invoice	Fair Price
Tri-coat paint, Signature	$300	$258	$270
Cartier	NC	NC	NC
Monotone paint, Signature	NC	NC	NC
Engine block heater	60	52	54
Y-spoke alloy wheels, Signature	NC	NC	NC
Full-size spare tire	220	190	198

MAZDA

Mazda Miata

	Retail Price	Dealer Invoice	Fair Price
2-door convertible	$18450	$16730	—
Destination charge	450	450	450

Fair prices not available at time of publication. Prices are for vehicles distributed by Mazda Motor of America, Inc. Prices may be higher in areas served by independent distributors.

Standard Equipment:

1.8-liter DOHC 4-cylinder engine, 5-speed manual transmission, 4-wheel disc brakes, driver- and passenger-side air bags, cloth reclining bucket seats, tachometer, oil pressure and coolant temperature gauges, trip odometer, intermittent wipers, AM/FM/cassette, digital clock, dual outside mirrors, center storage console w/cup holder, dual courtesy lights, remote fuel door and decklid releases, cargo light, 185/60HR14 tires, styled steel wheels.

Optional Equipment:

4-speed automatic transmission	850	739	—
Requires Popular Equipment Pkg. or Leather Pkg.			
Anti-lock brakes	900	765	—
Requires Popular Equipment Pkg. or Leather Pkg.			
Air conditioning	900	720	—
Detachable hardtop	1500	1215	—
Includes rear defogger. Requires Popular Equipment Pkg. or Leather Pkg.			
Sensory Sound System	875	700	—
Requires Popular Equipment or Leather Pkg.			
Premium sound system w/CD player	675	540	—
Popular Equipment Pkg. with 5-speed	2090	1756	—
with automatic	1700	1428	—

Power steering, power mirrors, leather-wrapped steering wheel, headrest speakers, limited-slip differential (5-speed), power windows, cruise control, power antenna, alloy wheels.

Prices are accurate at time of publication; subject to manufacturer's change.

MAZDA

	Retail Price	Dealer Invoice	Fair Price
Power Steering Pkg.	$300	$252	—
Variable-assist power steering, wheel trim rings.			
Leather Pkg., 5-speed	2985	2507	—
automatic	2595	2180	—
Popular Equipment Pkg. plus tan interior with leather seating surfaces, tan vinyl top.			
R Pkg.	1500	1260	—
Limited-slip differential, sport suspension, front and rear spoilers, alloy wheels. Requires manual transmission. Not available with Popular Equipment Pkg., Power Steering Pkg., or Leather Pkg.			
Floormats	80	58	—

Mazda Millenia

	Retail Price	Dealer Invoice	Fair Price
4-door notchback	$27995	$24657	—
L 4-door notchback w/Leather Pkg.	31395	27334	—
S 4-door notchback	34395	29597	—
Destination charge	450	450	450

Fair price not available at time of publication. Prices are for vehicles distributed by Mazda Motor America, Inc. Prices may be higher in areas served by independent distributors.

Standard Equipment:

Base: 2.5-liter DOHC V-6 engine, 4-speed automatic transmission, anti-lock 4-wheel disc brakes, driver- and passenger-side air bags, automatic climate control, variable-assist, power steering, cruise control, cloth reclining bucket seats, 8-way power driver's seat, power tilt steering wheel with touch controls, console, tachometer, power windows and locks, heated power mirrors, variable intermittent wipers, anti-theft alarm, AM/FM/cassette, illuminated visor mirrors, rear defogger, illuminated entry system, fuel-door and decklid release, cargo lights, fog lamps, floormats, 205/65HR15 tires, alloy wheels. **L** adds: leather upholstery, 4-way power front passenger seat, remote keyless entry, power glass moonroof. **S** adds: 2.3-liter DOHC Miller-cycle V-6 engine, traction control, 215/55VR16 tires.

Optional Equipment:

4-Seasons Package,			
base, L	600	504	—
S	300	252	—
Traction control (base), heated front seats, heavy-duty wipers, heavy-duty starter, extra capacity windshield washer tank.			
Bose audio system with			
CD changer, L, S	1200	960	—

MAZDA

	Retail Price	Dealer Invoice	Fair Price
White pearl metallic paint, base with Leather Pkg., L, S	$350	$294	—
Deep sea metallic paint, base with Leather Pkg., L, S	175	147	—

1995 Mazda MPV

	Retail Price	Dealer Invoice	Fair Price
L 4-door van	$21595	$19458	$19958
LX 4-door van	22475	20251	20751
LXE 4-door van	24865	22404	22904
LX 4WD 4-door van	25870	23309	23809
LXE 4WD 4-door van	28095	25314	25814
Destination charge	480	480	480

Prices are for vehicles distributed by Mazda Motor of America, Inc. Prices may be higher in areas served by independent distributors.

Standard Equipment:

L: 3.0-liter V-6 engine, 4-speed automatic transmission, 4-wheel disc brakes, anti-lock rear brakes, driver-side air bag, variable-assist power steering, cloth reclining front bucket seats, removable reclining 2-passenger middle seat, folding 3-passenger rear seat, tachometer, map pockets, remote fuel door release, tinted glass, 195/75R15 tires, wheel covers. **LX** adds: power mirrors, tilt steering column, cruise control, rear defogger, 6-speaker AM/FM/cassette, digital clock, power windows and door locks, variable intermittent wipers, intermittent rear wiper/washer, color-keyed grille. **LXE** adds: leather upholstery, leather-wrapped steering wheel, 2-tone paint, Towing Pkg., 215/65R15 tires, alloy wheels. **4WD models** add: part-time 4-wheel drive, 4-Seasons Pkg., heavy duty cooling fan, conventional spare tire, 215/65R15 tires (LX), alloy wheels (LX).

Optional Equipment:

Single air conditioning, L	900	738	828
LX Preferred Equipment Group 1LX	700	595	644

Air conditioning, privacy glass, floormats.

LX Preferred Equipment Group 2LX	1400	1190	1288

Replaces air conditioning in Group 1LX with front and rear air conditioning.

LXE Preferred Equipment Group, 2WD	2000	1700	1853
4WD	1550	1318	1436

Front and rear air conditioning, remote keyless entry, privacy glass, floormats, special alloy wheels, 215/65R15 tires (2WD).

Prices are accurate at time of publication; subject to manufacturer's change.

MAZDA

	Retail Price	Dealer Invoice	Fair Price
Power glass moonroof, LX, LXE	$1200	$1020	$1106
Towing Pkg., LX 2WD	595	506	560
LX 4WD	495	421	467

Transmission oil cooler, automatic load leveling, heavy duty cooling fan (2WD), conventional spare (2WD).

4-Seasons Pkg., 2WD	350	298	330

Rear heater, large-capacity windshield washer tank, heavy duty battery.

Alloy Wheel Pkg., LX 2WD	495	421	467

215/65R15 tires, alloy wheels.

Extra cost paint, LX	350	298	330
Floormats, L	100	70	88

Mazda MX-6

	Retail Price	Dealer Invoice	Fair Price
2-door notchback	$19595	$17457	$17957
LS 2-door notchback	22850	20392	21192
Destination charge	450	450	450

Prices are for vehicles distributed by Mazda Motor of America, Inc. Prices may be higher in areas served by independent distributors.

Standard Equipment:

Base: 2.0-liter DOHC 4-cylinder engine, 5-speed manual transmission, variable-assist power steering, driver- and passenger-side air bags, cloth reclining front bucket seats, driver's-seat thigh support adjustment, 60/40 folding rear seat with armrest, console with storage, power windows and door locks, cruise control, power mirrors, visor mirrors, AM/FM/cassette, tachometer, coolant temperature gauge, trip odometer, tilt steering column, intermittent wipers, door pockets, tinted glass, remote fuel door and decklid releases, rear defogger, cargo lights, reading lights, front and rear stabilizer bars, 195/65R14 tires, full wheel covers. **LS** adds: 2.5-liter DOHC V-6 engine, 4-wheel disc brakes, air conditioning, power steel sunroof, anti-theft alarm, variable intermittent wipers, 6-speaker audio system, leather-wrapped steering wheel, power antenna, remote keyless entry, fog lights, mud guards, floormats, 205/55VR15 tires, alloy wheels.

Optional Equipment:

4-speed automatic transmission	800	696	760
Anti-lock brakes, base	950	808	903
LS	800	680	760

Base includes 4-wheel disc brakes and requires Popular Equipment Group.

Air conditioning, base	900	720	854
Leather Pkg., LS	1095	876	1045

Leather/vinyl sport bucket seats, power driver's seat, heated outside mirrors.

MAZDA

	Retail Price	Dealer Invoice	Fair Price
Popular Equipment Group, base	$2145	$1802	$2038

Air conditioning, power steel sunroof, anti-theft alarm, variable intermittent wipers, 6-speaker audio system, power antenna, remote keyless entry, alloy wheels.

Rear spoiler	375	300	356
Floormats, base	80	56	75

Mazda Protege

	Retail Price	Dealer Invoice	Fair Price
DX 4-door notchback	$11695	$11145	$11695
LX 4-door notchback	12995	12106	12606
ES 4-door notchback	14695	13516	14016
Destination charge	450	450	450

Prices are for vehicles distributed by Mazda Motor of America, Inc. Prices may be higher in areas served by independent distributors.

Standard Equipment:

DX: 1.5-liter DOHC 4-cylinder engine, 5-speed manual transmission, driver- and passenger-side air bags, variable-assist power steering, cloth/vinyl reclining front bucket seats, rear seat headrests, tilt steering wheel, console, driver footrest, dual remote mirrors, tinted glass, rear defogger, remote fuel door release, trip odometer, color-keyed bumpers and grille, child safety rear door locks, intermittent wipers, cargo light, body-side moldings, 175/70R13 tires. **LX** adds: cruise control, AM/FM/cassette, velour upholstery, split folding rear seat, remote decklid release, tachometer, digital clock, power windows and door locks, power mirrors, map lights, passenger-side vanity mirror, front side storage trays, full wheel covers. **ES** adds: 1.8-liter DOHC 4-cylinder engine, 4-wheel disc brakes, air conditioning, sport front bucket seats, 185/65HR14 tires.

Optional Equipment:

4-speed automatic transmission	800	720	760
Anti-lock brakes, LX, ES	800	680	760
Convenience Pkg., DX	1575	1292	1496

Air conditioning, AM/FM/cassette, floormats.

Luxury Pkg., LX	1145	939	1088

Air conditioning, raised console armrest (automatic transmission-equipped models), floormats.

Premium Pkg., ES	1195	956	1135

Alloy wheels with locks, power sunroof.

Touring Pkg., ES	105	84	100

Floormats, raised console armrest. Requires automatic transmission.

Prices are accurate at time of publication; subject to manufacturer's change.

MAZDA

	Retail Price	Dealer Invoice	Fair Price
Power sunroof, LX	$700	$560	$665
Floormats	80	64	76

Mazda 626

	Retail Price	Dealer Invoice	Fair Price
DX 4-door notchback	$15495	$14521	$15121
LX 4-door notchback	17695	16053	16653
LX V-6, 4-door notchback	19895	18032	18632
ES V-6, 4-door notchback	22795	20445	21045
Destination charge	450	450	450

Prices are for vehicles distributed by Mazda Motor of America, Inc. Prices may be higher in areas served by independent distributors.

Standard Equipment:

DX: 2.0-liter DOHC 4-cylinder engine, 5-speed manual transmission, variable-assist power steering, driver- and passenger-side air bags, cloth reclining front bucket seats, 60/40 folding rear seat with armrest, console with armrest and storage, tachometer, coolant temperature gauge, trip odometer, tilt steering wheel, intermittent wipers, dual remote mirrors, door pockets, tinted glass, remote fuel door and decklid releases, rear defogger, passenger-side visor mirror, body-side moldings, 195/65R14 tires, full wheel covers. **LX** adds: air conditioning, power windows and locks, cruise control, power mirrors, AM/FM/cassette, dual visor mirrors w/illuminated passenger-side mirror, map lights. **LX V-6** adds: 2.5-liter DOHC V-6 engine, 4-wheel disc brakes, variable intermittant wipers, floormats, 205/55HR15 tires, alloy wheels. **ES** adds: anti-lock brakes, 8-way power driver's seat, anti-theft alarm, remote keyless entry, power moonroof, power antenna, dual illuminated visor mirrors, leather seats, heated power mirrors, fog lamps.

Optional Equipment:

4-speed automatic transmission	800	696	760
Anti-lock brakes, LX	950	808	903
LX V-6	800	680	760
LX includes rear disc brakes.			
Convenience Pkg., DX	1215	972	1154
Air conditioning, AM/FM/cassette, floormats.			
Luxury Pkg., LX	1750	1400	1663
Power moonroof, heated power mirrors, anti-theft alarm, 6-speaker sound system, assist grips, remote keyless entry, floormats, alloy wheels.			
Premium Pkg., LX V-6	2095	1676	1990
Anti-lock brakes, power driver's seat, power moonroof, heated power mirrors, anti-theft alarm, 6-speaker sound system, assist grips, remote keyless entry.			
Floormats, LX	80	58	76

MERCEDES-BENZ

Mercedes-Benz C-Class

	Retail Price	Dealer Invoice	Fair Price
C220 4-door notchback	$29900	—	—
C280 4-door notchback	35250	—	—
C36 4-door notchback	51000	—	—
Destination charge	595	595	595

Dealer invoice and fair price not available at time of publication.

Standard Equipment:

C220: 2.2-liter DOHC 4-cylinder engine, 4-speed automatic transmission, anti-lock 4-wheel disc brakes, driver- and passenger-side air bags, power steering, automatic climate control, cruise control, power windows and locks, keyless entry system with remote decklid release, heated power mirrors, cloth 10-way power driver's seat, 10-way manual adjustable passenger seat, split folding rear seat with trunk pass-through, center storage console, folding rear armrest, rear head restraints, leather-wrapped steering wheel and shifter, cellular phone and CD pre-wiring, tinted glass, anti-theft system, fog lamps, 8-speaker AM/FM/cassette, tachometer, coolant temperature gauge, trip odometer, outside temperature indicator, digital clock, cup holders, lighted visor mirrors, rear defogger, seat pockets, burl walnut interior trim, first aid kit, floormats, 195/65HR15 all-season tires, alloy wheels. **C280** adds: 2.8-liter DOHC 6-cylinder engine, Bose sound system, power passenger seat. **C36** adds: 3.6-liter DOHC 6-cylinder engine, leather upholstery, power glass sunroof, 225/45ZR17 front and 245/40ZR17 rear tires.

Optional Equipment:

C1 Option Pkg., C220	1200	—	—
C280, C36	2150	—	—

Electronic Traction System (C220), ASR acceleration slip control (C280, C36), headlamp washer/wipers, heated front seats.

C2 Option Pkg.	340	—	—

Split folding rear seat with trunk pass-through and ski sack.

C3 Option Pkg., C220, C280	1970	—	—

Leather upholstery, power glass sunroof, telescopic steering wheel.

C4 Option Pkg., C220	950	—	—

Bose sound system, 10-way power passenger seat, automatic day/night rearview mirror.

C5 Option Pkg.	1495	—	—

Integrated cellular telephone and 6-disc CD changer.

Anti-theft alarm system	610	—	—
Headlamp washer/wipers	330	—	—
Bose sound system, C220	550	—	—

Prices are accurate at time of publication; subject to manufacturer's change.

CONSUMER GUIDE®

MERCEDES-BENZ

	Retail Price	Dealer Invoice	Fair Price
Power glass sunroof, C220, C280	$1070	—	—
Telescopic steering wheel	160	—	—
Power passenger seat, C220	590	—	—
Power front seat orthopedic backrests (each), C220, C280	380	—	—
Automatic day/night rearview mirror	125	—	—
Metallic paint	595	—	—

Mercedes-Benz E-Class

	Retail Price	Dealer Invoice	Fair Price
E300 Diesel 4-door notchback	$39900	$34710	—
E320 4-door notchback	43500	37840	—
E420 4-door notchback	49900	—	—
Destination charge	595	595	595

Dealer invoice, fair price, and E420 optional equipment not available at time of publication.

Standard Equipment:

E300 Diesel/E320: 3.0-liter DOHC 6-cylinder diesel engine (E300 Diesel), 3.2-liter DOHC 6-cylinder engine (E320), 4-speed automatic transmission, front and side air bags, anti-lock 4-wheel disc brakes, Electronic Traction System, variable-assist power steering, cruise control, automatic climate control, power adjustable steering column with memory, power front seats with memory, leather upholstery (E320), cloth upholstery (E300), rear headrests, seat pockets, anti-theft alarm system, power windows and door locks, remote keyless entry, 8-speaker AM/FM/cassette with active bass, dual power mirrors with memory, automatic day/night rearview mirror, tinted glass, rear defogger, visor mirrors, active charcoal ventilation filter, leather-wrapped steering wheel, cellular phone and CD pre-wiring, cup holders, first aid kit, fog lamps, universal garage-door opener, outside temperature indicator, burl walnut interior trim, 215/55R16 tires, alloy wheels. **E420 4-door** adds to E320 4-door: 4.2-liter DOHC V-8 engine, 5-speed automatic transmission, ASR acceleration slip control, Bose sound system, xenon headlamps.

Optional Equipment:

E1 Option Pkg., E300, E320	750	—	—
Heated front seats, headlamp wiper/washer.			
E2 Option Pkg., E300, E320	1050	—	—
Bose sound system, orothopedic front seats.			
E3 Option Pkg., E300	1970	—	—
Leather upholstery, power glass sunroof.			
E5 Option Pkg., , E300, E320	1495	—	—
Integrated cellular telephone and 6-disc CD changer.			

MERCEDES-BENZ

	Retail Price	Dealer Invoice	Fair Price
Power glass sunroof, E300, E320	$1070	$931	—
Leather upholstery, E300 Diesel	1675	1457	—
ASR acceleration slip control, E320	1200	1044	—
Bose Premium Sound System, E300, E320	550	478	—
Headlamp washers/wipers	330	287	—
Power rear window sunshade	425	370	—
Xenon headlamps, E300, E320	950	826	—
Requires headlamp washer/wipers or E1 Option Pkg.			
Metallic paint	685	552	—

Mercedes-Benz S-Class

	Retail Price	Dealer Invoice	Fair Price
S320 4-door notchback (119.7-inch wheelbase)	$62700	—	—
S320 4-door notchback (123.6-inch wheelbase)	65900	—	—
S420 4-door notchback	73900	—	—
S500 4-door notchback	87500	—	—
S500 2-door notchback	91900	—	—
S600 4-door notchback	130300	—	—
S600 2-door notchback	133300	—	—
Destination charge	595	595	595
Gas Guzzler Tax, S420,	1300	1300	1300
S500	1700	1700	1700
S600	2600	2600	2600

Dealer invoice and fair price not available at time of publication.

Standard Equipment:

S320: 3.2-liter 6-cylinder engine, 5-speed automatic transmission, power steering, anti-lock 4-wheel disc brakes, driver- and passenger-side air bags, Electronic Traction System, anti-theft alarm, power windows and door locks, automatic climate control, tinted glass, Bose Beta AM/FM/cassette, CD and cellular phone pre-wiring, leather upholstery, power front bucket seats with 3-position memory, power telescopic steering column with memory, leather-wrapped steering wheel and shift knob, rear defogger, cruise control, headlamp wipers/washers (123.6-inch wheelbase), intermittent wipers, power glass sunroof, fog lights, power memory mirrors, automatic day/night memory rearview mirror, outside temperature indicator, tachometer, coolant temperature and oil pressure gauges, trip odometer, remote keyless entry and decklid release, front and rear center armrests with cup holders, rear-seat head restraints, front reading lights, rear reading lights (4-door), first aid kit, seat pockets, lighted visor mirrors, floormats,

Prices are accurate at time of publication; subject to manufacturer's change.

MERCEDES-BENZ • MERCURY

235/60HR16 tires, alloy wheels. **S420** adds: 4.2-liter DOHC V-8 engine, ASR acceleration slip control. **S500** adds: 5.0-liter DOHC V-8 engine, rear axle level control, heated front seats, heated rear seats (4-door), automatic courtesy seat adjustment (2-door), active charcoal ventilation filter, leather/burl-walnut shifter (2-door), rear storage console (2-door). **S600** deletes ASR acceleration slip control, rear-axle level control; and adds to S500: 6.0-liter DOHC V-12 engine, Adaptive Damping System, Electronic Stability Program, power rear seats (4-door), rear air conditioner (4-door), 10-disc CD changer, integrated cellular telephone, power rear window sunshade, upgraded leather interior, orthopedic front backrests, leather/burl-walnut shifter.

Optional Equipment:

	Retail Price	Dealer Invoice	Fair Price
Rear air conditioner, S320, S420, S500	$1950	—	—
NA 2-door models.			
Adaptive Damping System, 500	2200	—	—
ASR acceleration slip control, 320	1200	—	—
Electronic Stability Program, 420, 500	1870	—	—
Power rear window sunshade (std. 600)	490	—	—
Orthopedic front backrests, each (std. 600)	380	—	—
4-place power seating, 500 4-door, 600 4-door	5460	—	—
Power rear seat, S500 4-door	1700	—	—
Heated front seats, 320, and 420	595	—	—
Active charcoal ventilation filter, 320, and 420	530	—	—
Rear axle level control, 320, and 420	910	—	—
Headlamp washers, 320 119.7-inch wheelbase	330	—	—
Portable cellular telephone	930	—	—
Metallic paint	NC	NC	NC

MERCURY

Mercury Cougar

	Retail Price	Dealer Invoice	Fair Price
XR7 2-door notchback	$17430	$15933	$16433
Destination charge	510	510	510

Standard Equipment:

3.8-liter V-6, 4-speed automatic transmission, power steering, driver- and passenger-side air bags, air conditioning, reclining front bucket seats with power lumbar support, cloth and leather upholstery, floor storage console

MERCURY

with cup holders, tilt steering wheel, intermittent wipers, tinted glass, AM/FM/cassette, oil pressure and coolant temperature gauges, voltmeter, tachometer, center console with storage, power windows and mirrors, rear armrest, door map pockets, color-keyed bodyside moldings, bumpers and door trim panels, rear heater ducts, visor mirrors, 205/70R15 tires, wheel covers.

Optional Equipment:

	Retail Price	Dealer Invoice	Fair Price
4.6-liter V-8 engine	$1130	$1006	$1017

Includes variable-assist power steering, heavy duty battery. Requires Pkg. 262A.

Traction-Lok axle	95	85	86

NA with Traction Assist. Requires option pkg.

Anti-lock 4-wheel disc brakes	570	507	513

Requires option pkg.

Automatic air conditioning	155	138	140

Requires automatic headlamp on/off delay, option pkg.

Preferred Pkg. 260A	505	450	455

Cruise control, Power Lock Group, rear defogger, front floormats, 215/70R15 tires, alloy wheels.

Preferred Pkg. 262A	1340	1194	1206

Pkg. 260A plus 4.6-liter V-8 engine, variable-assist power steering, power driver's seat, leather-wrapped steering wheel, illuminated entry, heavy-duty battery.

Group 1	200	178	180

Rear defogger, front floormats.

Group 2	685	610	617

Cruise control, Power Lock Group, alloy wheels, 215/70R15 tires.

Group 3	455	407	410

Power driver's seat, leather-wrapped steering wheel, illuminated entry.

Luxury Light Group	200	178	180

Interior courtesy lights, engine compartment light, lighted visor mirrors. Requires option pkg.

Sport Appearance Group	115	102	104

Geometric-spoke alloy wheels, non-functional luggage rack. Requires option pkg.

Automatic headlamp on/off delay	70	62	63

Requires automatic air conditioning and option pkg.

Keyless entry system, Pkg. 260A	270	240	243
Pkg. 262A	190	169	171

Includes illuminated entry.

Power moonroof	740	658	666

Includes dual reading lights, pop-up air deflector, sunshade, rear tilt-up. Requires Luxury Light Group, option pkg.

Premium electronic AM/FM/cassette	290	258	261

Includes amplifier and premium speakers. Requires option pkg.

Prices are accurate at time of publication; subject to manufacturer's change.

MERCURY

	Retail Price	Dealer Invoice	Fair Price
Premium electronic AM/FM/CD player	$430	$383	$387
Includes amplifier and premium speakers. Requires option pkg.			
Power antenna	85	76	77
Requires option pkg.			
Power driver's seat, Pkg. 260A	290	258	261
Power passenger seat	290	258	261
Requires power driver's seat, option pkg.			
Individual leather seats	490	436	441
Requires dual power seats and option pkg.			
Leather-wrapped steering wheel, Pkg. 260A	90	80	81
Anti-theft alarm system	145	129	131
Requires keyless entry system, option pkg.			
Heavy duty battery, Pkg. 260A	25	23	24
Traction Assist	210	187	189
Requires anti-lock brakes, option pkg.			
Tri-coat paint	225	201	203
Engine block heater	20	18	19
Requires option pkg.			
Chrome Wheels	580	516	522
Includes 215/70R15 tires. Requires option pkg.			

Mercury Grand Marquis

	Retail Price	Dealer Invoice	Fair Price
GS 4-door notchback	$21975	$20555	$21055
LS 4-door notchback	23385	21826	22326
Destination charge	580	580	580

Standard Equipment:

GS: 4.6-liter V-8, 4-speed automatic transmission, 4-wheel disc brakes, power steering, driver- and passenger-side air bags, air conditioning, cloth twin comfort lounge seats with power recliners, 6-way power driver's seat, dual front and rear folding armrests, power windows and mirrors, solar-control tinted glass, AM/FM/cassette, right visor mirror, intermittent wipers, rear defogger, digital clock, tilt steering wheel, oil pressure and coolant temperature gauges, voltmeter, trip odometer, Luxury Sound Insulation Pkg., auxiliary power outlet, automatic parking brake release, 215/70R15 all season whitewall tires, wheel covers. **LS** adds: upgraded upholstery and door trim, rear seat headrests, driver's seat power lumbar adjuster.

Optional Equipment:

Anti-lock brakes w/Traction-Assist	670	596	603
Automatic climate control, LS	175	156	158
Rear air suspension, LS	270	240	243

MERCURY

	Retail Price	Dealer Invoice	Fair Price
Preferred Pkg. 157A, GS (credit)	($860)	($764)	($764)

Cruise control, Power Lock Group, illuminated entry, floormats, radial-spoke wheel covers.

Preferred Pkg. 172A, LS (credit)	(80)	(71)	(71)

Pkg. 157A plus bodyside paint stripe, leather-wrapped steering wheel, Luxury Light Group (includes underhood light, dual dome/map lights, rear reading lights, dual secondary sun visors, lighted visor mirrors), alloy wheels, remote keyless entry, cornering lights.

Preferred Pkg. 173A, LS	1730	1537	1557

Pkg. 172A plus anti-lock brakes with Traction-Assist, Electronic Group (includes digital instrumentation, tripminder computer, heavy duty battery), automatic climate control, automatic day/night mirror, premium electronic cassette player, power front passenger's seat.

Group 1, GS	555	495	500
LS	260	232	234

Cruise control, floormats, radial-spoke wheel covers (GS).

Group 2	385	343	347

Power Lock Group (includes power locks, remote decklid release), illuminated entry.

Group 3, LS	1075	956	968

Luxury Light Group, bodyside paint stripe, leather-wrapped steering wheel, cornering lights.

Luxury Light Group	190	169	171

Includes dual dome/map lights, rear reading lights, dual secondary sun visors, lighted visor mirrors.

Electronic Group, LS	455	405	410

Digital instrumentation, tripminder computer. Requires Automatic climate control, premium cassette player.

Feature Car, LS w/Pkg. 173A	NC	NC	NC

6-way power passenger seat, leather upholstery, "Flying M" embroidery, unique seat trim.

Keyless entry system	240	213	216

Requires Group 2.

Handling Pkg., LS	1020	908	918
with option pkg.	600	534	540

Includes rear air suspension, tuned suspension, larger stabilizer bars, dual exhaust, 3.27 axle ratio, 225/60R16 whitewall tires, alloy wheels. NA with Trailer Tow III.

Trailer Tow III Pkg., LS	900	801	810

Includes rear air suspension, heavy duty battery, dual exhaust, trailer towing wiring harness, engine, power steering, and transmission oil coolers, conventional spare tire, 3.27 Traction-Lok axle. Requires alloy wheels. NA with Handling Pkg.

Bodyside paint stripe	60	54	55

Prices are accurate at time of publication; subject to manufacturer's change.

MERCURY

	Retail Price	Dealer Invoice	Fair Price
Power front passenger's seat, LS	$360	$321	$324
Includes power lumbar support and recliners for both front seats.			
Leather seat trim, LS	646	574	581
Requires power front passenger's seat.			
Premium electronic cassette player, LS	360	321	324
Requires automatic climate control.			
Conventional spare tire, LS	185	165	167
with Handling Pkg.	240	213	216
Includes alloy wheel.			
Cast alloy wheels, LS	NC	NC	NC
Requires Group 3.			
Engine block heater	25	23	24

Mercury Mystique

	Retail Price	Dealer Invoice	Fair Price
GS 4-door notchback	$14330	$13154	—
LS 4-door notchback	15705	14377	—
Destination charge	510	510	510

Fair price not available at time of publication.

Standard Equipment:

GS: 2.0-liter DOHC 4-cylinder engine, 5-speed manual transmission, driver- and passenger-side air bags, power steering, front and rear stabilizer bars, solar-control tinted glass, cloth reclining front bucket seats with 4-way adjustable headrests, console, split folding rear seat, coolant temperature gauge, tachometer, trip odometer, day/night rearview mirror, color-keyed bumpers and bodyside moldings, AM/FM radio, power mirrors, intermittent wipers, remote decklid release, front seatback and door map pockets, passenger assist handles, passenger compartment air filtration system, visor mirrors, 185/70R14 tires. **LS** adds: 10-way power driver's seat, cassette player, rear defogger, heated mirrors, power antenna, fog lights, floormats, 205/60R15 tires, alloy wheels.

Optional Equipment:

4-speed automatic transmission	815	725	—
Traction control	805	716	—
Includes anti-lock brakes.			
Anti-lock brakes	570	507	—
Air conditioning	780	694	—
Cruise control	215	191	—
Preferred Pkg. 370A, GS	915	814	—
Air conditioning, rear defogger, cassette player, heated mirrors, power antenna.			

MERCURY

	Retail Price	Dealer Invoice	Fair Price
Preferred Pkg. 371A, GS	$1505	$1340	—

Pkg. 370A plus power door locks and windows, cruise control, light group.

Preferred Pkg. 372A, GS	2450	2182	—

Pkg. 371A plus 2.5-liter V-6 engine. Includes 4-wheel disc brakes, sport suspension, low-profile tires.

Preferred Pkg. 381A, LS	2250	2003	—

2.5-liter V-6 engine (includes 4-wheel disc brakes, sport suspension, low-profile tires), air conditioning, power door locks and windows, cruise control, Light Group (lighted visor mirrors, trunk compartment light, map lights, illuminated entry), remote keyless entry, leather-wrapped steering wheel.

Comfort/Convenience Group 1, GS	270	240	—

Rear defogger, heated mirrors, power antenna.

Comfort/Convenience Group 2, GS	945	841	—
LS	780	694	—

Cassette player (GS), air conditioning.

Comfort/Convenience Group 3, GS	675	601	—
LS	865	770	—

Remote keyless entry (LS), power door locks and windows, Light Group.

Power door locks and light group,			
GS with Pkg. 370A	335	299	—
Young America Edition decor group, LS	1050	935	—

Monochromatic white clearcoat paint, color-keyed grille and wheels, blue and white leather upholstery, decklid spoiler, badging, upgraded front floormats. Requires Pkg. 381A.

Sport Appearance Pkg., GS	675	601	—

Rear spoiler, alloy wheels, 205/60R15 tires.

Leather upholstery, LS	595	530	—
10-way power driver's seat,			
GS with Pkgs. 371A or 372A	330	294	—
Power sunroof	595	530	—

NA GS with Pkg. 370A.

Remote keyless entry	190	169	—

NA GS with Pkg. 370A.

Premium cassette player, GS	295	263	—
GS with Group 2, LS	130	116	—

Includes amplifier.

CD player, GS	435	387	—
GS with Group 2, LS	270	240	—

Includes amplifier.

Rear defogger, GS	170	151	—

Includes heated mirrors.

Rear spoiler	345	307	—

Prices are accurate at time of publication; subject to manufacturer's change.

MERCURY

	Retail Price	Dealer Invoice	Fair Price
Floormats, GS	$45	$40	—
Alloy wheels, GS	425	379	—
Includes 205/60R15 tires.			
Engine block heater	20	18	—

Mercury Sable

	Retail Price	Dealer Invoice	Fair Price
GS 4-door notchback	$18995	$17391	—
LS 4-door notchback	21295	19472	—
GS 5-door wagon	20015	18298	—
LS 5-door wagon	22355	20381	—
Destination charge	550	550	550

Fair price not available at time of publication.

Standard Equipment:

GS: 3.0-liter V-6 engine, 4-speed automatic transmission, power steering, driver- and passenger-side air bags, air conditioning, cloth reclining front bucket seats with center seating console, front and rear armrests, 60/40 split folding rear seat, center console w/cupholders, coin holders, and cassette storage, solar-control tinted glass, remote decklid release, variable intermittent wipers, rear defogger, tachometer, coolant temperature gauge, trip odometer, illuminated entry, digital clock, power heated mirrors, power windows, tilt steering wheel, AM/FM radio, dual visor mirrors, air filter, seat map pockets, 205/65R15 tires, wheel covers. **Wagon** has 4-wheel disc brakes, luggage rack, power antenna, cargo tie-downs, cargo light. **LS** adds to GS: 3.0-liter DOHC V-6 engine, reclining bucket seats with power lumbar support and 4-way adjustable headrests, power driver's seat, cloth/leather upholstery, cassette player, power door locks, rear air ducts, Passive Anti-Theft System, remote fuel door release, lighted visor mirrors, leather-wrapped shift handle, automatic headlamp on/off delay, Light Group, alloy 5-spoke wheels. **LS wagon** adds to LS and GS wagon: cargo net.

Optional Equipment:

Anti-lock 4-wheel disc brakes, GS, LS w/Pkg. 460A	570	507	—
Automatic air conditioning, LS	175	156	—
Power moonroof, LS	740	658	—
Preferred Pkg. 450A, GS	210	187	—
Cruise control, cassette player, power door locks, floormats.			
Preferred Pkg. 451A, GS	810	721	—
Pkg. 450A plus power driver's seat, Light Group, alloy wheels.			
Preferred Pkg. 460A, LS	150	134	—
Cruise control, leather-wrapped steering wheel, floormats.			

MERCURY

	Retail Price	Dealer Invoice	Fair Price
Preferred Pkg. 461A, LS	$860	$766	—
Pkg. 460A plus anti-lock 4-wheel disc brakes, remote keyless entry w/perimeter anti-theft system.			
Preferred Pkg. 462A, LS 4-door	1915	1704	—
LS wagon	1730	1540	—
Pkg. 461A plus JBL audio system (4-door), Premium Sound system (wagon), automatic air conditioning, chrome wheels.			
Group 1, GS	260	232	—
LS	350	312	—
Cruise control, leather-wrapped steering wheel (LS), floor mats.			
Group 2, GS	450	402	—
Cassette player, power door locks.			
Group 3, GS	700	623	—
6-way power driver's seat, Light Group, alloy wheels.			
Wagon Group, wagon	255	227	—
Cargo-area cover, rear wiper/washer. GS requires power door locks (Group 2).			
Light Group, GS w/Pkg. 450A	45	41	—
Courtesy, reading, map, and dome lights.			
Remote keyless entry, GS	190	169	—
Remote keyless entry w/perimeter anti-theft system, LS w/Pkg. 460A	440	392	—
Premium Sound AM/FM/cassette, LS wagon	315	280	—
Requires automatic air conditioning.			
JBL Audio System, LS 4-door	500	446	—
Requires automatic air conditioning.			
CD changer, LS	595	530	—
Sedan requires JBL Audio System. Wagon requires Premium Sound.			
6-way power driver's seat, GS	340	302	—
Rear-facing third seat, wagon	200	178	—
Leather bucket seats, LS	990	881	—
Cloth/leather bucket seats with center seating console, LS	NC	NC	NC
Integrated child seat, wagon	135	120	—
Cellular telephone	650	579	—
Heavy duty suspension, wagon	25	23	—
Rear wiper/washer, wagon	255	227	—
Includes cargo-area cover.			
Cargo tie-down net, GS wagon	40	36	—
Daytime running lights	40	36	—
Full-size spare tire	125	112	—
Not available on wagons.			
Alloy wheels, GS	315	280	—
Chrome wheels, LS	580	516	—

Prices are accurate at time of publication; subject to manufacturer's change.

CONSUMER GUIDE®

MERCURY

	Retail Price	Dealer Invoice	Fair Price
Heavy duty battery	$30	$27	—
Engine block heater	35	31	—

Mercury Tracer

	Retail Price	Dealer Invoice	Fair Price
4-door notchback	$11755	$11016	$11216
5-door wagon	12285	11490	11690
LTS 4-door notchback	13625	12709	13009
Destination charge	390	390	390

Standard Equipment:

1.9-liter 4-cylinder engine, 5-speed manual transmission, driver- and passenger-side air bags, motorized front shoulder belts, power steering, cloth reclining front bucket seats, 60/40 split rear seatback, AM/FM radio, tachometer, trip odometer, digital clock, console, coolant temperature gauge, low fuel warning light, door map pockets, variable intermittent wipers, visor mirrors, tinted glass, 175/65R14 tires, wheel covers. **Wagon** adds: power mirrors, cargo cover, rear defogger, rear wiper/washer. **LTS** adds: 1.8-liter DOHC engine, 4-wheel disc brakes, sport suspension, tilt steering column, cassette player, cloth reclining sport bucket seats, Light Group (includes illuminated visor mirrors, dual map lights, trunk and engine compartment lights, rear door courtesy light), remote decklid release, cruise control, leather-wrapped steering wheel, front air dam, rear spoiler, 185/60HR14 tires, alloy wheels.

Optional Equipment:

Preferred Pkg. 540A, base 4-door	395	351	356
wagon	135	121	122
Remote decklid release (4-door), rear defogger (4-door), Light Group, power mirrors (4-door), air conditioning.			
Preferred Pkg. 541A, base 4-door	1125	1000	1013
wagon	860	765	774
Pkg. 540A plus AM/FM/cassette, Convenience Group, Power Group.			
Preferred Pkg. 555A, LTS	930	827	837
Air conditioning, Power Group.			
Power moonroof, LTS	525	468	473
Integrated child seat	135	120	122
NA LTS.			
4-speed automatic transmission	815	725	734
Anti-lock brakes, LTS	570	507	513
Power Group, base	520	463	468
Power door locks and windows.			
Convenience Group	355	316	320
Tilt steering wheel, cruise control.			

MERCURY

	Retail Price	Dealer Invoice	Fair Price
Trio Pkg., base 4-door	NC	NC	NC
wagon	$210	$187	$189
Leather-wrapped steering wheel, decklid spoiler (4-door), alloy wheels.			
Power moonroof	525	468	473
Integrated child seat	135	120	122
NA LTS.			
Cassette player, base	165	147	149
Premium sound system	60	54	55
Requires cassette player.			
CD player, base w/Pkg. 540A	325	290	293
base w/Pkg. 541A, LTS	160	143	144
Includes premium sound system.			
Luggage rack, wagon	110	98	99

Mercury Villager

	Retail Price	Dealer Invoice	Fair Price
GS 4-door van	$19940	$18072	$18872
LS 4-door van	24300	21908	22708
Nautica 4-door van	26390	23729	24529
Destination charge	555	555	555

Standard Equipment:

GS: 3.0-liter V-6 engine, 4-speed automatic transmission, driver- and passenger-side air bags, anti-lock brakes, power steering, tilt steering column, cloth reclining front bucket seats, 3-passenger bench seat, cloth upholstery, AM/FM/cassette, tachometer, coolant temperature gauge, trip odometer, dual outside mirrors, visor mirrors, solar-tinted glass, variable-intermittent wipers, rear wiper/washer, color-keyed bumpers and bodyside moldings, cornering lamps, rear storage bin, front door map pockets, floormats, 205/75R15 all-season tires, wheel covers. **LS** adds: front air conditioning, 2-passenger middle and 3-passenger rear bench seats, cruise control, power windows, mirrors, and locks, Light Group, privacy glass, rear defogger, luggage rack, lighted visor mirrors, seatback map pockets, rear cargo net, lockable underseat storage bin, 2-tone paint, color-keyed bodyside molding w/chrome strip. **Nautica** adds: quad captain's chairs, leather upholstery, unique exterior paint, color-keyed bodyside molding w/yellow Mylar insert, unique grille, white alloy wheels, duffle bag.

Optional Equipment:

Front air conditioning, GS	855	727	787
Front air conditioning, GS	855	727	787
Anti-theft system	100	85	92
Requires remote keyless entry.			
Cruise control, base GS	225	191	207

Prices are accurate at time of publication; subject to manufacturer's change.

MERCURY

	Retail Price	Dealer Invoice	Fair Price
Auxiliary rear air conditioning with rear heater, GS	$465	$395	$428

Includes front air conditioning, rear seat fan and temperature controls. Requires 7-passenger seating (included in option pkgs.).

Automatic temperature control	645	548	593

Includes front and auxiliary rear air conditioning. NA GS w/Pkg. 691A or standard radio.

Preferred Equipment Pkg. 691A, GS	1250	1062	1150

Front air conditioning, 7-passenger seating, power windows and door locks, cruise control, rear defogger, power mirrors.

Preferred Equipment Pkg. 692A, GS	2900	2464	2668

Pkg. 691A plus power driver's seat, rear air conditioning and rear heater, remote keyless entry, flip-open liftgate window, privacy glass, luggage rack, underseat storage bin, alloy wheels.

Preferred Equipment Pkg. 695A, LS	740	628	681

Power driver's seat, rear air conditioning with rear heater, cassette player, leather-wrapped steering wheel w/radio controls, remote keyless entry, illuminated visor mirrors, flip-open liftgate window, deluxe alloy wheels.

Preferred Equipment Pkg. 696A, LS	2040	1734	1877

Pkg. 695A plus automatic air conditioning, power passenger seat, quad captain's seats, heated power mirrors, headlamp delay system, electronic instrumentation.

Preferred Equipment Pkg. 697A, Nautica	1430	1215	1316

Automatic air conditioning with rear air conditioning and heater, power front seats, cassette player, leather-wrapped steering wheel w/radio controls, flip-open liftgate window, heated power mirrors, electronic instrumentation, remote keyless entry w/headlamp delay system, electronic instrumentation, illuminated visor mirrors.

Light Group, GS w/ Pkg. 692A	165	140	152

Overhead dual map lights, dual liftgate lights, front door step lights, power rear vent windows, under instrument panel lights with time delay. Requires rear defogger and 7-passenger bench seat or quad captain's chairs.

Handling Suspension	85	73	79

Includes 215/70R15 performance tires, firm ride suspension, rear stabilizer bar. Requires alloy wheels. NA GS w/Pkg. 691A.

Trailer Towing Pkg.	250	213	230

Includes heavy duty battery, conventional spare tire, 3500-pound trailer rating.

Power windows and locks, GS	570	484	524

Requires 7-passenger seating.

Power mirrors, GS	100	85	92
Heated power mirrors, LS	50	43	47

MERCURY

	Retail Price	Dealer Invoice	Fair Price
Power moonroof, LS, Nautica	$775	$659	$714
7-passenger seating, GS	330	281	304
Quad captain's chairs, LS	610	518	561
with leather	865	735	796
Requires auxiliary rear air conditioning and rear heater.			
Integrated child seats, GS w/option pkg.,			
LS w/Pkg. 695A	240	204	221
LS w/Pkg. 696 A (credit)	(235)	(200)	(200)
Requires 7-passenger seating.			
8-way power driver's seat	395	336	363
Includes power lumbar support.			
4-way power front passenger's seat	195	166	179
Requires 8-way power driver seat. NA GS.			
Electronic instrumentation, LS	245	208	225
Requires automatic temperature control, remote keyless entry w/headlamp delay system. NA w/standard radio.			
Remote keyless entry, GS	175	149	161
Requires power windows and locks.			
Remote keyless entry and headlamp delay systems, LS	350	298	322
Requires automatic temperature control. NA w/standard radio.			
Rear defogger, GS	170	144	156
Flip open liftgate window	115	97	106
Requires rear defogger.			
Privacy glass, GS	415	352	382
Requires rear defogger.			
Illuminated visor mirrors, base LS	25	21	23
Premium Sound cassette player, GS	310	263	285
Includes rear radio controls with front seat lockout, dual mini headphone jacks, cassette/CD storage console. NA Pkg. 691A.			
Premium Sound CD/cassette player,			
GS w/Pkg. 692A	680	578	626
LS, Nautica	370	314	340
Supersound CD/cassette player, LS and Nautica	865	735	796
Premium Sound CD/cassette player plus power antenna, subwoofer speaker. NA Pkg. 695A.			
Leather wrapped steering wheel, base LS	320	272	294
Luggage rack, GS	145	123	133
Underseat storage bin, GS	30	26	28
Monotone paint, LS (credit)	(135)	(115)	(115)
Alloy wheels, GS	395	336	363
NA Pkg. 691A.			
Deluxe alloy wheels, GS w/alloy wheels	40	34	37
LS	395	336	363

Prices are accurate at time of publication; subject to manufacturer's change.

MITSUBISHI

Mitsubishi Eclipse

	Retail Price	Dealer Invoice	Fair Price
RS 3-door hatchback, 5-speed	$14970	$13015	—
RS 3-door hatchback, automatic	15670	13630	—
GS 3-door hatchback, 5-speed	17330	15071	—
GS 3-door hatchback, automatic	18030	15685	—
GS-T 3-door hatchback, 5-speed	20940	18213	—
GS-T 3-door hatchback, automatic	21780	18947	—
GSX 3-door hatchback, 5-speed	23910	20560	—
GSX 3-door hatchback, automatic	24740	21270	—
Destination charge	420	420	420

Fair price not available at time of publication.

Standard Equipment:

RS: 2.0-liter DOHC 4-cylinder engine, 5-speed manual or 4-speed automatic transmission, driver- and passenger-side air bags, power steering, cloth reclining front bucket seats, 5-way adjustable driver's seat w/memory recliner, center storage console, folding rear seat, map lights, remote fuel door and rear hatch releases, tachometer, trip odometer, low fluid warning lights, AM/FM radio, digital clock, tinted glass, rear defogger, dual remote mirrors, color-keyed bumpers and front air dam, full wheel covers, 195/70HR14 tires. **GS** adds: 4-wheel disc brakes, 6-way adjustable driver's seat, split folding rear seat, tilt steering column, cassette player, color-keyed power mirrors, rear wiper/washer, color-keyed rear spoiler, lower bodyside cladding, fog lights, cargo cover and net, 205/55HR16 tires. **GS-T** adds: turbocharged and intercooled engine, engine oil cooler, air conditioning, cruise control, turbo boost gauge, Infinity 8-speaker AM/FM/cassette/CD player with amplifier, power door locks and windows, bright dual exhaust outlets, sport-tuned shock absorbers, alloy wheels. **GSX** adds: permanent all-wheel drive, limited-slip differential, power driver's seat, leather-wrapped steering wheel, Leather Pkg., 215/55VR16 tires (manual transmission), 205/55VR16 tires (automatic transmission).

Optional Equipment:

Air conditioning, RS, GS	891	731	—
Anti-lock brakes	716	587	—
NA RS.			
Preferred Equipment Pkg. PM, RS	1479	1213	—
Air conditioning, rear spoiler, cargo cover, alloy wheels.			
Preferred Equipment Pkg. PH, GS	1560	1279	—
Air conditioning, cruise control, power windows and door locks.			

MITSUBISHI

	Retail Price	Dealer Invoice	Fair Price
Alarm system	$334	$274	—
Includes remote keyless entry. NA RS.			
Remote keyless entry	136	89	—
GS requires PH Pkg. NA RS.			
Leather Pkg., GS, GS-T	457	375	—
Leather front seats.			
Infinity 8-speaker AM/FM/cassette with amplifier, GS	427	350	—
CD player, RS, GS	442	310	—
RS requires cassette player or PM Pkg.			
10-disc CD changer	769	499	—
Power sunroof with sunshade	731	599	—
Cargo net, RS	26	17	—
Floormats	49	32	—
Mudguards	93	61	—
Alloy wheels, GS	348	285	—
Includes wheel locks.			
Wheel locks, RS, GS	32	21	—
RS requires Pkg. PM.			

Mitsubishi Galant

	Retail Price	Dealer Invoice	Fair Price
S 4-door notchback, 5-speed	$14920	$13275	$13775
S 4-door notchback, automatic	15810	14068	14568
ES 4-door notchback, automatic	19790	16820	17320
LS 4-door notchback, automatic	22860	19426	19926
Destination charge	420	420	420

Standard Equipment:

S: 2.4-liter 4-cylinder engine, 5-speed manual or 4-speed automatic transmission, driver- and passenger-side air bags, power steering, 5-way adjustable driver's seat, tinted glass, cloth and vinyl upholstery, rear defogger, tilt steering column, center console armrest with storage, driver-side door map pocket, cup holders, remote fuel door and decklid releases, driver-side visor mirror, intermittent wipers, tachometer, coolant temperature gauge, fog lights, black bodyside moldings, manual remote outside mirrors, digital clock, 185/70HR14 all-season tires, full wheel covers. **ES** adds: 4-speed automatic transmission, air conditioning, cruise control, power windows and door locks, AM/FM/cassette, automatic power diversity antenna, remote keyless entry system, HomeLink remote control transmitter, color-keyed power mirrors, folding rear seat with center armrest, full cloth upholstery and door trim, passenger-side visor mirror, door map pockets, floormats, cargo net. **LS** adds: power glass sunroof with sun shade, automatic air conditioning, power driver's seat, leather upholstery, Infinity audio

Prices are accurate at time of publication; subject to manufacturer's change.

MITSUBISHI

system w/graphic equalizer, intermittent wipers, fog lamps, ETACS-IV (includes ignition key illumination, seat belt warning timer/chime, headlight on warning chime, rear defogger timer, fade out dome light), illuminated driver's-side visor mirror, front seatback map pockets, 195/60HR15 all-season tires, alloy wheels.

Optional Equipment:

	Retail Price	Dealer Invoice	Fair Price
Anti-lock brakes	$965	$791	$869
S requires Preferred Equipment Pkg.			
Air conditioning, S	902	740	812
Preferred Equipment Pkg., S	2305	1890	2075
Air conditioning, power windows and door locks, AM/FM/cassette, cruise control, trunk trim, door armrest and storage pockets.			
Premium Pkg., ES	1664	1361	1498
Power sunroof, graphic equalizer, six speakers, upgraded upholstery, fog lamps, 195/60R15 tires, alloy wheels.			
Luxury Group, LS	612	502	551
Air conditioning, Infinity audio system.			

Mitsubishi 3000GT

	Retail Price	Dealer Invoice	Fair Price
3-door hatchback, 5-speed	$30680	—	—
3-door hatchback, automatic	31620	—	—
SL 3-door hatchback, 5-speed	35830	—	—
SL 3-door hatchback, automatic	36760	—	—
SL Spyder 2-door convertible, automatic	57449	—	—
VR-4 3-door hatchback, 6-speed	45580	—	—
VR-4 Spyder 2-door convertible, 6-speed	64449	—	—
Destination charge	470	470	470

Dealer invoice and fair price not available at time of publication.

Standard Equipment:

3.0-liter DOHC V-6, 5-speed manual or 4-speed automatic transmission, 4-wheel disc brakes, power steering, driver- and passenger-side air bags, air conditioning, power windows, door locks and mirrors, ETACS alarm control system, cruise control, rear spoiler, 6-way adjustable cloth front bucket seats, split folding rear seat, center storage console with coin and cup holders, tachometer, coolant temperature and oil pressure gauges, voltmeter, trip odometer, remote fuel door and hatch releases, Mitsubishi/Infinity audio system with external amp and eight speakers, power antenna, tilt steering column, leather-wrapped steering wheel, manual shifter knob, and parking brake handle, fog lamps, variable intermittent wipers, rear intermittent wiper, visor mirrors, rear defogger, digital clock, tinted glass, cargo area cover, 225/55VR16 tires, alloy wheels. **SL** adds: anti-lock brakes, automatic climate control, leather seats, 7-way adjustable driver's seat with 5-

MITSUBISHI • NISSAN

way power adjustments, rear wiper/washer, remote keyless entry with anti-theft system, steering-wheel mounted radio controls, heated power mirrors, auxiliary power outlet. **VR-4** adds: turbocharged intercooled engine, 6-speed manual transmission, permanent 4-wheel drive, 4-wheel steering, limited-slip rear differential, automatic climate control, Active Aero with retractable front air dam extension and motorized rear spoiler, turbo boost gauge, engine oil cooler, lighted visor mirrors, 245/40ZR18 tires, chrome wheels. **Spyder** models add to SL and VR-4: power folding hardtop, automatic day/night mirror, fixed rear spoiler, CD changer, HomeLink remote control transmitter, 245/45ZR17 tires, chrome wheels.

Optional Equipment:

	Retail Price	Dealer Invoice	Fair Price
CD auto changer, hatchbacks	$699	$488	—
Manual sunroof, SL and VR-4	375	300	—
Power sunroof, SL	900	720	—
VR-4	525	420	—
Deletes electronically controlled suspension from VR-4.			
Chrome wheels, SL	600	480	—
Yellow pearl paint	313	250	—
Mud guards	130	85	—

NISSAN

Nissan Altima

	Retail Price	Dealer Invoice	Fair Price
XE 4-door notchback, 5-speed	$15649	$13942	$14442
XE 4-door notchback, automatic	16479	14682	15182
GXE 4-door notchback, 5-speed	16999	14970	15470
GXE 4-door notchback, automatic	17829	15701	16201
SE 4-door notchback, 5-speed	19299	16896	17396
SE 4-door notchback, automatic	20129	17623	18123
GLE 4-door notchback, automatic	20999	18384	18884
Destination charge	405	405	405

Standard Equipment:

XE: 2.4-liter DOHC 4-cylinder engine, 5-speed manual or 4-speed automatic transmission, driver- and passenger-side air bags, power steering, tilt steering column, rear defogger, dual cup holders, remote fuel door and decklid releases, cloth reclining bucket seats, center front console, tachometer, coolant temperature gauge, trip odometer, low fuel warning light, child safety rear door locks, tinted glass, power mirrors, front map pockets, visor mirrors, 205/60R15 tires, wheel covers. **GXE** adds: power windows with auto down driver's window, power locks, front seat console with armrest,

NISSAN

rear seat center armrest with trunk pass-through. **SE** adds: 4-wheel disc brakes, sport-tuned suspension, air conditioning, cruise control, front sport seats, AM/FM/cassette, power diversity antenna, digital clock, variable intermittent wipers, fog lights, front cornering lights, bodyside cladding and rear spoiler, power sunroof, front sport seats, leather-wrapped steering wheel and manual shift knob, alloy wheels. **GLE** adds to GXE: 4-speed automatic transmission, automatic temperature control, cruise control, upgraded velour upholstery, variable intermittent wipers, front cornering lights, theft deterrent system, AM/FM/cassette and CD player, power diversity antenna, digital clock, power sunroof, adjustable lumbar support, lighted visor mirrors, alloy wheels.

Optional Equipment:

	Retail Price	Dealer Invoice	Fair Price
Anti-lock brakes	$999	$854	$899
Requires option pkg. with XE and GXE.			
Cruise control, XE	249	213	224
Requires automatic transmission.			
Leather Trim Pkg., SE and GLE	1049	897	944
Includes leather-wrapped steering wheel on GLE.			
XE Opt. Pkg.	1899	1624	1709
Air conditioning, AM/FM/cassette with digital clock, cruise control.			
Power sunroof, GXE	849	726	764
Requires GXE Value Option Pkg.			
GXE Value Opt. Pkg.	1299	1111	1169
AM/FM/cassette with digital clock, air conditioning, cruise control, power antenna.			

Nissan Maxima

	Retail Price	Dealer Invoice	Fair Price
GXE 4-door notchback, 5-speed	$20999	$18709	—
GXE 4-door notchback, automatic	22679	19973	—
SE 4-door notchback, 5-speed	22679	19856	—
SE 4-door notchback, automatic	23679	20731	—
GLE 4-door notchback, automatic	26279	23007	—
Destination charge	405	405	405

Fair price not available at time of publication.

Standard Equipment:

GXE: 3.0-liter DOHC V-6 engine, 5-speed manual transmission, driver- and passenger-side air bags, 4-wheel disc brakes, air conditioning, power steering, power windows with auto-down driver's window, power locks, cruise control, tilt steering column, velour cloth reclining bucket seats, multi-adjustable driver's seat with cushion tilt adjustment, center console w/cupholders, fold-down rear armrest, front door map pockets, rear defogger, power mirrors, illuminated entry, child-safety rear door locks, remote

NISSAN

trunk and fuel filler releases, tinted glass, tachometer, coolant temperature gauge, trip odometer, digital clock, AM/FM/cassette audio system with power diversity antenna, visor vanity mirrors, map light, color-keyed body-side moldings, full wheel covers, 205/65R15 tires. **SE** adds: sport-tuned suspension, fog lamps, body-colored rear spoiler, leather-wrapped steering wheel and shift knob, black-out exterior trim, alloy wheels, 215/60R15 tires. **GLE** adds to GXE: 4-speed automatic transmission, automatic air conditioning, 8-way power driver's seat, 4-way power front-passenger seat, leather seating surfaces, leather-wrapped steering wheel and shift knob, simulated wood trim on console and around power window/lock buttons, automatic temperature control, remote keyless entry, dual illuminated visor vanity mirrors, variable intermittent wipers, remote keyless entry system with trunk release, security system, Bose 6-speaker cassette/CD audio system, 205/65R15 tires, alloy wheels.

Optional Equipment:

	Retail Price	Dealer Invoice	Fair Price
Anti-lock brakes	$999	$854	—

NA GXE with 5-speed manual transmission.

Leather Trim Pkg., SE	1349	1153	—

Includes leather seats, 4-way power front passenger seat, automatic temperature control, passenger-side seatback pocket. Requires Security and Convenience Pkg., power sunroof and Bose 6-speaker audio system.

Cold Weather Pkg.	199	174	—

Includes heated front seats, heated outside mirrors, heavy-duty battery, low windshield washer fluid warning light. GLE requires anti-lock brakes. SE and GXE require anti-lock brakes and Security and Convenience Pkg. NA GXE with 5-speed manual transmission.

Security and Convenience Pkg., SE, GXE	699	612	—

Includes 8-way power driver's seat, remote keyless entry system, power trunk release, security system, illuminated visor vanity mirrors, variable intermittent wipers, chrome tailpipe tip (GXE), 205/60HR15 tires (GXE). SE requires power sunroof. NA GXE with 5-speed manual transmission.

Bose 6-speaker cassette/CD audio system	799	700	—

Requires Security and Convenience and power sunroof. NA GXE with 5-speed manual transmission.

Power sunroof	899	768	—

NA GXE with 5-speed manual transmission.

Nissan Pathfinder
Prices not available at time of publication.

Standard Equipment:

XE: 3.3-liter V-6 engine, 5-speed manual transmission, driver- and passenger-side air bags, power steering, anti-lock brakes, reclining front bucket

Prices are accurate at time of publication; subject to manufacturer's change.

NISSAN

seats, 60/40 split folding rear seat with reclining seatbacks and head restraints, cloth upholstery, center storage console with armrest, rear folding armrest, AM/FM/CD player with six speakers, diversity antenna, digital clock, tilt steering column, rear defogger, tachometer, coolant temperature gauge, trip odometer, tinted windows, dual outside mirrors, variable intermittent wipers, rear intermittent wiper/washer, remote fuel-door release, cup holders, auxiliary power outlets, concealed storage bin, front and rear stabilizer bars, rear heat ducts (4WD), map lights, cargo light, cargo cover (4WD), 235/70R15 all-season tires, chromed steel wheels, full-size spare tire. **SE** adds: cruise control, adjustable driver's seat including seat-cushion tilt and lumbar support, moquette upholstery, heated power mirrors, power door locks and windows, remote keyless entry, anti-theft system, power antenna, privacy glass, seatback and door map pockets, luggage rack, chrome grille and upper bumper, tubular step rail, fog lamps, rear wind deflector, black mudguards, cargo net and cover, 265/70R15 all-season tires, alloy wheels. **LE** deletes tubular step rail, rear wind deflector and adds: 4-speed automatic transmission, limited slip differential (4WD), automatic air conditioning, leather upholstery, heated front seats (4WD), passenger-side illuminated visor mirrors, HomeLink remote control transmitter, running boards, color-keyed mudguards and lower bumper, 235/70R15 all-season tires.

Nissan Quest

	Retail Price	Dealer Invoice	Fair Price
XE 7-passenger	$20899	$18297	$20099
GXE 7-passenger	25699	22499	24899
Destination charge	405	405	405

Standard Equipment:

XE: 3.0-liter V-6 engine, 4-speed automatic transmission, driver- and passenger-side air bag, front air conditioning, power steering, cloth reclining front bucket seats, 2-passenger middle bench seat and 3-passenger rear bench seat w/seatback tray tables, rear defogger, tilt steering column, dual mirrors, tachometer, trip odometer, variable intermittent wipers, rear intermittent wiper/washer, color-keyed bodyside moldings, visor mirrors, cornering lamps, door map pockets, AM/FM/cassette, diversity antenna, digital clock, tinted glass, carpeted front and rear floormats, console with cassette/CD storage, tilt-out middle and rear quarter windows, rear storage compartment, full wheel covers, 205/75R15 all-season tires. **GXE** adds: anti-lock brakes, rear air conditioning, rear heater controls, cruise control, power driver's seat, dual middle row captain's chairs, power locks and windows, power rear quarter windows, automatic headlight control, upgraded upholstery and door trim panels, power heated mirrors, illuminated visor mirrors, upgraded radio with rear controls, leather-wrapped steering wheel w/audio controls, remote keyless entry w/security system, power antenna, luggage rack, side and rear privacy glass, map lights, lockable underseat storage, cargo net, alloy wheels.

NISSAN

Optional Equipment:

	Retail Price	Dealer Invoice	Fair Price
Handling Pkg., GXE	$539	$460	$496

Tuned springs and shock absorbers, rear stabilizer bar, wiring harness, full-size spare tire, 215/70R15 tires. Requires Luxury Pkg.

Power and Privacy Glass Pkg., XE	1249	1068	1149

Power windows, locks, and heated mirrors, side and rear privacy glass.

Convenience Pkg., XE	579	496	533

Cruise control, remote keyless entry w/security system, rear audio controls, lighted right visor mirror, lockable underseat storage, roof rack, cargo net. Requires Power and Privacy Glass Pkg.

Touring Pkg., XE	999	854	919

6-disc CD changer, leather-wrapped steering wheel w/radio controls, wiring harness, full-size spare tire, alloy wheels. Requires rear air conditioning, Convenience Pkg.

Rear air conditioning, XE	649	555	597

Requires Convenience Pkg.

Anti-lock brakes, XE	699	598	643

Requires Convenience Pkg.

Leather Trim Pkg., GXE	1299	1111	1195

Leather upholstery, 4-way power passenger seat. Requires Luxury Pkg.

Luxury Pkg., GXE	1249	1068	1149

6-disc CD changer, semi-automatic air conditioning, power sunroof.

Child seat,	199	170	183

Requires rear air conditioning, anti-lock brakes.

2-tone paint, GXE	299	255	275

Nissan Sentra

	Retail Price	Dealer Invoice	Fair Price
Base 4-door notchback, 5-speed	$11499	$10897	—
XE 4-door notchback, 5-speed	13529	12542	—
XE 4-door notchback, automatic	14329	13283	—
GXE 4-door notchback, 5-speed	14459	12957	—
GXE 4-door notchback, automatic	15259	13674	—
GLE 4-door notchback, 5-speed	15229	13646	—
GLE 4-door notchback, automatic	16029	14363	—
Destination charge	405	405	405

Fair price not available at time of publication.

Standard Equipment:

Base: 1.6-liter DOHC 4-cylinder engine, 5-speed manual transmission, driver- and passenger-side air bags, cloth reclining front bucket seats, console, tinted glass, tilt steering column, coolant temperature gauge, trip odometer, rear defogger, front door map pockets, color-keyed grille, auxiliary power outlet, 155/80R13 tires. **XE** adds: 5-speed manual or 4-speed automatic

Prices are accurate at time of publication; subject to manufacturer's change.

NISSAN

transmission, power steering, air conditioning, AM/FM/cassette, digital clock, intermittent wipers, remote trunk and fuel door releases, dual exterior mirrors, passenger-side visor mirror, color-keyed bumpers, 175/70R13 tires, wheel covers. **GXE** adds: cruise control, split folding rear seat, upgraded interior trim, power windows and door locks, power mirrors. **GLE** adds: power glass sunroof, velour seat trim, center armrest (with automatic transmission), remote keyless entry, security alarm, tachometer, color-keyed bodyside moldings, 175/65R14 tires, alloy wheels.

Optional Equipment:

	Retail Price	Dealer Invoice	Fair Price
Anti-lock brakes, GXE, GLE	$999	$854	—
Includes 4-wheel disc brakes.			

Nissan 200SX

	Retail Price	Dealer Invoice	Fair Price
Base 2-door notchback, 5-speed	$12449	$11797	—
Base 2-door notchback, automatic	13249	12555	—
SE 2-door notchback, 5-speed	14869	13324	—
SE 2-door notchback, automatic	15669	14041	—
SE-R 2-door notchback, 5-speed	16069	14400	—
SE-R 2-door notchback, automatic	16869	15117	—
Destination charge	405	405	405

Fair price not available at time of publication.

Standard Equipment:

Base: 1.6-liter DOHC 4-cylinder engine, 5-speed manual or 4-speed automatic transmission, power steering, driver- and passenger-side air bags, cloth reclining front bucket seats, console, power mirrors, tinted glass, tilt steering column, tachometer, coolant temperature gauge, trip odometer, rear defogger, intermittent wipers, front door map pockets, remote trunk and fuel door releases, color-keyed grille and bumpers, auxiliary power outlet, 175/70R13 tires, wheel covers. **SE** adds: air conditioning, cruise control, split folding rear seat, upgraded interior trim, AM/FM/cassette, digital clock, power windows and door locks, fog lights, color-keyed bodyside moldings, mirrors, and door handles, 175/65R14 tires, alloy wheels. **SE-R** adds: 2.0-liter DOHC 4-cylinder engine, 4-wheel disc brakes, limited-slip differential, remote keyless entry, security alarm, leather-wrapped steering wheel and shifter knob, lower bodyside cladding, decklid spoiler, 195/55R15 tires.

Optional Equipment:

Anti-lock brakes, SE, SE-R	999	854	—
SE includes 4-wheel disc brakes.			
Popular Equipment Pkg., base	1449	1239	—
Air conditioning, AM/FM/cassette, digital clock.			

NISSAN • OLDSMOBILE

	Retail Price	Dealer Invoice	Fair Price
Power sunroof, SE, SE-R	$449	$384	—
Requires decklid spoiler.			
Decklid spoiler, SE	149	127	—

OLDSMOBILE

Oldsmobile Achieva

	Retail Price	Dealer Invoice	Fair Price
2-door notchback (Series I)	$13495	$12888	—
2-door notchback (Series II)	14495	13553	—
4-door notchback (Series II)	14495	13553	—
2-door notchback (Series III)	16495	15423	—
4-door notchback (Series III)	16495	15423	—
Destination charge	500	500	500

Fair price not available at time of publication.

Standard Equipment:

Series I: 2.4-liter DOHC 4-cylinder engine, 5-speed manual transmission, anti-lock brakes, driver- and passenger-side air bags, power steering, air conditioning, Passlock theft-deterrent system, cloth reclining front bucket seats, console with storage armrest, cupholders, and auxiliary power source, tilt steering wheel, intermittent wipers, tachometer, engine-coolant temperature gauge, AM/FM radio, Rear Aero Wing Pkg., tinted glass, rear defogger, programmable power locks, remote fuel door and decklid releases, illuminated entry/exit, reading/map/courtesy lights, visor mirrors, map pockets, color-keyed bodyside moldings, daytime running lamps, floormats, 195/70R14 tires, wheel covers. **Series II** deletes Rear Aero Wing Pkg. and adds: cassette player, manual right/remote left mirror (4-door). **2-door** adds: Rear Aero Wing Pkg. **Series III** adds to Series II 4-door: 4-speed automatic transmission w/ Enhanced Traction System, driver's-side lumbar support, cruise control, rear-window grid antenna, dual power mirrors, power windows, 195/65R15 touring tires. **2-door** adds: rear spoiler.

Optional Equipment:

3.1-liter V-6, Series II, III	457	393	—
Includes variable-effort power steering. Series II requires cruise control and 4-speed automatic transmission.			
5-speed manual transmission, Series III (credit)	(795)	(684)	(684)
4-speed automatic transmission, Series II	795	684	—
Includes Enhanced Traction System.			

Prices are accurate at time of publication; subject to manufacturer's change.

OLDSMOBILE

	Retail Price	Dealer Invoice	Fair Price
Cruise control, Series II	$225	$194	—
Requires 3.1-liter V-6 engine.			
Sport Pkg., Series III	745	641	—
Includes power sunroof, leather-wrapped steering wheel and shifter, fog lamps.			
6-way power driver's seat, Series III	270	232	—
Split folding rear seat, Series III	150	129	—
Rear Aero Wing Pkg., Series II 4-door	224	193	—
Series III 4-door	125	108	—
Rear spoiler, power mirrors, rear-window grid antenna.			
Remote keyless entry, Series III	125	108	—
CD player, Series III	160	138	—
Automatic tone control, six speakers.			
CD/cassette player, Series III	260	224	—
Automatic tone control, six speakers.			
Alloy wheels, Series II	391	336	—
Series III	285	245	—
Includes 195/65R15 touring tires.			
195/65R15 touring tires, Series II	106	91	—
Includes includes wheel covers.			
Engine block heater	18	15	—

Oldsmobile Aurora

	Retail Price	Dealer Invoice	Fair Price
4-door notchback	$34360	$31783	—
Destination charge	640	640	640

Fair price not available at time of publication.

Standard Equipment:

4.0-liter DOHC V-8 engine, 4-speed automatic transmission, anti-lock 4-wheel disc brakes, driver- and passenger-side air bags, traction control, variable-assist power steering, automatic climate control system with inside/outside thermometer, dual exhaust outlets, solar-control tinted glass, cruise control, AM/FM/cassette with CD player, integrated antenna, steering-wheel climate and radio touch controls, leather-wrapped steering wheel, leather upholstery, interior wood trim, center storage console with leather-wrapped shifter and auxiliary power source, overhead storage console, power front bucket seats with power lumbar support and 2-position memory for driver's side, folding rear armrest with trunk pass-through, power windows, automatic programmable door locks, power memory mirrors with defoggers, automatic day/night rearview mirror, lighted visor mirrors, power fuel-door and deck-lid release, intermittent wipers, tilt steering wheel, Pass-Key theft deterrent system, Twilight Sentinel automatic headlamp con-

OLDSMOBILE

trol, fog lamps, cornering lamps, remote keyless illuminated entry/exit system, Driver Information System, tachometer, engine-coolant temperature gauge, trip odometer, oil level sensor, universal garage-door opener, rear defogger, color-keyed bodyside moldings, cargo net, front and rear floormats, 235/60R16 tires, alloy wheels.

Optional Equipment:

	Retail Price	Dealer Invoice	Fair Price
Power sunroof	$995	$856	—
Bose Acoustimass Sound System	1131	973	—
Includes 12-disc CD changer, woofer, six additional speakers.			
Heated driver and front passenger seats	295	254	—
235/60VR16 tires	395	340	—
Includes 3.71 axle ratio.			
White diamond paint	395	340	—
Chrome wheels	800	688	—

Oldsmobile Bravada

	Retail Price	Dealer Invoice	Fair Price
5-door wagon	$29505	$27292	—
Destination charge	490	490	490

Fair price not available at time of publication.

Standard Equipment:

4.3-liter V-6 engine, 4-speed automatic transmission, permanent 4-wheel drive, 4-wheel anti-lock brakes, driver-side air bag, air conditioning, power steering, cruise control, front reclining bucket seats with power lumbar adjustment, 6-way power driver's seat, split folding rear bench seat, leather upholstery, AM/FM/cassette with graphic equalizer and six speakers, power antenna, digital clock, tilt steering wheel, power windows, rear defogger, tachometer, oil pressure and coolant temperature gauges, voltmeter, trip odometer, power mirrors, center console with storage armrest and dual cup holders, overhead storage console with trip computer, compass, reading lamps, outside temperature gauge, and universal garage-door opener, tinted windows, illuminated visor mirrors, remote keyless entry, intermittent wipers, door and seatback map pockets, auxiliary power outlets, rear air deflector, color-keyed bumpers and body-side moldings, front tow hooks, 5-wire trailer-towing electrical harness, luggage rack, Twilight Sentinel automatic headlamps, fog lamps, daytime running lamps, floormats, cargo net and cover, striping, 235/70R15 all-season tires, alloy wheels, full-size spare tire.

Optional Equipment:

CD player		124	107	—
Towing Pkg.		210	181	—
Heavy-duty suspension and hazard lights, 7-wire electrical harness, platform hitch, engine-oil cooler.			

Prices are accurate at time of publication; subject to manufacturer's change.

OLDSMOBILE

Oldsmobile Cutlass Ciera

	Retail Price	Dealer Invoice	Fair Price
4-door notchback (Series I)	$14455	$13805	—
4-door notchback (Series II)	16455	15385	—
5-door wagon	17455	16320	—
Destination charge	540	540	540

Fair price not available at time of publication.

Standard Equipment:

Series I: 2.2-liter 4-cylinder engine, 3-speed automatic transmission, anti-lock brakes, driver-side air bag, power steering, air conditioning, 55/45 bench seat with armrest and power seatback recliners, cupholders, automatic power locks, tilt steering wheel, AM/FM/cassette, digital clock, engine-coolant temperature gauge, tinted glass, left remote and right manual mirrors, rear defogger, intermittent wipers, illuminated entry/exit system, reading/courtesy lights, map pockets, bodyside moldings, visor mirrors, floormats, 185/75R14 whitewall tires, wheel covers. **Series II** adds: 3.1-liter V-6 engine, 4-speed automatic transmission, power windows, cruise control, power mirrors. **Wagon** adds: rear air deflector, roof rack, rear-facing third seat, locking rear storage compartment.

Optional Equipment:

3.1-liter V-6 engine, Series I	810	697	—
Includes 4-speed automatic transmission.			
Cruise control, Series I	225	194	—
Power driver's seat, Series II, wagon	305	262	—
Remote keyless entry, Series II	185	159	—
Wagon	125	108	—
Engine block heater	18	15	—
185/75R14 tires (credit), Series I	(48)	(41)	—
195/75R14 tires	NC	NC	NC
195/75R14 whitewall tires	40	34	—
Wire wheel covers, Series II, wagon	240	206	—
NA with 195/75R14 tires.			
Alloy wheels, Series II, wagon	295	254	—
Includes 195/75R14 tires.			

Oldsmobile Cutlass Supreme

	Retail Price	Dealer Invoice	Fair Price
2-door notchback (Series I)	$17455	$16670	—
4-door notchback (Series I)	17455	16670	—
2-door notchback (Series II)	18455	17255	—
4-door notchback (Series II)	18455	17255	—
2-door notchback (Series III)	18960	17728	—
4-door notchback (Series III)	18960	17728	—

OLDSMOBILE

	Retail Price	Dealer Invoice	Fair Price
2-door notchback (Series IV)	$20160	$18850	—
4-door notchback (Series IV)	20160	18850	—
Destination charge	540	540	540

Fair price not available at time of publication.

Standard Equipment:

Series I: 3.1-liter V-6 engine, 4-speed automatic transmission, anti-lock brakes, driver- and passenger-side air bags, power steering, air conditioning, cruise control, cloth reclining front bucket seats, tilt steering wheel, tachometer, center console with storage armrest and cup holders, automatic programmable door locks, AM/FM/cassette w/four speakers, digital clock, power windows, power mirrors, rear defogger, intermittent wipers, engine-coolant temperature gauge, illuminated entry system, courtesy/reading lights, Pass-Key theft-deterrent system, fog lamps, map pockets, visor mirrors, floormats, 205/70R15 tires, wheel covers. **Series II** adds: leather-wrapped steering wheel, remote keyless entry system, 215/60R16 tires, alloy wheels. **Series III** adds: variable-assist steering, split folding rear seat, lighted visor mirrors, 6-speaker audio system, power antenna. **Series IV** adds: automatic front/rear air conditioning with inside/outside thermometer, 6-way power driver's seat, cassette/CD player, steering-wheel radio and air-conditioning controls, leather upholstery.

Optional Equipment:

55/45 front seats, Series I	NC	NC	NC
3.4-liter DOHC V-6, Series III, IV	1223	1052	—
Includes sport suspension, rear spoiler (2-door notchback), dual exhaust outlets, 225/60R16 tires.			
Power sunroof, Series IV	695	598	—
6-way power driver's seat, Series III	270	232	—
55/45 front seats, Series I, II, III	NC	NC	NC
NA with Series I 2-door notchback or 3.4-liter DOHC V-6 engine.			
CD player, Series II, III	100	86	—
Series II includes four speakers, Series III includes six speakers.			
CD/cassette player, Series II, III	200	172	—
Series II includes four speakers, Series III includes six speakers.			
Engine block heater	18	15	—

Oldsmobile Eighty Eight

	Retail Price	Dealer Invoice	Fair Price
4-door notchback	$20405	$19487	—
LS 4-door notchback	22810	21327	—
LSS 4-door notchback	26010	24319	—

Prices are accurate at time of publication; subject to manufacturer's change.

OLDSMOBILE

	Retail Price	Dealer Invoice	Fair Price
Destination charge, base, LS	$590	$590	$590
LSS	640	640	640

Fair price not available at time of publication.

Standard Equipment:

3.8-liter V-6 engine, 4-speed automatic transmission, driver- and passenger-side air bags, anti-lock brakes, power steering, high capacity engine cooling, air conditioning, cruise control, 55/45 cloth front seat with storage armrest and reclining seatback, power windows, driver's-side remote and passenger-side manual mirrors, tinted glass with solar-control windshield and rear window, rear defogger, intermittent wipers, AM/FM radio with digital clock, power antenna, auxiliary power source, tilt steering wheel, Pass-Key theft-deterrent system, power decklid release, power door locks, coolant temperature gauge, trip odometer, courtesy lights, front door map pockets, illuminated entry/exit, Twilight Sentinel headlight control, daytime running lamps, color-keyed bodyside moldings, floormats, cargo net, 205/70R15 tires, wheel covers. **LS** adds: cassette player, remote keyless entry system, programmable door locks, 8-way power driver's seat with power recliner, power mirrors, lighted visor mirrors, reading lights, alloy wheels. **LSS** adds: dual-zone air conditioning, variable-effort power steering, traction control, automatic load-leveling touring suspension, 8-way power passenger seat with power recliner, rear seat w/trunk pass through, leather upholstery, leather-wrapped steering wheel with touch controls for radio and air conditioning, automatic day/night rearview mirror, floor console with storage armrest, overhead storage console, rear-seat storage armrest, cupholders, foglamps, tachometer, 225/60R16 tires.

Optional Equipment:

Supercharged 3.8-liter V-6 engine, LSS	1022	879	—
Traction control system, LS	175	151	—
Power driver's seat, base	350	301	—
Requires cassette player.			
Power sunroof, LSS	995	856	—
Leather upholstery, LS	515	443	—
Cloth upholstery, LSS	NC	NC	NC
Alloy wheels, base	330	284	—
Chrome wheels, LSS	600	516	—
Cassette player, base	375	323	—
Cassette and CD players, LS, LSS	200	172	—
Engine block heater	18	15	—

OLDSMOBILE

Oldsmobile Ninety Eight

	Retail Price	Dealer Invoice	Fair Price
Regency Elite 4-door notchback (Series I)	$28160	$26330	—
Regency Elite 4-door notchback (Series II)	29260	27358	—
Destination charge	640	640	640

Fair price not available at time of publication.

Standard Equipment:

Regency Elite (Series I): 3.8-liter V-6 engine, 4-speed automatic transmission, anti-lock brakes, driver- and passenger-side air bags, power steering, dual-zone air conditioner with inside/outside temperature indicator, high capacity engine cooling, leather upholstery, 55/45 reclining front seat, 6-way power front seats with power recliners and lumbar support adjusters, front and rear seat storage armrests w/cupholders, overhead storage console w/reading lamps, cruise control, power windows and door locks, power mirrors, AM/FM/cassette with eight speakers, power antenna, steering wheel controls for radio and air conditioner, power remote fuel door and decklid releases, remote keyless entry system, coolant temperature gauge, trip odometer, tilt leather-wrapped steering wheel, automatic leveling suspension, tinted glass with solar control windshield and rear window, intermittent wipers, rear defogger, Pass-Key theft deterrent system, lighted visor mirrors, front door and seatback map pockets, illuminated entry/exit system, Twilight Sentinel headlight control, daytime running lamps, cargo net, floormats, 205/70R15 whitewall tires, alloy wheels. **Regency Elite (Series II)** adds: traction control, electronic instrument cluster, cornering lamps, driver's seat and outside mirror memory controls, automatic day/night rearview mirror, automatic day/night driver's-side heated outside mirror, compass, power decklid pulldown.

Optional Equipment:

Traction control, Series I	175	151	—
Power sunroof, Series II	995	856	—
Cassette/CD player	200	172	—
Cloth seat trim	NC	NC	NC
Engine block heater	18	15	—

Oldsmobile Silhouette

	Retail Price	Dealer Invoice	Fair Price
4-door van (Series I)	$21355	$19967	—
4-door van (Series II)	22655	21182	—
Destination charge	545	545	545

Fair price not available at time of publication.

Standard Equipment:

Series I: 3.4-liter V-6 engine, 4-speed automatic transmission, anti-lock

Prices are accurate at time of publication; subject to manufacturer's change.

OLDSMOBILE • PLYMOUTH

brakes, driver-side air bag, power steering, front air conditioning, cruise control, power windows and door locks, 4-way adjustable driver's seat, 7-passenger seating (front bucket seats, three middle and two rear modular seats), center console with locking storage, overhead console, power mirrors, tachometer, coolant temperature and oil pressure gauges, voltmeter, trip odometer, remote keyless entry system, AM/FM/cassette, digital clock, tilt steering wheel, tinted glass with solar control windshield, intermittent wipers, rear wiper/washer, rear defogger, fog lamps, reading lights, roof rack, color-keyed bodyside moldings, visor mirrors, front door map pockets, floormats, cargo area auxiliary power outlet, cargo net, 205/70R15 tires, alloy wheels. **Series II** adds: power sliding door, 6-way power driver's seat, leather upholstery, steering wheel with auxiliary radio controls.

Optional Equipment:

	Retail Price	Dealer Invoice	Fair Price
Touring suspension	$205	$176	—
Integrated child seat	125	108	—
Integrated dual child seats	225	194	—
Rear air conditioning	450	387	—
Power sliding door, Series I	350	301	—
Towing Pkg.	355	305	—

Includes traction control system, engine and transmission oil coolers, 5-lead wiring harness.

	Retail Price	Dealer Invoice	Fair Price
CD player, Series I	256	220	—
Series II	226	194	—
Engine block heater	18	15	—

PLYMOUTH

Plymouth Voyager

	Retail Price	Dealer Invoice	Fair Price
Base 4-door van, SWB	$16575	$15096	—
Base Grand 4-door van	17825	16221	—
SE 4-door van, SWB	19270	17468	—
Grand SE 4-door van	20010	18144	—
Destination charge	560	560	560

Fair price not available at time of publication. SWB denotes standard wheelbase.

Standard Equipment:

Base: 2.4-liter DOHC 4-cylinder engine, 3-speed automatic transmission, driver- and passenger-side air bags, power steering, tinted glass, cloth reclining front bucket seats, 3-passenger rear bench seat (SWB), folding 2-passenger middle bench seat (Grand), folding 3-passenger rear bench seat

PLYMOUTH

(Grand), AM/FM radio, digital clock, trip odometer, dual exterior mirrors, variable intermittent wipers, variable intermittent rear wiper/washer, visor mirrors, 205/75R14 tires, wheel covers. **SE** adds: 4-speed automatic transmission, anti-lock brakes, cruise control, tilt steering column, folding 2-passenger middle bench seat with armrest (SWB), deluxe cloth upholstery, cassette player, tachometer, heated power mirrors, storage drawer below passenger seat, dual horns, additional sound insulation, cargo net, 215/65R15 tires.

Optional Equipment:

	Retail Price	Dealer Invoice	Fair Price
Anti-lock brakes, base	$415	$353	—
Pkg. 22T/24T, base	605	514	—
base Grand	255	217	—

Air conditioning, 7-passenger Seating Group (folding 2-passenger middle bench seat, folding 3-passenger rear bench seat) (base), rear sound insulation, storage drawer below passenger seat, Light Group (interior courtesy lights, map lights, rear auxiliary power outlet), passenger-seatback assist strap, dual horns. Pkg. 24T requires 3.0-liter V-6 engine.

Pkg. 23B/24B, SE SWB	470	400	—
Pkg. 23B/28B, SE Grand	470	400	—

Air conditioning, CYN 7-passenger Deluxe Seating Group (reclining/folding 2-passenger middle bench seat and 3-passenger rear bench seat with adjustable headrests), Light Group, rear defogger. Pkg. 24B requires 3.0-liter V-6 engine. Pkg. 28B requires 3.3-liter V-6 engine.

Pkg. 28C, SE	1120	952	—

Pkg. 23B/24B plus Rallye Decor Group (solar-control glass, Rallye decals, striping, body-color grille and door handles, alloy wheels). Requires 3.3-liter V-6 engine.

Pkg. 24D, SE SWB	1190	1012	—
Pkg. 24D/28D, SE Grand	1190	1012	—

Pkg. 23B/24B plus power windows and door locks, power rear quarter vent windows, lighted visor mirrors, added sound insulation, floormats. Pkg. 24D requires 3.0-liter engine and 3-speed automatic transmission. Pkg. 28D requires 3.3-liter V-6 engine.

Pkg. 28E, SE	1895	1611	—

Pkg. 24D/28D plus Rallye Decor Group. Requires 3.3-liter V-6 engine.

3.0-liter V-6 engine, base	770	655	—
SE	520	442	—

Requires 3-speed automatic transmission. Base requires Pkg. 24T. SE requires Pkg. 24B.

3.3-liter V-6 engine, SE	815	693	—

Requires option pkg.

3-speed automatic transmission, Grand SE	(250)	(213)	(213)

Requires option pkg. 24B or 24D.

CYE 7-passenger Seating Group, base SWB	350	298	—

Folding 2-passenger middle bench seat, folding 3-passenger rear bench seat.

Prices are accurate at time of publication; subject to manufacturer's change.

CONSUMER GUIDE®

PLYMOUTH

	Retail Price	Dealer Invoice	Fair Price
CYK 7-passenger Seating Group, base	$285	$242	—

Reclining/folding 2-passenger middle bench seat with two integrated child seats and adjustable headrests, Folding 3-passenger middle bench seat. Requires option pkg.

CYR Deluxe 7-passenger Seating Group, SE	225	191	—

CYN Deluxe 7-passenger Seating Group with two integrated child seats in middle bench. Requires option pkg.

CYS Deluxe 7-passenger Seating Group, SE	745	633	—

Reclining/folding middle bucket seats and rear 3-passenger bench seat with adjustable headrests. Requires Pkg. 24D/28D or 28E.

Climate Group 1	860	731	—

Air conditioning.

Climate Group 2	450	383	—

Air conditioning, solar-control glass, windshield wiper de-icer. Requires option pkg.

Climate Group 3,

Grand SE w/Pkg. 23B/28B	1130	961	—
Grand SE w/Pkg. 28D	1020	867	—
Grand SE w/Pkg. 28D with Loading & Towing Group 3	955	811	—

Rear heater and air conditioning, overhead console.

Convenience/Security Group 1, base	435	370	—

Cruise control, tilt steering, power mirrors. Requires option pkg.

Convenience/Security Group 2, base	750	638	—
SE	315	268	—

Group 1 plus power locks. Requires option pkg.

Convenience/Security Group 3, SE	685	582	—

Group 1 plus power windows and rear quarter vent windows. Requires option pkg.

Convenience/Security Group 4, SE	235	200	—

Remote keyless entry, illuminated entry, headlight-off delay. Requires Pkg. 24D, 28D, or 28E.

Convenience/Security Group 5, SE	385	327	—

Group 3 plus security alarm. Requires Pkg. 24D, 28D or 28E.

Loading & Towing Group 1	110	94	—

Full-size spare tire. Requires option pkg.

Loading & Towing Group 2, SE	180	153	—

Group 1 plus heavy load/firm ride suspension. Requires option pkg.

Loading & Towing Group 3, Grand SE	445	378	—

Group 2 plus Heavy Duty Trailer Tow Group (heavy duty battery alternator, brakes, and radiator, heavy duty transmission oil cooler, trailer wiring harness). Requires Pkg. 28D.

PLYMOUTH • PONTIAC

	Retail Price	Dealer Invoice	Fair Price
Rear defogger,			
base w/o Convenience/Security Group	$195	$166	—
base w/Convenience/Security Group, SE	230	196	—
Includes windshield wiper de-icer.			
Sliding driver's side door	500	425	—
Requires option pkg.			
AM/FM/Cassette, base	170	145	—
10-speaker cassette player w/equalizer, SE	335	285	—
Requires Pkg. 24D, 28D, or 28E.			
10-speaker cassette/CD w/equalizer, SE	730	621	—
Requires Pkg. 24D, 28D, or 28E.			
Roof rack	175	149	—
Requires option pkg.			
Extra-cost paint	100	85	—
Engine block heater	35	30	—
Smoker's Group	15	13	—
Cigarette lighter, ash trays.			
Alloy wheels, Grand SE w/option pkg.	415	313	—

PONTIAC

Pontiac Bonneville

	Retail Price	Dealer Invoice	Fair Price
SE 4-door notchback sedan	$21589	$19538	$20038
SSE 4-door notchback sedan	26559	24036	24536
Destination charge	590	590	590

Standard Equipment:

SE: 3.8-liter V-6 engine, 4-speed automatic transmission, anti-lock brakes, power steering, driver- and passenger-side air bags, cruise control, air conditioning, cloth 45/55 reclining front seats with storage armrest, tilt steering wheel, power windows with driver-side express down, power door locks, AM/FM radio, digital clock, tinted glass, left remote and right manual mirrors, coolant temperature and oil pressure gauges, voltmeter, tachometer, trip odometer, daytime running lights, Twilight Sentinel, Lamp Group (includes rear courtesy lights, rear assist handles, headlamp-on warning, trunk light), rear defogger, intermittent wipers, color-keyed bodyside moldings, Pass-Key II theft-deterrent system, visor mirrors, fog lights, floormats, 215/65R15 tires, wheel covers. **SSE** adds: dual exhaust, variable-assist power steering, electronic load leveling, automatic climate control, 45/45 cloth bucket seats with center storage console and rear air conditioning vents, overhead console with power outlet, 6-way power driver's seat, rear

Prices are accurate at time of publication; subject to manufacturer's change.

PONTIAC

center armrest with cup holders, heated power mirrors, 6-speaker cassette player with equalizer and steering wheel controls, leather-wrapped steering wheel, power antenna, Driver Information Center, remote decklid release, rear spoiler, remote keyless entry system, color-keyed lower body cladding, accessory emergency road kit (includes spot light, first aid kit, air hose, windshield scraper, gloves), illuminated entry, lighted visor mirrors, trunk net, 225/60R16 tires, alloy wheels.

Optional Equipment:

	Retail Price	Dealer Invoice	Fair Price
Supercharged 3.8-liter V-6 engine, SE	$1362	$1212	$1226
SSE	1342	1194	1208
SSE with Group 1SB	1167	1039	1050

Requires traction control. SE requires Group 1SD. SSE includes SSEi Supercharger Pkg. (engine plus boost gauge, driver-selectable shift controls, 2.97 axle ratio, SSE badging and floormats, 225/60HR16 tires).

Option Group 1SB, SE	836	744	752

Variable-effort power steering, illuminated entry, cassette player, 6-way power driver's seat, power mirrors, remote decklid release, trunk net.

Option Group 1SC, SE	1287	1145	1158

Group 1SB plus automatic climate control, remote keyless entry system, leather-wrapped steering wheel, lighted visor mirrors.

Option Group 1SD, SE	3057	2721	2751

Group 1SC plus Sport Luxury Edition equipment (3.06 rear axle ratio, 6-speaker stereo system with power antenna, 45/45 leather bucket seats, rear spoiler, 225/60R16 tires, 5-blade alloy wheels).

Option Group 1SB, SSE	1250	1113	1125

6-way power passenger seat, head-up display, automatic day/night rearview mirror, traction control, 8-speaker sound system, anti-theft alarm.

Performance and Handling Pkg., SE

with Group 1SC	1183	1053	1065
with Group 1SD	775	690	698
with Group 1SD and supercharged 3.8-liter V-6 engine	600	534	—

Computer Command Ride, traction control, electronic load leveling, 3.06 rear axle ratio (with std. engine), 225/60R16 touring tires (with std. engine) or 225/60R16 tires (with supercharged engine), alloy wheels. Includes bucket seats.

Rear decklid spoiler, SE	110	98	99
Rear decklid spoiler delete (credit)	(110)	(98)	(98)

SE requires Group 1SD.

Traction control	175	156	158

SE requires option group, bucket seats, alloy wheels.

Power glass sunroof, SE	995	886	896
SE with bucket seats, SSE	981	873	883

SE requires alloy wheels, option group.

PONTIAC

	Retail Price	Dealer Invoice	Fair Price
Cloth 45/45 bucket seats, SE	$314	$279	$283
with Group 1SC	218	194	196
with Group 1SD	NC	NC	NC

Includes center storage console and rear air conditioning vents, lighted visor mirrors, overhead console with power outlet.

	Retail Price	Dealer Invoice	Fair Price
Leather 45/45 bucket seats, SE			
with Group 1SB	1213	1080	1092
with Group 1SC	1067	950	960

Includes center storage console and rear air conditioning vents, rear seat storage armrest, leather-wrapped steering wheel, overhead console with power outlet.

	Retail Price	Dealer Invoice	Fair Price
45/45 leather bucket seats, SSE	779	693	701
45/45 articulating leather bucket seats, SSE with Group 1SB	1024	911	922
6-way power driver's seat, SE	305	271	275
6-way power passenger seat	305	271	275

SE requires option group.

	Retail Price	Dealer Invoice	Fair Price
Remote keyless entry system, SE with Group 1SB	135	120	122
Cassette player, SE	195	174	176
CD player, SE	295	263	266
with option group, SSE	100	89	90

Includes 6-speaker system. SSE w/Group 1SB includes 8-speaker system.

	Retail Price	Dealer Invoice	Fair Price
Cassette player with equalizer and steering wheel controls, SE with Group 1SB or 1SC	385	343	347
with leather upholstery and Group 1SB or 1SC	335	298	302
with Group 1SD	150	133	135
CD player with equalizer and steering wheel controls, SE with Group 1SB or 1SC	485	432	437
with leather upholstery and Group 1SB or 1SC	435	387	392
with Group 1SD	250	223	225
SSE	100	89	90

SSE includes 8-speaker sound system.

	Retail Price	Dealer Invoice	Fair Price
6-speaker sound system, SE	100	89	90
Leather-wrapped steering wheel with radio controls, SE with Group 1SB	175	156	158
with leather upholstery, or with Group 1SC or 1SD	125	111	113
Anti-theft alarm	190	169	171

SE requires Group 1SC or 1SD.

Prices are accurate at time of publication; subject to manufacturer's change.

PONTIAC

	Retail Price	Dealer Invoice	Fair Price
Power antenna, SE	$85	$76	$77
Requires option group.			
Computer Command Ride, SSE with Group 1SB	380	338	342
16-inch gold or silver crosslace alloy wheels	324	288	292
w/Group 1SD or 1SC w/Performance and Handling Pkg.	NC	NC	NC
SE requires 225/60R16 tires.			
225/60R16 blackwall touring tires, SE	84	75	76

Pontiac Firebird

	Retail Price	Dealer Invoice	Fair Price
3-door hatchback	$15614	$14287	$15114
2-door convertible	22444	20536	21944
Formula 3-door hatchback	19464	17810	18964
Formula 2-door convertible	25284	23135	24784
Trans Am 3-door hatchback	21414	19594	20914
Trans Am 2-door convertible	27364	25038	26864
Destination charge	505	505	505

Standard Equipment:

Base: 3.8-liter V-6 engine, 5-speed manual transmission, anti-lock brakes, power steering, driver- and passenger-side air bags, rear stabilizer bar, cloth reclining front bucket seats, folding rear bench seat, tilt steering wheel, center console with storage, lamp and cup holder, remote hatch release, AM/FM/cassette, intermittent wipers, solar-control tinted glass, front air dam, rear decklid spoiler, left remote and right manual mirrors, coolant temperature and oil pressure gauges, tachometer, voltmeter, trip odometer, Pass-Key II theft-deterrent system, dual reading lamps, visor mirrors, front floormats, 215/60R16 tires, alloy wheels. **Convertible** adds: air conditioning, cruise control, automatic power door locks, power windows, cassette with equalizer, power mirrors, power top with glass rear window and defogger, 3-piece tonneau cover, rear floormats. **Formula** adds to base hatchback: 5.7-liter V-8 engine, 6-speed manual transmission, 4-wheel disc brakes, air conditioning, performance suspension, 3.42 axle ratio, limited-slip differential, 235/55R16 touring tires, bright silver alloy wheels. **Formula convertible** adds: cruise control, power mirrors, power windows, automatic power door locks, cassette with equalizer, power top with glass rear window and defogger, rear floormats. **Trans Am** adds to Formula hatchback: cruise control, power windows, 4-way manually adjustable driver's seat, leather-wrapped steering wheel, shift knob, and parking brake handle, cassette with equalizer, power mirrors, automatic

PONTIAC

power door locks, rear defogger, color-keyed bodyside moldings, fog lights.
Trans Am convertible adds: 6-speaker sound system and power antenna, steering wheel radio controls, power top with glass rear window, remote keyless entry system, rear floormats, 245/50ZR16 tires.

Optional Equipment:

	Retail Price	Dealer Invoice	Fair Price
4-speed automatic transmission	$790	$703	$727

Base hatchback requires option group.

Traction control, Formula, Trans Am	450	401	414

NA with 245/50ZR16 performance tires. Formula hatchback requires option group.

Option Group 1SB, base hatchback	1078	959	992

Air conditioning, cassette player with equalizer, manual 4-way adjustable driver's seat, color-keyed bodyside moldings, rear floormats.

Option Group 1SC, base hatchback	2499	2224	2299

Hatchback Group 1SB plus power windows, automatic power door locks, power mirrors, cruise control, remote keyless entry system, power antenna, leather-wrapped steering wheel with radio controls, rear defogger.

Option Group 1SB, Formula hatchback	1184	1054	1089

Cassette player with equalizer, power windows, automatic power door locks, power mirrors, cruise control, manual 4-way adjustable driver's seat, rear defogger, color-keyed bodyside moldings, rear floormats.

Option Group 1SC, Formula hatchback	1604	1428	1476

Hatchback Group 1SB plus remote keyless entry, power antenna, leather-wrapped steering wheel with radio controls.

Option Group 1SB, base and Formula convertibles	580	516	534

Remote keyless entry, premium cassette player with equalizer, power antenna, leather-wrapped steering wheel with radio controls, remote keyless entry, manual 4-way adjustable driver's seat, color-keyed bodyside moldings, rear floormats.

3800 Performance Pkg., base	535	476	492

Limited-slip differential, 4-wheel disc brakes, faster-ratio steering gear, dual-outlet exhaust, 3.42 rear axle ratio (with automatic transmission), 235/55R16 tires, 5-spoke aloy wheels. Hatchback requires option group.

Ram Air Performance and Handling Pkg., Formula and Trans Am hatchbacks	2995	2666	2755

Ram Air induction system, functional hood scoops, dual oval exhaust outlets, 275/40ZR17 tires, 5-spoke alloy wheels. Requires upgraded decklid spoiler.

Cruise control, base hatchback with Group 1SB	225	200	207
Rear defogger, base and Formula hatchbacks	170	151	156
Removable locking hatch roof	970	863	892

Requires option group with base and Formula.

Prices are accurate at time of publication; subject to manufacturer's change.

PONTIAC

	Retail Price	Dealer Invoice	Fair Price
Hatch roof sunshades	$25	$22	$23
Content theft alarm	90	80	83

Requires remote keyless entry system. Base hatchback requires option group.

Rear performance axle,
Formula, Trans Am	175	156	161

Includes 3.23 axle ratio. Requires 4-speed automatic transmission, 245/50ZR16 tires. Formula hatchback requires option group.

Upgraded decklid spoiler,
Trans Am hatchback	395	352	363

Color-keyed bodyside moldings,
base, Formula	60	53	55

Power mirrors,
base and Formula hatchbacks	96	85	88

Requires power door locks and windows. Base requires option group.

Automatic power door locks,
base and Formula hatchbacks	220	196	202

Base requires option group.

Power windows,
base and Formula hatchbacks	290	258	267

Base requires option group.

Cassette player with equalizer, hatchbacks	73	65	67

Premium cassette player with equalizer,
Trans Am hatchback	115	102	106
base and Formula convertibles	50	45	46

Includes 6- (convertibles) or 10-speaker (hatchbacks) sound system. Hatchbacks require power door locks and windows, option group.

CD player with equalizer,
base and Formula hatchbacks	173	154	159
Trans Am hatchback, base and Formula convertibles	100	89	92

NA convertibles with Group 1SB.

Premium CD player with equalizer,
hatchbacks	215	191	198
base and Formula convertibles with option group	150	134	138
Trans Am convertible	100	89	92

Includes 6- (convertibles) or 10-speaker (hatchbacks) sound system. Hatchbacks require power door locks and windows. Base and Formula hatchbacks require option group.

Trunk-mounted
CD changer	595	530	547

Requires cassette player with equalizer. Base hatchback requires option group.

PONTIAC

	Retail Price	Dealer Invoice	Fair Price
Power antenna	$85	$76	$78

Base and Formula hatchbacks require Group 1SB.

	Retail Price	Dealer Invoice	Fair Price
Leather-wrapped steering wheel with radio controls, base, Formula	200	178	184
Trans Am hatchback	125	111	115

Base and Formula hatchbacks require Group 1SB, optional radio.

Cloth articulating bucket seats, Trans Am	330	294	304
Leather articulating bucket seats, base and Formula hatchbacks	804	716	740
convertibles, Trans Am hatchback	829	738	763

Requires premium audio system. Base and Formula require Group 1SB (convertibles) or Group 1SC (hatchbacks).

4-way manual driver's seat, base, Formula	35	31	32
6-way power driver's seat, base, Formula	305	271	281
base and Formula with option group, Trans Am	270	240	248

NA with articulating seats, leather upholstery.

Remote keyless entry system (std. Trans Am convertible)	135	120	124

Requires power windows, power door locks and power mirrors. Base hatchback requires option group.

235/55R16 touring tires, base	132	117	121
245/50ZR16 tires, Formula, Trans Am hatchback	225	200	207

Hatchbacks require traction control.

245/50ZR16 performance tires, Formula, Trans Am	225	200	207

NA with traction control.

Chrome 5-spoke wheels	500	445	460

Base requires 3800 Performance Pkg.

Rear floormats (std. Trans Am convertible)	15	13	14

Pontiac Grand Am

	Retail Price	Dealer Invoice	Fair Price
SE 2-door notchback	$13499	$12352	$12752
SE 4-door notchback	13499	12352	12752
GT 2-door notchback	15499	14182	14582
GT 4-door notchback	15499	14182	14582
Destination charge	500	500	500

Standard Equipment:

SE: 2.4-liter DOHC 4-cylinder engine, 5-speed manual transmission, anti-lock brakes, driver- and passenger-side air bags, power steering, daytime

Prices are accurate at time of publication; subject to manufacturer's change.

PONTIAC

running lights, cloth reclining front bucket seats, center console with armrest, storage and coin holder, overhead compartment, left remote and right manual mirrors, front door map pockets, AM/FM radio, tinted glass, automatic power door locks, Passlock theft-deterrent system, remote fuel door and decklid releases, fog lights, color-keyed bodyside moldings, tachometer, voltmeter, trip odometer, illuminated entry, visor mirrors, rear seat headrests, floormats, 195/70R14 tires, wheel covers. **GT** adds: air conditioning, 6-way power driver's seat, leather-wrapped tilt steering wheel, intermittent wipers, decklid spoiler, 205/55R16 tires, alloy wheels.

Optional Equipment:

	Retail Price	Dealer Invoice	Fair Price
3.1-liter V-6 engine	$395	$352	$359
Requires 4-speed automatic transmission. SE also requires air conditioning and 15- or 16-inch tires.			
4-speed automatic transmission	795	708	723
Includes traction control.			
Air conditioning, SE	830	739	755
Option Group 1SB, SE	1630	1451	1483
Air conditioning, cruise control, cassette player, intermittent wipers, rear defogger, tilt steering wheel.			
Option Group 1SC, SE 2-door	2353	2094	2141
SE 4-door	2418	2152	2200
Group 1SB plus variable-effort power steering, power windows, power mirrors, split folding rear seat, remote keyless entry.			
Option Group 1SB, GT	652	580	593
Cruise control, cassette player, rear defogger, variable-effort power steering.			
Option Group 1SC, GT 2-door	1313	1169	1195
GT 4-door	1378	1226	1254
Group 1SB plus power windows, power mirrors, split folding rear seat, remote keyless entry.			
Sport Interior Group, SE w/cloth upholstery	220	196	200
GT w/cloth upholstery	170	151	155
SE w/leather upholstery and Group 1SB	845	752	769
SE w/leather upholstery and Group 1SC	695	619	632
GT w/leather upholstery and Group 1SB	795	708	723
GT w/leather upholstery and Group 1SC	645	574	587
Leather or upgraded cloth upholstery, split folding rear seat (w/leather upholstery), driver-seat lumbar adjuster, seat back pockets, 4-way manual seat adjuster, leather-wrapped steering wheel (SE), shift knob, and parking brake handle, reading and courtesy lamps, sunvisor extensions. Requires option group.			
Cruise control	225	200	205
Rear defogger	170	151	155
6-way power driver's seat	340	303	309
Requires Group 1SC with SE and GT.			

PONTIAC

	Retail Price	Dealer Invoice	Fair Price
Power windows, SE and GT with Group 1SB			
2-door	$290	$258	$264
4-door	355	316	323
Power sunroof	595	530	536
Requires option group.			
Split folding rear seat,			
SE and GT with Group 1SB	150	134	137
Tilt steering wheel, SE	145	129	132
Intermittent wipers, SE	65	58	59
Remote keyless entry system,			
SE and GT with Group 1SB	135	120	123
Requires power windows.			
Cassette player	195	174	177
Cassette player with equalizer	305	271	278
with option group	110	98	100
CD player with equalizer	405	360	369
with option group	210	187	191
Cassette and CD players with equalizer	600	534	546
with option group	405	360	369
Steering wheel radio controls	125	111	114
Requires option group.			
Rear decklid spoiler, SE	150	134	137
Rear decklid spoiler delete, GT (credit)	(150)	(134)	(134)
195/65R15 tires, SE	131	117	119
205/55R16 tires, SE	223	198	203
15-inch alloy wheels, SE	275	245	250
16-inch alloy wheels, SE	300	267	273
Engine block heater	18	16	17

Pontiac Grand Prix

	Retail Price	Dealer Invoice	Fair Price
SE 4-door notchback	$17089	$15636	$16136
SE 2-door notchback	18359	16798	17298
Destination charge	540	540	540

Standard Equipment:

4-door: 3.1-liter V-6 engine, 4-speed automatic transmission, 4-wheel disc brakes, driver- and passenger-side air bags, power steering, air conditioning, power windows, automatic power door locks, 45/55 cloth reclining front seat with folding armrest, integrated rear seat headrests, AM/FM radio, Pass-Key II theft-deterrent system, tachometer, trip odometer, coolant temperature gauge, tilt steering wheel, left remote and right manual mirrors, tinted glass, intermittent wipers, fog lights, day/night rearview mirror, door

Prices are accurate at time of publication; subject to manufacturer's change.

PONTIAC

map pockets, 205/70R15 tires, wheel covers. **2-door** adds: dual exhaust outlets, sport suspension, cruise control, cloth reclining bucket seats with storage console, cassette player, leather-wrapped steering wheel with radio controls, power mirrors, rear defogger, remote decklid release, lower aero skirting, wheel flares, visor mirrors, front and rear floormats, 225/60R16 performance tires, alloy wheels.

Optional Equipment:

	Retail Price	Dealer Invoice	Fair Price
Anti-lock brakes	$450	$401	$405
Option Group 1SB, 4-door	742	660	668

Cruise control, rear defogger, power mirrors, cassette player, remote decklid release, visor mirrors.

Option Group 1SC, 4-door	1937	1724	1743

Group 1SB plus anti-lock brakes, 6-way power driver's seat, leather-wrapped steering wheel with radio controls, remote keyless entry, power antenna, floormats.

GT Performance Pkg., 4-door
with Group 1SB	2275	2025	2048
with Group 1SC	1825	1624	1643

3.4-liter DOHC V-6 engine, anti-lock brakes, sport suspension, dual exhaust outlets, variable-assist power steering, bucket seats, hood louvers, GT nameplates, 225/60R16 tires, alloy wheels.

GTP Performance Pkg., 2-door	1635	1455	1472

3.4-liter DOHC V-6 engine, anti-lock brakes, variable-effort power steering, hood louvers, GTP nameplates.

White Special Edition Pkg., 2-door	295	263	266

Decklid spoiler, white 5-spoke alloy wheels, striping. Requires white exterior paint and GTP Performance Pkg.

Polished 5-spoke Wheel Pkg., 2-door	495	441	446

Decklid spoiler, polished 5-spoke alloy wheels, silver striping. Requires white, red, black, or teal metallic exterior paint, GTP Performance Pkg.

6-way power driver's seat	305	271	274
Cruise control, 4-door	225	200	202
Remote decklid release, 4-door	60	53	54
Rear defogger, 4-door	170	151	153
Power glass sunroof	646	575	581

Requires custom interior.

Trip computer	199	177	179

Requires anti-lock brakes. 4-door requires option group.

Head-up instrument display	250	223	225

Requires anti-lock brakes. 4-door requires option group.

Remote keyless entry	135	120	121

4-door requires option group and remote decklid release.

Visor mirrors, 4-door	14	12	13
Bucket seats, 4-door	70	62	63

PONTIAC

	Retail Price	Dealer Invoice	Fair Price
Custom interior, 4-door with bench seat			
with Group 1SB	$488	$434	$439
with Group 1SC	393	350	354

45/55 reclining front bench seat with storage armrest, upgraded cloth upholstery, leather-wrapped steering wheel, front overhead console with front and rear reading lights, door courtesy lights, rear seat pass through, rear folding armrests, lighted visor mirrors, trunk net, floormats.

Custom interior, with bucket seats			
4-door with Group 1SB	588	523	529
4-door with Group 1SC	493	439	444
4-door with Group 1SB and GT Pkg.	518	461	466
4-door with Group 1SC and GT Pkg.	423	376	381
2-door	391	348	352

Replaces 45/55 front bench seat with custom bucket seats.

Custom interior, with leather bucket seats			
4-door with Group 1SB	1063	946	957
4-door with Group 1SC	968	862	871
4-door with Group 1SB and GT Pkg.	993	884	894
4-door with Group 1SC and GT Pkg.	898	799	808
2-door	866	771	779

Adds leather upholstery. Requires power driver's seat.

Cassette player, 4-door	195	174	176
Cassette player with equalizer,			
4-door with Group 1SB	325	289	293
4-door with Group 1SB and custom interior	275	245	248
4-door with Group 1SC	150	134	135
2-door	175	156	158

Includes leather-wrapped steering wheel with radio controls (4-door), 8-speaker sound system. 4-door requires option group.

CD player, 4-door	295	263	266
4-door with option group	100	89	90
2-door	125	111	113
CD player with equalizer,			
4-door with Group 1SB	425	378	383
4-door with Group 1SB and custom interior	375	334	376
4-door with Group 1SC	250	223	225
2-door	275	245	248

Includes leather-wrapped steering wheel with radio controls (4-door), 8-speaker sound system. 4-door requires option group.

Steering wheel radio controls, 4-door	175	156	157
4-door with custom interior	125	111	112

Includes leather-wrapped steering wheel and shift lever. Requires radio with cassette or CD player and option group.

Prices are accurate at time of publication; subject to manufacturer's change.

PONTIAC

	Retail Price	Dealer Invoice	Fair Price
Power antenna	$85	$76	$77
Rear decklid spoiler, 2-door	175	156	158
Dual exhausts, 4-door	90	80	81
Requires option group.			
Alloy wheels, 4-door	259	231	233
215/60R16 touring tires, 4-door	112	100	101
Requires alloy wheels.			
Front and rear floormats, 4-door	45	40	40
Engine block heater	18	16	17

Pontiac Sunfire

	Retail Price	Dealer Invoice	Fair Price
SE 2-door notchback	$11504	$10641	—
SE 4-door notchback	11674	10798	—
SE 2-door convertible	17734	16404	—
GT 2-door notchback	13214	12223	—
Destination charge	495	495	495

Fair price not available at time of publication.

Standard Equipment:

SE: 2.2-liter 4-cylinder engine, 5-speed manual transmission, driver- and passenger-side air bags, anti-lock brakes, power steering, daytime running lights, cloth reclining front bucket seats, center console with storage armrest, folding rear seat, tinted glass, AM/FM radio, tachometer, coolant temperature and oil pressure gauges, trip odometer, dual exterior mirrors, visor mirrors, front door map pockets, floormats, 195/70R14 tires, wheel covers. **Convertible** adds: 3-speed automatic transmission, air conditioning, tilt steering wheel, rear decklid spoiler, remote decklid release, power top, trunk net, reading lights, 195/65R15 tires. **GT** adds to SE 2-door: 2.4-liter DOHC 4-cylinder engine, tilt steering wheel, rear decklid spoiler, black painted roof, 205/55R16 tires, alloy wheels.

Optional Equipment:

2.4-liter DOHC 4-cylinder engine, SE	395	352	—
4-door requires 4-speed automatic transmission. NA with 3-speed automatic transmission.			
3-speed automatic transmission, SE notchbacks	550	490	—
NA with 2.4-liter DOHC 4-cylinder engine.			
4-speed automatic transmission, notchbacks	795	708	—
convertible	245	218	—
Includes traction control.			

PONTIAC

	Retail Price	Dealer Invoice	Fair Price
5-speed manual transmission, convertible (credit)	($550)	($490)	($490)

Requires 2.4-liter DOHC 4-cylinder engine.

	Retail Price	Dealer Invoice	Fair Price
Air conditioning, notchbacks	795	708	—
Option Group 1SB, SE notchbacks	1305	1161	—

Air conditioning, cassette player, tilt steering wheel, rear defogger.

Option Group 1SB, convertible	741	659	—

Cassette player, rear defogger, power mirrors, intermittent wipers, cruise control.

Option Group 1SC, SE notchbacks	1675	1491	—

Group 1SB plus cruise control, intermittent wipers, Convenience Pkg.

Option Group 1SC, convertible	1511	1345	—

Group 1SB plus cassette player with equalizer and steering wheel radio controls, remote keyless entry system, power windows and door locks.

Option Group 1SD, SE, 2-door	2531	2253	—
4-door	2636	2346	—

Group 1SC plus cassette player with equalizer and steering wheel radio controls, remote keyless entry system, power mirrors, windows and door locks.

Option Group 1SB, GT	1616	1438	—

Air conditioning, cassette player, cruise control, intermittent wipers, rear defogger, power mirrors, Convenience Pkg.

Option Group 1SC, GT	2386	2124	—

Group 1SB plus cassette player with equalizer and steering wheel radio controls, remote keyless entry system, power windows and door locks.

Convenience Pkg., SE notchbacks	80	71	—
with remote keyless entry system	69	61	—
with power sunroof	41	36	—
with remote keyless entry system and power sunroof	30	27	—

Remote decklid release, trunk net, reading lamps, overhead console. Requires Group 1SB. Deletes: remote decklid release with remote keyless entry system, overhead console with power sunroof.

Sport Interior Pkg., notchbacks	95	85	—
convertible	145	129	—

Vinyl trim (convertible), leather seat side bolsters and seatback map pockets, leather-wrapped steering wheel, parking brake handle and shifter, driver's seat lumbar support adjuster. Notchbacks require option group.

Cruise control	225	200	—

SE notchbacks require option group 1SB.

Rear defogger	170	151	—
Power door locks, 2-doors	210	187	—

Prices are accurate at time of publication; subject to manufacturer's change.

PONTIAC

	Retail Price	Dealer Invoice	Fair Price
4-door	$250	$223	—
SE notchbacks require option group.			
Power windows, 2-doors	265	236	—
4-door	330	294	—
Requires option group, remote keyless entry system, power door locks. SE 2-door notchback requires Group 1SC.			
Remote keyless entry system,			
SE notchbacks with Group 1SB	135	120	—
SE notchbacks with Group 1SC, convertible and GT with Group 1SB	124	110	—
Requires power door locks.			
Cassette player	195	174	—
Cassette player with equalizer	230	205	—
with option group	35	31	—
CD player with equalizer	330	294	—
SE notchbacks with Group 1SB or 1SC, convertible and GT with Group 1SB	135	120	—
SE notchbacks with Group 1SD, convertible and GT with Group 1SC	100	89	—
Steering wheel radio controls	125	111	—
Requires option group. SE notchbacks requires Group 1SC.			
Decklid spoiler, SE 2-door notchback	95	85	—
Tilt steering wheel, SE notchbacks	145	129	—
Power sunroof, SE 2-door notchback with Group 1SB, GT	595	530	—
SE 2-door notchback, with Group 1SC or 1SD, GT with option group.	556	495	—
Replaces overhead console when ordered with Convenience Pkg. SE requires Group 1SC or 1SD.			
195/65R15 touring tires, SE notchbacks	131	117	—
Alloy wheels, SE	275	245	—
Requires 195/65R15 tires.			

Pontiac Trans Sport

	Retail Price	Dealer Invoice	Fair Price
SE 4-door van	$19394	$17552	$18052
Destination charge	545	545	545

Standard Equipment:

SE: 3.4-liter V-6 engine, 4-speed automatic transmission, anti-lock brakes, driver-side air bag, power steering, front air conditioning, 4-way adjustable driver's seat, front reclining bucket seats, 3-passenger middle seat, cloth upholstery, tinted glass with solar-control windshield, tachometer, coolant temperature and oil pressure gauges, voltmeter, trip odometer, AM/FM

PONTIAC

radio, Lamp Group (includes overhead console map lights, rear reading lights, cargo area lights, underhood light), left remote and right manual mirrors, door and seatback pockets, intermittent wipers, fog lamps, rear wiper/washer, black roof paint, visor mirrors, floormats, 205/70R15 tires, wheel covers.

Optional Equipment:

	Retail Price	Dealer Invoice	Fair Price
Rear air conditioning and heater with Group 1SC, 1SD, or 1SE	$450	$401	$403

Requires 7-passenger seating, deep-tint glass.

	Retail Price	Dealer Invoice	Fair Price
Automatic level control, with Group 1SC	200	178	179
with Group 1SD	170	151	152

Includes rear saddle bags. Requires 205/70R15 touring tires.

Option Group 1SB	588	523	529

Cruise control, cassette player, power mirrors, tilt steering wheel.

Option Group 1SC	1683	1497	1515

Group 1SB plus automatic power door locks, power windows with driver-side express down, rear defogger, 7-passenger seating, deep-tint glass.

Option Pkg. 1SD	2263	2014	2037

Group 1SC plus 6-way power driver's seat, remote keyless entry system, roof rack.

Option Pkg. 1SE	3367	2997	3030

Group 1SD plus automatic level control, cassette player with equalizer, leather wrapped steering wheel with radio controls, overhead console, self-sealing 205/70R15 touring tires, alloy wheels.

Rear defogger	170	151	152
Deep-tint glass, with Group 1SB	245	218	220
Pop-up glass sunroof, with Group 1SC, 1SD or 1SE	300	267	269

NA with overhead console.

Roof rack	175	156	157

Includes rear saddle bags.

Automatic power door locks, with Group 1SB	300	267	269
6-way power driver's seat, with Group 1SC	270	240	242
Power windows with driver-side express down, with Group 1SB	275	245	246

Requires automatic power door locks.

Power sliding side door, with Groups 1SC, 1SD or 1SE	350	312	314

Requires remote keyless entry.

Remote keyless entry system, with Group 1SC	135	120	121

Prices are accurate at time of publication; subject to manufacturer's change.

CONSUMER GUIDE®

PONTIAC • RANGE ROVER

	Retail Price	Dealer Invoice	Fair Price
Cassette player	$140	$125	$126

NA with Group 1SE.

Cassette player with equalizer, with Group 1SD ... 315 280 284
Includes leather-wrapped steering wheel with radio controls.

CD player with equalizer, with Group 1SD ... 541 481 485
with Group 1SE ... 226 201 203
Includes leather-wrapped steering wheel with radio controls.

Overhead console, with Groups 1SC or 1SD ... 175 156 157
NA with sunroof. Requires remote keyless entry.

7-passenger seating ... 705 627 632
with leather upholstery ... 870 774 780
Three second row and two third row modular seats, cargo area net. Leather upholstery requires Group 1SD or 1SE.

Integral child seat ... 125 111 112
Requires 7-passenger seating.

Two integral child seats ... 225 200 202
Requires 7-passenger seating.

Trailer towing provisions, with Group 1SC, 1SD or 1SE ... 150 134 135
Includes wiring harness and heavy duty cooling. Requires 205/70R15 touring tires.

2-tone paint ... 125 111 112
Requires 205/70R15 touring tires and alloy wheels.

205/70R15 touring tires ... 35 31 31

Self-sealing touring tires ... 185 165 166

Alloy wheels ... 259 231 233
Requires 205/70R15 touring tires.

Silver-colored wheels ... 259 231 233
Engine block heater ... 18 16 17

RANGE ROVER

Range Rover 4.0 SE/4.6 HSE

	Retail Price	Dealer Invoice	Fair Price
4.0 SE 5-door wagon	$55000	$48700	—

RANGE ROVER • SAAB

	Retail Price	Dealer Invoice	Fair Price
4.6 HSE 5-door wagon	$62000	$54600	—
Destination charge	625	625	625

Fair price not available at time of publication.

Standard Equipment:

4.0 SE: 4.0-liter V-8, 4-speed automatic transmission, permanent 4-wheel drive, electronic two-speed transfer case, electronic traction control, anti-lock 4-wheel disc brakes, driver- and passenger-side air bags, power steering, automatic load-levelling suspension, automatic climate control with dual temperature controls and interior air filtration system, leather heated 10-way power front bucket seats with armrests and power lumbar support adjusters, split folding rear bench seat, center console with storage, leather-wrapped tilt steering wheel, cruise control, 11-speaker AM/FM/cassette/CD with 6-disc changer, diversity antenna, and steering wheel-mounted controls, remote fuel door release, power glass sunroof, heated power mirrors, tinted glass, heated windshield and rear window, power windows and door locks, remote keyless entry with memory seat and mirror system, anti-theft alarm system, variable intermittent wipers with heated washer nozzles, rear wiper/washer, heated power headlight wiper/washers, computer message center, automatic day/night rearview mirror, lighted visor mirrors, map lights, trailer hitch and wiring harness, burl walnut interior trim, cargo cover, front spoiler, front and rear fog lights, 225/65HR16 tires, full-size spare tire, alloy wheels. **4.6 HSE** adds: 4.6-liter V-8 engine, chrome exhaust outlets, body-flush mud flaps, 225/55HR18 tires.

Optional Equipment:

Beluga black paint, 4.0 SE		300	250	—

SAAB

Saab 900

	Retail Price	Dealer Invoice	Fair Price
S 3-door hatchback	$23995	—	—
S 5-door hatchback	24695	—	—
S 2-door convertible	33995	—	—
SE 3-door hatchback	28995	—	—
SE 5-door hatchback	29695	—	—
SE 5-door hatchback, V-6	31195	—	—
SE 2-door convertible	39995	—	—
SE 2-door convertible, V-6	42495	—	—
Destination charge	495	495	495

Prices are accurate at time of publication; subject to manufacturer's change.

SAAB

Fair price and dealer invoice not available at time of publication.

Standard Equipment:

S: 2.3-liter DOHC 4-cylinder engine, 5-speed manual transmission, anti-lock 4-wheel disc brakes, driver- and passenger-side air bags, front seatbelt pre-tensioners, daytime running lights, power steering, air conditioning, cruise control, power door and trunk locks, theft alarm system, power windows, automatic power antenna, power top and boot cover (convertible), telescopic steering wheel, front fog lamps, rear fog lamp, heated power mirrors, rear defogger, intermittent wipers, solar-control tinted glass, AM/FM/cassette, trip computer, cellular phone pre-wiring (hatchbacks), CD changer pre-wiring, cloth (hatchbacks) or leather (convertible) heated reclining front bucket seats, driver's seat manual lumbar adjustment, folding rear seat, front console with storage, removable cup and coin holder, headlamp wipers/washers, rear wiper/washer (hatchbacks), tachometer, analog clock, front spoiler, front and rear stabilizer bars (hatchbacks), tool kit, bodyside moldings, rear spoiler (3-door), floormats, 195/60VR15 tires, alloy wheels. **SE adds:** 2.0-liter turbocharged DOHC 4-cylinder engine, leather upholstery (hatchbacks), leather-wrapped shift-knob and boot (hatchbacks), power front seats with driver's side memory, automatic air conditioning, power glass sunroof (hatchbacks), premium sound system, CD changer (convertible), Saab Car Computer, sport suspension, 205/50ZR16 tires. **V-6 models add:** 2.5-liter DOHC V-6, automatic transmission, traction control, 195/60VR15 tires.

Optional Equipment:	Retail Price	Dealer Invoice	Fair Price
4-speed automatic transmission	$995	—	—
Power glass sunroof, S hatchbacks	995	—	—
Leather upholstery, S hatchbacks	1295	—	—
Includes leather-wrapped shift knob and boot.			
Child booster seats, 5-doors	250	—	—

Saab 9000	Retail Price	Dealer Invoice	Fair Price
CS 5-door hatchback	$31395	—	—
CSE Turbo 5-door hatchback	37695	—	—
CSE V-6 5-door hatchback	40195	—	—
Aero 5-door notchback	41195	—	—
Destination charge	495	495	495

Fair price and dealer invoice not available at time of publication.

Standard Equipment:

CS: 2.3-liter turbocharged DOHC 4-cylinder engine, 5-speed manual transmission, anti-lock 4-wheel disc brakes, driver- and passenger-side air bags,

SAAB • SATURN

daytime running lights, power steering, automatic climate control, removable AM/FM/cassette, cruise control, telescopic steering wheel, cloth reclining heated bucket seats, folding rear seat, power door locks and windows, anti-theft alarm system, dual heated power mirrors, automatic power antenna, remote decklid release, tachometer, trip odometer, intermittent wipers, headlamp wipers/washers, rear wiper/washer, solar-control tinted glass, dual visor mirrors, rear defogger, locking center storage console with cupholders, overhead console with swivel map light, front and rear fog lamps, courtesy lights, dual rear reading lights, lighted visor mirrors, front spoiler, analog clock, floormats, 195/65TR15 tires, alloy wheels. **CSE Turbo** adds: 200-horsepower 2.3-liter turbocharged engine with intercooler, leather upholstery, power front seats with driver-side memory, power glass sunroof, turbo boost gauge, leather-wrapped steering wheel and shift boot cover, Saab Car Computer with digital clock, Harmon/Kardon audio system with CD player, 195/65VR15 tires. **CSE V-6** adds: 3.0-liter DOHC V-6 engine, 4-speed automatic transmission, traction control. **Aero** deletes V-6 engine, rear fog lamp, and traction control, and adds: 225-horsepower 2.3-liter turbocharged 4-cylinder engine with 5-speed manual transmission or 200-horsepower 2.3-liter turbocharged 4-cylinder engine with 4-speed automatic transmission, aerodynamic body trim, sport suspension, wood interior trim, rear seat pass-through, rear spoiler, 205/55ZR16 tires.

Optional Equipment:

	Retail Price	Dealer Invoice	Fair Price
4-speed automatic transmission, CS, CSE Turbo, Aero	$1045	—	—
Power glass sunroof, CS	1115	—	—
Leather/Power Seat Pkg., CS	2095	—	—

Leather upholstery, leather-wrapped steering wheel and shift boot cover, power front seats.

SATURN

Saturn Coupe

	Retail Price	Dealer Invoice	Fair Price
SC1 2-door notchback, 5-speed	$12195	$10610	—
SC1 2-door notchback, automatic	13025	11332	—
SC2 2-door notchback, 5-speed	13295	11567	—
SC2 2-door notchback, automatic	14125	12289	—
Destination charge	390	390	390

Fair price not available at time of publication.

Standard Equipment:

SC1: 1.9-liter 4-cylinder engine, 5-speed manual or 4-speed automatic

Prices are accurate at time of publication; subject to manufacturer's change.

SATURN

transmission, driver- and passenger-side air bags, power steering, cloth reclining front bucket seats, 60/40 folding rear seatback, coolant temperature gauge, tachometer, trip odometer, tilt steering wheel, tinted glass, intermittent wipers, rear defogger, AM/FM radio, remote fuel door and decklid releases, door pockets, digital clock, right visor mirror, front and rear consoles, dual remote outside mirrors, wheel covers, 175/70R14 tires. **SC2** adds: 1.9-liter DOHC engine, variable-assist power steering, driver's seat height and lumbar support adjustments, sport suspension, locking storage armrest, retractable headlamps, striping, 195/60R15 tires.

Optional Equipment:

	Retail Price	Dealer Invoice	Fair Price
Anti-lock brakes	$795	$692	—
Includes traction control, rear disc brakes.			
Air conditioning	920	800	—
Option Pkg. 1, SC1	1815	1579	—
Air conditioning, cruise control, power windows and door locks, remote keyless entry, power right outside mirror.			
Option Pkg. 2, SC2	2110	1836	—
Option Pkg. 1 plus teardrop II alloy wheels.			
Power sunroof	690	600	—
Cassette player	220	191	—
Cassette player w/equalizer and premium coaxial speakers	365	318	—
Premium coaxial speakers	75	65	—
Cruise control	260	226	—
Fog lights	155	135	—
Leather upholstery, SC2	690	600	—
Includes leather-wrapped steering wheel.			
Rear spoiler	225	196	—
Sawtooth alloy wheels, SC1	410	357	—
Teardrop II alloy wheels, SC2	295	257	—

Saturn Sedan/Wagon

	Retail Price	Dealer Invoice	Fair Price
SL 4-door notchback, 5-speed	$10495	$9131	—
SL1 4-door notchback, 5-speed	11395	9914	—
SL1 4-door notchback, automatic	12225	10636	—
SL2 4-door notchback, 5-speed	12295	10697	—
SL2 4-door notchback, automatic	13125	11419	—
SW1 5-door wagon, 5-speed	11995	10436	—
SW1 5-door wagon, automatic	12825	11158	—
SW2 5-door wagon, 5-speed	12895	11219	—
SW2 5-door wagon, automatic	13725	11941	—
Destination charge	390	390	390

Fair price not available at time of publication.

SATURN

Standard Equipment:

SL: 1.9-liter 4-cylinder engine, 5-speed manual transmission, driver- and passenger-side air bags, cloth reclining front bucket seats, 60/40 folding rear seatback, tachometer, coolant temperature gauge, trip odometer, tilt steering wheel, tinted glass, intermittent wipers, rear defogger, AM/FM radio, remote fuel door and decklid (notchback) releases, door pockets, digital clock, right visor mirror, front console, child-safety rear door locks, wheel covers, 175/70R14 tires. **SL1** adds: 5-speed manual or 4-speed automatic transmission, power steering, dual outside mirrors, upgraded interior trim. **SL2** adds: 1.9-liter DOHC engine, variable-assist power steering, driver's seat height and lumbar support adjustments, sport suspension, upgraded upholstery, 185/65R15 touring tires. **SW1** adds to SL1: rear wiper/washer. **SW2** adds to SW1: 1.9-liter DOHC engine, variable-assist power steering, driver's seat height and lumbar support adjustments, sport suspension, upgraded upholstery, cargo cover, 185/65R15 touring tires.

Optional Equipment:

	Retail Price	Dealer Invoice	Fair Price
Anti-lock brakes	$795	$692	—
Includes traction control, rear disc brakes.			
Air conditioning	920	800	—
Option Pkg. 1, SL1, SW1, SW2	1940	1688	—
Air conditioning, cruise control, power windows and door locks, remote keyless entry, power right outside mirror.			
Option Pkg. 2, SL2	2250	1958	—
Option Pkg. 1 plus sawtooth alloy wheels.			
Power sunroof, SL1, SL2	690	600	—
Cassette player, SL	250	218	—
SL1, SL2, SW1, SW2	220	191	—
Cassette player w/equalizer and premium coaxial speakers, SL	395	344	—
SL1, SL2, SW1, SW2	365	318	—
Premium coaxial speakers	75	65	—
Power door locks	350	305	—
Includes remote keyless entry. NA on SL.			
Cruise control	260	226	—
NA on SL.			
Dual outside mirrors, SL	40	35	—
Fog lamps, SL2, SW2	155	135	—
Leather upholstery, SL2, SW2	690	600	—
Includes leather-wrapped steering wheel.			
Rear spoiler, SL2	195	170	—
Cargo cover, SW1	75	65	—
Floormats	55	48	—
Sawtooth alloy wheels, SL2, SW2	310	270	—

Prices are accurate at time of publication; subject to manufacturer's change.

SUBARU

SUBARU

Subaru Legacy	Retail Price	Dealer Invoice	Fair Price
Brighton 5-door wagon, AWD	$16495	$15365	$15865
L 4-door notchback	17195	15587	16087
L 5-door wagon	17895	16207	16507
Outback 5-door wagon, AWD	21995	19689	20189
LS 4-door notchback, AWD	22095	19778	20278
LS 5-door wagon, AWD	22795	20398	20898
GT 4-door notchback, AWD	22295	19995	20495
GT 5-door wagon, AWD	22995	20575	21075
LSi 4-door notchback, AWD	24795	22171	22671
LSi 5-door wagon, AWD	25495	22791	23291
Destination charge	495	495	495

Prices are for vehicles distributed by Subaru of America. Prices may be higher in areas served by independent distributors.

Standard Equipment:

Brighton: 2.2-liter 4-cylinder engine, 5-speed manual transmission, full-time all-wheel drive, driver- and passenger-side air bags, cloth reclining front bucket seats, air conditioning, storage console, variable-assist power steering, tilt steering column, 4-speaker AM/FM/cassette, digital clock, trip odometer, temperature gauge, tinted glass, rear defogger, intermittent wipers, rear wiper/washer, remote fuel door and decklid releases, body-side moldings, child safety rear door locks, 185/70SR14 all-season tires, wheel covers. **L** deletes full-time all-wheel drive and rear wiper/washer, and adds: front-wheel drive, split folding rear seat, power mirrors, power windows and door locks, tachometer, right visor mirror. **Outback** adds: full-time all-wheel drive, anti-lock 4-wheel disc brakes, cruise control, roof rack, fog lights, 2-tone paint, upgraded cloth interior, cargo hooks, cargo area power outlet, 205/70SR15 white-lettered tires, alloy wheels. **LS** adds to L: 4-speed automatic transmission, full-time all-wheel drive, anti-lock 4-wheel disc brakes, cruise control, power moonroof with sunshade, power antenna, variable intermittent wipers, map light, 195/60HR15 all-season tires, alloy wheels. **GT** adds: 2.5-liter DOHC 4-cylinder engine, fog lights, rear spoiler, ground effects. **GT wagon** deletes power moonroof; adds roof rack. **LSi** adds to LS: 2.5-liter DOHC 4-cylinder engine, 6-speaker compact disc player, leather upholstery, security system. **LSi wagon** adds: roof rack. **All wagons** add: rear wiper/washer, cargo cover (except Brighton).

Optional Equipment:

2.5-liter DOHC 4-cylinder engine, Outback	1000	884	900

Includes 4-speed automatic transmission.

SUBARU • SUZUKI

	Retail Price	Dealer Invoice	Fair Price
4-speed automatic transmission, Brighton, L	$800	$714	$720
Requires AWD or Active Safety Group.			
Cold Weather Pkg., Outback	400	355	360
Includes heated front seats, dual heated outside mirrors, engine-block heater.			
All-wheel drive, L	1000	743	900
Active Safety Group, L	1700	1368	1550
Anti-lock brakes (includes rear disc brakes), AWD, cruise control.			
Metallic paint	NC	NC	NC

SUZUKI

1995 Suzuki Esteem

	Retail Price	Dealer Invoice	Fair Price
GL 4-door notchback, 5-speed	$11399	$10715	—
GL 4-door notchback, automatic	12399	11655	—
GLX 4-door notchback, 5-speed	12699	11937	—
GLX 4-door notchback, automatic	13699	12877	—
GLX 4-door notchback with option pkg., 5-speed	14399	13535	—
GLX 4-door notchback with option pkg., automatic	15399	14475	—
Destination charge	390	390	390

Fair price not available at time of publication.

Standard Equipment:

GL: 1.6-liter 4-cylinder engine, 5-speed manual or 4-speed automatic transmission, driver- and passenger-side air bags, power steering, cloth and vinyl reclining front bucket seats, console, folding rear seat, intermittent wipers, tinted glass, rear defogger, trip odometer, remote fuel door and decklid releases, front door map pockets, dual exterior mirrors, 155/80R13 tires. **GLX** adds: cloth upholstery, split folding rear seat, AM/FM/cassette, tachometer, power windows, door locks, and mirrors, color-keyed bumpers, passenger-side visor mirror, mud flaps, 175/70R13 tires, wheel covers. **GLX with option pkg.** adds: anti-lock brakes, air conditioning, cruise control.

Options are available as dealer-installed accessories.

Suzuki Sidekick

	Retail Price	Dealer Invoice	Fair Price
JS 2WD 2-door conv., 5-speed	$12899	$12254	$12454
JS 2WD 2-door conv., automatic	13499	12824	13024
JX 4WD 2-door conv., 5-speed	14669	13642	13842

Prices are accurate at time of publication; subject to manufacturer's change.

SUZUKI

	Retail Price	Dealer Invoice	Fair Price
JX 4WD 2-door conv., automatic	$15269	$14200	$14400
JS 2WD 5-door, 5-speed	14399	13391	13791
JS 2WD 5-door, automatic	15349	14274	14674
JX 4WD 5-door, 5-speed	15999	14559	14959
JX 4WD 5-door, automatic	16949	15423	15823
JX Sport 4WD 5-door, 5-speed	17999	16379	16779
JX Sport 4WD 5-door, automatic	18999	17289	17689
JLX Sport 4WD 5-door, 5-speed	18999	17289	17689
JLX Sport 4WD 5-door, automatic	19999	18199	18599
Destination charge, 2-door	375	375	375
5-door	390	390	390

Standard Equipment:

JS 2-door: 1.6-liter 4-cylinder engine, 5-speed manual or 3-speed automatic transmission, driver- and passenger-side airbags, power steering, cloth reclining front bucket seats and folding rear seat, center console w/cup holders, tilt steering column, front door map pockets, fuel tank skid plate, folding canvas top, tinted glass, dual outside mirrors, intermittent wipers, tachometer, trip odometer, daytime running lights, carpeting, spare-tire carrier w/full-size spare, 195/75R15 tires. **JX 2-door** adds: part-time 4WD, 2-speed transfer case, power mirrors, remote fuel-door release, passenger-side visor mirror, 205/75R15 tires. **JS 5-door** adds to JS 2-door: 5-speed manual or 4-speed automatic transmission, split folding rear seat, AM/FM/cassette, rear defogger, passenger-side visor mirror. **JX 5-door** adds to JX 2-door: 5-speed manual or 4-speed automatic transmission, split folding rear seat, AM/FM/cassette, rear defogger. **JX Sport** adds: 1.8-liter DOHC 4-cylinder engine, 4-wheel anti-lock brakes, air conditioning, power windows and door locks, security alarm system, 215/65R16 tires. **JLX Sport** adds: automatic locking front hubs, cruise control, rear wiper/washer, map lights, spare tire lock, deluxe spare-tire cover, alloy wheels.

Optional Equipment:

4-wheel anti-lock brakes	600	540	—

Other options are available as dealer-installed accessories.

1995 Suzuki Swift

	Retail Price	Dealer Invoice	Fair Price
3-door hatchback, 5-speed	$8699	$8003	—
3-door hatchback, 5-speed w/anti-lock brakes	9259	8518	—
3-door hatchback, automatic	9349	8601	—
3-door hatchback, automatic w/anti-lock brakes	9909	9116	—

SUZUKI • TOYOTA

	Retail Price	Dealer Invoice	Fair Price
Destination charge	$360	$360	$360

Fair price not available at time of publication.

Standard Equipment:

1.3-liter 4-cylinder engine, 5-speed manual or 3-speed automatic transmission, driver- and passenger-side air bags, cloth reclining front bucket seats, folding rear seat, tinted glass, intermittent wipers, rear defogger, trip odometer, front console, dual outside mirrors, wheel covers, 155/80R13 tires. ABS-equipped models add anti-lock brakes.

Options are available as dealer-installed accessories.

TOYOTA

Toyota Avalon	Retail Price	Dealer Invoice	Fair Price
XL 4-door notchback, front bucket seats	$23418	$20303	—
XL 4-door notchback, front bench seat	24228	21005	—
XLS 4-door notchback	27448	23517	—
Destination charge	420	420	420

Fair price not available at time of publication. Prices are for vehicles distributed by Toyota Motor Sales, U.S.A., Inc. The dealer invoice, fair price, and destination charge may be higher in areas served by independent distributors.

Standard Equipment:

XL: 3.0-liter DOHC V-6 engine, 4-speed automatic transmission, 4-wheel disc brakes, driver- and passenger-side air bags, power steering, air conditioning, cruise control, cloth 6-way adjustable front bucket seats or power split bench seat with storage armrest, rear headrests, AM/FM/cassette, power windows and door locks, power mirrors, tinted glass, tilt steering column, auto-off headlamps, rear defogger, front door pockets, cup holders, 205/65HR15 all-season tires, full-size spare tire. **XLS** adds: anti-lock brakes, automatic temperature control, 7-way power front bucket seats or power split bench seat with storage armrest, premium cassette player with six speakers and equalizer, theft-deterrent system, remote keyless entry, illuminated entry, variable intermittent wipers, leather-wrapped steering wheel and shift knob, alloy wheels.

Optional Equipment:

Anti-lock brakes, XL	980	804	—

Prices are accurate at time of publication; subject to manufacturer's change.

TOYOTA

	Retail Price	Dealer Invoice	Fair Price
Theft-deterrent system, XL	$220	$176	—
Includes remote keyless entry.			
Leather Trim Pkg., XL with bucket seats	1910	1562	—
XL with bench seat	1060	848	—
XLS	1005	804	—

Leather seat and simulated leather door trim. XL adds leather-wrapped steering wheel and shift knob. XL requires alloy wheels. NA 7-way power front bucket seats

	Retail Price	Dealer Invoice	Fair Price
7-way power front bucket seats, XL with bucket seats	850	714	—
NA with Leather Trim Pkg.			
Power moonroof, XL	1000	800	—
XLS	980	784	—
Includes map light.			
Premium cassette player, XL	250	188	—
Includes six speakers and equalizer.			
Premium cassette player and CD changer, XL	1470	1103	—
XLS	1220	915	—
Includes seven speakers and equalizer.			
Diamond white pearlescent paint	210	179	—
Includes bronze-tint glass.			
Mudguards	60	48	—
Alloy wheels, XL	435	348	—

Toyota Camry

	Retail Price	Dealer Invoice	Fair Price
DX 2-door notchback, 5-speed	$16468	$14445	$14968
DX 2-door notchback, automatic	17268	15147	15768
LE 2-door notchback, automatic	19878	17233	18378
LE V-6 2-door notchback, automatic	22158	19210	20658
SE V-6 2-door notchback, automatic	23828	20659	22328
DX 4-door notchback, 5-speed	16758	14700	15258
DX 4-door notchback, automatic	17558	15402	16058
LE 4-door notchback, automatic	20168	17485	18668
LE 5-door wagon, automatic	21608	18734	20108
XLE 4-door notchback, automatic	22278	19314	20778
SE V-6 4-door notchback, automatic	24118	20910	22618
LE V-6 4-door notchback, automatic	22448	19462	20948
LE V-6 5-door wagon, automatic	23918	20736	22418
XLE V-6 4-door notchback, automatic	25038	21707	23538
Destination charge	420	420	420

Prices are for vehicles distributed by Toyota Motor Sales, U.S.A., Inc. The dealer invoice, fair price, and destination charge may be higher in areas served by independent distributors.

TOYOTA

Standard Equipment:

DX: 2.2-liter DOHC 4-cylinder engine, 5-speed manual or 4-speed automatic transmission, driver- and passenger-side air bags, power steering, tachometer, coolant temperature gauge, trip odometer, cloth reclining front bucket seats, split folding rear seat with armrest, remote fuel door and trunk releases, rear defogger, dual remote outside mirrors, front door pockets, tilt steering column, cup holders, auto-off headlamps, intermittent wipers, AM/FM radio, tinted glass, 195/70HR14 all-season tires. **LE** adds: 2.2-liter DOHC 4-cylinder or 3.0-liter DOHC V-6 engine, 4-speed automatic transmission, 6-way manual driver's seat, air conditioning, cruise control, power windows, door locks, and mirrors, cassette player, power antenna, upgraded interior trim, cargo cover (wagon), rear wiper (wagon), door courtesy lights (2-door), 205/65HR15 all-season tires (V-6). **SE** adds to DX: 3.0-liter DOHC V-6 engine, 4-speed automatic transmission, air conditioning, cruise control, cassette player, power antenna, power windows, door locks, and mirrors, sport suspension, rear spoiler, leather-wrapped steering wheel, shift knob, and parking brake handle, passenger-side visor mirror, illuminated entry, 205/65VR15 all-season tires, alloy wheels. **XLE** adds to LE: anti-lock brakes, 7-way power driver's seat, illuminated entry, lighted visor mirrors, variable intermittent wipers, alloy wheels. V-6 models have 4-wheel disc brakes.

Optional Equipment:

	Retail Price	Dealer Invoice	Fair Price
Anti-lock brakes, 4-cylinder models	1100	902	1045
Includes rear disc brakes.			
LE V-6, SE V-6	950	779	903
Anti-lock brakes with folding third seat,			
LE 4-cylinder wagon	1445	1178	1373
LE V-6 wagon	1295	1055	1230
Includes cargo-area cover.			
Air conditioning, DX	1005	804	955
Value Pkg., DX 4-door	1355	1219	1287
DX 2-door	1255	1129	1192
Air conditioning, Power Pkg., floormats.			
Collector's Edition with two tone paint,			
LE V-6	4980	3062	4731
Diamond white metallic/flaxen pearl two tone, Leather Trim Pkg., CD player, gold trim, wood dash trim, floormats, alloy wheels.			
Power Pkg., DX 4-door	770	616	732
DX 2-door	670	536	637
Power windows, door locks, and mirrors, courtesy lamp (2-door).			
Power driver's seat, LE 2-door	250	210	238
LE wagon	370	311	352
Folding third seat, 4-cylinder wagon	495	399	470
V-6 wagon	345	276	328
Includes cargo area cover.			

Prices are accurate at time of publication; subject to manufacturer's change.

TOYOTA

	Retail Price	Dealer Invoice	Fair Price
Leather Trim Pkg., LE 4-door	$1450	$1160	$1378
LE 2-door	1310	1048	1245
XLE	1300	1040	1235
SE	1005	804	955

Leather seat and door trim, power driver's seat (LE 2-door), power passenger seat (XLE), leather-wrapped steering wheel (LE, XLE), adjustable headrest, leather-wrapped parking brake handle (4-cylinder models).

Cruise control, DX	290	232	276
Power moonroof	1000	800	950

Includes map lights and sunshade. NA DX.

Cassette player, DX	225	169	214
Premium AM/FM/cassette	250	188	238

NA DX.

Premium cassette player and CD changer	1195	896	1135

NA DX.

Mudguards	60	48	57
Alloy wheels, LE	415	332	394
LE V-6	435	348	413

Toyota Celica

	Retail Price	Dealer Invoice	Fair Price
ST 2-door notchback, 5-speed	$16958	$14789	$15389
ST 2-door notchback, automatic	17758	15486	16086
GT 2-door notchback, 5-speed	19468	16878	17478
GT 2-door notchback, automatic	20268	17572	18172
ST 3-door hatchback, 5-speed	17318	15103	15703
ST 3-door hatchback, automatic	18118	15800	16400
GT 3-door hatchback, 5-speed	19978	17320	17920
GT 3-door hatchback, automatic	20778	18014	18614
GT 2-door convertible, 5-speed	24178	21202	21802
GT 2-door convertible, automatic	24978	21896	22496
Destination charge	420	420	420

Prices are for vehicles distributed by Toyota Motor Sales, U.S.A., Inc. The dealer invoice, fair price, and destination charge may be higher in areas served by independent distributors.

Standard Equipment:

ST: 1.8-liter DOHC 4-cylinder engine, 5-speed manual or 4-speed automatic transmission, driver- and passenger-side air bags, power steering, cloth 4-way adjustable front sport seats, center console with armrest, split folding rear seat, dual cup holders, digital clock, rear defogger, remote fuel door and trunk/hatch releases, map lights, coolant temperature gauge, tachometer, trip odometer, intermittent wipers, auto-off headlamps, tinted glass,

TOYOTA

dual outside mirrors, AM/FM radio with four speakers, visor mirrors, cargo area cover (hatchback), 185/70R14 all-season tires, wheel covers. **GT** adds: 2.2-liter DOHC 4-cylinder engine, 4-wheel disc brakes, cassette player with six speakers, power antenna, power windows and door locks, tilt steering column, intermittent rear wiper (hatchback), upgraded door and interior trim, engine oil cooler (5-speed), 205/55VR15 all-season tires. **Convertible** adds: power top, glass rear window.

Optional Equipment:

	Retail Price	Dealer Invoice	Fair Price
Anti-lock brakes	$850	$697	$808
Requires cruise control.			
Air conditioning	1005	804	955
Power Pkg., ST	525	420	499
Power windows and door locks. Requires cruise control.			
Leather Trim Pkg.	1085	868	1031
Leather sport seats, leather-wrapped steering wheel and manual shift knob, leather door trim. NA ST.			
Sport Pkg. w/leather, GT 3-door hatchback	1630	1304	1549
Adds Leather Pkg. seats to Sport Pkg. Requires cruise control.			
Rear spoiler, hatchbacks	415	332	394
ST requires intermittent rear wiper.			
Intermittent rear wiper, ST hatchback	170	139	162
Power sunroof	760	608	722
NA convertible.			
Cruise control, GT	290	232	276
ST	395	316	375
Cassette player, ST	335	257	318
Premium cassette player, GT			
notchback, hatchback	250	190	238
convertible	195	146	185
Includes graphic equalizer and six speakers.			
Cassette and CD player, GT			
notchback, hatchback	1335	1004	1268
convertible	1280	960	1216
Includes graphic equalizer and eight speakers.			
Fog lamps, ST	100	80	95
Contoured rocker panels, ST 2-door, hatchbacks	200	160	190
Alloy wheels, GT	435	348	413
ST	675	540	641

Toyota Corolla

	Retail Price	Dealer Invoice	Fair Price
4-door notchback, 5-speed	$12728	$11554	$12054
4-door notchback, automatic	13228	12008	12508

Prices are accurate at time of publication; subject to manufacturer's change.

TOYOTA

	Retail Price	Dealer Invoice	Fair Price
DX 4-door notchback, 5-speed	$13908	$12198	$12698
DX 4-door notchback, automatic	14708	12899	13399
DX 5-door wagon, 5-speed	15058	13206	13706
DX 5-door wagon, automatic	15858	13910	14410
Destination charge	420	420	420

Prices are for vehicles distributed by Toyota Motor Sales, U.S.A., Inc. The dealer invoice, fair price, and destination charge may be higher in areas served by independent distributors.

Standard Equipment:

1.6-liter DOHC 4-cylinder engine, 5-speed manual or 3-speed automatic transmission, driver- and passenger-side air bags, cloth reclining front bucket seats, console with storage, coolant temperature gauge, trip odometer, remote decklid and fuel door releases, auto-off headlights, cup holders, color-keyed bumpers, wheel covers, tinted glass, 175/65R14 all-season tires. **DX** adds: 1.8-liter DOHC 4-cylinder engine, 5-speed manual or 4-speed automatic transmission, power steering, passenger visor mirror, cloth door trim with map pockets, full cloth seats with headrests, rear seat headrests, 60/40 split folding rear seat, dual remote mirrors, bodyside moldings, rear luggage lamp, digital clock, intermittent wipers, rear defogger, rear cargo cover and power hatch lock (wagon), 185/65R14 all-season tires.

Optional Equipment:

Anti-lock brakes	825	677	742
Air conditioning	950	760	855
Power steering, base	270	231	243
Value Pkg., base	892	803	847
Air conditioning, power steering, floormats.			
Value Pkg., DX 4-door	1837	1653	1745
wagon	1747	1572	1660
Air conditioning, tilt steering column (4-door), Power Pkg., deluxe AM/FM/cassette with four speakers, floormats.			
Convenience Pkg., base	1220	991	1159
Includes power steering, air conditioning.			
Tilt steering column, DX	170	145	153
Power sunroof, DX 4-door	595	476	536
Includes map light.			
Rear wiper, wagon	195	160	176
Radio Prep Pkg.	100	75	90
Includes two speakers, wiring harness, antenna.			
AM/FM radio with four speakers	390	293	351
AM/FM/cassette with four speakers	615	461	554

TOYOTA

	Retail Price	Dealer Invoice	Fair Price
Power Pkg., DX 4-door	$780	$624	$702
DX wagon	640	512	576
Power windows and door locks.			
Tachometer, DX 4-door, DX 5-speed wagon	70	56	63
Cruise control, DX	290	232	261
Includes variable intermittent wipers.			
All Weather Guard Pkg., base, 5-speed	265	215	239
base, automatic	255	207	230
DX	70	59	63
Heavy duty rear defogger, battery, heater and wiper motor, 4.5-liter windshield washer tank. Base with automatic includes rear defogger with timer.			
Integrated child seat, DX 4-door	125	100	113
Rear window defogger, base	185	148	167
Body-side molding, base	50	40	45
DX 4-door	20	16	18
NA with black mudguards.			
Black mudguards, DX	60	48	54
NA with body-side moldings.			
Color-keyed mudguards, DX 4-door	80	64	72
Requires body-side moldings.			
Full wheel covers, base	120	96	108
Alloy wheels, DX 4-door	415	332	374

Toyota Land Cruiser

	Retail Price	Dealer Invoice	Fair Price
5-door 4WD wagon	$40258	$34287	—
Destination charge	420	420	420

Fair price not available at time of publication. Prices are for vehicles distributed by Toyota Motor Sales, U.S.A., Inc. The dealer invoice, fair price, and destination charge may be higher in areas served by independent distributors.

Standard Equipment:

4.5-liter DOHC 6-cylinder engine, 4-speed automatic transmission, permanent 4-wheel drive, anti-lock 4-wheel disc brakes, driver- and passenger-side air bags, power steering, air conditioning, cruise control, cloth reclining front bucket seats, middle seat center armrests, folding rear seat, rear seat headrests, power windows and door locks, power mirrors, rear step bumper, console with storage, rear defogger and intermittent wiper/washer, remote fuel door release, tinted glass, rear heater, AM/FM/cassette, power antenna, digital clock with stopwatch and alarm, auto-off headlamps, skid plates for fuel tank and transfer case, tilt steering column, front and rear tow hooks, tachometer,

TOYOTA

voltmeter, oil pressure and coolant temperature gauges, trip odometer, variable intermittent wipers, passenger-side lighted visor mirror, transmission oil cooler, trailer towing wiring harness, 275/70R16 tires.

Optional Equipment:

	Retail Price	Dealer Invoice	Fair Price
Premium cassette w/CD player	$945	$709	—
Includes equalizer.			
Leather Trim Pkg.	4280	3455	—
Leather seats and door trim, leather-wrapped steering wheel and transfer case knob, leather-covered center console, power seats, Third Seat Pkg.			
Black Pkg.	150	127	—
Black paint, chrome outside mirrors and door handles. NA 2-tone paint.			
Differential locks	825	681	—
Lockable front and rear differentials.			
Power moonroof	1185	948	—
Third Seat Pkg.	1515	1212	—
Includes split folding rear third seat, rear 3-point seat belts, cloth headrests, child-safety hatch lock, privacy glass, rear assist grip, sliding rear quarter windows. NA Leather Trim Pkg.			
Alloy wheels		525	420	—
2-tone paint		285	228	—

Toyota Paseo

	Retail Price	Dealer Invoice	Fair Price
2-door notchback, 5-speed	$13038	$11569	—
2-door notchback, automatic	13838	12279	—
Destination charge	420	420	420

Fair price not available at time of publication. Prices are for vehicles distributed by Toyota Motor Sales, U.S.A., Inc. The dealer invoice, fair price, and destination charge may be higher in areas served by independent distributors.

Standard Equipment:

1.5-liter DOHC 4-cylinder engine, 5-speed manual or 4-speed automatic transmission, power steering, driver- and passenger-side air bags, cloth reclining bucket seats, door map pockets, tinted glass, tachometer, coolant temperature gauge, trip odometer, digital clock, variable intermittent wipers, dual remote mirrors, AM/FM radio, rear defogger, cup holders, color-keyed bumpers, remote trunk and fuel door releases, folding rear seat, 185/60R14 tires, wheel covers.

Optional Equipment:

Anti-lock brakes	850	697	—
NA with cruise control.			

TOYOTA

	Retail Price	Dealer Invoice	Fair Price
Air conditioning	$925	$740	—
Cruise control	290	232	—
NA with anti-lock brakes.			
Pop-up glass moonroof	410	328	—
Includes sunshade and storage pouch.			
Power Pkg.	525	420	—
Power windows and door locks.			
Cassette player with four speakers	225	169	—
All-Weather Guard Pkg.	70	59	—
Heavy-duty battery, rear defogger with timer, and heater.			
Alloy wheels	415	332	—
Poly-cast wheels	115	92	—
Rear spoiler	415	332	—

Toyota Previa

	Retail Price	Dealer Invoice	Fair Price
DX S/C 2WD	$24318	$21207	$21907
LE S/C 2WD	28858	25020	25707
DX S/C All-Trac	27858	24153	24853
LE S/C All-Trac	32198	27915	28615
Destination charge	420	420	420

Prices are for vehicles distributed by Toyota Motor Sales, U.S.A., Inc. The dealer invoice, fair price, and destination charge may be higher in areas served by independent distributors.

Standard Equipment:

DX: 2.4-liter supercharged 4-cylinder engine, 4-speed automatic transmission, driver- and passenger-side air bags, power steering, tilt steering column, cloth reclining front bucket seats, console with storage, 2-passenger center seat, 3-passenger split-folding rear seat, AM/FM radio, rear defogger, variable intermittent wipers, rear intermittent wiper/washer, auto-off headlamps, tinted glass, digital clock, dual outside mirrors, tilt-out rear quarter windows, wheel covers, 215/65R15 all-season tires, full-size spare tire. **LE** adds: dual air conditioners, 4-wheel disc brakes, cruise control, power windows and door locks, power mirrors, cassette player, upgraded upholstery and interior trim, passenger-side lighted visor mirror. **All-Trac** adds: permanently engaged 4-wheel drive.

Optional Equipment:

Anti-lock brakes, DX	1135	931	1022
LE	980	804	882

DX includes 4-wheel disc brakes. Requires cruise control. DX requires Value Pkg. 1.

Prices are accurate at time of publication; subject to manufacturer's change.

TOYOTA

	Retail Price	Dealer Invoice	Fair Price
Dual air conditioners, DX	$1735	$1388	$1562
Value Pkg. 1, DX	1765	1588	1633
LE	455	410	421

Air conditioning (DX), cruise control (DX), Power Pkg. (DX), cassette player (DX), privacy glass, anti-lock brakes (LE). NA Security Pkg.

Value Pkg. 2, LE	775	698	717

Pkg. 1 plus captain's chairs.

Value Pkg. 3, LE	1305	1175	1207

Pkg. 1 plus leather captain's chairs.

Power Pkg., DX	775	620	698

Power windows, door locks, and mirrors.

Privacy glass	425	340	383
Cruise control, DX	305	244	275
Cassette player, DX	225	169	203
Premium cassette player, LE	280	210	252

Includes seven speakers. Requires Value Pkg. 1, 2, or 3.

Premium cassette and CD players, LE	1265	949	1139

Includes nine speakers and programmable equalizer. Requires Value Pkg. 1, 2, or 3.

Dual moonroofs, LE 2WD	1610	1288	1449

Includes sunshade and rear spoiler.

Captain's chairs with armrests, LE	870	696	783
Leather Trim Package, LE	1900	1520	1710

Includes captain's chairs. NA Value Pkgs.

Security Pkg., DX	995	796	896
LE	220	176	198

Anti-theft system, Power Pkg. (DX). NA Value Pkg 1 (DX).

Alloy wheels, LE	435	348	392

Toyota RAV4

Prices not available at time of publication.

Standard Equipment:

3-door: 2.0-liter DOHC 4-cylinder engine, 5-speed manual transmission (with center differential lock), permanent 4WD, driver- and passenger-side air bags, power steering, reclining cloth front bucket seats, split folding and reclining rear seat, dual outside mirrors, rear defogger, tachometer, trip odometer, console with cup holders, intermittent front and rear wipers, door pockets, body-side cladding, 215/70R16 tires, styled steel wheels. **5-door** adds: 5-speed manual transmission (with center differential lock) or 4-speed automatic transmission, 5-passenger seating, seatback pockets.

TOYOTA

Toyota Tercel

	Retail Price	Dealer Invoice	Fair Price
Standard 2-door notchback, 4-speed	$10348	$9656	—
Standard 2-door notchback, automatic	11048	10310	—
DX 2-door notchback, 5-speed	11598	10640	—
DX 2-door notchback, automatic	12308	11298	—
DX 4-door notchback, 5-speed	11908	10931	—
DX 4-door notchback, automatic	12618	11583	—
Destination charge	420	420	420

Dealer invoice and fair price not available at time of publication. Prices are for vehicles distributed by Toyota Motor Sales, U.S.A., Inc. The dealer invoice, fair price, and destination charge may be higher in areas served by independent distributors.

Standard Equipment:

Standard: 1.5-liter DOHC 4-cylinder engine, 4-speed manual or 3-speed automatic transmission, driver- and passenger-side air bags, vinyl reclining front bucket seats, coolant temperature gauge, left outside mirror, center console, color-keyed grille, 155/80SR13 tires. **DX** adds: 5-speed manual or 4-speed automatic transmission, cloth reclining seats, cloth door trim, dual outside mirrors, trip odometer, tinted glass, cup holders, full wheel covers.

Optional Equipment:

Anti-lock brakes	850	697	—
Includes larger temporary spare tire.			
Air conditioning	925	740	—
Rear defogger	185	148	—
Power steering, DX	270	231	—
Power Pkg., DX 4-door	640	512	—
DX 2-door	525	420	—
Power windows and door locks.			
Value Equipment Pkg. VQ, DX	905	814	—
Power steering, Convenience Pkg., AM/FM/cassette with four speakers, color-keyed bumpers, floormats.			
Value Equipment Pkg. VP, DX	1530	1377	—
Pkg VQ plus air conditioning.			
Value Equipment Pkg. VP, standard	968	871	—
Air conditioning, power steering, passenger-side mirror, floormats.			
Convenience Pkg., DX	365	293	—
Intermittent wipers, digital clock, remote mirrors, 60/40 folding rear seatback, remote fuel door and decklid releases.			
AM/FM radio with two speakers	245	184	—
with four speakers, DX	390	293	—
AM/FM/cassette with four speakers, DX	615	461	—

Prices are accurate at time of publication; subject to manufacturer's change.

TOYOTA • VOLKSWAGEN

	Retail Price	Dealer Invoice	Fair Price
All Weather Guard Pkg.	$255	$215	—
Heavy duty battery, heater, starter, and rear defogger.			
Color-keyed bumpers, DX	95	76	—

Toyota 4Runner

Prices not available at time of publication.

Standard Equipment:

Base 2WD/4WD: 2.7-liter DOHC 4-cylinder engine, 5-speed manual or 4-speed automatic transmission, 4WDemand part-time 4WD (4WD models), power steering, driver- and passenger-side air bags, cloth bucket seats, 50/50 split folding rear seat, AM/FM radio with four speakers, tachometer, voltmeter, oil pressure gauge, trip odometer, intermittent wipers, power rear window, tinted windows, cup holders, passenger-side visor mirror, front and rear mudguards, 225/75R15 tires, styled steel wheels. **SR5 2WD/4WD** adds: 3.4-liter DOHC V-6 engine, anti-lock brakes, tilt steering column, cassette player, rear defogger, variable intermittent wipers, power door locks and mirrors, rear wiper, digital clock, spring rear antenna, rear cup holders, map and courtesy lights, privacy glass, chrome bumpers and grille. **Limited 4WD** adds: air conditioning, cruise control, upgraded brakes, differential lock (automatic transmission), sport seats, power driver's seat, leather upholstery, cassette player with six speakers, power windows, remote 4-wheel drive selector, wood interior trim, leather-wrapped steering wheel and shift knob, All-Weather Guard Equipment Pkg. (heavy-duty battery, starter, and wiper motor, large wiper-fluid reservoir), body-side cladding, fender flares, running boards, floormats, 265/70R16 tires, alloy wheels.

VOLKSWAGEN

Volkswagen Jetta/Golf	Retail Price	Dealer Invoice	Fair Price
Golf GL 5-door hatchback	$13150	$12141	12641
GTI 3-door hatchback	16000	14742	15242
GTI VR6 3-door hatchback	19685	18176	18676
Jetta GL 4-door notchback	14250	12934	13434
Jetta GLS 4-door notchback	16300	14765	15265
Jetta GLX 4-door notchback	20610	19020	19520
Destination charge	425	425	425

VOLKSWAGEN

Standard Equipment:

Golf GL and Jetta GL: 2.0-liter 4-cylinder engine, 5-speed manual transmission, driver- and passenger-side air bags, power steering, cloth reclining bucket seats, driver's seat height adjustment, 60/40 split folding rear seat, anti-theft alarm, central power locking system with remote hatch and fuel door releases, tachometer, center console with storage, cup holders, daytime running lights, dual manual remote mirrors, variable intermittent wipers, rear defogger, rear wiper/washer (Golf), visor mirrors, grille and bodyside molding, rear spoiler (Golf), cargo cover, 185/60HR14 all-season tires, full wheel covers. **GTI** adds: anti-lock 4-wheel disc brakes, air conditioning, 8-speaker AM/FM/cassette, cloth sport seats, power glass sunroof, dark-tinted tail light lenses, reading light, 195/60HR14 all-season tires, 5-spoke alloy wheels. **GTI VR6** adds: 2.8-liter V-6 engine, close-ratio 5-speed manual transmission, sport suspension, traction control, power windows and mirrors, cruise control, trip computer, tilt steering wheel, leather-wrapped steering wheel, 205/50HR15 tires, Pinanfarina-style alloy wheels. **Jetta GLS** adds to Jetta GL: air conditioning, AM/FM/cassette, cruise control, power windows, heated power mirrors, tilt steering wheel, trunk light. **Jetta GLX** adds: 2.8-liter V-6 engine, close-ratio 5-speed manual transmission, anti-lock 4-wheel disc brakes, sport suspension, traction control, cloth sport seats, power sunroof, Bose 6-speaker AM/FM/cassette, leather-wrapped steering wheel, fog lamps, trip computer, reading lights, rear spoiler, 205/50HR15 tires, Bugatti-style alloy wheels.

Optional Equipment:

	Retail Price	Dealer Invoice	Fair Price
4-speed automatic transmission	$875	$856	$866
Includes 195/60HR14 tires. NA GTI VR6.			
Cold Weather Pkg., Jetta GLS, GLX	250	218	225
Heated front seats and windshield washer nozzles. GLX requires leather upholstery.			
Air conditioning, GL models	860	750	817
Leather upholstery, GTI VR6	550	480	495
Jetta GLX	800	698	720
Anti-lock 4-wheel disc brakes	775	727	751
AM/FM/cassette, GL models	485	423	437
Includes eight speakers.			
Bose 6-speaker AM/FM/cassette, Jetta GLS	375	313	338
CD changer	495	412	446
Power sunroof w/sunshade	590	516	531
Clearcoat metallic paint	175	153	158

Volkswagen Passat

	Retail Price	Dealer Invoice	Fair Price
GLS 4-door notchback	$18490	$16657	—
TDI 4-door notchback	19430	17498	—

Prices are accurate at time of publication; subject to manufacturer's change.

VOLKSWAGEN • VOLVO

	Retail Price	Dealer Invoice	Fair Price
TDI 5-door wagon	$19860	$17882	—
GLX 4-door notchback	21890	19694	—
GLX 5-door wagon	22320	20078	—
Destination charge	425	425	425

Fair price not available at time of publication.

Standard Equipment:

GLS: 2.0-liter 4-cylinder, 5-speed manual transmission, 4-wheel disc brakes, driver- and passenger-side air bags, air conditioning, power steering, power windows and door locks, heated power mirrors, cruise control, 8-speaker AM/FM/cassette with theft-deterrent system, remote fuel door release, power decklid release, rear reading lights, child-safety rear door locks, cloth reclining front bucket seats with adjustable height, thigh and lumbar supports, 60/40 folding rear seatback, rear armrest, center storage console, tachometer, coolant temperature gauge, digital clock, interior pollen filter, rear defogger, tinted glass, variable-speed intermittent wipers, front door and seatback pockets, tilt steering column, lighted visor mirrors, daytime running lamps, color-keyed bumpers and bodyside moldings, rear spoiler, alarm system, 195/60HR14 tires, wheel covers. **TDI** adds: 1.9-liter turbodiesel engine. **GLX** adds: 2.8-liter V-6 engine, anti-lock brakes, traction control, trip odometer, trip computer, leather-wrapped steering wheel, shift knob and parking brake handle, fog lights, 215/50HR15 all-season tires, 8-spoke alloy wheels. **Wagon** deletes power decklid release and rear spoiler, and adds cargo cover, rear wiper/washer, remote tailgate release, black roof rails.

Optional Equipment:

4-speed automatic transmission	$800	$777	—
Anti-lock brakes, GLS and TDI	775	727	—
Leather upholstery, GLX	875	764	—
6-disc CD changer, notchbacks	495	412	—
Power glass sunroof	855	746	—
All-Weather Package, GLX	325	284	—

Includes heated front seats and windshield washer nozzles. Requires leather upholstery.

Metallic paint	N/C	N/C	N/C

VOLVO

Volvo 850

	Retail Price	Dealer Invoice	Fair Price
4-door notchback, 5-speed	$26125	$23925	—

VOLVO

	Retail Price	Dealer Invoice	Fair Price
4-door notchback, automatic	$27100	$24900	—
5-door wagon, 5-speed	27425	25225	—
5-door wagon, automatic	28400	26200	—
4-door notchback w/Grand Luxury Pkg., 5-speed	27150	24850	—
4-door notchback w/Grand Luxury Pkg., automatic	28125	25825	—
5-door wagon w/Grand Luxury Pkg., 5-speed	28450	26150	—
5-door wagon w/Grand Luxury Pkg., automatic	29425	27125	—
GLT 4-door notchback, 5-speed	29200	26800	—
GLT 4-door notchback, automatic	30175	27775	—
GLT 5-door wagon, 5-speed	30500	28100	—
GLT 5-door wagon, automatic	31475	29075	—
Turbo 4-door notchback, automatic	32650	29700	—
Turbo 5-door wagon, automatic	33950	33950	—
Platinum Limited Edition Turbo 4-door notchback, automatic	36885	33685	—
Platinum Limited Edition Turbo 5-door wagon, automatic	38335	35135	—
Destination charge	495	495	495

Fair price not available at time of publication.

Standard Equipment:

Base: 2.4-liter DOHC 5-cylinder engine, 5-speed manual or 4-speed automatic transmission, front and side air bags, anti-lock 4-wheel disc brakes, air conditioning with dual climate control, power steering, cruise control, tilt/telescoping steering wheel, tinted glass, rear-window defroster, digital clock, intermittent wipers, cloth reclining front bucket seats, 8-way manually adjustable driver's seat, fully folding passenger seat, 60/40 fold-down rear seat with armrest, integrated child booster seat (wagon), power windows and door locks, heated power mirrors, 6-speaker AM/FM/cassette with anti-theft circuitry, power antenna (notchback), integrated window antenna (wagon), remote decklid (notchback) or rear hatch (wagon) release, remote fuel door release, daytime running lights, rear fog light, 195/60R15 tires. **Grand Luxury Pkg.** adds: 8-way power driver's seat with 3-position memory, remote keyless entry with alarm, 6-spoke alloy wheels. **GLT** adds: power glass sunroof, automatic climate control, 8-speaker AM/FM/full-logic cassette, velour upholstery. **Turbo** adds: turbocharged 2.3-liter DOHC 5-cylinder engine, 4-speed automatic transmission, trip computer, leather-wrapped steering wheel, 205/50ZR16 tires, 5-spoke alloy wheels. **Platinum Limited Edition** adds: TRACS traction-control system, power pas-

Prices are accurate at time of publication; subject to manufacturer's change.

VOLVO

senger seat, heated front seats, leather upholstery, CD player, headlamp wiper/washer, ambient temperature gauge, burled walnut interior trim, pearl white platinum paint.

Optional Equipment:

	Retail Price	Dealer Invoice	Fair Price
Sport Pkg., base, GLT, Turbo	$725	$580	—
Sport suspension, fog lights, rear spoiler. NA wagons.			
Touring Pkg., base, GLT	395	315	—
Trip computer, leather-wrapped steering wheel.			
Grand Touring Pkg., base w/Grand Luxury Pkg., GLT, Turbo	1485	1185	—
Power passenger seat, CD player, wood instrument panel and console trim.			
Cold Weather Pkg., base, GLT, Turbo	485	385	—
Heated front seats, headlamp wiper/washer, ambient temperature gauge.			
TRACS traction-control system and Cold Weather Pkg., base, GLT, Turbo	810	645	—
Automatic Load Leveling, GLT wagon	495	395	—
CD player, GLT	485	385	—
Leather upholstery, base, GLT, Turbo	1195	955	—
Velour upholstery, base	200	160	—
Power driver's seat, base	495	395	—
8-way power driver's seat with 3-position memory.			
Decklid spoiler, notchbacks	385	305	—
Automatic climate control, base w/Grand Luxury Pkg.	350	280	—
Sport suspension, Platinum Limited Edition notchback	175	140	—
6-spoke alloy wheels, base	400	320	—
Platinum Limited Edition	NC	NC	NC
205/55ZR16 all-season tires, Turbo models	NC	NC	NC

Volvo 960

	Retail Price	Dealer Invoice	Fair Price
960 4-door notchback	$33960	$31260	—
960 5-door wagon	35260	32560	—
Destination charge	495	495	495

Fair price not available at time of publication.

Standard Equipment:

2.9-liter DOHC 6-cylinder engine, 4-speed automatic transmission, anti-lock 4-wheel disc brakes, automatic locking differential, power steering, front and side air bags, automatic climate control, power glass sunroof, reclining front bucket seats, 8-way power driver's seat with 3-position memory, 8-

VOLVO

way power front passenger seat, rear-seat trunk pass through (notchback), 60/40 split folding rear seat (wagon), integrated child booster seat (wagon), power windows and locks, cruise control, leather upholstery (wagon), tailored leather upholstery (notchback), heated power mirrors, 8-speaker (notchback) or 6-speaker (wagon) AM/FM/cassette with anti-theft circuitry, power antenna (notchback), integrated window antenna (wagon), clock, tachometer, coolant temperature gauge, trip odometer, tinted glass, rear defogger, intermittent wipers, remote decklid release, remote keyless entry and alarm system, walnut interior trim (notchback), leather-wrapped tilt steering wheel, seatback and door map pockets, illuminated visor mirrors, tool kit, headlight wiper/washers, front fog lamps, daytime running lights, rear fog light, color-keyed luggage rack (wagon), cargo tie-down hooks (wagon), locking storage compartment (wagon), floormats, front and rear stabilizer bars, 195/65HR15 tires (wagon), 205/55VR16 tires (notchback), alloy wheels.

Optional Equipment:

	Retail Price	Dealer Invoice	Fair Price
CD player	$485	$315	—
Cold Weather Pkg.	395	255	—
Heated front seats, ambient temperature gauge.			
Tailored leather upholstery, wagon	250	250	250